Theological Themes of Psalms

Theological Themes of Psalms

The Theology of the Book of Psalms

by

Robert D. Bell

WIPF & STOCK · Eugene, Oregon

THEOLOGICAL THEMES OF PSALMS
The Theology of the Book of Psalms

Wipf & Stock
An Imprint of Wipf and Stock Publishers
199 W. 8th Ave., Suite 3
Eugene, OR 97401

www.wipfandstock.com

PAPERBACK ISBN: 978-1-5326-5416-9
HARDCOVER ISBN: 978-1-5326-5417-6
EBOOK ISBN: 978-1-5326-5418-3

Manufactured in the U.S.A.   04/18/18

To my wife,
Kathryn Kruse Bell,
who is God's great blessing to me and who has
provided valuable editing for my writing

Table of Contents

Theological Themes of Psalms

Theological Themes of Psalms

Abbreviations

General Terms

#	number of occurrences
1CS	First Common (Masculine or Feminine) Singular
2MP	Second Masculine Plural
2MS	Second Masculine Singular
impv	imperative & imperatives
LXX	Septuagint (ancient Greek translation of the OT)
MT	Masoretic Text (official medieval Jewish vowel-pointed Hebrew text)
MSS	manuscripts
n.	note
NT	New Testament
OT	Old Testament
p. & pp.	page & pages
Ps.	Psalm/Psalms
sg	singular
v.	verse
vv.	verses
x	times

Bibliography

ABD	*The Anchor Bible Dictionary*, ed. David Noel Freedman, 6 vols. (New York: Doubleday, 1992)
BDB	Francis Brown, S. R. Driver, and C. A. Briggs, *Hebrew and English Lexicon of the Old Testament* (Oxford: Clarenden, 1907)
BibSac	*Bibliotheca Sacra*
DCH	*The Dictionary of Classical Hebrew,* ed. David J. A. Clines, 8 vols. (Sheffield : Sheffield Academic Press, 1993–2011)
EBC	*The Expositor's Bible Commentary*, revised edition, ed. Tremper Longman III and David E. Garland
EDBT	*Evangelical Dictionary of Biblical Theology*, ed. Walter A. Elwell (Grand Rapids: Baker Books, 1996)
GKC	E. Kautzsch, ed., *Gesenius' Hebrew Grammar*, trans. A. E. Cowley, 2nd ed. (Oxford: Clarendon, 1910)
HALOT	Ludwig Koehler and Walter Baumgartner, *The Hebrew and Aramaic Lexicon of the Old Testament*, trans. M. E. J. Richardson, 2 vols. (Leiden: Brill, 2001).
IBHS	Bruce K. Waltke and M. O'Connor, *An Introduction to Biblical Hebrew Syntax* (Winona Lake: Eisenbrauns, 1990)
ICC	The International Critical Commentary
ISBEr	*International Standard Bible Encyclopedia*, ed. G. W. Bromiley, rev. ed. 4 vols. (Grand Rapids: Eerdmans, 1979–1988)
JBL	*Journal of Biblical Literature*
JETS	*Journal of the Evangelical Theological Society*
JSOT	*Journal for the Study of the Old Testament*
JSOTSup	Journal for the Study of the Old Testament Supplement Series, ed. David J. A. Clines and Philip R. Davies
NAC	The New American Commentary, ed. E. Ray Clendenen

NDBT   *New Dictionary of Biblical Theology*, ed. T. Desmond Alexander and Brian S. Rosner (Downers Grove: InterVarsity, 2000)

NIDOTTE   *New International Dictionary of Old Testament Theology & Exegesis*, ed. Willem A. VanGemeren, 5 vols. (Grand Rapids: Zondervan, 1977)

NIVAC   The NIV Application Commentary: From Biblical Text … to Contemporary Life, ed. Terry Muck

PiH   *Psalterium iuxta Hebraeos* (Jerome's translation of Psalms from the Hebrew)

TDNT   Gerhard Kittel and Gerhard Friedrich, eds. *Theological Dictionary of the New Testament,* trans. and ed. Geoffrey W. Bromiley, 10 vols. (Grand Rapids: Eerdmans, 1964–76)

TDOT   G. Johannes Botterweck, Helmer Ringgren, Heinz-Josef Fabry, eds., *Theological Dictionary of the Old Testament*, trans. David E. Green and others, 15 vols. (Grand Rapids: William B. Eerdmans, 1974–2006)

TLOT   Ernst Jenni and Claus Westermann, eds. *Theological Lexicon of the Old Testament,* trans. Mark E. Biddle. 3 vols. (Peabody, MA: Hendrickson Publishers, 1997)

TWOT   *Theological Wordbook of the Old Testament*, ed. R. Laird Harris, 2 vols. (Chicago: Moody, 1980)

WBC   Word Biblical Commentary, ed. Bruce M. Metzger, David A. Hubbard, and Glenn W. Barker

WHS   *Williams' Hebrew Syntax,* 3rd ed., revised and expanded by John C. Beckman (Toronto: University of Toronto Press, 2007)

ZPEB   *The Zondervan Pictorial Encyclopedia of the Bible*, ed. Merrill C. Tenney, 5 vols. (Grand Rapids: Zondervan, 1975)

Theological Themes of Psalms

Bibliography of Commentaries

Alexander   Joseph A. Alexander, *Commentary on Psalms* (1864; reprint, Grand Rapids: Kregel, 1991)

Allen   Leslie C. Allen, *Psalms 101–150*, rev. ed., vol. 21 of WBC (Dallas: Word, 2002)

Anderson   A. A. Anderson, *The Book of Psalms*, 2 vols. New Century Bible (London: Oliphants, 1972)

Barnes   Albert Barnes, *Notes on the Old Testament, Explanatory and Practical: Psalms*, ed. Robert Frew, 3 vols. (London: Blackie & Son, 1870–1872)

Boice   James Montgomery Boice, *Psalms: An Expositional Commentary*, 2 vols. (Grand Rapids: Baker Books, 2005)

Briggs   Charles Augustus Briggs and Emilie Grace Briggs, *A Critical and Exegetical Commentary on the Book of Psalms*, 2 vols. ICC (New York: Charles Scribner's Sons, 1906–1907)

Broyles   Craig C. Broyles, *Psalms*, New International Biblical Commentary (Peabody, MA: Hendrickson, 1999)

Calvin   John Calvin, *Commentary on the Book of Psalms*, trans. James Anderson, 5 vols. (Grand Rapids: Eerdmans, 1949)

Cohen   A. Cohen, *The Psalms: Hebrew Text & English Translation with an Introduction and Commentary*, in Soncino Books of the Bible, ed. A. Cohen (London: Soncino, 1945)

Craigie   Peter C. Craigie, *Psalms 1–50*, 2nd ed., vol. 19 of WBC

Dahood   Mitchell Dahood, *Psalms*, vols. 16–17A of The Anchor Bible, ed. William Foxwell Albright and David Noel Freedman (New York: Doubleday, 1965–70)

Delitzsch   Franz Delitzsch, *Biblical Commentary on the Psalms*, trans. Francis Bolton, 3 vols. (1887; reprint, Grand Rapids: Eerdmans, n.d.)

Eaton   John Eaton, *The Psalms: A Historical and Spiritual Commentary with an Introduction and New Translation* (London: Continuum, 2005)

Fausset   A. R. Fausset, *Job–Isa.*, vol. 3 of *A Commentary on the Old and New Testaments*, by Robert Jamieson, A. R. Fausset, and David Brown (Grand Rapids: Eerdmans, 1945)

Futato   Mark D. Futato, *The Book of Psalms, The Book of Proverbs*, vol. 7 of Cornerstone Biblical Commentary, ed. Philip W. Comfort (Carol Stream, IL: Tyndale House Publishers, 2009)

Goldingay   John Goldingay, *Psalms*, 3 vols., Baker Commentary on the Old Testament, ed. Tremper Longman III (Grand Rapids: Baker Academic, 2006–08)

Grogan   Geoffrey W. Grogan, *Psalms*, in The Two Horizons Old Testament Commentary (Grand Rapids: Eerdmans, 2008)

Harman   Allan Harman, *Psalms*, 2 vols. Mentor Commentary (Ross-shire, Scotland: Christian Focus, 2011)

Hossfeld & Zenger   Frank-Lothar Hossfeld and Erich Zenger, *A Commentary on Psalms*, ed. Klaus Baltzer, trans. Linda M. Maloney, vols. 15B & 15C of Hermeneia—a Critical and Historical Commentary on the Bible (Minneapolis: Fortress Press, 2005 & 2011)

Jennings & Lowe   A. C. Jennings, *The Psalms, with Introductions and Critical Notes*, assisted in parts by W. H. Lowe, 2 vols., 2nded. (London: Macmillan and Co., 1884)

Kidner   Derek Kidner, *Psalms: An Introduction and Commentary*, vols. 15 & 16 of Tyndale Old Testament Commentaries (1973 & 1975; reprint, Downers Grove: InterVarsity Press, 2008)

Kirkpatrick   A. F. Kirkpatrick, *The Book of Psalms*, The Cambridge Bible for Schools and Colleges (Cambridge: The University Press, 1902)

Theological Themes of Psalms

Kraus Hans-Joachim Kraus, *A Continental Commentary: Psalms,* trans. Hilton C. Oswald, 2 vols. (Minneapolis: Fortress Press, 1993)

Leupold H. C. Leupold, *Exposition of the Psalms* (Grand Rapids: Baker Book House, 1959)

Mays James Luther Mays, *Psalms,* Interpretation: A Biblical Commentary for Teaching and Preaching (Louisville: John Knox, 1994)

Moll Carl Bernhard Moll, *The Psalms,* trans. Charles A. Briggs and others, vol. 9 of *Lange's Commentary on the Holy Scriptures,* ed. Philip Schaff (1872; reprint, Grand Rapids: Zondervan, n.d.)

Murphy James G. Murphy, *A Critical and Exegetical Commentary on the Book of Psalms* (Andover: Warren F. Draper, 1875)

Perowne J. J. Stewart Perowne, *The Book of Psalms: A New Translation, with Introductions and Notes, Explanatory and Critical,* 5th edition, 2 vols. (London: George Bell and Sons, 1882–1883)

Rawlinson G. Rawlinson, "Exposition," in *Psalms,* 3 vols. The Pulpit Commentary (London; New York: Funk & Wagnalls Company, 1909).

Ross Allen P. Ross, *A Commentary on the Psalms,* 3 vols., in Kregel Exegetical Library (Grand Rapids: Kregel, 2011–15)

Spurgeon C. H. Spurgeon, *The Treasury of David,* 6 vols. (1869; reprint, Grand Rapids: Zondervan, 1966)

Steveson Peter A. Steveson, *Psalms* (Greenville, SC: Bob Jones University Press, 2007)

Tate Marvin Tate, *Psalms 51–100,* rev. ed., vol. 20 of WBC (Dallas: Word, 1998)

VanGemeren Willem A. VanGemeren, *Psalms,* vol. 5 of *EBC* (Grand Rapids: Zondervan Publishing House, 2008)

Waltner	James H. Waltner, *Psalms*, Believers Church Bible Commentary (Scottdale, PA: Herald Press)
Weiser	Artur Weiser, *The Psalms*, trans. Herbert Hartwell, The Old Testament Library (London: SCM Press, 1962)

English Versions

ASV	American Standard Version (New York: Thomas Nelson & Sons, 1901)
CEV	Contemporary English
ESV	English Standard Version
HCSB	Holman Christian Standard Bible
JPS	Jewish Publication Society of America Tanakh (OT)
KJV	The King James Version (1611)
NAB	New American Bible
NASB	New American Standard Bible
NEB	New English Bible
NET	NET Bible
NIV	New International Version
NJB	New Jerusalem Bible
NLT	New Living Translation
NRSV	New Revised Standard Version of the Bible
RSV	Revised Standard Version
TEV	Today's English Version
YLT	*Young's Literal Translation of the Holy Bible*, 3rd ed. (1898; Grand Rapids: Baker Book House, 1953)

Preface

Biblical theology is the science that seeks to analyze what God has revealed in the holy Scriptures and then proclaims these theological truths in propositional form. These truths fall into three main categories: (1) God, (2) man, and (3) salvation. The Bible concentrates on four main theological propositions: (1) God has spoken to mankind; (2) Man has rebelled against his Creator and sinned; (3) God threatens and carries out judgments because of sin;[1] but the good news is that (4) in compassion God has provided salvation for mankind.

Nature of a Book Theology

One of the methods of biblical theology is a book theology. It seeks to display the theological themes that occur in a book of the Bible and to present the data supporting those themes. A Biblical verse has a context within what precedes and follows it. We could call this its vertical context. But it also has a horizontal context: its themes are related to the other parts of the book that treat the same themes.[2] By presenting a book's theological themes, a book theology provides this horizontal context for the verses in a Biblical book.

It may appear that Psalms contains a miscellaneous collection of poems written over a long period by many different authors, but actually, careful study reveals a unifying element. The Holy Spirit as the real Author behind a series of human poets who focused on one key topic with a related

---

[1] Propositions two and three are two sides of one theme and relate to both the God and man categories.

[2] For a diagram and further explanation of this concept, see Robert D. Bell, *The Theological Messages of the Old Testament Books* (Greenville, SC: BJU Press, 2010), 7–8.

1

group of themes.[3] Since Psalms focuses on worship and prayer, the theological truths about God (His attributes and works) abound in the book's poems.[4] Furthermore, Psalms presents also truths about mankind. The psalmists set their hopes on what God has promised to do, the key event being the universal rule of the Messiah, who is God Himself as well as David's descendent.

The theological value of Psalms has often been recognized. Geoffrey W. Grogan speaks of "a coherent theological perspective": "This means that although the immediate literary context for any one word, phrase, verse or stanza is the particular psalm in which it is to be found, each psalm needs also to be interpreted within the context of the whole book. In some ways, therefore, a theology of the psalms is like a biblical theology."[5] Martin Luther called the Psalms "a little Bible. In it is comprehended most beautifully and briefly everything that is in the entire Bible. It is really a fine enchiridion or handbook."[6] Included are the truths about mankind's inward state: Calvin called Psalms, "An Anatomy of all the Parts of the Soul."[7]

Quotations in the New Testament

The significance of the theological message of Psalms is evident in the frequent use the New Testament makes of this book. It is difficult to nail

---

[3] Grogan put it this way: "... there is an important uniting feature. This consists of a series of convictions that the writers have in common.... They all concern the God of the psalmists ..." (p. 232).

[4] O. Palmer Robertson has argued that each of the five Books of Psalms progressively develops major themes. *The Flow of the Psalms: Discovering Their Structure and Theology* (Phillipsburg: P&R, 2015). His focus is on whole psalms; in this book I have concentrated on individual verses, parts of verses, and key words.

[5] "Psalms," *NDBT*, 203.

[6] "Preface to the Psalter," in of *Luther's Works*, vol. 35, ed. E. Theodore Bachmann (Philadelphia: Muhlenberg Press, 1960), 253.

[7] "There is not an emotion of which any one can be conscious that is not here represented as in a mirror. Or rather, the Holy Spirit has here drawn to the life all the griefs, sorrows, fears, doubts, hopes, cares, perplexities, in short, all the distracting emotions with which the minds of men are wont to be agitated." The psalmists "draw, each of us to the examination of himself in particular, in order that none of the many infirmities to which we are subject, and of the many vices with which we abound, may remain concealed. It is certainly a rare and singular advantage, when all lurking places are discovered, and the heart is brought into the light, purged from that most baneful infection, hypocrisy" (1:xxxvii).

down exactly how many quotations of and allusions to the Psalms there are in the New Testament. Delitzsch says there are about seventy;[8] Waltner claims that 60 psalms provide the New Testament with 93 quotes;[9] Henry M. Shires claims seventy cases introduced by formulas and sixty without.[10] Other works provide lists of references: the UBS NT has 79;[11] Leopold Sabourin itemizes 112 quotations;[12] a key reference work tabulates 67;[13] a collection of articles charts 118 quotations and allusions.[14] Another list carefully distinguishes between "formal quotations," allusions, and paraphrases.[15] Table P.1 below charts 58 cases where the NT uses some introductory word or words to introduce information from Psalms, clearly indicating a direct or indirect quote. Table P.2 provides a list of 25 places where the NT author directly quotes Psalms without an introductory formula, and Table P.3 adds seven more instances of quoted portions by some other speaker. Thus my total would be 90 quotations. The tables help us identify the key Messianic psalms: 2, 8, 16, 22, and 110, which was quoted six times and alluded to one additional time.

Organization of This Book Theology

Table P.4 charts this book's arrangement, referring first to the three main categories of theology mentioned above in the first paragraph. In the table they are called topics. The next column divides this book according to the four main theological propositions, called principles in the table. Next are 28 themes that run through Psalms; these are the chapter titles of this book.

---

[8] 1:48.   [9] Page 25.

[10] *Finding the Old Testament in the New* (Philadelphia: Westminster, 1974), 126.

[11] Barbara Aland and others, eds., *The Greek New Testament*, 5th ed. (Stuttgart: Deutsche Bibelgesellschaft, 2014), 858–59.

[12] *The Psalms: Their Origin and Meaning*, updated ed. (New York: Alba House, 1974), 164–70.

[13] Gleason L. Archer and Gregory Chirichigno, *Old Testament Quotations in the New Testament* (Chicago: Moody Press, 1983), 56–89.

[14] Steve Moyise and Maarten J. J. Menken, eds., *The Psalms in the New Testament* (London: T & T Clark International, 2004), 249–50.

[15] Robert G. Bratcher, ed., *Old Testament Quotations in the New Testament*, rev. ed. (n.p.: United Bible Societies, 1967), vii.

Theological Themes of Psalms

Table P.1 Direct Psalm Quotes Introduced in the New Testament

#	Psalm	NT Reference	Introductory Word(s)
1	2:1-2	Acts 4:25-26	said
2	2:7	Acts 13:33	written
3	2:7	Heb. 1:5	say
4	2:7	Heb. 5:5	said
5	5:9	Rom. 3:13	written (v. 10)
6	8:2	Matt. 21:16	read
7	8:4-6	Heb. 2:6-8	saying (somewhere)
8	8:6	1 Cor. 15:27	for
9	10:7	Rom. 3:14	written (v. 10)
10	14:1-3; 53:1-3	Rom. 3:10-12	written (v. 10)
11	16:8-11	Acts 2:25-28 (31)	says of Him
12	16:10	Acts 13:35	says
13	18:49	Rom. 15:9	written
14	19:4	Rom. 10:18	indeed they have
15	22:15	John 19:28	Scripture … be fulfilled
16	22:18	John 19:24	fulfill the Scripture
17	22:22	Heb. 2:12	saying
18	24:1	1 Cor. 10:26	for
19	32:1-2	Rom. 4:7-8	David also speaks
20	34:12-16	1 Pet. 3:10-12	for
21	34:20	John 19:36	fulfill the Scripture
22	35:19	John 15:25	fulfill the word …
23	36:1	Rom. 3:18	written (v. 10)
24	40:6-8	Heb. 10:5-7	says
25	41:9	John 13:18	Scripture … fulfilled
26	44:22	Rom. 8:36	written
27	45:6-7	Heb. 1:8-9	says … of the Son (v. 6)
28	51:4	Rom. 3:4	written
29	68:18	Eph. 4:8	says
30	69:4	John 15:25	fulfill the word … written …
31	69:9	John 2:17	written
32	69:9	Rom. 15:3	written
33	69:22-23	Rom. 11:9-10	David says
34	69:25	Acts 1:20	written … Psalms
35	78:2	Matt. 13:35	fulfill …
36	82:6	John 10:34	written in your Law
37	94:11	1 Cor. 3:20	written (v. 19) … and again
38	95:7-11	Heb. 3:7-11 (15) (18)	Holy Spirit says
39	95:7-8	Heb. 4:7	said before
40	95:11	Heb. 4:3 (5)	just as He has said
41	102:25-27	Heb. 1:10-12	says (v. 7) … And
42	104:4	Heb. 1:7	He says
43	109:8	Acts 1:20	written in … Psalms
44	110:1	Matt. 22:44; Mk. 12:36; Lk. 20:42-43	saying/said/says
45	110:1	Acts 2:34-35	says
46	110:1	1 Cor. 15:25	for … says
47	110:1	Heb. 1:13	He ever said
48	110:4	Heb. 5:6	He says also in another passage
49	110:4	Heb. 7:17	attested
50	112:9	2 Cor. 9:9	written
51	116:10	2 Cor. 4:13	written
52	117:1	Rom. 15:11	says … again

#	Psalm	NT Reference	Introductory Word(s)
53	118:6	Heb. 13:6	(We confidently say)
54	118:22-23	Matt. 21:42; Mk. 12:10-11; Lk. 20:17	read/read/written
55	118:22	1 Pet. 2:7	Scripture (v. 6) …
56	132:11	Acts 2:30	had sworn …
57	135:14	Heb. 10:30	said … and again
58	140:3	Rom. 3:13	written (v. 10)

Table P.2 Quoted Allusions from Psalms in the New Testament

#	Psalm	NT Reference	Number of Words Quoted
1	2:8-9	Rev. 2:26-27	Hebrew 8/ Greek 10
2	2:9	Rev. 12:5	Hebrew 3/ Greek 4
3	2:9	Rev. 19:15	Hebrew 3/ Greek 5
4	4:4	Eph. 4:26	Hebrew 3/ Greek 4
5	6:8	Matt. 7:23; Lk. 13:27	Hebrew 5/ Greek 7/6
6	8:6	Eph. 1:22	Hebrew 4/ Greek 6
7	9:8	Acts 17:31 (also 96:13 & 98:9)	Hebrew 3/ Greek 5
8	22:1	Matt. 27:46; Mk. 15:34	Hebrew 4/ Aramaic 4
9	22:7	Matt. 27:39; Lk. 23:35	Hebrew 7/Greek 4/2
10	22:8	Matt. 27:43	Hebrew 7/Greek 5
11	22:18	Matt. 27:35; Mk. 15:24; Lk. 23:34	Hebrew 7/ Greek 5/7/6
12	31:5	Lk. 23:46	Hebrew 3/ Greek 7
13	34:8	1 Pet. 2:3	Hebrew 4/ Greek 5
14	42:5, 11	Matt. 26:38; Mk. 14:34	Hebrew 2/ Greek 3
15	62:12	Matt. 16:27	Hebrew 3/ Greek 6
16	62:12	Rom. 2:6	Hebrew 3/ Greek 6
17	62:12	2 Tim. 4:14	Hebrew 2/ Greek 5
18	69:21	Matt. 27:48; Mk. 15:36	Hebrew 2/Greek 2
19	86:9	Rev. 15:4	Hebrew 5/ Greek 8
20	89:3-4	Acts 2:30	Hebrew 4/ Greek 8
21	110:1	Matt. 26:64; Mk. 14:62; Lk. 22:69	Hebrew 2/ Greek 3
22	118:26	Matt. 23.39; Lk. 13:35	Hebrew 4/ Greek 6
23	146:6	Acts 4:24	Hebrew 9/ Greek 13
24	146:6	Acts 14:15	Hebrew 9/ Greek 14
25	146:6	Rev. 10:6	Hebrew 8/ Greek 11

Table P.3 Allusions to Psalms by Other Speakers

#	Psalm	NT Reference	Speaker
1	78:24	John 6:31	crowd
2	89:36	John 12:34	crowd
3	91:11-12	Matt. 4:6; Lk. 4:10	Satan
4	103:17	Lk 1:50	Mary
5	107:9	Lk 1:53	Mary
6	118:25-26	Matt. 21:9; Mk. 11:9-10; Lk. 19:38; John 12:13	crowd
7	148:1	Matt. 21:9; Mk. 11:10	crowd

Theological Themes of Psalms

Table P.4 Organization Chart

Topic	Principle	Theme	Chapter
God (theology)	Revelation [12]	Speech	1
		Instruction	2
		Wisdom	3
		Creation	4
		Blessing	5
		Greatness	6
		Holiness	7
		Wrath	8
		Justice	9
		Compassion	10
		Love & Faithfulness	11
		Protection	12
Man (anthropology)	Sin [4]	Iniquity	13
		Pride	14
		The Wicked	15
		The Enemies	16
	Judgment [4]	Punishment	17
		Imprecation	18
		Affliction	19
		Prayer	20
Salvation (soteriology)	Deliverance [8]	Redemption	21
		Hope	22
		The Righteous	23
		Joy	24
		Praise	25
		Worship	26
		Life	27
		Sovereignty	28

Arrangement of Psalms into Five Books

The edition of the book of Psalms that has providentially come down to us has been divided into five groups, known as "books."[16] Robertson has presented charts in color to indicate how the books advance the themes introduced in Psalms 1 and 2, thus indicating the significance of these books for theology.[17] My work on themes in Psalms, therefore, has given some attention to these divisions (especially, statistically). Table P.5 lists the psalms, verses, and Hebrew words in each of the five books. Many of the

---

[16] We know this from ancient church and Jewish witnesses. See Delitzsch, 3:14–19; Rawlinson, ii–iii; Gerald Henry Wilson, *The Editing of the Hebrew Psalter* (Chico, CA: Scholars Press, 1985), 199–228.

[17] *Flow*, 303–10.

statistical tables in the following chapters of this volume have double lines to indicate the Psalm book divisions.

Table P.5 The Five Books in Psalms

Books	Psalms	Verses	Words
I	1-41	616 (25.03%)	5097 (26.75%)
II	42-72 (31)	465 (18.89%)	3838 (20.14%)
III	73-89 (17)	358 (14.55%)	2689 (14.11%)
IV	90-106 (17)	321 (13.04%)	2411 (12.65%)
V	107-150 (44)	701 (28.48%)	5020 (26.34%)
totals:	150	2461	19,055

Note that in this book theology Psalm commentaries are referenced only by last name and page number. Their bibliography information is listed above in the last section of Abbreviations (Bibliography of Commentaries). Scripture translations not identified in this book are from the King James Version (KJV) or are the author's own very literal translations. The context will generally identify the latter cases (by the use of "literally"). Since Hebrew words are spelled out in the Masoretic script, the transliterations that usually follow are intended only to provide an approximate pronunciation and do not indicate a letter for letter match with the Hebrew; thus some Hebrew letters are not distinguished from each other (for example, both ט and some תs are transliterated as "t"). Both א and ע are treated as silent but indicated by single quote marks (distinguished as ' for א and ' for ע). The velar fricative ח is indicated by "kh."

1

Speech

Theology is the study of God. It is thus appropriate for a book theology to focus on Him. In Psalms His personal name, Yahweh (usually indicated in English translations by "LORD"),[1] occurs 689 times (not counting 6x in the Psalm titles). Additionally, there are five common titles used for Yahweh in Psalms: God (אֱלֹהִים, *'Elowhiym*; 351x), another Hebrew word for God (אֵל, *'Eyl*; 68x), Lord (אֲדֹנָי, *'Adownay*; 63x), a shortened form of Yahweh, Yah (יָהּ, *Yah*; 43x), and Most High (עֶלְיוֹן, *'Elyown*; 21x).[2] Table A1.3 lists some titles that occur just a few times in Psalms, including the verses where Yahweh or God is connected to the armies of heaven ("LORD of hosts," KJV). Thus God is mentioned by name or title well over 1200 times. If we include all the references to Him by means of pronouns, then there are well over 2500 cases where something is being said about God. Every single psalm mentions Him at least once.[3]

But what does the book of Psalms say about God? When we open our Bible, a truth that jumps out for us right in the very beginning is that God has spoken. We get to the third verse of the first book, and we find the simple words, "And God said" (Gen. 1:3a). As we proceed through this collection of books, we find this claim repeated thousands of times. Although

---

[1] Notice the small caps. This practice appropriately follows the Jewish traditional routine of avoiding the pronunciation of the name by substituting the title אֲדֹנָי (*'Adownay*–"Lord") or אֱלֹהִים (*'Elowhiym*–"God"). See Table A1.1 in Appendix A for a complete list of the verses in Psalms where this name appears.

[2] See Table A1.2 for a list of all verses in Psalms where these five terms occur.

[3] The name Yahweh does not appear in 19 psalms (see Table A.1, last column), but in each instance one of the three Hebrew words for "God" occurs.

we tend to think of Psalms as a book that records what the saints have said to God in prayer or to each other for instruction or encouragement, the fact is that in at least 29 passages we find direct quotations from God recorded for us. The human authors of the psalms claim that God said something and they wrote it down.

The doctrine of inspiration (2 Tim. 3:16; 2 Pet. 1:19–21) teaches that all Scripture is God's word; therefore, direct quotations of God or Christ are not more inspired or authoritative than the rest of Scripture. When the New Testament quotes the Old Testament as Scripture, it does not distinguish between direct quotations of God and the remainder of the texts that Moses and the prophets wrote. The claim of the Bible is that what the Holy Spirit inspired the prophets and apostles to write is truly God's very word. Since there are no quotation marks in the original manuscripts, it is sometimes difficult to distinguish between Christ's very words and the apostles' declarations in the Gospels.[4] In the Old Testament the distinction is not always clear between God's direct speech and the prophets' written inspired statements.[5] This is also the case sometimes in Psalms. Thus what follows is not making a claim of superiority for the quotations of God over the psalmists' words, which the Holy Spirit inspired.

Cases of Divine Speech

It is common to find copies of the Bible in which the words of Jesus Christ are printed in red. What is rare, however, is to see a Bible in which all God's direct quotations appear in the color red. In 1980 under the title *The King James Bible Red Lettered,* a little-known edition of the Authorized Version appeared that met the challenge.[6] Table 1.1 lists the references in Psalms for these quotations from the 2001 edition. The double lines in the

---

[4] A key example would be John 3. Where do the words of Jesus end and the Apostle John's testimony about the Son of God begin? See Gerald L. Borchert, *John 1–11,* vol. 25A of NAC (Nashville: Broadman & Holman, 1996), 179–80.

[5] For example, in Isaiah 42 does the direct quote that starts in v. 14 end at v. 16 or v. 20? Compare NASB with HCSB.

[6] (Nashville: Christian Bible Society, 1980). Produced anonymously, this work has since surfaced in various printings, editions, and revisions. For example, *The King James Red Letter Bible—Large Print Special Study Edition* (Goodyear, Ariz.: G.E.M., 2001); *Holy Bible: King James Version Easy Reader (KJVER)* (Goodyear, Ariz.: Global Evangelism Ministry, 2010). This publication's web cite (www.swordbible.org) offers a large variety of formats.

table indicate the book divisions in Psalms; notice that each of the five books has about the same number of quotes. As this edition acknowledges,[7] there are some difficulties identifying these because the original text does not use quotation marks and 14 of the 29 are not formally introduced. In these cases an interpreter has to make a judgment based on pronoun usage in the text that indicates that God is directly speaking. What we find are first-person pronouns (I, Me, My) that cannot be referring to the psalmist author.

Many of these cases are fairly obvious with general agreement that God must be speaking: for example, 46:10 ("Be still, and know that I am God: I will be exalted among the heathen ….); 50:7–15 ("Hear, O my people, and I will speak; O Israel, and I will testify against thee: I am God …."); 89:3–4 ("I have made a covenant with my chosen, I have sworn unto David my servant …"). Several other cases, however, call for special comment. (1) Psalm 27:8 contains three short clauses: "to You my heart said"; "Seek [2MP imperative] My face"; and "Your face, Yahweh, I will seek" (literal translations). Because of the difficult syntax many commentators and translators resort to emending the text,[8] but it is better to accept the MT and understand David as introducing a divine quotation.[9] Various translations add an additional clause like "When You said" (NASB, KJV, ASV, ESV, RSV) to make this clear, suggesting that the second clause is parenthetical to explain why David voiced the first clause; thus the third clause completes the first.

(2) In Psalm 32 after David addresses God as his "hiding place" (v. 7), suddenly there is another voice: "I will instruct thee …" (vv. 8–9). Without any introduction David records what God said in response to him.[10] Critics sometimes look at such cases as occasions when one who is worshipping the Lord suddenly receives what he thinks is a divine oracle.[11]

---

[7] From the "Preface": "The reader should be aware, however, that the red lettering is only 'suggestive,' and … scholars … will differ …" (p. v.).

[8] For a brief discussion of this, see Ross, 1:630–31.

[9] See Alexander, 130.

[10] VanGemeren says, "The sudden shift from the encouragement of God's protection (vv. 6–7) to the exhortation to wise living (vv. 9–11) is due to a word from the Lord. The personal pronoun 'I' does not come originally from the mouth of the psalmist. He quotes Yahweh …" (p. 315). But the references to Yahweh in vv. 10–11 must indicate that the quote ended in v. 9.

[11] For example, see Kraus: "Upon closer investigation, the individual statements in vv. 8–9 clearly show themselves to be divine utterances …. Against the

Theological Themes of Psalms

We must acknowledge, however, that not all conservative commentators are in agreement about this. For example, Perowne claims that it is the psalmist who is giving the instruction.[12]

(3) In Psalm 75 the abrupt change of pronouns between the first two verses clearly marks a switch from the psalmist to God even though there is no introduction of a new speaker. What is not clear, however, is where God's statement ends. The pronoun "I" (4 times in vv. 2–4) indicates that at least three verses are a direct statement from God, but when does the psalmist begin speaking again (v. 5, v. 6, or v. 7)?[13] Generally, the commentators and translations end the quotation before the word כִּי (*kiy,* "for"; v. 6) since it would possibly indicate a transition to a new thought.[14] The last verse of the psalm is even more difficult. Is it the psalmist who says, "All the horns of the wicked also will I cut off" (v. 10a)? Various commentators have declared that it is,[15] but Kidner argues that "in view of the emphasis on the one Judge, more probably this echoes God's own proclamation of 4 and 5."[16] Asaph, the author of this psalm, has no authority nor power to punish the wicked himself; it is Yahweh that promises to do this Himself.

---

argument of Delitzsch [who regards David as the speaker here], we should be reminded that an individual song of thanksgiving takes all of its perceptions from the conclusive divine oracle, which not infrequently is quoted in the Psalms" (1:371). Anderson says, "It is possible that ... the author is quoting the word of Yahweh which he received when he besought God during the time of affliction" (1:258).

[12] "The transition here to the direct form of address in the first person is certainly abrupt. Some have supposed that these are the words of God; but perhaps David himself speaks with something of a father's warning" (1:302). Steveson agrees with him (p. 130).

[13] See the lengthy discussion about all the different ideas from various commentators in Moll, 426.

[14] See the NET note on v. 4 about this Hebrew particle.

[15] For example, Calvin, 3:192; Alexander, 328–29; Rawlinson, 2:91; Steveson, 292; and VanGemeren, 579. Their basic argument is that "such a sudden, unmotivated shift of person is scarcely feasible" (Leupold, 547). The idea would be that the psalmist wants to act as God's instrument in eliminating the wicked.

[16] 16:302. Broyles agrees: "we should probably read it as a resumption of the divine oracle .... Yahweh is the one who hews off horns that would exalt themselves and exalts those who entrust—with praise—that prerogative to him" (p. 311).

12

(4) In Psalm 82 God, after being introduced in the first verse by the psalmist, is clearly speaking in the sixth verse, but where does His speech commence? Some regard Asaph as the one who says, "How long …?" (v. 2).[17] Others who view the first part as God's inquiry and indictment (vv. 2–4) raise questions about the middle verses (vv. 5–6).[18] There is an additional question about the fifth verse: a comment about the rulers or their victims?[19] It is best to view this verse as describing the "gods" and to see the first and last verses of the psalm as Asaph's bracketing of the divine word against human rulers (vv. 2–7),[20] which interrogates (v. 2), reprimands (vv. 3–4), describes (v. 5), and passes judgment on them (vv. 6–7).

(5) At the end of Psalm 87, we find the short clause "all my springs are in thee"(v. 7b). Who is saying this, and what is the antecedent of "thee"? Is the speaker God or the psalmist? Most commentators understand that the speakers are the singers mentioned at the verse's beginning,[21] but why switch from the plural to the singular ("my")? The switch from the first half of the verse to the second is so jarring that some have wanted to emend the Masoretic text. Another possibility is that the latter clause is actually the title of a song the musicians sing.[22] Context requires that "thee" refers to Zion, rather than to God. Since God has spoken earlier (v. 4), it is possible that the psalmist concludes the psalm with another statement from God about Zion. This is how the *Red Letter Bible* understands the clause. Thus God declares that His life-giving and holy springs will be in Zion (Ezek. 47:1, 8–9).

There are five additional cases that are more debatable. Table 1.2 lists these, indicating what there is in the context to suggest that God is speaking directly. (1) In the second psalm the concluding verses (vv. 10–12) appear to come from the psalmist, but what man has the authority to proclaim this threat and blessing? It makes more sense to say that though the

---

[17] For example, Steveson, 321. He does this on the basis that "Selah" marks a change of speakers.

[18] For example, Tate, 336–38. He ends up assigning the first verse to a someone in "the congregation" (v. 1) and the second to God.

[19] Kidner opts for the latter (16:329).

[20] Among those who agree with this analysis are Broyles, 335; Delitzsch, 2:549; Harmon, 2:620; and Weiser, 559.

[21] For example, Fausset, 287 & 289; Leupold, 626; Steveson, 340.

[22] Cohen, 284.

Theological Themes of Psalms

Table 1.1 Direct Quotations of God in Psalms (29 Cases)

Psalm	Verses	Words	Introductory Words: Hebrew	English (literal)
2:6	1	7	אָז יְדַבֵּר	Then He will speak (v. 5)
2:7b–9	2.5	19	אָמַר אֵלַי	He said to me
12:5	.8	10	יֹאמַר יְהוָה	Yahweh says
27:8b	.2	2		[none]
32:8–9	2	21		[none]
46:10	1	9		[none]
50:5	1	7	יִקְרָא	He shall call (v. 4)
50:7–15	9	63		[none]
50:16b–23	7.7	62	וְלָרָשָׁע אָמַר אֱלֹהִים	And to the wicked God said
60:6b–8	2.7	25	אֱלֹהִים דִּבֶּר	God has spoken
68:22b–23	1.7	13	אָמַר אֲדֹנָי	The Lord said
75:2–5	4	28		[none]
75:10	1	7		[none]
81:6–16	11	82	עֵדוּת	a testimony (v. 5)
82:2–7	6	42		[none]
87:4	1	12		[none]
87:7b	.6	3		[none]
89:3–4	2	14		[none]
89:19b–37	18.6	121	אָז דִּבַּרְתָּ־בְחָזוֹן	Then You spoke in a vision
90:3b	.4	3	וַתֹּאמֶר	And You said
91:14–16	3	20		[none]
95:8–11	4	34		[none]
105:11	.9	7	לֵאמֹר	saying
105:15	1	6		[none]
108:7b–9	2.7	25	אֱלֹהִים דִּבֶּר	God spoke
110:1b	.8	8	נְאֻם יְהוָה	the declaration of Yahweh
110:4b	.6	7	נִשְׁבַּע יְהוָה	Yahweh has sworn
132:11b–12	1.4	19	נִשְׁבַּע־יְהוָה	Yahweh has sworn
132:14–18	5	33		[none]
totals:	93.6	709	15	15

psalmist writes the words the Holy Spirit speaks directly here.[23] (2) The words of 14:4 most likely are a quote from the One who looked down to inspect mankind (v. 2).[24] (3) In Psalm 21 David begins by addressing and praising

---

[23] Boice says, "it is perhaps not overly whimsical to follow Ironside at this point …, since he speaks of 'four voices' in the psalm: those of the world, God the Father, God the Son, and God the Holy Spirit" (1:26).

[24] Cohen says simply, "In this verse God speaks" (p. 34). Barnes, however, regards this verse as spoken by the psalmist (p. 116).

Yahweh (vv. 1–6); then he states a fact about his faith (v. 7). Another shift occurs in the following verses: we have what has the appearance of a divine oracle delivered to David (vv. 8–12).[25] The last verse of the psalm shifts back to addressing the Lord (v. 13). (4) Some commentators have recognized 27:14 as a divine oracle that gives the Holy Spirit's response to David's prayer.[26] (5) The first five verses of Psalm 101 present David's resolve to live righteously, but the remaining verses (5–8) of the psalm seem to go beyond what David himself could ever do: knowing about secrets and proud attitudes (v. 5), watching over all the faithful (v. 6), and quickly destroying the wicked (v. 8). Is this a psalm that moves from David to the divine Messiah and His knowledge and actions? On the other hand this may be another case of an oracle from Yahweh after David has made his pledge.[27]

Table 1.2 Possible Additional Direct Divine Quotations

Psalm	Verses	Words	Hint
2:10–12	3	26	addressing kings (Who can do this?)
14:4	1	12	"My people" (Who can say this?)
21:8–12	5	38	"Your," & "You" (Who can find and destroy?)
27:14	1	9	"Wait" (Who can require faith?)
101:5–8	4	45	"My," "Me," & "I" (Who sees and destroys?)
totals:	14	130	

Propositions

Recording 839 words of direct quotations from God, the108 verses in Psalms listed in the two tables provide us with some significant theological insight. First and obviously, we note that (1) *God has indeed spoken to*

[25] "In what appears to be a divine oracle the king is told of the power he may wield against his enemies and foes." Broyles, 114. Ross recognizes that vv. 8–10 introduce a new speaker who addresses David, but he thinks it is a congregational spokesman (1:516). The other possibility is that these words are spoken to God. That is how NASB handles vv. 10–12 by capitalizing the second person pronouns.

[26] Kraus argues that this verse can not be the psalmist admonishing himself (the pronoun is 2MS not 1CS) or others (sg pronoun), but "a word of God by which the petitioner is encouraged to be firm and strong" (1:337). Kidner says, "this may even be the Lord's answering oracle" (15:139).

[27] John S. Kselman views the psalm as a dialogue and has set forth "the thesis that the 'I' of vv. 6-7 (and perhaps v. 8) is no longer the voice of the king, but of Yahweh, in the form of a divine oracle to the king." "Psalm101: Royal Confession and Divine Oracle," *JSOT* 33 (1985): 45–62.

mankind in normal words that mankind can understand. Verbs that indicate ordinary verbal communication appear several times to introduce the quotations: אמר (*'amar*, "to say"; 2:7; 12:5; 50:16; 68:22; 90:3; 105:11), דבר (*davar*, "to speak"; 2:5; 60:6; 89:19; 108:7), קרא (*qara'*, "to call"; 50:4). David used the noun נאם (*ne'um*, "declaration"; 110:1) once.

Many of the quotations occur in situations where the psalmist is petitioning or otherwise speaking to God and God enters into a dialogue with him. Thus we may say that (2) *God sometimes answers the prayers of saints directly with His word.* The so-called "answering oracle"[28] occurs in 12:5; 27:8; 32:8–9; 60:6; 108:7–9, and elsewhere. In Psalm 12 David has cried for help, and he gets an answer. In Psalm 27 David says, "hear" (v. 7), and he gets an answer. In Psalm 32 David testifies, "Thou art my hiding place" (v. 7), and the Lord speaks to him.[29] In Psalm 60 David says, "save" and "hear" (v. 5b), and God answers! In Psalm 108 David praises Yahweh (v. 3) and says, "Be thou exalted," and God speaks to him. The significance of this for us is that when we speak to God in prayer, we need then to open our Bibles and read, expecting the Holy Spirit to guide us to some verses and illumine our hearts that He is answering or speaking to us from the Scripture.

These direct quotations include cases when (3) *God has spoken directly about His plan.* In Psalms this is especially the case concerning the Davidic Covenant. Two of the longer quotations contain the specific promises God made to David: 89:19b–37 and 132:11–18, the latter focusing on the Lord's plans for Zion as "a lamp for David" (v. 17). In Psalm 2 the Lord states His blueprint for the messianic kingdom (vv. 6–9). In 46:10 Yahweh declares His plan to be universally glorified in the earth,[30] thus frustrating all His enemies' conspiracies (v. 6a). That plan God has not hidden from the wicked.

Furthermore, (4) *God has spoken directly to the wicked to warn them about the coming judgment.* Yahweh communicates to the rebellious kings in wrath (2:5) and informs them that the Messiah will "dash them in pieces like

---

[28] Eaton uses this expression four times in his commentary (pp. 89, 137, 227, and 396). Earlier Sigmund Mowinckel had used it in *The Psalms in Israel's Worship*, trans. D. R. Ap-Thomas (Oxford: Basil Blackwell, 1962), 2:77 and 149.

[29] Kidner notes that God's reply is not just to David, but "… through to the rest of us, since the command of verse 9 is in the plural" (15:152).

[30] God "bids them to 'desist' from their schemes and their rebellious and divisive ambitions, and to recognize where true power lies." Eaton, 191.

a potter's vessel" (v. 9b). Psalm 105:15 reports what God said to a pagan king concerning Abraham (Gen. 20:7). In Psalm 50, where the second and third longest quotes appear, He first admonishes His people who have been mistaken about the place of sacrifices (vv. 7–15); then Asaph records what God explicitly said "unto the wicked" (v. 16), and we have 62 words from the Lord that describe their sins and warn of their judgment (being torn to pieces, v. 22). Significantly, God mentions the possibility of deliverance from the coming destruction for a person who repents by changing his way (v. 23).[31] In another psalm by Asaph God speaks directly to the proud and wicked (75:4), warning them (v. 5) and announcing His personal judgment (v. 2). The most alarming statement to the wicked is the one God the Son makes in 101:7–8.

God also has something to say to the saints. (5) *The Lord encourages the righteous by directly promising to rescue them.* When David prayed for help, he heard God tell him what He would do for the one in need of salvation: "Now I will arise …; I will set him in the safety for which he longs" (12:5b, NASB). David knew the value of that promise because God's words are "pure" (v. 6).[32] The certainty of such promises is enhanced by God's faithfulness in the past: the Lord testifies directly about how He rescued Israel from Egypt (81:6–7, 10a). God directly promises deliverance from "the depths of the sea" (68:22) and victory over enemies (v. 23).[33] In Psalm 91 after the psalmist encourages the one who trusts in the Lord (vv. 9–11), suddenly God speaks with no introduction to promise deliverance in answer to prayer (vv. 14–16).[34] Indeed, God proceeds beyond His act of rescuing by expressly promising that "the horns of the righteous shall be exalted" (75:10b).

Additionally, (6) *God has words of instruction for the saints.* "I will instruct thee and teach thee in the way which thou shalt go: I will guide thee

---

[31] "The *idea* here is, that where there is a true desire to find the way of truth and salvation, God will impart needful instruction." Barnes, 2:80–81.

[32] That "expression removes the alloy of undependability. Man may often intend to do well and may promise help but may fall short of keeping his promise because of human frailty. Not so God." Leupold, 132.

[33] Boice recognizes the brutality of v. 23 and points out that "if this is a messianic reference, if we are to think not of Israel's enemies primarily but of God's enemies, then it is appropriate to think of such a complete destruction and rejoice in it" (2:562).

[34] These verses develop "an arresting climax as the psalmist carries the voice of God himself speaking of his beloved one in the third person …." Eaton, 327.

with mine eye" (32:8). He directly tells them not to harden their hearts as the Israelites did in the wilderness (95:8). On the positive side is the instruction to "wait on the LORD" (27:14).

We could make a further claim that (7) *God has something to say to everyone.* Psalms presents Him issuing a series of direct invitations. "Seek ye my face" (27:8a). "Be still, and know that I am God" (46:10a). Moses reported God's sincere bidding: "Return, ye children of men" (90:3b). Each of these are plural imperatives, addressed to all mankind.

New Testament Echoes

In the New Testament we notice cases where the very voice of God was heard on earth. At Christ's baptism God testified: "This is my beloved Son, in whom I am well pleased" (Matt. 3:17). At the Transfiguration the disciples heard that same voice: "This is my beloved Son, in whom I am well pleased; hear ye him" (Matt. 17:5). John 12:28–30 records another case of direct speech from God. Paul affirms that when he cried out to the Lord requesting deliverance from his thorn in the flesh (2 Cor. 12:7–8), God spoke to him: "My grace is sufficient for thee: for my strength is made perfect in weakness" (v. 9). The book of Hebrews begins with the affirmation that God has indeed spoken to mankind in the past (1:1) and that now He speaks to us by His Son (v. 2), who is indeed Immanuel, God with us. The claim of the writers of the Gospels is that they have recorded the very words of this Immanuel (hence red-letter editions of the NT). But it is not just the Gospels that record these direct quotes from Jesus: we find a number of them in Acts (1:4b–5, 7b–8; 9:4b–6, 11–12, 15–16; 11:16b; 18:9b–10; 20:35c; 22:7b–8, 10b, 18b, 21b; 23:11b; 26:14b–18). Paul quotes Christ a couple of times in his letters (1 Cor. 11:24b–25; 1 Tim. 5:18b).[35] Of course, Revelation contains a number of quotations in chapters 1–3 and 22. If we look at all these words of Christ, we will find Him affirming the seven propositions above.

A fitting conclusion to this theme of God's speaking to mankind is what the psalmist tells the Lord in Psalm 89: "Then You spoke in a vision to Your saints, and You said ..." (89:19a, literal translation). This is indeed good news! God chose to communicate with fallen people. When our first parents sinned, God could have punished them on the spot, but He came and spoke to them. We then have the first proclamation of the gospel (Gen. 3:15).

---

[35] Another case may be 1 Cor. 7:10 though we might consider this to be an indirect quote.

2

Instruction

God has spoken. When we say that, we naturally think about God's law delivered to Moses on Mount Sinai. The Hebrew word for "law" is תּוֹרָה (towrah),[1] related to a verb (ירה, yarah) that means "to teach" or "to instruct." As God has spoken to mankind, right from the beginning after creation, He instructed humans about His requirements and blessings (Gen. 1:28–30; 2:16–17). In fact, everything that the Lord has said to mankind could, in a broad sense, be called "instruction." God's word is always instructive for both the ungodly and the godly. The verb for instruction (ירה, yarah) appears twice in Psalm 25. The Lord "instructs sinners in the way" (v. 8, NASB), and He "instructs" those who fear Him (v. 12). Psalms has much to say about the Lord's instruction: over 200 verses treat the subject of God's word.

When the book of Psalms speaks about God's law, it is referring not just to the law of Moses as God's word but also to itself. In other words, the Psalms themselves are God's word. There are certain indications in the Old Testament that what the psalmists are saying has been inspired by the Holy Spirit. In a Davidic psalm recorded in 2 Samuel 23, David makes the following claim: "The Spirit of the LORD spake by me, and his word was in my tongue" (v. 2).[2] In Psalm 49 the author exhorts everyone to listen to his

---

[1] " 'Law' (*tôrâ*) in the broad sense refers to any 'instruction' flowing from the revelation of God as the basis for life and action." VanGemeren, 220.

[2] In v. 1 "*Oracle of David* ... indicates that David is speaking as a prophet, and uttering a divine word. This is expressly stated in verses 2–3.... Before the divine word is cited, a fourfold ascription makes certain that the Lord is known to be its source." Joyce G. Baldwin, *1 and 2 Samuel: An Introduction and Commentary*, TOTC (Downers Grove: InterVarsity, 1988), 311. The four indications of divine origin are "Spirit ... spake," "his word was in my tongue," "God ... said," and "the Rock ... spake."

19

poem because his "mouth shall speak of wisdom" (v. 3). This is really a claim that the Holy Spirit has revealed divine truth to him: "For the LORD giveth wisdom: out of his mouth cometh knowledge and understanding" (Prov. 2:6). Significantly, Psalm 49 speaks about the afterlife, providing instructions to us in the form of information that could only be known by revelation from God.

The New Testament clearly indicates the divine inspiration of Psalms. Our Lord based one of His arguments on the wording of Psalm 82:6, calling it a part of the "Law"; then He says, "the scripture cannot be broken" (John 10:34–35). Matthew 22:43 records Jesus saying that David was in the Spirit[3] when he called his messianic Son "Lord" (Ps. 110:1). Peter affirmed that David prophesied in writing Psalm 16:8–11 (Acts 2:30–31). The book of Hebrews opens with the declaration that God in the past spoke through prophets (1:1); then the author proceeds to quote from the Psalms five times in the first chapter, implying that the psalmists were indeed prophets.

Synonyms for the Word of God

As we search Psalms to gather information about what the book says about the word of God, we soon realize that there are a number of synonyms for this basic term. The book of Psalms uses eight main synonyms to refer to this instruction He has provided for mankind. In Psalm 119 these words occur 176 times, more than twice as many times as the occurrences in the rest of the book. Table 2.1 below lists these eight terms in the order of their first appearance in that psalm. Table 2.2 charts the remaining 75 uses of the synonyms for this concept.

The first synonym appearing in Psalm 119 is "law" (תּוֹרָה, towrah) from "instruct," and like this word many of the other synonyms derive from verbs. The KJV uses "testimonies" to translate the second synonym, which is the Hebrew word עֵדוּת ('eyduwth),[4] normally plural but used in the singular five times (19:7; 78:5; 81:5; 119:88; 122:4); the associated verb means "to

---

[3] "And when David used that term he was *inspired by the Spirit* (literally just 'in [the] Spirit'), i.e. he spoke as a prophet." R. T. France, *Matthew: An Introduction and Commentary*, Tyndale New Testament Commentaries (Downers Grove: InterVarsity Press, 1985), 325.

[4] By their vowel pointing the Masoretes distinguished this noun from a similar noun with the same meaning: עֵדָה ('eydah), 19x in Psalms. The LXX, however, did not make a distinction, always translating the two forms in the same way (with a form of the word μαρτυριον), just as our English translations do.

Table 2.1 Synonyms for Instruction in Psalm 119

Hebrew words:	תּוֹרָה towrah	עֵדֹת 'eydoth	פִּקּוּדִים piqquwdiym	חֻקִּים khuqqiym	מִצְוֹת mitswowth	מִשְׁפָּטִים mishpatiym	דָּבָר davar	אִמְרָה 'imrah
section	**law**	**witnesses**	**rules**	**statutes**	**commands**	**customs**	**word**	**saying**
1 (א)	1	2	4	5 8	6	7		
2 (ב)		14	15	12 16	10	13	9 16	11
3 (ג)	18	22 24		23	19 21	20	17	
4 (ד)	29	31	27	26	32	30	25 28	
5 (ה)	34	36	40	33	35	39		38
6 (ו)	44	46	45	48	47 48	43	42 43	41
7 (ז)	51 53 55		56	54		52	49	50
8 (ח)	61	59	63	64	60	62	57	58
9 (ט)	70 72		69	68 71	66		65	67
10 (י)	77	79	78	80	73	75	74	76
11 (כ)	85	88	87	83	86		81	82
12 (ל)	92	95	93 94		96	91	89	
13 (מ)	97	99	100 104		98	102	101	103
14 (נ)	109	111	110	112		106 108	105 107	
15 (ס)	113	119		117 118	115	120	114	116
16 (ע)	126	125	128	124	127			123
17 (פ)	136	129	134	135	131		130	133
18 (צ)	142	138 144	141		143	137	139	140
19 (ק)	150	146 152		145	151	149	147	148
20 (ר)	153	157	159	155		156 160	160	154 158
21 (ש)	163 165	167 168	168		166	164	161	162
22 (ת)	174		173	171	172 176	175	169	170 172
totals:	25	23	21	22	22	20	23	19

witness" or "to testify." How does a noun like this become a synonym for law or instruction? It turns out that one of the meanings of the verb is "to declare openly" or "to confirm a truth by oath": in that sense a law openly declared is a testimony. A sign that says, "Warning: Bridge Out!" is a witness that confirms a truth. God's covenant with Israel, which contained His laws, was confirmed by God's oath (Deut. 28:9). In a context of judgment God addresses Israel and says, "I will testify against thee" (50:7).[5] That is why the word "testimony" can parallel the word "law" in 19:7 and 78:5. God has affirmed His law; thus it is a witness to the fact of sin and judgment. The plural form "testimonies" indicates that the individual laws are each a warning in the form of an instruction that one must obey.

---

[5] At the end of his life Moses claimed the he was testifying to Israel concerning "all the words of this law" (Deut. 32:46).

The third synonym in Psalm 119 is the plural word פִּקּוּדִים (*piqquwdiym*), usually translated "precepts," related to the verb "to inspect" (פקד, *paqad*). Scrutinizing is the action of an overseer or supervisor, one who investigates the work or behavior of others to determine if they are in conformity with their instructions, procedures, or the rules that are supposed to govern their conduct.[6] The fourth is חֻקִּים (*khuqqiym*),[7] usually translated "statutes." Its corresponding verb means "to inscribe" by using a chiseling tool. This reminds us that God's laws were originally engraved on stone to indicate their permanence (Exod. 31:18).[8]

The fifth term, מִצְוֹת (*mitswowth*), "commands," always appears in this book as a plural, except for 19:8 and 119:96. Of course, its cognate verb is "to command." The focus is on the fact that God is an authority that gives orders to mankind. The sixth synonym is another plural, מִשְׁפָּטִים (*mishpatiym*), frequently translated "judgments" (KJV, ASV, NASB, HCSB). Related to the verb "to judge" (שׁפט, *shaphat*), the noun, however, has developed semantically in a couple of directions. When a judge hands down a decision, hopefully exhibiting justice and wisdom, he should make the same decision in an equivalent case, thus establishing legal precedent. As the courts hand down these "judgments" over the years, legal precedence grows, and we may speak of judicial customs, instead of "judgments."[9] This particular meaning eventually developed to the extent that the Hebrew noun could refer to any kind of "custom": for example, note the NRSV translation of the singular in 119:132 ("... be gracious to me, as is your custom toward those who love your name"). We can therefore speak of God's laws as His "customs,"[10] His legal precedents, standard procedures for mankind. Tables

---

[6] The noun "is a general term for the responsibilities that God places on his people." *TWOT*, 2:732. It only occurs in the book of Psalms, just three times outside of 119.

[7] Six times the word is sg (2:7; 81:4; 94:20; 99:7; 105:10; 148:6). A homonym ("bosom") occurs in 74:11.

[8] The permanence is highlighted in 148:6b. God "hath made a decree which shall not pass." Calvin says, "he gave that law to them which remains inviolable" (5:306).

[9] The word also developed the meaning of "justice": for example, "I have done justice and righteousness" (119:121, NASB).

[10] See Osborne Booth, "The Semantic Development of the Term מִשְׁפָּט in the Old Testament," *JBL* 61 (1942):105-110. He claims that the word means

2.1 and 2.2 list just the 33 cases (out of a total of 65) of this term in Psalms where its singular (twice: 81:4; 119:160[11]) or plural is used to refer to God's law, omitting references to justice (like 119:121) or to judgment (like 119:84).

The last two terms are interesting in that one is a very common noun that has produced a cognate verb and the other is a noun whose origin is from a very common verb. In meaning there is really little difference between them. The noun דָּבָר (*davar*), usually translated "word," has generated the denominative verb[12] דבר (*davar*), "to speak," used over a thousand times in the Hebrew Bible. The other noun, אִמְרָה (*'imrah*, "saying"), originated from the verb אמר (*'amar*), "to say," and is usually translated "word";[13] however, its usage in Psalm 119 points to the nuanced meaning of "promise"; the Geneva Bible translated it this way ten times, and the NAB used "promise" for all of its 19 occurrences in 119.[14] The singular and plural forms of דָּבָר (*davar*) occur 67 times in Psalms, but not all of these refer to God's

---

"custom" 26x in the OT, but I am counting the cases of his meaning 6 ("commandment of God") in this category. Booth claims that the concept of "custom" was original ("As custom does not develop from law, but law from custom, it is probable that the meaning of this word traveled in the same direction.") whereas I believe that "judgment" was first. The semantic changes all happened before the time of Moses; therefore, the texts that we have can not be used to trace the development.

Kidner points out that the term "is based on a court's recorded decisions and therefore comes to mean not only judgments (in both senses of that word) but Scripture, as God's will revealed" (15:165).

[11] In this verse there is strong textual evidence from various Hebrew MSS as well as the LXX, Syriac, Targum, and *PiH* that the plural is the correct reading. In fact, the very expression in this verse (מִשְׁפַּט צִדְקֶךָ) appears in the plural (מִשְׁפְּטֵי צִדְקֶךָ) in 119:7, 62, 106, and 164. Interestingly, the Geneva Bible, the KJV, and modern English translations use the plural in v. 160.

[12] In English we often verbify nouns: for example, "she likes to dust the house." Hebrew uses a morphological change in the noun to accomplish this: the consonantal root of the noun morphologically marked as a Piel verb. See *IBHS* §24.4. I maintain that the verb דבר (*davar*) is a Piel denominative. "The verb *dābar* ('speak') is derived from the noun …." VanGemeren, 220.

[13] Ross regards it as simply "a poetic variant" of דָּבָר (3:477).

[14] The KJV, however, used the word "promise" only twice in Psalms, once for אֹמֶר (*'owmer*) in 77:8 and once for דבר (*davar*) in 105:42. In Psalm 119 NIV and ESV translate אִמְרָה (*'imrah*) as "promise" eleven and twelve times, respectively.

instructions. In Psalm 119 every occurrence but one (v. 42a) fits this theme, but in the rest of the Psalter this is not the case. Many refer to man's words (for example, 55:21). Table 2.2 lists just those verses that treat in some way God's instructions.

Table 2.2 Synonyms for Instruction in Other Psalms

Hebrew words: Psalm	תּוֹרָה towrah law	עֵדוּת 'eyduwth witness	פִּקּוּדִים piqquwdiy rules	חֻקִּים khuqqiym statutes	מִצְוֹת mitswowth commands	מִשְׁפָּטִים mishpatiym customs	דְּבָר davar word	אִמְרָה 'imrah saying
1:	2 [2]							
2:				7				
10:						5		
12:								6 [2]
17:							4	
18:				22		22		30
19:	7	7	8		8	9		
25:		10						
33:							4 6	
36:						6		
37:	31							
40:	8							
48:						11		
50:				16				
56:							4 10	
72:						1		
78:	1 5 10	5 56			7			
81:		5		4		4		
89:	30			31	31	30		
93:		5						
94:	12			20				
97:						8		
99:		7		7				
103:			18				20 [2]	
105:	45			10 45		5 7	8 28 42	19
106:						12 24		
107:							20	
111:			7					
112:					1			
122:		4						
130:							5	
132:		12						
138:								2
147:				19		19 20	15 18 19	15
148:				6			8	
totals:	11	9	3	11	4	13	18	6

The theme of God's instructions utilizes some additional terms that can be identified by parallelism to the eight main synonyms. In Psalm 119, where almost every verse contains some reference to God's word, the third verse uses the plural of the term דֶּרֶךְ (*derek*), "way": "... they walk in his ways," paralleling "testimonies" in the second verse and "precepts" in the fourth verse. A similar phenomenon occurs in 119:36–38 ("testimonies," "ways," and "word"). Also in this psalm we find "way" connected with four of the main synonyms in the following phrases: "the way of thy testimonies/precepts/commandments/statutes" (vv. 14, 27, 32, 33). Literally, this word refers to a road; then by metonymy it came to mean "journey"; from this it developed metaphorically to refer to behavior. Hence, when David says that God "made known his ways unto Moses" (103:7), he is speaking about conduct that pleases the Lord.[15] God has prescribed such behavior by His laws; therefore, the word דֶּרֶךְ (*derek*), either singular or plural, can be a reference to instruction. Table 2.3 lists 17 such cases out of the 66 occurrences of this word in Psalms. Key examples are the instances when "way" is the object of a verb meaning "to teach": "What man is he that feareth the LORD? him shall [God] teach [ירה (*yarah*)] in the way ..." (25:12); "Then will I teach [למד (*lamad*)] transgressors thy ways" (51:13a); "cause me to know [*hiphil* of ידע (*yada'*)] the way wherein I should walk" (143:8b).[16] In each of these cases the psalmist is speaking about a knowledge of the Lord's law or instruction given by revelation.

---

[15] Conceivably in this particular verse, the "ways" could be a reference to God's own way of behavior or operating, as Moses mentions in Exod. 33:13 ("show me now thy ways, that I may know thee," ASV). See Moll, 525. Calvin says, "for these *ways*, which he says had been shown to Moses, were nothing else than the deliverance wrought for the people until they entered the promised land. He selected this as an instance of God's righteousness and judgment, surpassing all others, to prove that God always shows himself righteous in succouring those who are oppressed" (4:132). But Barnes counters, "God had *revealed his will;* that this had been done in an indubitable manner to Moses; and that these revelations had been recorded by him for the instruction and guidance of his people. The word *'ways'* here means his laws; his methods of administration; the principles on which he governs mankind, and the conditions on which he will save men. There is no higher ground of gratitude to God than the fact that he has given a revelation to mankind" (3:76).

[16] Additionally "way" occurs after ירה (*yarah*) in 27:11; 32:8; 86:11, after למד (*lamad*) in 25:9, and after of ידע (*yada'*) in 25:4 (in this case, "ways"). Note that the key synonym "statutes" (חֻקִּים, *khuqqiym*) occurs as the object of למד

25

Theological Themes of Psalms

Table 2.3 Additional Terms in Psalms for God's Instructions

Hebrew	English	#	References	Total in Psa
דֶּרֶךְ way		17	18:21; 25:4, 9, 12; 27:11; 32:8; 37:34; 51:13; 81:13; 86:11; 95:10; 103:7; 119:3, 37; 128:1; 138:5; 143:8	66
עֵצָה counsel		5	33:11; 73:24; 106:13; 107:11; 119:24	11
אֹרַח path		3	25:4, 10; 119:15	14
אֵמֶר word		3	78:1; 107:11; 138:4	7
אֹמֶר word		2	68:12; 77:8	4
נְאֻם declaration		1	110:1	2

The synonym of דֶּרֶךְ (*derek*), "way," is אֹרַח (*'owrakh*), "path"; 3 of its 14 uses in Psalms have reference to God's instructions. For example, "I will meditate in thy precepts, and have respect unto thy ways [אֹרְחֹתֶיךָ]" (119:15). Because of a parallelism between "words of God" and "counsel of the most High" in 107:11, it is evident that what God instructs can be called His "advice," עֵצָה (*'eytsah*), a term used in this way four other times in the book.[17] Table 2.3 also lists the occurrences of three infrequent synonyms for the noun דָּבָר (*davar*), "word": אֵמֶר (*'eymer*), אֹמֶר (*'owmer*), and נְאֻם (*ne'um*), better translated as "declaration" or "oracle." For each of these words only some of the usages are relevant for the theme of divine instruction.

Characteristics of God's Word

The 254 verses in 47 different psalms listed above in the three tables provide us with a wealth of information about the subject of God's instructions for mankind. The Holy Spirit has indicated four characteristics. Primacy belongs to the fact that (1) God's word is true. This is indicated primarily by the term צֶדֶק (*tsedeq*), "righteousness." This Hebrew noun indicates that someone or something has met a standard.[18] In regard to words or communication, that standard is truthfulness.[19] Psalm 119 attributes

---

(*lamad*), "teach," six times in Psalm 119 (vv. 12, 26, 64, 68, 124, and 136) and once with ירה (*yarah*), "instruct" (v. 33).

[17] In 119:24b literally "the men of my counsel"; that is, "counselors." Calvin comments: the psalmist "did not rely on his own judgment simply, but took counsel from the word of God" (4:418).

[18] See Harold G. Stigers, "צֶדֶק (*sedeq*)," *TWOT* 2:752–55.

[19] Because several of the terms for God's communication refer to His laws, we could argue that the standard is justice; however, it seems inconceivable that a just

"righteous" to the various synonyms ten times (vv. 7, 62, 75, 106, 123, 138, 144, 160, 164, and 172), mainly "judgments" (5x). The psalmists explicitly say that God's word is true at least four times by using the noun אֱמֶת (*'ameth*), "truth."[20] "The judgments [מִשְׁפָּטִים (*mishpatiym*)] of the LORD are true" (19:9); "your law/commands/words is/are true" (119:142, 151, 160, NIV). Additionally, in Psalm 25 if אָרְחוֹת (*'arekhowth*), "ways," in verse 10 can be connected to its synonym דֶּרֶךְ (*derek*), "way," in verse 9, where the term refers to God's communication (because this is what He "teaches"), then we have the statement "All the paths [His instructions] of the LORD are … truth."[21]

Another way to express the verity of God's instructions is the use of the word יָשָׁר (*yashar*), "upright": "For the word of the Lord is right" (33:4) and "upright are thy judgments" (119:137b). The Geneva Bible recognized the connotation of the Hebrew verb אָמַן (*'aman*), "reliable," and translated 111:7 as "all his statutes are true."[22] Thus we can recognize that "sure" means "true" also in 19:7 ("testimony") and 93:5 ("testimonies"). The word, however, that really stresses this characteristic is תָּמִים (*tamiym*), "perfect," applied to the "law" in 19:7 and when referring to communication, indicating absolute veracity.[23]

This veracity is part of what makes feasible the next characteristic. (2) God's word is immutable. Lies are eventually rejected and not

---

law could not also meet the standard of truth. Calvin's comment on 119:7 is appropriate: "the prophet commends God's law on account of the thorough perfection of the doctrine contained in it" (4:406). Only doctrine that is true can be perfect.

[20] It is common for the Hebrew language to use various nouns to function as descriptive in the way we use our adjectives. This is done usually by joining the attribute noun to the construct state of the noun it modifies. For example, Hebrew "hill of thy holiness" equals English "thy holy hill" (49:3). Thus the noun אֱמֶת (*'ameth*) appears in the expression "God of truth" (31:5), which means "faithful God" or "the true God." Ross, 1:691.

[21] In verse 10 Delitzsch ties the word "truth" to "the certainty of [God's] promises" (1:344). Ross says, "God is faithful to his covenant promises" (1:601), which would include the idea that the promises are true.

[22] Delitzsch says the Lord's "testimony" is "raised above all doubt in its declarations, and verifying itself in its threatenings and promises" (1:286).

[23] "It is flawless. It is without error. There is no misleading or unnecessary instruction. It is sound, consistent, unimpaired, and genuine." Ross, 1:478.

remembered; books full of false theories and incorrect statements are discarded. The truth, however, endures. "LORD, Your word is forever; it is firmly fixed in heaven" (119:89, HCSB; see also KJV, ESV, NET). It does not pass away: "he hath made a decree which shall not pass" (148:6b). It does not fall like error: His "counsel … standeth for ever" (33:11a). Yes, what God says is eternal: "every one of thy righteous judgments endureth for ever" (119:160).

Furthermore, (3) God's word is powerful. Psalm 29:4a tells us, "The voice of the LORD is powerful." His word was the means of creation: "By the word of the LORD were the heavens made; and all the host of them by the breath of his mouth" (33:6). It is also the means of the preservation of the earth, for all things have to obey His orders: "They continue this day according to thine ordinances: for all are thy servants" (119:91).[24] Psalm 147 states that God merely "sends forth His command/word to the earth" (vv. 15, 18), and things happen. When people were in great trouble, God "sent his word, and healed them" (107:20a).

Finally, (4) God's word is wonderful. "Thy commandment is exceeding broad" (119:96b). The expression רְחָבָה מְאֹד (*rekhavah me'owd*), "very wide," indicates that the law is immeasurable,[25] that it is profound,[26] containing numerous spiritual implications. Christ made some of these explicit for us (Matt. 5:21–48). Another passage uses a different metaphor to indicate that God's revelation is unfathomable: "thy judgments are a great deep" (36:6b).[27] Thus we look with amazement at God's Law, indeed at the whole of Scripture. Three times in 119 the author uses words from the Hebrew root פלא (*pala'*, "to be marvelous, extraordinary, or difficult") to specify this characteristic: "Open thou mine eyes, that I may

---

[24] "They have humbly to obey God's judicial decisions … because these declarations, long since formulated in the Law, are unalterably valid, as being words of God, and sure from eternity." Moll, 591–92.

[25] "The idea of breadth must involve the thought that the scope of this divine Word is simply without parallel as far as other earthly things and values are concerned." Leupold, 843.

[26] "Verse 96 (like Job 28:3) emphasizes the mystery of divine wisdom …." Hossfeld & Zenger, 15C:276.

[27] Concerning this reference Ross says, "his wisdom and knowledge are unsearchable…. no one can possibly get to the bottom of God's decisions, let alone understand them" (1:791).

behold wondrous things out of thy law" (v. 18); "Make me to understand the way of thy precepts: so shall I talk[28] of thy wondrous works" (v. 27); "Thy testimonies are wonderful" (v. 129a).

Propositions

Of course, each of these characteristics has been stated above as a proposition, but this section will treat four of the many propositions which express actions rather than attributes. With regard to His word God acts on mankind, and the saints react. Constantly, the psalmists tell us that (1) *God has revealed His word to mankind.* "The Lord gave the word" (68:11a).[29] This is also the request for the king: "Give the king thy judgments [laws]" (72:1). In Psalm 119 God's statutes are the object of the verb לָמַד (*lamad*), "teach," 7x in requests by the psalmist: "teach me thy statutes" (vv. 12, 26, 64, 68, 108,[30] 124, and 135). Additionally in verse 33 he says, "Teach me [*hiphil* of יָדַע (*yada'*), 'cause me to know'], O Lord, the way of thy statutes." And the author of this psalm affirmed that God has indeed done that: "for thou hast taught me" (vv. 102 & 171, using different Hebrew verbs; also 71:17). Other ways of making this request are "grant me thy law graciously" (119:29b) and "Incline my heart unto thy testimonies" (v. 36). In 147:19 three of the synonyms are the direct objects of God's reporting: "He sheweth his word unto Jacob, his statutes and his judgments unto Israel."

(2) *The saints habitually think about God's word.* That is their first reaction to God's revelation. They must remember what God has said and consciously meditate on divine revelation. "Remember … the judgments uttered by His mouth" (105:5, NASB). God approves of "those that remember his precepts to do them" (103:18b). The psalmist affirms that he "remembered thy judgments of old" (119:52). Many times this idea is stated in the negative: the psalmist has not forgotten God's instruction (119:16, 61, 83, 93, 109, 141, 153, 176). What makes this possible is his constant meditation on God's word: the verb (שִׂיחַ, *siyakh*) occurs in 119:15, 23, 27,

---

[28] The other five times this verb occurs in 119 the KJV translated it as "meditate." Scripture is wonderful because "The word opens up the greatness of God's acts in creation and in redemption" (VanGemeren, 865).

[29] In context this verse specifically refers to a word of victory, but its wording appropriately states this proposition.

[30] In v. 108 the object is מִשְׁפָּטִים (*mishpatiym*), "judgments," rather than חֻקִּים (*khuqqiym*).

48, 78, and 148; the noun (שִׂיחָה, *siykhah*) occurs in verses 97 and 99. In fact, meditation about God's instructions seems to be the defining characteristic of the righteous person: "and in his law doth he meditate [a different verb here: הגה, *hagah*] day and night" (1:2b).[31]

(3) *The saints emotionally react to God's word by delighting in and loving it.* The first part of Psalm 1:2 is "But his delight [חֵפֶץ, *kheyphets*] is in the law of the LORD."[32] The verb חפץ (*khaphats*), "to delight," appears twice in reference to God's instructions: "Blessed is the man … that delighteth greatly in his commandments" (112:1); "Make me to go in the path of thy commandments; for therein do I delight" (119:35). In Psalm 119 a different verb (שׁעע, *sha'a'*) for this concept appears three times: "I will delight myself in thy statutes/commandments" (vv. 16a, 47a); "I delight in thy law" (v. 70b). The noun (שַׁעֲשֻׁעִים, *sha'eshu'iym*)[33] related to this second verb occurs five times: "my delight" (vv. 24 [thy testimonies], 77, 92, & 174 [thy law], and 143 [thy commandments]). Relative to this proposition are two verses that speak about joy over the Lord's "customs" (48:11; 97:8).[34] Closely connected to this pleasure is the heart-felt love for the word: in Psalm 119 the author expresses his love ten times for Yahweh's "law" (vv. 97, 113, 163), "testimonies" (vv. 119, 167), "precepts [פִּקּוּדִים, *piqquwdiym*]" (v. 159), "commands" (vv. 47, 48, 127), or "word [אִמְרָה, *'imrah*]" (v. 140).[35]

(4) *The saints are regularly obedient to God's word. The emotional response leads to actions.* Repeatedly in Psalm 119 there is the promise to "keep" the word: verses 8, 33, 34, 44, 57, 69, 106, 145, and 146 (at least 9x). Furthermore, there are the psalmist's affirmations that he has done this: verses 55, 56, 60, 67, 100, 129, 167, and 168. For this action Hebrew uses two

---

[31] "This half-aloud reading and rereading are really the process of musing or meditating …." Leupold, 36.

[32] "Instead of finding his happiness in the society and the occupations of the wicked, he finds it in the truth of God." Barnes, 1:4.

[33] The plural form of this term is intensive: "sheer delight." GKC §124e. Alexander views the plural as "denoting fulness and completeness" (p. 493).

[34] Many commentators miss this reference to delight in the word because they understand "judgments" in another sense. For example, concerning 48:11 Calvin says, the psalmist "makes use of the word judgment, because God, who undertook the cause of his Church, openly showed that he was the enemy of her oppressors, and that he would repress their presumption and audacity" (2:230).

[35] In this verse the psalmist refers to himself as "thy servant" rather than "I."

verbs (שָׁמַר, *shamar*; נָצַר, *natsar*), which appear in parallel (for example, 105:45) and are semantically equivalent.[36] Sometimes these verbs have been translated as "guard" (for example, NASB 20 and 2x respectively; for example, 91:11), and that would give a better picture of what is involved with this concept. Guarding requires conscious diligence as well as a carefulness about one's actions; thus "guarding a commandment" cannot be done casually, but requires a careful attention that avoids even an accidental violation. Only in this fashion can one achieve integrity of conduct.

New Testament Echoes

The terms "law" (νόμος, *nomos*, 194x) and "word" (λόγος, *logos*, 330x) are extremely common in the New Testament, though many of these uses do not relate to God's instructions (for example, Rom. 7:21 and Col. 3:17). In New Testament usage "Law" can refer to the holy Scriptures of the Old Testament (for example, John 12:34 and Rom. 3:19), attesting to the idea that all of God's communication with mankind is instruction.

The Septuagint translated the eight Hebrew synonyms of Psalm 119 by using seven different Greek words.[37] The 175 Hebrew nouns in Table 2.1 are matched by 173 uses of these Greek terms.[38] The following verses represent some of the significant uses in the New Testament of these seven Greek synonyms for God's instructions. (1) Christ affirmed both the permanence and truthfulness of the Law (νόμος, *nomos*): "Til heaven and earth pass, one jot or one tittle shall not pass from the law till all be fulfilled" (Matt. 5:18). (2) In Matthew 24:14 we find an example of God's word serving as a testimony of the truth: "And this gospel of the kingdom shall be preached in all the world for a witness [μαρτύριον, *marturion*] unto all nations." (3) Christ did not hesitate to identify the two greatest

---

[36] Keith N. Schoville, "נצר," *NIDOTTE*, 3:148.

[37] Two additional Greek synonyms (διάταξις, *diataksis*; "command," and κρίσις, *krisis*; "judgment") were used to translate מִשְׁפָּטִים (*mishpatiym*, "judgments" or "rules"), vv. 91 and 137.

[38] Although some of these match the Hebrew exactly (for example, μαρτυρία [*marturia*] for עֵדֹת ['*eydowth*], "witnesses" 23x), there are some inconsistencies: for example, νόμος (*nomos*), "law," for תּוֹרָה (*towrah*) 25x, but once for דָּבָר (*davar*), "word," in v. 57. The LXX used δικαιώματά (*dikaiōmata*), "regulations," for both חֻקִּים (*khuqiym*) (22x) and פִּקּוּדִים (*piqudiym*) (5x), which was translated as εντολάς (*entolas*), "laws," the other 16x.

commandments (ἐντολάς, *entolas*) in the Law (Matt. 22:37–39). (4) These instructions are identified with the revelation God gave to Moses: "Then verily the first covenant had also ordinances [δικαιώματα, *dikaiōmata*] of divine service, and a worldly sanctuary" (Heb. 9:1). (5) In Romans 11 Paul employs the special use of κρίματα (*krimata*), "judgments,"[39] for God's customs or directives: "how unsearchable are his judgments, and his ways past finding out" (v. 33). (6) The New Testament affirms the effectiveness of God's word: "For the word [λόγος, *logos*] of God is quick, and powerful, and sharper than any twoedged sword, piercing even to the dividing asunder of soul and spirit, and of the joints and marrow, and is a discerner of the thoughts and intents of the heart" (Heb. 4:12). (7) We find four cases of the word λόγια (*lōgia*) being used for the oracles of God (Acts 7:38; Rom. 3:2; Heb. 2:12; 1 Pet. 4:11).

As a fitting conclusion to this study of God's instructions, let us each affirm with the psalmist, "O how love I thy law! it is my meditation all the day" (119:97). May our love not terminate with just thoughts, but may it prompt us to spread the good news, to evangelize: "My tongue shall speak of thy word: for all thy commandments are righteousness" (119:172).

---

[39] Many NT exegetes understand this term as referring to God's work of judgment. For example, Robert Jewett and Roy David Kotansky say, " 'God's judgments' (τὰ κρίματα αὐτοῦ) comprise actions against oppressors and in behalf of the oppressed ...." *Romans: A Commentary*, ed. Eldon Jay Epp, vol. 45 of Hermeneia (Minneapolis: Fortress Press, 2006), 717. William Sanday and Arthur C. Headlam also see this as "not judicial decisions, but judgements on the ways and plans of life." *A Critical and Exegetical Commentary on the Epistle to the Romans*, 5th ed., ICC (Edinburgh: T. & T. Clark, 1902), 340. But William Hendriksen is correct in saying that the reference is to "God's sovereign decisions, decrees, disposals." *Exposition of Paul's Epistle to the Romans*, vol. 6 of New Testament Commentary (Grand Rapids: Baker Book House, 1980-1981), 386. See also James Montgomery Boice, *Romans* (Grand Rapids: Baker Book House, 1991-1995), 3:1434.

3

Wisdom

God's instruction of mankind has its basis in His wisdom. He knows what is best for His creatures. When He speaks to human beings, as words emanate from His mouth, so does wisdom. This theme connects with that of the previous chapter, "Instruction," because wisdom is tied closely to the Torah or Law. The theme of wisdom, however, does not dominate the book of Psalms by means of key words. The standard word חָכְמָה (*khokmah*), which occurs 149 times in the Old Testament, is found only six times in Psalms. Related words occur only seven more times. Near the end of the book the psalmist uses one of the synonyms (תְּבוּנָה, *tevuwnah*) for wisdom and declares that God's "understanding is infinite" (147:5). This is the clearest statement in Psalms about this attribute of God. The expression translated "infinite" is literally "without number": it is impossible for us to calculate how great His wisdom is; He is omniscient! Psalms develops the wisdom of God theme by tying it to God's instruction and to His creation. Of course, the twelve wisdom psalms are also relevant for this topic.

The Wisdom of Instruction

God has not kept His wisdom to Himself, but has communicated part of it to mankind by giving us instructions. Proverbs begins with a wise father instructing his son (1:1–9) and then continues with a personification of Wisdom calling to the simple ones and offering them counsel (1:20–33). At that point we realize that Solomon is writing under inspiration with words of divine wisdom. In Psalms Asaph can say, "I will open my mouth in a parable: I will utter dark sayings of old" (78:2) only because God's Spirit has inspired him and those that wrote earlier Scripture (v. 3).[1] As another psalmist

---

[1] I understand the "we" in v. 3a to refer to Asaph and other psalmists, who heard their message from the Holy Spirit. Note that the "we" in v. 4, not simply "I,"

reflects on what he writes under inspiration,[2] he describes it as speaking wisdom (49:3).[3] As David ponders God's revelation to him, he refers to God's teaching him wisdom: "in the hidden part thou shalt make me to know wisdom" (51:6b). All references in Psalms referring to God's law, therefore, are indications that there is wisdom behind those instructions. That means the focus of Psalm 119 on the delights found in God's word (for example, v. 47) are at the same time the pleasures of contemplating God's wisdom. Psalm 19:7–11 also focuses on the law and makes a direct connection to wisdom: "making wise the simple" (v. 7d). Of course, references to God's counsel presuppose that His advice is wise. Asaph is confident that his Lord guides him in this life by counseling him (73:24a). Actually, God's laws act as counsellors (119:24), but often people spurn that counsel (107:11), refusing "to walk in his law" (78:10). As a result, the Psalmist concludes, "Therefore their days did he consume in vanity, and their years in trouble" (v. 33).

The Wisdom of Creation

The psalmists explicitly connect God's wisdom to His work of creation in two passages. "O LORD, how manifold are thy works! in wisdom hast thou made them all: the earth is full of thy riches" (104:24).[4] The last word in the verse (קִנְיָן, *qinyan*) is usually translated as "creatures" (NIV, ESV, HCSB, NAB) and refers to possessions, either purchased or created. The variety and intricacy of what God has created required immeasurable wisdom on His part. The second passage focuses on the skill of creating the celestial objects: "To him that by wisdom made the heavens" (Psalm 136:5a). Here the word תְּבוּנָה (*tevuwnah*, "understanding") can be translated as "skill" (NASB). The following verses describe His skillful acts: He "stretched out the earth above the waters"; "made ... the sun to rule by day"; "the moon

---

refers to the communication that Asaph provides in vv. 5ff. What the "fathers have told us" certainly includes the writings of Moses.

[2] "He knew that the Spirit of truth and wisdom spoke through him." Spurgeon, 2:369.

[3] The word for wisdom in this verse is plural (חָכְמוֹת, *khokmowth*). This is a plural of amplification (GK, § 124e), indicating extraordinary or especially great wisdom. The same usage applies to the word "understanding" (תְּבוּנוֹת, *tevuwnowth*), "profound insight or understanding" (Delitzsch, 2:110).

[4] "All nature yields a manifold science, of which it is the concrete embodiment, proving the universal intelligence of the Maker." Murphy, 543.

and stars to rule by night" (vv. 6–9). Some other psalms that describe creation also indicate the Creator's wisdom. When David says, "The heavens declare the glory of God; and the firmament sheweth his handiwork" (19:1), a significant portion of that glory is the wisdom that is revealed in the things He has made.[5] We marvel at the skill that put the earth, moon, and planets in their orbits. That wonder is there in 8:3, where David says, "When I consider thy heavens, the work of thy fingers, the moon and the stars, which thou hast ordained." When the psalmist exclaims, "Indeed, the world is firmly established, it will not be moved" (93:1b, NASB), he uses the same expression that appears in 104:5 (בַּל־תִּמּוֹט, *bal-timmowt*; literally, "it cannot not be shaken"). Since Psalm 104 is clearly about creation, 93:1 can be understood in the same way.[6] If the earth's orbit and speed were erratic, ocean tides and our counting of time would be chaotic. Psalm 104 proceeds to provide numerous examples of God's wise control of the forces of nature to make provision for the needs of plants, animals, and mankind (vv. 10–23).

The Wisdom Psalms

Scholarly studies in Psalms often refer to a group called "wisdom psalms," those that have some of the characteristics of the wisdom literature in Proverbs, Job, and Ecclesiastes. There is, however, much disagreement over what requirement a particular psalm must meet to fall into this category. There is some consensus on a short list (37, 49, 112, and 128), but wide differences in lists of nine or more. In fact, some scholars even dispute whether it is proper to speak of wisdom psalms.[7] One way to identify them is by wisdom motifs, indicated by special wisdom vocabulary.[8] This

---

[5] "The glory of God is the sum of his revealed perfections ...." Alexander, 87.

[6] "This 'act of establishing' is the actual work of creation." Kraus, 2:234.

[7] James L. Crenshaw has said, "My own research in the Psalter leads me to question the very category of wisdom psalms. ... Perhaps we should limit ourselves to what can definitely be affirmed: some psalms resemble wisdom literature in stressing the importance of learning, struggling to ascertain life's meaning, and employing proverbial lore." *The Psalms: An Introduction* (Grand Rapids: Eerdmans, 2001), 94.

[8] C. Hassell Bullock has expanded R. B. Y. Scott's list of terms and used them to analyze nine psalms that have a claim to this category. *Encountering the Book*

terminology includes references to wisdom, understanding, the law, parables, fearing God, a contrast of the righteous and wicked, and the blessing that comes from being wise. Table 3.1 provides a list of twelve possible psalms that fall into this category and indicates some of the characteristic wisdom vocabulary in each psalm. Psalm 37 is loaded with wisdom terms. The last three psalms in the list are rather short. As indicated by the double lines, wisdom psalms appear in four of the books of Psalms, with special concentration in Book V. It is quite evident that these sub-themes primarily concern wisdom as it applies to mankind. The attribute of God's wisdom is not usually transparent in these wisdom psalms, but it is there if we meditate on God's communication to man.

Table 3.1 Listing of Wisdom Psalms

Psalm	Key Words in the KJV (v. #)
1:	blessed (v. 1), law (v. 2)
19:	law (v. 7), wise (v. 7), fear of the Lord (v. 9)
37:	righteous/wicked (4x), consider (v. 10), wisdom (v. 30), law (v. 31)
49:	wisdom (v. 3), understanding (vv. 3, 20), parable (v. 4), wise (v. 10)
73:	understood (v. 17), counsel (v. 24)
78:	law (vv. 1, 5, 10), parable (v. 2), skilfulness (v. 72)
111:	fear of the Lord (v. 10), wisdom (v. 10), understanding (v. 10)
112:	blessed (v. 1), feareth the Lord (v. 1)
119:	blessed (vv. 1–2), law (25x), counsellors (v. 24), wiser (v. 98)
127:	blessed (v. 5)
128:	blessed (vv. 1–2), feareth the Lord (vv. 1, 4), days of thy life (v. 5)
133:	blessing (v. 3), life for evermore (v. 3)

New Testament Echoes

The Greek word for wisdom (σοφία, *sophia*) occurs over 50 times in the New Testament, 15 times in 1 Corinthians 1–2. Paul marvels at the magnitude of God's wisdom (Rom. 11:33), and the church exists to manifest this wisdom to the angelic beings (Eph. 3:10). From His childhood Christ was "filled with wisdom" (Luke 2:40). His wisdom amazed the people of His hometown (Matt. 13:54). As the great Prophet, Christ in His communications to mankind has greater wisdom than Solomon (Matt. 12:42). Jesus referred to Himself as "the wisdom of God" (Luke 11:49).

---

of Psalms: A Literary and Theological Introduction (Grand Rapids: Baker Academic, 2001), 203–07.

Furthermore, Paul specifically identified Jesus Christ with wisdom: "Christ the power of God, and the wisdom of God"; "Jesus Christ, who of God is made unto us wisdom ..." (1 Cor. 1:24, 30). Additionally, some of the wisdom psalms are quoted in the New Testament: 19:4 (Rom. 10:18), 78:2 (Matt. 13:35), and 112:9 (2 Cor. 9:9).

The concluding book in the New Testament gives us a glimpse into heaven as John records for us the scene: a scroll sealed with seven seals in the hand of God. No one in heaven is found worthy to open the book until the Lamb of God takes it. The inhabitants of heaven sing a new song, "Worthy is the Lamb that was slain to receive power, and riches, and wisdom, and strength, and honour, and glory, and blessing" (Rev. 5:12). As the seals are opened, the righteous judgments of God begin to be loosed on the earth. But God's wisdom will not allow His faithful servants to suffer the penalty which the Lamb has already paid. God stops the progress of the judgment to seal His 144,000 faithful servants among Israel. An innumerable multitude from all nations as well as heavenly beings fall on their faces before the throne, "saying, Amen: Blessing, and glory, and wisdom, and thanksgiving, and honour, and power, and might be unto our God for ever and ever. Amen" (Rev. 7:12). The book of Revelation gives us a detailed description of God's judgment, but we also see the wisdom of God in a new creation: a Holy City coming down from heaven where God will finally be able to dwell with His people (21:2). The laws that by God's wisdom sustained the first earth will be changed. This new creation will not need the sun or the moon, for there will be no night, and the Lamb will be its light (21:23). Familiar elements such as fruit trees will be there, but they will bear twelve different fruits according to the month (22:2). The river will flow from the throne of God, not from the top of a mountain (22:1). Just the function of a three-dimensional city in a cubical form (21:16) is unimaginable to us, but the wisdom of God will construct it.

In conclusion, we call attention to the fact that the Holy Spirit, who has communicated wisdom to mankind, exhorts us to be wise. "Who is wise? Let him give heed to these things, and consider the lovingkindnesses of the LORD" (107:43, NASB). We all need to reflect on God's wise instruction and focus on the Lord's goodness and faithfulness. The instructive wisdom of Psalm 111 challenges us to contemplate God's creative wisdom: "Great are the works of the LORD, studied by all who delight in them" (v. 2, ESV); "He hath made his wonderful works to be remembered" (v. 4a). The psalmist speaks of redemption (v. 9), and in the last verse comes back to wisdom's great slogan: "The fear of the LORD is the beginning of wisdom" (v. 10a).

4

Creation

The first three chapters have prepared us for the theme of God's work of creation. The act of God's speaking (Chapter 1) led to heavenly bodies coming into existence: "he commanded, and they were created" (148:5b). The instructions He gave (Chapter 2) were the means of creation: "By the word of the LORD were the heavens made" (33:6a). Two of the twelve wisdom psalms (78 & 119) have something to say about creation. Of course, the book of Psalms connects God's wisdom (Chapter 3) to His creative acts: "O LORD, how manifold are thy works! in wisdom hast thou made them all" (104:24a); "To him that by wisdom made the heavens" (136:5a).[1]

The Psalms frequently celebrate this theme and praise God for this particular work of His. The doctrine of creation appears in 33 psalms, occurring in 51 different verses. Every one of the five Books in Psalms treats this subject in at least three psalms, with dominance in the last two Books (17 verses in Book IV, 15 in Book V). Since the Bible itself begins with creation and because creation is the first of God's awesome works, it is a fitting topic in praising the Lord and appears in four of the five concluding hallelujah psalms (146:6; 147:8; 148:5; 149:2).

Vocabulary of Creation

The normal Hebrew verb for "create" (ברא, *bara*) occurs six times in Psalms (see Table 4.1 below). By noting parallels to this word, we discover additional terms for this theme. The poetry of Isaiah 45:18a gives us three synonyms: "For thus saith the LORD that **created** the heavens; God himself

---

[1] In the second verse the word translated as "wisdom" in the KJV is actually the Hebrew term תְּבוּנָה (*tebuwnah*, "understanding"). This is the only place in the KJV where this term is translated as "wisdom," but Hebrew parallelism indicates that it is indeed another way of referring to the concept of wisdom. Note the following passages: Exod. 36:1; Ps. 49:3; Prov. 2:2; 3:13; 8:1; Jer. 51:15 (and various others).

that **formed** the earth and **made** it; he hath **established** it ..." (my emphasis). The verb עָשָׂה (*'asah*, "to make") is a very general term that occurs over 2500 times in the Old Testament, over 100 times in Psalms, where it specifically refers to creation 17 times. Parallel to it in 95:5 is the verb יָצַר (*yatsar*, "to form"), used for God's creative activity in five out of its seven occurrences in Psalms. It can designate the activity of a potter with his clay. In 74:17b English versions (KJV, ASV, NASB, ESV, HCSB, and NIV)[2] usually translate it as "made." In this same context the third synonym from Isaiah 45:18 appears: "The day is thine, the night also is thine: thou hast prepared the light and the sun" (74:16). This verb כוּן (*kuwn*, "to establish") indicates founding or setting up something firmly, for example, of a man setting up a city (Hab. 2:12) or of establishing an altar (Ezra 3:3).

The psalmists make use of four additional verbs for creation (listed in Table 4.1 below). Parallel to כוּן (*kuwn*) in 24:2 is the term יָסַד (*yasad*, "to found"): "For he has **founded** [the earth] upon the seas, and **established** it upon the floods" (my emphasis). Six out its ten occurrences in Psalms refer to creative action. Parallel to עָשָׂה (*'asah*) in 95:5 is יָצַר (*yatsar*, "to form"): "The sea is his, and he **made** it: and his hands **formed** the dry land." This verb refers to creation an additional four times in Psalms. When David asks the Lord to "create ... a clean heart" in him, the parallel is "renew a right spirit within me" (51:10). The verb חָדַשׁ (*khadash*) could be translated "make anew" or "create something new."[3] The same verbs are parallel in 104:30. The verb קָנָה (*qanah*), which normally means "to buy" or "to acquire" can rarely mean "to create,"[4] as it does in 139:13.[5] An additional

---

[2] An exception is NET: "you created the cycle of summer and winter," with its note giving the literal "you formed them."

[3] Notice what Pieter A. Verhoef says about the new spirit of Ezek. 11:19 in connection with Ps. 51:10, 12 and Jer. 31:33. It "will be fully realized in the 'new creation' of the NT (2 Cor 5:17; cf. also Rom 6:4; 7:6; Eph 2:15; 4:24) ...." "חדשׁ," *NIDOTTE*, 2:35–36.

[4] See the lengthy discussion by W. H. Schmidt, "קנה *qnh* to acquire," *TLOT*, 1151–53.

[5] The cognate noun (קִנְיָן, *qinyan*) to this verb occurs in 104:24c, possibly with the meaning "creation." "The earth is full of your creatures" (ESV). Better yet is the full translation of the verse in NET: "How many living things you have made, O LORD! You have exhibited great skill in making all of them; the earth is full of the living things you have made." This is how the LXX understood the word. But

verse counted in the totals but not noted in the table is 90:2, which uses the verbs יָלַד (*yalad*) and חִיל (*khiyl*): "Before the mountains were brought forth [literally, "were born"], or ever thou hadst formed [literally, "brought forth by labor pains"] the earth and the world, even from everlasting to everlasting, thou art God." Also, five verbs not included in the table are used in contexts of creation and in parallel with verbs in the table: (1) נטע (*nata'*), "planted the ear" (94:9); (2) נטה (*natah*), "stretchest out the heavens" (104:2); (3) רקע (*raqa'*), "stretched out the earth" (136:6); (4) סכך (*sakak*), "wove me in my mother's womb" (139:13); (5) עמד (*hiphil* of *'amad*), "stablished them for ever" (148:6). These provide pictures of the ease of God's creative work: like planting a shoot, spreading a piece of cloth, hammering a piece of metal, weaving cloth, or hanging a door.

Table 4.1 Terminology in Psalms for Creation

Hebrew	English	#	References	Totals: Ps./all OT
בָּרָא create		6	51:10; 89:12, 47; 102:18; 104:30; 148:5	6/54
עָשָׂה make		17	33:6; 86:9; 95:5, 6; 96:5; 100:3; 104:19, 24; 115:15; 119:73; 121:2; 124:8; 134:3; 136:5, 7; 146:6; 149:2	110/2640
כּוּן establish		11	8:3; 24:2; 65:6, 9; 74:16; 89:37; 93:1; 96:10; 119:73, 90; 147:8	53/218
יָסַד found		6	24:2; 78:69; 89:11; 102:25; 104:5, 8	10/44
יָצַר form		5	33:15; 74:17; 94:9; 95:5; 104:26	7/45
חָדַשׁ renew		2	51:10; 104:30	3/10
קָנָה create		1	139:13	3/85
מַעֲשֶׂה work		8	8:3, 6; 19:1; 28:5; 33:4; 103:22; 111:2; 143:5	39/235
פֹּעַל work		2	111:3; 143:5	11/37
פְּעֻלָּה work		1	28:5	3/14

Table 4.1 also lists three additional terms. The cognate noun to the verb עָשָׂה (*'asah*) is מַעֲשֶׂה (*ma'eseh*; "work"), a word occurring over 235 times in the Old Testament, 39 times in Psalms. In at least eight passages referring to God's creative deeds.[6] In 28:5 מַעֲשֶׂה is parallel to the noun

normally this word means "possessions" or "property," connected to the common meaning for the verb ("to buy"). This sg noun occurs ten times in the OT, and in every case the meaning "possessions" fits appropriately. See Kidner's note (16:405).

[6] When David said "marvellous are thy works" in 139:14, he may have had in mind works of creation, not just his own origins in the womb. "From this particular instance [his own formation] David is led to refer in general to all the

פְּעֻלָּה (*pe'ullah*) and in 143:5 to the noun פֹּעַל (*pow'al*). The latter refers to creation also in 111:3.[7]

Propositions

The many verses in Table 4.1 provide us with at least seven propositions, some of them rather obvious but nevertheless important. (1) *God's work of creation is still active and ongoing.* In various of the passages it is difficult to discern between what God did in the original creation and what He is still doing in His work of preservation.[8] The psalmist describes the ongoing growth of plant life as creation: "Thou sendest forth thy spirit, they are created: and thou renewest the face of the earth" (104:30). Procreation becomes labeled as creation: "For you created my inmost being" (139:13, NIV).[9] The close connection between creation and preservation appears also in 102:18b and 149:2a.

(2) *The means of creation is God's spoken word.* "By the word of the LORD were the heavens made; and all the host of them by the breath of his mouth" (33:6). I believe that God the Father gave commands like "Let there be light" (Gen. 1:3), and God the Son implemented the orders: "for he commanded, and they were created" (148:5b). In the next verse the psalmist also calls the command a "decree" (חֹק, *khoq*).

---

works of God, which are just so many wonders fitted to draw our attention to him." Calvin, 5:214.

[7] Alexander contends that "*His work* means specifically here what he does for the protection and deliverance of his people" (pp. 469–70). Kidner says, "Here God's work … is more likely to mean His providential acts …; but Isaiah 45:9–13 reminds us not to draw too sharp a line between what He has made and what He is doing, which are all of a piece" (16:432). The mention of "great" and "splendor and majesty" (ESV) in vv. 2–3 would signal for us a reference to God's creative action. See 96:5–6, where the same expression "splendor and majesty" (הוֹד־וְהָדָר, *howd-wehadar*) occurs in the context of "the LORD made the heavens."

[8] Patrick D. Miller says, "the distinction between God as creator and God as Lord of history is more a convenience for the sake of systematizing our theological categories than it is a real distinction…. God's activity in creation and history are parts of a whole." *Interpreting the Psalms* (Philadelphia: Fortress Press, 1986), 74.

[9] "But it was not mother nature mysteriously at work when the human being began to take shape and form in the body of the mother. God was at work there, weaving together the substances that go to make up a human being." Leupold, 946.

(3) *Creation clearly displays God's attributes of wisdom and power.* The psalmists explicitly state that what God made He did by wisdom and understanding (104:24; 136:5). David affirms to God that "You created [כוּן, *kuwn*] the mountains by your power" (65:6, NET). John Calvin noted that "When a man, from beholding and contemplating the heavens, has been brought to acknowledge God, he will learn also to reflect upon and to admire his wisdom and power as displayed on the face of the earth, not only in general, but even in the minutest plants."[10] God's creation power is in contrast to "the idols of the heathen" (135:15): "to him who alone doeth great wonders" (136:4). "For all the gods of the nations are idols: but the LORD made the heavens" (96:5). Does not this verse express the same concept found in Jeremiah 10:11–12? "The gods that have not made the heavens and the earth, even they shall perish from the earth …. He hath made the earth by his **power**, he hath established the world by his **wisdom**, and hath stretched out the heavens by his discretion" (my emphasis).

(4) *As the Creator, God acts as a beneficent Father.* Just as a loving father gives good gifts to his children (Matt. 7:11), so God in His creative work has blessed His human and animal creation. The creation verse 65:9 proclaims, "Thou visitest the earth, and waterest it: thou greatly enrichest it with the river of God, which is full of water: thou preparest [כוּן, *kuwn*] them corn, when thou hast so provided [כוּן, *kuwn*] for it." This term for "establishing" by creation or preservation occurs again in 68:9 in reference to God's sending His rain to restore parched land (see ESV). The psalmist uses the term again as he praises God, "who prepareth rain for the earth, who maketh grass to grow upon the mountains. He giveth to the beast his food …" (147:8b–9a). It is most significant that when 33:5 says that "the earth is full of the goodness of the LORD," it is in the context of creation (vv. 6–7).[11]

(5) *The work of creation is a key subject in the practice of glorifying God.* Psalm 104, often called the great creation psalm, begins and ends with an

---

[10] 1:309. Speaking of God's ways in 77:13, Calvin exclaims: "And yet, the utmost point to which we can ever attain is, to contemplate with admiration and reverence the hidden wisdom and power of God, which, while they shine forth in his works, yet far surpass the limited powers of our understanding" (3:218–19).

[11] In 33:4–5 "What is that *word* and *work* that is faithful, righteous, just, and loving? One would expect it to be the Lord saving Israel, delivering the poor. But in a move that is fraught with theological significance, … [it] is said to be *the creation of the universe* (vv. 6–7). The beginning of the faithful love of God and the justice of God … is the beginning of everything" (his emphasis). Miller, 75–76.

exhortation to praise Yahweh (see Geneva and NET). In the 32 psalms that mention God's creative work (Table 4.1), we find words of praise in 24 of them (Table 25:1). If the expression "his mighty acts" (גְבוּרֹתָיו, *gevuwrowthayw*) in 150:2 refers to creative acts, then each of the closing hallelujah psalms glorify God for creation (146:6; 147:8; 148:5; 149:2). The righteous praise God for His work of creation (33:1–6), but the Lord will judge the wicked "because they regard not the works of the LORD, nor the operation of his hands" (28:5a). If they do not acknowledge that He is the Creator, then certainly there is no praise for Him on their lips!

(6) *The work of creation involves an order which is continuing.* This proposition is similar to the first, but differs since here we are not speaking about an ongoing work (preservation) but just the original acts that maintain stability. The key word for this proposition is כון (*kuwn;* "establish"). Semantically, this term specifies preparation, arrangement, and permanence. The verb indicates the setting up of something so that it will be steady (fixed) and lasting.[12] In creation God "set in place" or "established" (HCSB) the sun (74:16), the moon (8:3; 89:37), and the stars (8:3; 74:16). He put these heavenly bodies into a particular fixed orbit where they continue "forever, a faithful witness in the sky" (89:37b, HCSB). Furthermore, God has founded (יסד, *yasad*) and established the earth (אֶרֶץ, *erets*) (24:1–2; 65:9; 104:5; 119:90), also called "the world" (תֵבֵל, *teyveyl*) in 24:1; 93:1; and 96:10; therefore, "it cannot be moved" (93:1; 96:10, ASV). At creation God put our world in a stable orbit, where it has neither accelerated or decelerated for thousands of years; therefore, we are not tossed about. David noted that God "by his strength setteth fast the mountains" (65:6), and there they have stood for millennia. The Lord has instituted weather patterns: He "prepares rain for the earth" (147:8). Biologically, there is stability[13] in man's bodily nature because of creation (119:73). In the beginning God programmed mankind's DNA, and that structure is still determining our natural formation.

(7) *The Psalms emphasize that God is the Creator of mankind.* At least forty of the creation verses identify God as the agent of creation. This is one

---

[12] "Five somewhat different connotations can be discovered in the usages of this root, all having basic theological significance. These connotations move from provision [or formation] through preparation and establishment to fixity and rightness." John N. Oswalt, "כון (*kûn*)," *TWOT,* 1:433.

[13] Kidner notes that there is "an emphasis on giving a thing its firm constitution" (16:462).

of those obvious points. In eleven of these cases mankind is the object of that act (33:15; 51:10; 86:9; 89:47; 94:9; 95:6; 100:3; 102:18; 119:73; 139:13; and 149:2): God created man. This is important because the book of Psalms has accentuated it. A portion of 89:47 is actually the explicit statement of this fact: literally, "You created all the sons of mankind." As our Creator, God rightfully owns us: "Acknowledge that Yahweh is God. He made us, and we are His" (100:3a, HCSB).

New Testament Echoes

By using the Greek equivalents of the three key Hebrew verbs for God's creative activity, the New Testament reaffirms the doctrine of creation. Revelation uses κτίζω (*ktizō*) in three significant statements: "for thou hast created all things, and for thy pleasure they are and were created" (4:11b); "And sware by him that liveth for ever and ever, who created heaven, and the things that therein are, and the earth, and the things that therein are, and the sea, and the things which are therein ..." (10:6); and "worship him that made heaven, and earth, and the sea, and the fountains of waters" (14:7b). We find this same verb in a verse proclaiming God's goodness in His creation: "... meats, which God hath created to be received with thanksgiving of them which believe and know the truth" (1 Tim. 4:6), and Colossians 1:16 identifies Christ as this Creator. The Greek verb for "make" (ποιέω, *poieō*) occurs in reference to creation in two important passages: "the living God, which made heaven, and earth, and the sea, and all things that are therein" (Acts 14:15b); "worship him that made heaven, and earth, and the sea, and the fountains of waters" (Rev. 14:7b). The Greek verb that matches the Hebrew term "establish" is καταρτίζω (*katartizō*):[14] "Through faith we understand that the worlds were framed by the word of God" (Heb. 11:3a).

In the fifth book of Psalms David and other psalmists proclaim five times that Yahweh is עֹשֶׂה שָׁמַיִם וָאָרֶץ, literally "Maker of heaven and earth" (115:15; 121:2; 124:8; 134:3; and 146:6). This is a fitting summary statement of the book's creation theme.

---

[14] In Psalms this is the LXX word that translates כּוּן (*kuwn*, "to establish") in 74:16 and 89:37.

5

Blessing

When God created the world and then man and woman in His image, He blessed them (Gen. 1:28). In fact, He had already blessed the creatures He had made on the fifth day (Gen. 1:22). After the Flood God again blesses mankind (Gen. 9:1) and more specifically Abraham's descendants (Gen. 12:2–3). We really cannot think of the blessing of God without being conscious of His goodness and His kindhearted giving. In the Genesis 1 account the author states seven times that God observed that the work of creation was "good" (vv. 4, 10, 12, 18, 21, 25, and 31). In the book of Psalms there is this same connection between creation and God's goodness. The great creation psalm proclaims the Lord's kind provision for His creatures: "thou openest thine hand, they are filled with good" (104:28). Psalm 115 ties together God's blessing (vv. 12–15) with His creation act (v. 15), and 134:3 joins the two themes succinctly in a short verse ("The LORD that made heaven and earth bless thee out of Zion"). After affirming the fact of Yahweh's creation of mankind (100:3), another psalm first expresses thanksgiving (v. 4) and then proclaims the Creator's goodness (v. 5).

Briefly put, the Psalms announce that "God is good!" The theme begins in the very first word of Psalms ("Blessed"), and it climaxes in Psalm 147. This theme of goodness or blessing appears in 75 different psalms. The two tables below trace the significant occurrences of twelve Hebrew words in 154 different verses, a little over 6% of the verses in the book. The topic is predominant in Book V, where about a third of the verses appear and where 23 of the 43 psalms contain at least one verse, not surprising because praise is so prevalent in this Book and God's goodness is a primary topic for praise.

Vocabulary for Blessing

It takes some discerning thought to establish a list of terms in Psalms that would identify the verses on this theme of God's blessing and goodness.

Theological Themes of Psalms

Most of the relevant words have meanings and uses that fit other topics, and it is necessary to examine carefully many of the verse contexts. In some cases it is not even possible to be sure about the boundaries of these topics. Table 5.1 lists five key words that directly relate to God's beneficent nature or work. We must start, however, with three nouns listed in Table 5.2 that will lead us to the other words. The Hebrew word בְּרָכָה (*berakah*), "blessing," best represents the subject of this chapter. It appears 71 times in the Old Testament and nine times in Psalms, but only six of these are relevant here. One of these appears in a significant sentence: "The blessing of the LORD be upon you" (129:8b). In the very next sentence we find the verb related to this noun: "we bless you in the name of the LORD" (129:8c).[1] This verb, ברך (*barak*), "to bless," occurs over 300 times in the Old Testament, 74 times in Psalms, but many cases are not relevant for this chapter. When men "bless" God they are really praising Him. In a later chapter Table 25.1 lists those cases. There are, however, 24 uses of the verb in Psalms that refer to the benefits that God grants. In 112:1–2 we can recognize אַשְׁרֵי (*'asherey*), "blessed,"[2] as a synonym for ברך (*barak*),[3] which occurs at the end of verse two. The former word occurs 26 times in the book, 24 times[4] concerning advantages that come from God for someone.

---

[1] This is a greeting in which people express their hope or prayer that God will bless someone.

[2] The KJV translates this word as "happy" 18x. "As is sometimes expressed, what the world calls 'lucky' or 'fortunate' the Scriptures call *'aśrê*, with a decided emphasis on a life in right relationship with God." Michael L. Brown, "אַשְׁרֵי," *NIDOTTE*, 1:570. I maintain, however, that the fortunate situation is just that because of *God's* bestowal of advantages or benefits to the person. The Hebrew term is plural, and it is usually understood as an intensive plural ("O how very fortunate is …"), but we should regard it as a numerical plural: "O the benefits of …!" Significantly, the expression is never used of God, for He does not need to receive advantages from anyone (nor can He). The relevance of this word for this chapter is corroborated by the Aramaic Targum on Psalms, which translates it by using one of two nouns (טוב, טובי), meaning "goodness" or "benefit," or an adjective (טב), "good."

[3] Sigmund Mowinckel claims that there is no difference in meaning between these two words. *The Psalms in Israel's Worship*, trans. D. R. Ap-Thomas (Oxford: Basil Blackwell, 1962), 2:47.

[4] The two which are not included in the list are in Psalm 137:8–9, where the author declares a blessing on the one who avenges what Babylon has done to

The verb בָּרַך (*barak*) leads us in our search to two Hebrew nouns for the concept of goodness. At the end of 65:10 God blesses agriculture; then the next verse says, "Thou crownest the year with thy goodness." The promise of 128:5 is that "The LORD shall bless thee out of Zion: and thou shalt see the good ["prosperity," NASB; literally, "goodness"] of Jerusalem all the days of thy life." The nouns translated "goodness" in these verses are respectively טוֹבָה (*towvah*) and טוּב (*tuwv*). Though they are used in Psalms infrequently, they point to the etymologically related adjective טוֹב (*towv*), "good," which is often used substantively ("a good thing" or "benefit"). This last term is joined in 21:3 with word בְּרָכָה (*berakah*): "the blessings of goodness." The adjective טוֹב (*towv*) occurs almost 500 times in the Old Testament and 60 times in Psalms, 31 of which are relevant to God's goodness.

It is difficult to think of this goodness without being mindful of His giving. The two are explicitly connected in 84:11 ("the LORD will give grace and glory: no good thing will he withhold from them that walk uprightly"), 85:12a ("Yea, the Lord shall give that which is good"), and 104:28 ("when you give … they are filled with good things," NRSV). After David requests God to give him strength, he says, "Show me a sign of Your goodness [טוֹבָה, *towvah*]" (HCSB). In 115:15–16 the two verbs בָּרַך (*barak*) and נָתַן (*nathan*) are associated: "blessed by the LORD … He has given to the human race," HCSB). Thus the common verb נָתַן (*nathan*), "to give," used 94 times in Psalms, is relevant to our topic 31 times (spread over all five books).

The nouns טוֹבָה (*towvah*) and טוּב (*tuwv*) as well as the adjective טוֹב (*towv*) lead us to another important word. For the first noun the connection occurs in 86:15–17, for the second in 25:7, and for the third word in the familiar 23rd Psalm: "Surely goodness and mercy shall follow me all the days of my life" (v. 6a). Additionally, the psalmists associate טוֹב (*towv*) with this word in the repeated statement, "O give thanks unto the LORD; for he is good: for his mercy endureth for ever" (106:1; 118:1, 29; 136:1). Used 249 times in the Old Testament and 129 times in Psalms and usually translated as "mercy" or "lovingkindness," חֶסֶד (*khesed*) has two main meanings.[5]

Judah and kills the tyrant's infants. In this case the verses are a prophecy that Cyrus will overthrow Babylon. The blessings that God gives here are the successes of the conqueror and are connected to God's justice rather than to His grace. The rest of the cases all involve His gracious benevolence.

[5] This is the way the entry in *HALOT* has been divided: (1) "**joint obligation** between relatives, friends, host and guest, master and servant; closeness,

Theological Themes of Psalms

(1) This is an important covenant term, referring to benevolence in action because of a prior agreement or relationship—in other words, loyalty. Certainly references to God's faithfulness and probably appeals for His saving acts are indications that the word is being used in this sense.[6] (2) Sometimes, however, the term refers just to an act of kindness or love without calling attention to any covenant bond. In these cases the term can be parallel to "gracious" (חַנּוּן, *khannuwn*) and is really a synonym for "goodness." The KJV reflects this second meaning in the Old Testament fifty times by translating it as simply "kindness" (twice in Psalms) or "goodness" (7x in Psalms). It is this second category of occurrences in Psalms that I have attempted to chart in Table 5.1, while recognizing the difficulty of precisely making this distinction.[7] I identified 38 such uses, occurring in all five Books of Psalms, almost evenly divided except for Book III.

In Psalm 29:11 David says, "The LORD will give strength unto his people; the LORD will bless his people with peace," thus linking God's giving (נתן, *nathan*) and blessing (ברך, *barak*) with an additional term: שָׁלוֹם (*shalowm*), used 237 times in the Old Testament and 27 times in Psalms. In about seven of these cases it is an expression of God's goodness.[8] For example,

---

solidarity, **loyalty**"; (2) "in God's relationship with the people or an individual, **faithfulness, goodness, graciousness**" (1:336–337, their emphasis). The editors include a third category for the plural, which I regard as meaning simply "acts of loyalty or kindness."

[6] Those uses will be charted in Chapter 11 below.

[7] This difficulty arises in cases where the context mentions both (1) God's faithfulness or salvation and (2) God's goodness or blessing. For example, in Psalm 107, which uses חֶסֶד (*khesed*) six times, the psalmist focuses on the Lord's salvation ("the redeemed ... whom he hath redeemed," v. 2); therefore, I have not included these cases in the table even though the psalm begins with the expression "for he is good." Also Psalm 119:41 was not included because the verse mentions salvation. On the other hand, 106:1, 7 are included even though 106:4, 8 mention God's salvation since His merciful kindness seems to be in view rather than His covenant. But note that 106:45, which mentions the covenant, was not included. Obviously, God's faithfulness to His covenant promises is a part of His goodness, but this chapter concentrates on God's blessings, which have been upon mankind from the beginning, even before any covenant. Here again, however, blessing was definitely a part of the Noachian (Gen. 9:1–17) and Abrahamic (Gen. 12:1–3) covenants, and we must remember that the blessing mentioned in Psalms may be based on such covenants.

[8] Clause Westermann lists this term as primary among "additional words associated with blessing": "The concept of peace stands quite close to that of blessing

Table 5.1 Key Terms for Blessing

Hebrew words:	בְּרֵךְ *barak* to bless	אַשְׁרֵי *'asherey* fortunate	טוֹב *towv* good	נָתַן *nathan* to give	חֶסֶד *khesed* kindness
Psalm					
1:		1		8	
2:		12			
4:				7	
5:	12				7
17:					7
18:				35	
20:				4	
21:			3	2, 4	
23:			6		6
25:			8		6, 7
28:	9				
29:	11			11	
31:					7, 21
32:		1, 2			10
33:		12			
34:		8	8, 10		
37:	22			4	
40:		4			11
41:		1			
42:					8
45:	2				
51:					1
52:			9		1, 8
54:			6		
59:					16, 17
61:				5	
63:					3
65:	10	4			
66:					20
67:	1, 6, 7				
68:				35	
69:					16
72:	17				
73:			1		
77:					8
78:				24	
84:		4, 5, 12	11	11	
85:			12	7, 12	
86:			5	16	5, 15
89:		15			
90:					14
94:		12			18
100:			5		
103:			5		4, 8, 11
104:			28	27, 28	
105:				11, 44	

in the Old Testament." *Elements of Old Testament Theology,* trans. Douglas W. Stott (Atlanta: John Knox Press, 1982),113.

Theological Themes of Psalms

Hebrew words: Psalm	בָּרַךְ barak to bless	אַשְׁרֵי 'asherey fortunate	טוֹב towv good	נָתַן nathan to give	חֶסֶד khesed kindness
106:		3	1		1, 7
107:	38		1, 9		
109:	28				
111:				5	
112:	2	1	5		
115:	12 [3], 13, 15			16	
118:	26		1, 29		1, 2, 3, 4, 29
119:		1, 2	39, 65, 68, 72, 122		64
122:			9		
127:		5		2	
128:	4, 5	1, 2	2		
132:	15				
134:	3				
135:			3	12	
136:			1	21, 25	1
143:			10		
144:		15 [2]		10	2
145:			9	15	8
146:		5		7	
147:	13			9	11
totals:	24 (4/6/0/0/14)	24 (8/1/4/2/9)	31 (5/2/4/4/16)	29 (8/2/5/4/10)	38 (9/9/3/7/10)

Table 5.2 Additional Terms in Psalms for Blessing

Hebrew	English	#	References	Totals: Ps./all OT
בְּרָכָה	blessing	6	3:8; 21:3, 6; 24:5; 129:8; 133:3	9/71
טוּב	goodness	5	25:7; 27:13; 31:19; 65:4; 145:7	7/32
טוֹבָה	goodness	4	16:2; 65:11; 68:10; 86:17	8/67
יטב	to do good	3	51:18; 119:68; 125:4	7/117
שָׁלוֹם	peace	7	29:11; 35:27; 72:7; 85:8, 10; 119:165; 147:14	27/237
גְּמוּל	benefits	1	103:2	4/19
תַּגְמוּל	benefits	1	116:12	1/1

the sons of Korah desire a manifestation of Yahweh's kindness, mentioning His act of giving and His peace (85:7–8). Near the end of the Psalter we find another connection between blessing and peace (147:13–14). Additionally, the blessing theme includes two words that mean "benefit," listed below in Table 5.2. No doubt in other places Psalms touches on the theme without using one of the dozen words inventoried in the tables below. For example, Psalm 145, which uses four of the words, additionally includes two significant propositions of God's goodness. (1) "The LORD upholdeth all that fall, and raiseth up all those that be bowed down" (v. 14), and (2) "Thou openest thine hand, and satisfiest the desire of every living thing" (v. 16). Thus wherever we find fulfillment of human desires, prosperity, or deliverance from trouble, we are looking at God's blessing and goodness.

Propositions

The many verses listed in Tables 5.1 and 5.2 direct us to several theological generalizations. We begin with a proposition that should be obvious, but there is a human tendency to forget that (1) *because God is good, He is always doing good.*[9] In other words, His nature manifests itself in His actions. The psalmist puts it quite simply: "Thou art good, and doest good" (119:68). David affirms this: "For You, Lord, are good ... and abundant in lovingkindness [acts of love]" (86:5). The phrase "for the LORD is good" (כִּי־ יְהוָה טוֹב) describes His nature (34:8; 100:5; 135:3). The shorter form, "for he is good" (כִּי־טוֹב), occurs five times (106:1; 107:1; 118:1, 29; 136:1). In the contexts of many of these verses, the psalmists mention God's good actions, sometimes in general: "the mighty acts of the Lord" (106:2) and "magnificent, amazing deeds" (136:4, NET). Specifically, God's good deeds include provisions for those in need (34:9), rescue from enemies (107:2), responding to someone calling in distress (118:5), and election to be a part of His special treasure (135:4).[10] David says, "Good and upright is the LORD; therefore will he teach sinners in the way" (25:8). Later he exclaims about that characteristic in action: "Oh how great is thy goodness" (31:19a).

(2) *God has extended His goodness to all of His creation.* This proposition is explicit in 145:9. "The LORD is good to all: and his tender mercies are over all his works." This is what theologians call common grace.[11] David

---

[9] "The fact is that God is intrinsically good or he would not do good things." Ross, 1:753.

[10] Spurgeon notes concerning Israel, "Chosen they were; but mainly for this end, that they might be a peculiar people, set apart unto the service of the true God." Then he makes an application: "The love of God gives a new name and imparts a new value; for the comparison to a royal treasure is a most honourable one.... What an honour to the spiritual Israel that they are all this [wealth, delight, and glory] to the Lord their God!" (6:xxx).

[11] The key text for this is Matt. 5:45. Calvin's comments on this verse well describe this concept: "not only does God, with fatherly indulgence and clemency, forgive sin, but is good to all without discrimination.... Our sins having involved the whole world in the curse of God, there is everywhere an opportunity for the exercise of God's mercy, even in helping the brute creation" (5:276).

announces that God provides water for the earth, thus "blessing its growth" (65:9–10, ESV). He says to God, "Thou crownest the year with thy goodness; and thy paths drop fatness" (65:11).[12] Another psalm proclaims, "The land yields its harvest; God, our God, blesses us" (67:6, NIV). The expression of God's benevolence to all His creatures occurs also in 85:12; 104:27–28; 136:25; and 145:15. His common grace specifically to mankind finds expression in 100:5 ("to all generations") and 115:16b ("the earth hath he given to the children of men"). Indeed, "The earth is full of Your lovingkindness [acts of love]" (119:64a).

Yet (3) *God has especially provided His goodness to those who have a special relationship to Him.* Numerous times the psalmists mention God's people as the recipients of His blessing. For example, "thy blessing is upon thy people" (3:8b). Other cases include 28:9; 29:11; 68:35; 73:1 ("Israel"); 78:24 ("gave them food from heaven," NASB); 85:8 ("peace"); 105:44 ("gave them the lands"); and 115:12 ("he will bless the house of Israel"). God blesses those that fear Him: "Oh how great is thy goodness, which thou hast laid up for them that fear thee" (31:19). The psalmists return to this point repeatedly (103:11; 111:5; 115:13; 118:4; 128:4; 147:11). These persons are the "righteous" (5:12; 24:5), "those who walk uprightly" (84:11, NASB), including "them which put their trust" in God (17:7; 32:10; 34:8b; 52:8; 59:16). They "seek the LORD" (34:10; 119:2) because they are the "needy" (132:15, NASB), who hunger and thirst (107:9). In numerous instances it is the psalmist who, speaking with first-person pronouns, is the object of God's acts of kindness: "You have given gladness in my heart" (4:7, literal translation); "Thou hast also given me the shield of thy salvation" (18:35a); "Surely goodness and mercy shall follow me all the days of my life" (23:6a); and "the God of my mercy" (59:17c).[13]

(4) *God has responded with His goodness specifically to those who have asked for it.* Psalm 86:5 is the best proclamation of this proposition: "For thou, Lord, art good, and ready to forgive; and plenteous in mercy unto all them that call upon thee." Sometimes these requests are personal, from the psalmist using first-person pronouns: "Remember, O LORD, thy tender

---

[12] "The tracks would be those of the Lord's rain-cloud chariot (see 104:3). The sense of the text is that the tracks overflow with (the rains that produce an) abundance (of crops)." Futato, 218.

[13] "The God who has showed mercy [חָסַד, *khesed*] to me; he from whom all these favours have sprung." Barnes, 2:152.

mercies and thy lovingkindnesses;[14] ... according to thy mercy remember thou me for thy goodness' sake, O LORD" (25:6a, 7); "Have mercy upon me, O God, according to thy lovingkindness" (51:1a); "Blessed be God, which hath not turned away my prayer, nor his mercy from me" (66:20); "Hear me, O LORD; for thy lovingkindness is good: turn unto me according to the multitude of thy tender mercies" (69:16); "O turn unto me, and have mercy upon me; give [נָתַן, *nathan*] thy strength unto thy servant, ... Shew me a token for good [טוֹבָה, *towvah* ...]" (86:16–17); and "Be surety for thy servant for good: let not the proud oppress me" (119:122). Sometimes the requests are communal, the psalmists asking on behalf of the group: "Save thy people, and bless thine inheritance: feed them also, and lift them up for ever" (28:9); "Do good in thy good pleasure unto Zion: build thou the walls of Jerusalem" (51:18); "God be merciful unto us, and bless us" (67:1a); "O satisfy us early with thy mercy [חֶסֶד, *khesed*]" (90:14a); and "May you be blessed by the LORD" (115:15a, HCSB).[15]

God has not, however, responded reluctantly. (5) *God has delighted in bestowing His goodness for mankind.* The book of Psalms gives no indication that God is hesitant in His giving. In contrast with 5:4a ("For thou art not a God that hath pleasure in wickedness"), we hear David say, "Let the LORD be magnified, which hath pleasure in the prosperity [שָׁלוֹם, *shalowm*, "peace"] of his servant" (35:27b). After all, when God brought Israel out of Egypt, He said, "open thy mouth wide, and I will fill it" (81:10b). God's invitation seems to imply that He wants to bless: "And call upon me in the day of trouble: I will deliver thee, and thou shalt glorify me" (50:15).

That last verse points to another proposition. (6) *God has devised a purpose in bestowing His goodness.* The psalmists know what will result when God is gracious and giving: "God shall bless us; and all the ends of the earth shall fear him" (67:7). God's blessing leads also to the joy of His people: "You bless; ... Your servant shall be glad" (109:28, NASB); "O satisfy us early with

---

[14] This word is the plural of חֶסֶד, *khesed*, "acts of kindness." It "gives prominence to ... the positive blessings of grace." Murphy, 191.

[15] Some translations understand this sentence as an indicative ("Ye are blessed of the LORD," KJV). Verses 12–13 contain indicative verbs ("The LORD hath been mindful of us: he will bless us ..."), but verse 14 starts with a jussive ("May the LORD give you increase," NASB). Using the indicative, the psalmist calls attention to the fact of God's will. "To this fact wishes for blessings now immediately are attached" (Kraus, 2:381).

thy mercy; that we may rejoice and be glad all our days" (90:14). Ultimately, our joy results glorifying Him with our praise (for example, 71:22–23).

(7) *God has concentrated His goodness in the person and work of the Messianic King.* In Psalm 2 God the Father is willing to give a great inheritance to the King (v. 8). We also find God giving to David, the type of the King (18:35). In Psalm 20, which also points from the type to the Messianic King,[16] we see a request for God to grant [נתן, *nathan*] favors (v. 4). Psalm 21 is similar as its description of ultimate victory indicates Christ's end-time work.[17] Here we have an indication of God's blessings (vv. 3, 6) and of God's giving (v. 4). In yet another Messianic psalm God's blessing is upon the King, "fairer than the children of men" (45:2).[18] Psalm 72 continues this Messianic trend with God's blessing of peace: "In his days shall the righteous flourish; and abundance of peace so long as the moon endureth" (v. 7). It is through the Messiah that God will bless all people (72:17).[19]

New Testament Echoes

By using Greek equivalents of the six main Hebrew words, the New Testament corroborates the theme of God's blessing in Psalms. (1) ברך (*barak*)=εὐλογέω (*eulogeō*): Paul praises God the Father, "who hath blessed us with all spiritual blessings in heavenly places in Christ" (Eph. 1:3). He also says that believers "are blessed with faithful Abraham" (Gal. 3:9). God has called believers to "inherit a blessing [the noun εὐλογία, *eulogia*]" (1 Pet. 3:9). (2) אַשְׁרֵי (*'asherey*)=μακάριος (*makarios*): James declares that "Blessed is the man that endureth temptation: for when he is tried, he shall receive the crown of life, which the Lord hath promised to them that love him" (1:12). Paul quotes Psalm 32:1 and applies that declaration to Christians: "Blessed are they whose iniquities are forgiven, and whose sins are covered" (Rom. 4:7).

---

[16] Kidner comments concerning the office of the Lord's anointed (v. 6) that "In reality such a role must prove too big for any but the Messiah, whom it thus foreshadowed" (1:119).

[17] Ibid., 1:121–22.

[18] "On any hypothesis, except the Messianic one, this verse is unintelligible." Alexander, 210.

[19] Alexander ties this verse to the Abrahamic blessings and says "that the Messiah should be not only blessed himself, but a source of blessing to all nations" (p. 313).

(3) טוֹב (*towv*)=χρηστότης (*khrēstotēs*): Paul speaks about the great value of God's "goodness" (Rom. 2:4), and notes that in the future He will reveal "the exceeding riches of his grace in his kindness[20] toward us through Christ Jesus" (Eph. 2:7). The Geneva Bible has an interesting translation for this Greek word: "But when that *bountifulness* and that love of God our Savior toward man appeared" (Tit. 3:4). (4) נתן (*nathan*)=δίδωμι (*didōmi*): Christ compared God's generosity with what a fallen human father gives to his children (Lk. 11:13). James proclaims that the Lord "giveth to all men liberally, and upbraideth not" (1:5b), Paul mentions "the grace of God which is given you by Jesus Christ" (1 Cor. 1:4b), and Peter says that God "giveth grace to the humble" (1 Pet. 5:5b).

(5) חֶסֶד (*khesed*)=ἔλεος (*eleos*): Paul desired for God to show kindness[21] to the household of Onesiphorus (1 Tim. 1:16). Paul describes God as "rich in mercy, for his great love wherewith he loved us" (Eph. 2:4). (6) שָׁלוֹם (*shalowm*)=εἰρήνη (*eirēnē*): Paul prayed for the Lord to "give you peace always by all means" (2 Thess. 3:16b). John connected "grace," "mercy," and "peace" as coming to us from God (2 John 3).

An appropriate summation of this theme is a stretch of six verses that use four of the important terms for God's goodness. In one of the concluding praise psalms the author notes that the LORD "giveth [נתן, *nathan*] to the beast his food" (147:9). Then he observes that "Jehovah taketh pleasure … in those that hope in his lovingkindness [חֶסֶד, *khesed*]" (v. 11, ASV). Concerning Zion God has been blessing and will continue to bless [ברך, *barak*] its inhabitants (v. 13). "He maketh peace [שָׁלוֹם, *shalowm*] in thy borders, and filleth thee with the finest of the wheat" (v. 14).[22]

---

[20] KJV translates this Greek word (occurring 10x in the NT) as "kindness" four times and as "goodness" four times.

[21] The Greek noun usually means "mercy," but in certain contexts the NT uses the term the way the LXX used it in translating חֶסֶד (*khesed*). "Indeed, in a few instances ἔλεος has the original OT sense of the kindness which we owe one another in mutual relationships" (Rudolf Bultmann, "ἔλεος, ἐλεέω," *TDNT*, 2:482. Sometimes there is human kindness to another person with no prior relationship: an example would be the good Samaritan, who "shewed mercy" (Lk. 10:37).

[22] Calvin keeps coming back in his exposition of 147:9–14 to the term "goodness," concluding that the psalmist "commemorates the goodness of God as manifested to … his own Church, bountifully cherishing it, enriching it abundantly with all blessings, and preserving it in peace and safety from all harm" (5:297–99).

6

Greatness

God is good, but God is also great. That characteristic the Bible mentions and celebrates repeatedly. He is great in wisdom (Isa. 38:29), great in mercy or kindness (Psalm 57:10; 86:13; 103:11; 108:4; 145:8), great in wrath (Jer. 21:5), great in love (Eph. 2:4), great in His promises to us (2 Pet. 1:4), and in so many other ways. This chapter, however, will consider what the psalmists say about God's greatness in general. When we think of that greatness, we normally have in mind God's power, and it is noteworthy that Psalm 147:5 joins greatness and power together: "Great is our Lord, and of great power: his understanding is infinite."[1] Furthermore, David associates God's greatness with His glory: "for great is the glory of the LORD" (138:5b). When David said, "The heavens declare the glory of God" (19:1a), the characteristic of greatness immediately comes to our minds. Thus this chapter concentrates on God's power and glory, two concepts that the psalmists combine several times: "In God is my salvation and my glory: the rock of my strength" (62:7ab); "To see thy power and thy glory" (63:2a); and "They shall speak of the glory of thy kingdom, and talk of thy power" (145:11).[2]

The Psalms frequently mention this theme: it appears within 66 psalms in 144 distinct verses (5.85% of the verses in the book). Every one of the five Books in Psalms treats this subject in at least eleven psalms, with dominance in Books III and IV.[3] Each Book has at least two key psalms, each

---

[1] "Great in His omnipotence as in His omniscience." Murphy, 687. Although this verse also mentions God's wisdom, significantly power is first; the same sequence occurs in Isa. 40:28.

[2] Additionally, 29:3–4 juxtapose "glory" and "powerful" in consecutive verses.

[3] As calculated based on the percentage of the usage of vocabulary for the theme compared with the total words in each Book: 36 uses out of 2689 words (1.34

of which contains between four and seven verses on the topic (Psalms 24, 29, 59, 68, 78, 89, 96, 106, 107, 111, and 145). The theme starts with David calling Yahweh his "glory" (3:3)[4] and concludes with "Praise him for his **mighty** acts: praise him according to his excellent **greatness**" (150:2, emphasis added). The divine title best associated with God's greatness is "LORD of Hosts" (צְבָאוֹת יהוה, *Yahweh tseva'owth*)[5] used in eight psalms, seven of which contain verses on the subject of God's power (24, 46, 48, 59, 80, 84, and 89).[6] Another relevant title, used in just one psalm, is "the Mighty One of Jacob" (132:2, 5, NASB). Psalm 68:14 uses the name שַׁדַּי (*Shadday*), "the Almighty," in a context that mentions God's power four times (vv. 28, 33, 34, 35).[7]

Vocabulary for Greatness

The vocabulary for this theme is rich, with 20 different words in Psalms, occurring a total of 174 times. The common Hebrew adjective for "great" is גָּדוֹל (*gadowl*), used over 500 times in the Old Testament. In Psalms it occurs 30 times, but for the theme of God's greatness just 18 times, as indicated in Table 6.1. The nouns for "greatness" (גְּדוּלָה, *geduwllah*; גֹּדֶל, *gowdel*) occur infrequently, collectively just 25 times in the Old Testament. Table 6.2 lists the four relevant uses for these two words in Psalms.

%) and 28 out of 2411 (1.16 %). In sheer numbers of psalms, Book II contains 15 psalms out of 31, and Book V has 16 out of 44.

[4] Because "my glory" stands between the figure of a "shield" (for protection) and the action of having his head lifted (deliverance), David is probably referring to God's power to defend and rescue him. The expression "my glory" (כְּבוֹדִי, *kevowdiy*) occurs in a similar context in 62:7, where the context of God's power is explicit. Rawlinson notes this cross reference but understands the term as a reference to David's honor (1:18). VanGemeren's statements on this verse are significant: "The power of the Great King is referred to by the word 'glory' …. The king [David] puts his confidence in the protection that God alone can provide, because his glory is greater than any human power" (p. 102).

[5] "The title designates the LORD as the powerful God, as a warrior; the armies that are at his disposal are all the heavenly and earthly hosts …." Ross, 1:587, n. 26.

[6] The exception is 69:6, but in this psalm David cries out for deliverance from God (vv. 1, 14, 18, 29) because of "mighty" foes (v. 4), implying that he needed God's power to prevail.

[7] This title occurs also in 91:1 ("the shadow of the Almighty").

Table 6.1 Vocabulary

Hebrew words:	גָּדוֹל *gadowl* great	עֹז *'owz* power	גְּבוּרָה *gevuwrah* strength	נִפְלָאוֹת *niphla'owth* wonders	נוֹרָא *nowra'* awesome	כָּבוֹד *kavowd* glory
Psalm						
3:						3
9:				1		
19:						1
20:			6			
21:		1, 13	13			5
24:						7, 8, 9, 10 [2]
26:				7		
28:		7, 8				
29:		1, 11				1, 3, 9
40:				5		
45:					4	
46:		1				
47:	2				2	
48:	1					
54:			1			
57:						5, 11
59:		9, 16, 17				
61:		3				
62:		7, 11				7
63:		2				2
65:			6		5	
66:		3	7		3, 5	
68:		28, 33, 34, 35			35	
71:	19	7	16, 18	17		
72:				18		
74:		13				
75:				1		
76:	1				7, 12	
77:	13	14				
78:		26, 61		4, 11, 32		
80:			2			
81:		1				
84:		5				
85:						9
86:	10	16		10		
89:		10, 17	13		7	
90:		11				
93:		1				
95:	3					
96:	4	6, 7		3	4	3, 7
97:						6
98:				1		
99:	2, 3	4			3	
102:						15, 16
104:						31
105:		4		2, 5		
106:	21		2, 8	7, 22	22	
107:				8, 15, 21, 24, 31		
108:						5

Theological Themes of Psalms

Hebrew words:	גָּדוֹל	עֹז	גְּבוּרָה	נִפְלָאוֹת	נוֹרָא	כָּבוֹד
	gadowl	'owz	gevuwrah	niphla'owth	nowra'	kavowd
Psalm	great	power	strength	wonders	awesome	glory
110:		2				
111:	2			4	9	
113:						4
118:		14				
119:				27		
132:		8				
135:	5					
136:	4, 7			4		
138:	5	3				5
139:					14	
140:		7				
145:	3		4, 11, 12	5	6	5, 11, 12
147:	5					
150:		1	2			
totals:	18	41	15	25	15	28

Table 6.2 Additional Terms in Psalms for God's Greatness

Hebrew	Translit-eration	English	#	References	Totals: Ps./all OT
פֶּלֶא	pele'	wonders	6	77:11, 14; 78:12; 88:10, 12; 89:5	7/13
כֹּחַ	kowakh	power	4	29:4; 65:6; 111:6; 147:5	11/126
חַיִל	khayil	capacity	4	59:11; 110:3; 118:15, 16	18/245
אָמַץ	'amats	to be strong	3	80:15, 17; 89:21	3/7
גְדוּלָּה	geduwllah	greatness	2	145:3, 6	3/12
גֹּדֶל	gowdel	greatness	2	79:11; 150:2	2/13
עֱזוּז	'ezuwa	power	2	78:4; 145:6	2/3
אַבִּיר	'aviyr	powerful	2	132:2, 5	2/6
עָזַז	'azaz	to be strong	2	68:28; 89:13	4/11
חָזַק	khazaq	to be strong	1	147:13	5/290
חָזָק	khazaq	strong	1	136:12	2/56
עִזּוּז	'izzuwz	powerful	1	24:8	1/2
חֵזֶק	kheyzeq	strength	1	18:1	1/1
חָסִין	khesiyn	mighty	1	89:8	1/1

Terms denoting God's greatness in His power are more frequent. In the Hebrew there are many synonyms for the concept of power.[8] The most

---

[8] Robin Wakely lists 24 in his article: "כֹּחַ," *NIDOTTE*, 2:630. Of course, many of these words are infrequent and do not appear in Psalms.

common word in Psalms is עֹז (*'owz*), "power,"[9] used 41 times for God's power with significant occurrences in each of the five Books. Another word is גְּבוּרָה (*gevuwrah*), "strength," occurring in each book with a total of 15 times. Less common terms listed in Table 6.2 include three nouns כֹּחַ (*kowakh*), עֱזוּז (*'ezuwz*), and חֵזֶק (*kheyzeq*), which all mean "power" or "strength," as well as the adjectives אָבִיר (*'aviyr*), "powerful"; חָזָק (*khazaq*), "strong"; עִזּוּז (*'izzuwz*), "powerful"; and חָסִין (*khesiyn*), "mighty." Three verbs describe God's activity: אָמַץ (*'amats*), עָזַז (*'azaz*), and חָזַק (*khazaq*), "strengthen" (68:28; 80:15, 17; 89:21; 147:13). Another term relevant here is חַיִל (*khayil*), which basically means "capacity," whether in virtue (Prov. 31:10), wealth (Ps. 49:6, 10), or strength, especially the latter.[10] It occurs 18 times in Psalms, where in four cases it refers to the Lord's "power." The clearest case is 59:11,[11] but we may include also 110:3 and 118:15–16. In the two cases from Psalm 118 the KJV has "doeth valiantly," followed by most other translations, but HCSB has rendered the Hebrew as "strikes with power."

Another concept closely connected to God's greatness is His capability to do extraordinary feats, called "wonders" in the Bible. The psalmists employ two words for this: נִפְלָאוֹת (*niphla'owth*) is a feminine plural *niphal* participle that occurs 27 times in Psalms, 25 of which[12] refer to God's powerful activity; פֶּלֶא (*pele'*) is a collective noun used six times in the book.[13] The extraordinariness these terms describe is the unusual and sometimes supernatural power that God used in His special acts. As we humans observe such greatness, we naturally label these events as "miracles,"

---

[9] "Primarily this word is related to God. Strength is an essential attribute of God …." Carl Schultz, " 'ōz," *TWOT*, 2:660.

[10] In fact, H. Eising ("חַיִל *chayil*," *TDOT*, 4:349) and Robin Wakely ("חַיִל," *NIDOTTE*, 2:116) claim that the primary meaning is "strength, power."

[11] Eising says, "Thus this one passage indicates that *chayil* is not only effected by God, but is also one of his attributes. This conclusion is supported by the common use of *kōach* and *chayil* in parallel, whether in the human realm or as a gift of God …" (4:355). One of his examples for this parallel is 33:16.

[12] The exceptions are 119:18 ("wondrous things out of thy law") and 131:1 ("things too wonderful for me," ASV). The masculine plural participle occurs in 139:14 ("marvellous are thy works"), which could have been added the list.

[13] A seventh use is in 119:129, where the plural is used to describe God's "testimonies."

Theological Themes of Psalms

a term the NIV uses six times in Psalms (77:11, 14; 78:12; 105:5; 106:7, 22) to translate the two Hebrew words.

Humans tend to respond to such divine activity with astonishment (65:8, ESV), regarding God as "awesome," another way of designating His greatness. The Hebrew term for this is נוֹרָא (*nowra'*), a *niphal* participle from the verb יָרֵא (*yara'*), "to be afraid." This expression designates a mixed emotion, blending wonder with dread.[14] Table 6.1 above lists the 15 cases where this participle occurs in Psalms. Either or both the NET Bible and NASB use "awesome" to translate 14 of these: for example, "You answer our prayers by performing awesome acts of deliverance" (65:5a, NET), and "O God, You are awesome from Your sanctuary" (68:35a, NASB).[15] In the one exception (47:2) NET uses "awe-inspiring" while NRSV has "awesome."

Another significant word for this theme is כָּבוֹד (*kavowd*), normally translated "glory." Used 200 times in the Old Testament, it has three basic meanings: (1) wealth or assets, (2) splendor, and (3) honor. Theologically, it describes God's total assets or greatness[16] and by metonymy refer to His personal presence (associated with His "splendor"). In Psalms it appears 51 times, 31 of which concern the theme of the greatness of God: for example, "Be thou exalted, O God, above the heavens; let thy glory [that is, Your greatness] be above all the earth" (57:5).

Propositions

The numerous verses in the two tables above lead us to some significant and precious statements of fact about our God. The first one is simple and obvious: (1) *God is great!* The psalmist is sure about this: "I know that the LORD is great" (135:5). Four times in Psalms we find the simple sentence, גָּדוֹל יהוה (*gadowl Yahweh*; 48:1; 96:4; 135:5; 145:3), "great is the LORD."

---

[14] Concerning 47:2a ("For the LORD most High is terrible") Spurgeon says, "none can resist his power or stand before his vengeance; yet as these terrors are wielded on the behalf of his subjects, they are fit reasons for rejoicing. Omnipotence, which is terrible to crush, is almighty to protect" (2:352–53).

[15] "The manifestations which thou dost make of thyself when thou seemest to come forth from thine abode are *terrible*, or are fitted to fill the mind with awe." Barnes, 2:219.

[16] In reference to God, Scripture uses the word to indicate "that he is the most important or preeminent person in existence. And when the Bible refers to the glory of God, it is usually referring to all the evidence of God's preeminence and greatness ...." Ross, 1:474, n.

Once we find "Awesome [נוֹרָא, *nowra'*]is God" (68:35, ESV). We also find the statement, "the LORD, the Most High, is awesome" (47:2, NRSV).

The psalmists indicate clearly that (2) *it is most appropriate for us to acknowledge before God that He is great.* We should come before Him and say, "How great Thou art!" The psalmists address God in the second person and proclaim, "thou art great" (86:10) and "thou art very great" (104:1). David acknowledges this greatness by mentioning the Lord's miracles: "Many, O LORD my God, are thy wonderful works which thou hast done" (40:5a).After David says, "I love You, O LORD," he calls Him, "my strength [חֵזֶק, *kheyzeq*]" (18:1, NASB). In another place he addresses Him as "my Strength [עֹז, *'owz*]" (59:17, ESV). Another way to express this is to ask rhetorically, "O LORD God of hosts, who is a strong LORD like unto thee?" (89:8). The psalmists encourage others to speak to God in this fashion: "Say to God, "How awesome are your deeds! So great is your power ..." (66:3a, ESV). There is a call for both the heavenly spirits (29:1) and mankind (68:34; 96:7) to acknowledge God's greatness.[17] Involved in this recognition is our pondering this fact (119:27b). In contrast disobedient Israel failed to contemplate God's miracles (78:11; 106:7, 21). Relevant here is the fact that David actually encourages God to manifest His greatness: "Be thou exalted, LORD, in thine own strength" (21:13b; also 57:5).

(3) *The saints have an obligation to publicize God's greatness.* The psalmists admonish, "Declare his glory among the heathen, his wonders among all people" (96:3);[18] and "Let them praise thy great and terrible [awesome] name" (99:3). David says, "I will shew forth [סָפַר, *saphar*] all thy marvellous works" (9:1b); "But as for me, I shall sing of Your strength" (59:16a, NASB). The godly inform their children about the great powers of God (71:18;[19] 78:4; 145:12). The psalmist issues an invitation for people to

---

[17] Alexander explains: "To give in such connections, is to recognise something as belonging to another, to ascribe it to him. The form of expression is derived from Deut. 32:3 [ascribe ye greatness unto our God]" (p. 126). In Revelation this recognition is addressed to the Lord Himself (4:11).

[18] In the previous verse for the Hebrew verb translated as "show forth," the LXX uses the verb εὐαγγελίζω (*euangellizō*), from which we get our word "evangelize."

[19] "David ... beseeches God to assist him even to the end, that he may be able to commend to posterity the unintermitted course of the Divine goodness ...." Calvin, 3:95.

experience how great God is: "Come and witness God's exploits! His acts on behalf of people are awesome!" (66:5, NET).

(4) *God's greatness in power makes it possible for Him to effect salvation.* David knows about that special power to save: "he will hear him from his holy heaven with the saving strength of his right hand" (20:6); "God is our refuge and strength, a very present help in trouble" (46:1); "Save me, O God, by thy name, and judge me by thy strength" (54:1); "By awesome deeds You answer us in righteousness, O God of our salvation" (65:5a, NASB). In a number of cases the words of this theme (like "strength," "power," and "glory") are mentioned in the same context with words for redemption: for example, 28:8; 77:13–15; 106:8; 111:9; 118:15; 140:7. Naturally, the psalmists note the significance of God's great power in delivering Israel from Egypt (for example, 78:12, 26; 106:7–8, 23) and giving them victory in the conquest of Canaan (for example, 135:10–11; 136:18–20).

(5) *The great God exercises His power on behalf of even individuals.* In other words, God is not so big that He cannot concern Himself with merely one person. The sons of Korah spoke of an individual when they said, "Blessed is the man whose strength is in thee" (84:5). David uses the personal pronouns "my" and "me" as he describes God's use of power. He says, "But thou, O LORD, art a shield for me" (3:3a). Note the singular pronouns in the following testimony: "The LORD is my strength and my shield; my heart trusted in him, and I am helped" (28:7a). Psalmists whose names we do not even know testify that God's strength is personal for them: "thou art my strong refuge" (71:7b); "The LORD is my strength and song, and is become my salvation" (118:14).

(6) *Aware of God's greatness and His willingness to work on their behalf, the saints may boldly request His supernatural action.* In other words, the godly are not fearful or reluctant to ask the great God to demonstrate His power for their needs. Sometimes the request is for a group: "according to the greatness of thy power preserve thou those that are appointed to die" (79:11b); "stir up thy strength, and come and save us" (80:2b). In some cases it is individual: "O turn unto me, and have mercy upon me; give thy strength unto thy servant, and save the son of thine handmaid" (86:16). Additional verses include 108:5 and 110:2.[20] The psalmist even encourages others to ask for the help of divine power: "Seek the LORD, and his strength" (105:4a).

---

[20] Because the second half of this verse contains an imperative, we may interpret the imperfect form in the first half as a jussive: literally, "May Yahweh

(7) *God pours out His strength specially upon His anointed, the Messiah.* The Father has chosen to communicate His greatness to another and to magnify the divine-human Christ. As a divine Person, Christ is omnipotent in and of Himself, but as a human person, He receives greatness and power from God. Hebrews 2:8–9, quoting from Psalm 8, explains this. In this regard some of the verses in Psalms clearly focus on the type, David and the Davidic covenant: for example, "mine arm also shall strengthen him" (89:21b). Other passages, however, are prophetic, looking to the future Messiah: "His glory is great in thy salvation: honour and majesty hast thou laid upon him" (21:5);[21] "Let thy hand be upon the man of thy right hand, upon the son of man whom thou madest strong for thyself " (80:17).[22]

New Testament Echoes

The New Testament writers reaffirm each of these seven propositions. Theologically significant for the **first** proposition is Titus 2:13 ("the great God"). Concerning the **second** proposition Jude's closing doxology is really a prayer before God, acknowledging His greatness: "To the only wise God our Saviour, be glory and majesty, dominion" (v. 25). In Revelation the elders in heaven address God and say, "Thou art worthy, O Lord, to receive glory and honour and power" (4:11a). Later they call Him "Lord God Almighty" and say, "thou hast taken unto thee thy great power" (11:17). Revelation confirms the **third** proposition because we find the saints publicizing God's greatness in song: "Great and marvellous are thy works, Lord God Almighty" (15:3). John hears "a great voice of much people in heaven, saying, Alleluia; Salvation, and glory, and honour, and power, unto the Lord our God" (19:1).

The Apostle Peter asserts several times the **fourth** proposition, where God's power is connected with His saving acts: "Who are kept by the power of God through faith unto salvation ready to be revealed in the last time" (1 Pet. 1:5); "But the God of all grace, who hath called us unto his eternal glory

---

stretch out Your scepter of power from Zion." "Note how fully at one are the Lord (Yahweh) and this King. It is the Lord who wields the sceptre, it is the King who is urged to rule ..." (Kidner, 2:428).

[21] Perowne says, "we know that whatever was true of the glory, and dignity, and length of life of David as king of Israel, is far truer in its spiritual and eternal sense of Christ the Son of David" (1: 242).

[22] "There is no doubt here an outlook to the Messiah, for whom believing Jews had learned to look as the Saviour in time of trouble." Spurgeon, 3:391.

Theological Themes of Psalms

by Christ Jesus, after that ye have suffered a while, make you perfect, stablish, strengthen [implying His power], settle you" (5:10); and "According as his divine power hath given unto us all things that pertain unto life and godliness" (2 Pet. 1:3a). Paul exemplifies the **fifth** proposition as he individualizes the significance of God's power for himself: "Through mighty signs and wonders, by the power of the Spirit of God; … I have fully preached the gospel of Christ" (Rom. 15:19); "I can do all things through Christ which strengtheneth me" (Phil. 4:13); and "the Lord stood with me, and strengthened me" (2 Tim. 4:17a). Note the repeated use of the first-person pronoun "me." Peter individualizes God's greatness for a saint: "whoever serves … as one who is serving by the strength which God supplies" (1 Pet. 4:11).

The bold request of the **sixth** proposition appears in Paul's prayers for the Ephesians: "that ye may know what is the hope of his calling, and what the riches of the glory of his inheritance in the saints, and what is the exceeding greatness of his power to us-ward who believe, according to the working of his mighty power" (1:18–19), and "For this cause I bow my knees unto the Father … that he would grant you, according to the riches of his glory, to be strengthened with might by his Spirit in the inner man" (3:14–16). Paul prays similarly for the Colossians by mentioning "strengthened with all might, according to his glorious power" (1:9–11). The Messianic **seventh** proposition is evident beginning in Matthew's Gospel: "And then shall appear the sign of the Son of man in heaven: and then shall all the tribes of the earth mourn, and they shall see the Son of man coming in the clouds of heaven with power and great glory" (24:30). Some other instances are Luke's mention of an angel from God who strengthened Jesus in the Garden of Gethsemane (22:43) and the mention of Jesus "crowned with glory and honour" (Heb. 2:9).

Psalm 150:2 is a fitting conclusion to this study of God's greatness: "Praise him for his mighty acts: praise him according to his excellent greatness." The intellectual study of our God's magnitude must lead to an emotional response of joy and praise. How awesome He is! His greatness deserves great praise from all His rational creatures. We must not rob Him of His glory.

7

Holiness

The attribute of God's greatness bonds with His holiness, another attribute the psalmists spend time observing and honoring. Furthermore, God's holiness connects both to His goodness and His greatness.[1] Holiness is a somewhat difficult concept for theologians to explain clearly and accurately for us.[2] Its first appearance in the Bible is noteworthy. After six days of creation, "God blessed the seventh day, and sanctified it: because that in it he had rested from all his work which God created and made" (Gen. 2:3). The verb "sanctified" (קדשׁ, *qadash*, occurring 171x in the OT but not once in Psalms) is probably denominative (a verb originating from a noun), "to make holy" or "to consecrate." The Genesis context would indicate that the first six days are for common or ordinary activities, for mankind as the "ruler" of the creatures on earth (1:26, 28), but the seventh day was special: in contrast it was sacred. There is a distinction between God and His creation. There is a difference between the sacred and the secular (mundane). Another significant text is Numbers 16:38. "The censers of these sinners against their own souls, let them make them broad plates for a covering of the altar: for they offered them before the LORD, therefore they are hallowed: and they shall be a sign unto the children of Israel." Although because of His holiness God acted in judgment against the sinners who had consecrated (set aside for God) these objects, the objects nevertheless were holy because they were now God's special possession, no longer ordinary or mundane. The articles thus became a reminder that for man there is danger involved with God's holiness.

---

[1] "But the biblical viewpoint would refer the holiness of God not only to the mystery of his **power**, but also to his character as totally **good** and entirely without evil" (emphasis added). Thomas E. McComiskey, "קדשׁ," *TWOT*, 2:787.

[2] "One does not define God. Similarly, the idea of holiness is at once understandable and elusive." M. William Ury, "Holy, Holiness," *EDBT*, 340–41.

Theological Themes of Psalms

To some extent the concept of holiness involves the idea of separation, but words for holiness are never used in a non-religious sense to indicate separation, which is a common phenomenon among humans (for example, lepers were separated from society, but "holy" is not the terminology for this). The key is not separation but the distinction between divine and non-divine. Comparing Amos 4:2 with 6:8, we learn that "holiness" ("sworn by his holiness") is equivalent with God "Himself" ("sworn by himself").[3] Holiness is the general term for the essence of the divine,[4] the distinctive quality that differentiates God Himself from everything else, from all of His creation.[5] God's holiness indicates that He exists exclusively in a sacred environment.[6] Yahweh is thus unique and therefore somewhat mysterious. Holiness thus involves transcendence and a certain degree of unapproachableness. God told Moses, "Thou canst not see my face: for there shall no man see me, and live" (Exod. 33:20). Paul speaks about the Lord "dwelling in unapproachable light" (1 Tim. 6:16, HCSB). Because God is holy, even the seraphim cover themselves in His presence (Isa. 6:2). Separation is secondary to holiness since in itself it does not result in holiness, but it is a indispensable effect.[7] Finally, Psalm 24:3–4 link ethical purity to holiness, for "God is light, and in him is no darkness at all" (1 John 1:5).

Vocabulary for Holiness

The psalmists use three words containing the holiness root קדשׁ (*qadash*), two nouns and an adjective. Table 7.1 charts the 65 times these words occur in Psalms. The main word is an adjectival noun (קֹדֶשׁ, *qowdesh*) that can best be translated as "holiness." It often occurs in phrases like "the

---

[3] "For Yahweh to swear by his holiness means that he puts his divine personality on oath to carry out what he intends"; "He swears by himself בְּנַפְשׁוֹ, with a sense similar to בְּקָדְשׁוֹ 4.2." Erling Hammershaimb, *The Book of Amos: A Commentary*, trans. John Sturdy (Oxford: Basil Blackwell, 1970), 66, 102.

[4] "Holiness is what God is." Ury, 341.

[5] "God's holiness thus becomes an expression for his perfection of being that transcends everything creaturely." Jackie A. Naudé, "קדשׁ," *NIDOTTE*, 3:879.

[6] "The verb … connotes the state of that which belongs to the sphere of the sacred. Thus it is distinct from the common or profane." Thomas E. McComiskey, "קָדֵשׁ," *TWOT*, 1:786.

[7] "Separateness is often thought to be the basic meaning of holiness, but it is more its necessary consequence." Naudé, 3:885.

Table 7.1 Vocabulary

Hebrew words: Psalm	קֹדֶשׁ qowdesh holiness	adjunct or [translation]	קָדוֹשׁ qadowsh holy	[adjunct] or translation	מִקְדָּשׁ miqdash sanctuary
2:	6	mountain			
3:	4	mountain			
5:	7	temple			
11:	4	temple			
15:	1	mountain			
16:			3	saints	
20:	2	[sanctuary]			
20:	6	heaven			
22:			3	holy	
24:	3	place			
28:	2	sanctuary			
29:	2	beauty			
30:	4	memorial			
33:	21	name			
34:			9	saints	
43:	3	mountain			
46:			4	holy	
47:	8	throne			
48:	1	mountain			
51:	11	Spirit			
60:	6	*His*			
63:	2	[sanctuary]			
65:			4	[Your temple]	
68:					35
68:	5	habitation			
68:	17	[sanctuary]			
68:	24	[sanctuary]			
71:			22	Holy One	
73:					17
74:	3	[sanctuary]			
74:					7
77:	13	[sanctuary]			
78:			41	Holy One	
78:	54	border			
78:					69
79:	1	temple			
87:	1	mountain			
89:			5	saints	
89:			7	saints	
89:			18	Holy One	
89:	20	oil			
89:	35	*My*			
93:	5	house			
96:					6
96:	9	beauty			
97:	12	memorial			
98:	1	arm			
99:			3	holy	
99:			5	holy	

Hebrew words:	קֹדֶשׁ *qowdesh* holiness	adjunct or [translation]	קָדוֹשׁ *qadowsh* holy	[adjunct] or translation	מִקְדָּשׁ *miqdash* sanctuary
Psalm					
99:	9	mountain			
99:			9	holy	
102:	19	height			
103:	1	name			
105:	3	name			
105:	42	word			
106:			16	saint	
106:	47	name			
108:	7	*His*			
110:	3	beauties			
111:			9	[name]	
114:	2	[sanctuary]			
134:	2	[sanctuary]			
138:	2	temple			
145:	21	name			
150:	1	[sanctuary]			
totals:	45	(37) [9]	15	[2] (13)	5

mountain of His holiness," meaning simply "His holy mountain." The adjective (קָדוֹשׁ, *qadowsh*) occurs 15 times, three times as a descriptive title for God, "the Holy One," and five times as a substantive describing angels or godly Israelites ("saints"). The second noun (מִקְדָּשׁ, *miqdash*) is a term that refers to a place of holiness or "sanctuary." The first noun and the adjective are also used to refer to God's sanctuary. Five times there is the literal phrase "in the sanctuary" (בַּקֹּדֶשׁ, *baqqowdesh*; 63:2; 68:17, 24; 74:3; and 77:13), and once it says, "in his sanctuary" (150:1). Also we find "from the sanctuary" (20:2), "his sanctuary" (114:2), and "toward the sanctuary" (134:2, NET). In one case the noun modifies the word דְּבִיר (*deviyr*), "your most holy sanctuary" (28:2, ESV). This term refers to the holy of holies in the tabernacle or the temple. Twice the adjective is used as a substantive meaning "a holy place" (sanctuary): literally, "the holy [place] of the abodes of the Most High" (46:4); literally, "the holy [place] of Your temple" (65:4).

Propositions

The data in Psalms lead us to recognize at least seven propositions about the subject of holiness. (1) First, *holiness is an attribute of God.* The simple statement "thou art holy," with the adjective as predicate, occurs in 22:3. That adjective appears three times in Psalm 99, where we twice read the similar expression "holy is He" (vv. 3, 5; NASB). At the end of that psalm there is the full expression of this truth: "the LORD our God is holy" (v. 9).

(2) *God's holiness is closely associated with His magnificence or splendor.*
There are five passages that make this connection: 29:2; 93:4–5; 96:6, 9;
110:3. Table 7.2 lists five terms for this concept. In each of the five passages
a holiness term is juxtaposed with splendor or beauty. "Worship the LORD
in the splendor of *His* holiness" (29:2a & 96:9a, HCSB). The Hebrew term
here is הֲדָרָה (*hedarah*); though some have wanted to translate the phrase as
"holy array" (ASV, NASB, RSV) or "holy attire" (NET, Ross), there is
recognition that the word literally means "splendor."[8] The psalmist uses the
adjective אַדִּיר (*'addiyr*, "splendid")[9] to describe Yahweh; then in the next
verse he says, "holiness becometh thine house" (93:4–5). In Psalm 96:6 a
psalmist uses three of these terms (הוֹד, *howd*, "splendor"; הָדָר, *hadar*,
"majesty"; and תִּפְאֶרֶת, *tiph'ereth*, "beauty") and then refers them to the
Lord's sanctuary. In the Messianic Psalm 110 David refers to Christ's "holy
majesty" (v. 3, NIV).[10] Thus these Scriptures proclaim God's majestic
holiness, visible to creatures as simply very bright light, as Psalm 104:2
indicates.[11]

Table 7.2 Terms in Psalms for God's Magnificence

Hebrew	English	#	References	Total in Ps.
הָדָר	splendor	10	29:4; 45:3, 4; 90:16; 96:6; 104:1; 110:3; 111:3; 145:5, 12	13
הוֹד	splendor	7	8:1; 45:3; 96:6; 104:1; 111:3; 145:5; 148:13	8
אַדִּיר	splendid	4	8:1, 9; 76:5; 93:4	7
תִּפְאֶרֶת	beauty	3	78:61; 89:17; 96:6	4
הֲדָרָה	splendor	2	29:2; 96:9	2

[8] Kidner, 1:143; "The word ... usually refers to the LORD's glorious
appearance." Ross, 1:657. Furthermore, Ross rejects the proposal that Ugaritic
indicates the sense "array" (n. 15).

[9] "*Mighty* ... has the ring of majesty, as in Psalm 8:1 ...; and this psalm's
presentation of the majesty *on high* can add its own virile tone to our invocation of
God, 'who art in heaven.'" Kidner, 2:371.

[10] Calvin claims that by using this phrase David was implying "that all who
become Christ's subjects will not approach him as they would do an earthly king, but
as they would come into the presence of God himself" (4:302).

[11] Note that at Christ's transfiguration "his face did shine as the sun, and
his raiment was white as the light" (Matt. 17:2). Peter refers to this incident and
speaks of the "eyewitnesses of his majesty" (2 Pet. 1:16b).

(3) *God's holiness is connected to a location.* In Table 7.1 a study of the various words associated with the noun קֹדֶשׁ (*qowdesh*) reveals a predominance of terms indicating places: "mountain" (7x), "temple" (4x), "heaven" (20:6), "place" (24:3), "the holy of holies" (literally, "the inner room of Your holiness," 28:2),[12] "throne," (47:8), "habitation" (68:5), "border" (78:54), "height" (102:19), and "house" (93:5). This would signal the fact that the place where God chooses to manifest His presence is preeminently magnificent with His attribute of holiness.

(4) *God's holiness has a connection to what He says.* "God hath spoken in his holiness" (60:6a; 108:7a). Furthermore, 105:42 describes God's word as "holy" (דְּבַר קָדְשׁוֹ, literally, "the word of His holiness"). In 89:35 God says, "Once have I sworn by my holiness that I will not lie unto David."

(5) *God's holiness involves His action of deliverance for His saints.* When the Lord's anointed king goes into battle, there is the following assurance: "Now know I that the Lord saveth his anointed; he will hear him from his holy heaven with the saving strength of his right hand" (20:6). That help originates from God's holy place in heaven, represented on earth by His Zion sanctuary (v. 2). In Psalm 98 after mentioning that the Lord "hath done marvellous things," David speaks about salvation connected again to God's right hand; then he refers to His "holy arm" (v. 1), indicating a holy action involving strength.[13] After mentioning the Lord's redemption of His people, another psalmist creates a link by stating, "holy and reverend is his name" (111:9). When David prays, "take not thy holy spirit from me" (51:11), he is referring to the divine Person that speaks and acts by taking control of God's servants (prophets and the leaders for deliverance). In this case the Spirit is the One that has been empowering David's actions and is significantly called "the Spirit of Your holiness" (literal translation). This verse is the first instance in the Old Testament where the active Spirit of God is called holy.[14]

---

[12] The Hebrew word here is דְּבִיר (*deviyr*), used 16x to refer to the holy of holies, as 1 Kings 6:16 makes clear. It is usually translated as "sanctuary" by modern English versions. NJB renders it "Holy of Holies" in Ps. 28:2.

[13] "The 'marvelous things' … are the acts of the Lord done in his own power, metaphorically represented by 'his right hand' and 'his holy arm.' " VanGemeren, 731.

[14] Later in the 8th century, Isaiah twice used the exact same Hebrew expression (63:10–11). In each of the three cases the LXX translated the term with a

(6) *God associates His attribute of holiness with certain persons He has created, angels and the redeemed.* The plural adjective becomes a substantive describing angelic beings in Psalm 89. Because of the mention of "heaven" in verse 5a, we know that "the congregation of the saints" in 5b must be cherubim[15] surrounding God's throne. Verses 6–7 also refer to them. Regarding humans Psalm 106:16 refers to Aaron as "the saint of the LORD." David speaks of "the saints that are in the earth" (16:3),[16] and he exhorts, "O fear the Lord, ye his saints" (34:9), clearly referring to godly Israelites.

In a number of places the psalmists declare that (7) *God's holy name is a proper object of praise.* When the psalmists refer to God's holy name,[17] they are speaking about His holy nature or the fact that He is holy by reputation.[18] The concept of reputation is apparent in Psalm 30:4, where "unto the Lord" is parallel with the expression לְזֵכֶר קָדְשׁוֹ (*lezeyker qodshow,* literally, "to the memorial of His holiness"),[19] usually translated as "to his holy name"[20] (NASB, ESV, RSV, HCSB, NET, and NIV). We are exhorted,

---

noun and an adjective, followed by a personal pronoun in the genitive case ("the holy spirit of You/Him").

[15] Kirkpatrick points out that just like 89:5 Job 15:15 juxtaposes the terms "saints" with "heavens" to indicate angelic beings (p. 533).

[16] This label (קְדוֹשִׁים, *qedowshiym;* "holy ones") "denotes personal character, not as its primary meaning, but as the effect of a peculiar relation to God, as the objects of his choice, set apart from the rest of men for this very purpose." These are the ones who trust in God just as David has trusted. Alexander, 74.

[17] This happens seven times. Four times the text says literally, "the name of His holiness" (33:21; 103:1; 105:3; 145:21), and once it is "the name of Your holiness" (106:47). In 111:9 it says, "holy and reverend is his name"; the adjective occurs also in 99:3 (literally, "it/He is holy").

[18] "In Psalms the 'name' of the Lord refers most often to God's revealed nature, e.g., 9:2, 10; 18:49, but also to His reputation, e.g., 23:3; 25:11." Steveson, 25, n. 94. "The 'name of God' represented to Israel all that God was known to be, his nature and his reputation, revealed in his acts." Ross, 1:496.

[19] "The history of redemption is … an unfolding of the Name of Jahve and at the same time a setting up of a monument, an establishment of a memorial, and in fact the erection of a זֵכֶר קֹדֶשׁ; because all God's self-attestations, whether in love or in wrath, flow from the sea of light of His holiness." Delitzsch, 1:377.

[20] Calvin says, "I readily subscribe [to the idea] that memorial signifies the same thing as name; for God has assuredly rendered himself worthy of remembrance by his works …" (1:487). In Exod. 3:15 this term ("memorial") parallels "name."

therefore, to esteem God for this key attribute of His nature: "Let them praise thy great and terrible name; for it is holy" (99:3).[21]

New Testament Echoes

The New Testament confirms each of these seven propositions. (1) In Revelation 15:4 the saints in heaven exclaim, "for thou only art holy." (2) The New Testament describes Christ's second coming, a manifestation of the divine Son from God's holy sanctuary in heaven, as both glorious (Mark 8:38) and splendid ("the splendor of his coming," 2 Thess. 2:8, NIV). (3) Hebrews refers to heaven as "the holy place" (9:12; 10:19). Revelation connects holiness geographically to the new Jerusalem ("holy city," 21:2, 10).

(4) Paul naturally refers to God's spoken word as "holy" (Rom. 1:2, 7:12; 2 Tim. 3:15). (5) He refers also to God's action of calling as "holy" (2 Tim. 1:9). Furthermore, Hebrews speaks of the action of "eternal redemption" being connected with Christ's entrance "into the holy place" (9:12). (6) The New Testament makes mention of angels and frequently of believers as "saints" (for example, angels in 1 Thess. 3:13; believers in Rev. 5:8; 11:18). (7) Romans 15:9 quotes Psalm 89:49, which mentions praise for God's name without referring to holiness; similarly, there is the question "Who shall not fear thee, O Lord, and glorify thy name" (Rev. 15:4a). The praise of holiness, however, is evident when the four creatures (cherubim) "give glory and honor and thanks to him that sat on the throne" by saying, "Holy, holy, holy, Lord God Almighty" (Rev. 4:8–9).

It is most significant that the conclusion of the Psalter begins with "Praise ye the LORD. Praise God in his sanctuary" (150:1a), a reference to His holiness.[22] The psalmist continues by mentioning His works (v. 2a) and the additional attribute of greatness (v. 2b). Thus theologians are not off base when they claim that holiness is God's key attribute.[23] This being the case,

---

[21] In this verse the pronoun (הוּא, *huw'*) could refer either to God Himself or to His name (שֵׁם, *sheym*). Anderson, 2:695. Perowne prefers the former (p. 207), but Calvin decides for the latter (4:75) as does Steveson (p. 383). The latter is consistent with other verses mentioning the Lord's name.

[22] Ross considers this to be "a less convincing view" because of the parallelism in 1b ("firmament") (3:965).

[23] For example, "It does not seem proper to speak of one attribute of God as being more central and fundamental than another; but if this were permissible, the

76

we must focus our praise in this area as the seraphim do in heaven: "Holy, holy, holy, is the LORD of hosts" (Isa. 6:3).

Scriptural emphasis on the holiness of God would seem to justify its selection." Louis Berkhof, *Systematic Theology* (Grand Rapids: Eerdmans, 1938), 73.

8

Wrath

A holy God responds to sin with wrath. God's holiness involves an element of danger, and that danger is man's sinful disobedience that provokes the Lord's holy indignation. Of the 48 psalms that mention holiness, 14 contain some reference to God's anger.[1] Anger is certainly one of God's attributes, but it is commonly left out of lists of attributes generated by systematic theologians. The reason for this is the difficulty of perceiving wrath as an eternal characteristic (such as wisdom, love, and power) of the divine Being. God's attributes, however, must be understood not from a philosophical standpoint, but from how He has revealed Himself in Scripture.

The Old Testament repeatedly states that God has been or is angry,[2] and Psalms contains 50 verses that affirm that fact. God is a person, and persons have feelings; strong emotions are passions. One of the common passions is anger; therefore, we should not wonder that a personal God can get angry.[3] This emotion is not merely a feeling, however: God's wrath leads to action.

Vocabulary for Wrath

Most of the Hebrew vocabulary for the concept of wrath can refer to human anger, but in Psalms these words predominantly reference divine

---

[1] Compare Table 7.1 with the two tables below.

[2] "Words for anger occur 518x in the OT with Yahweh as the subject. This does not include several texts where Yahweh is clearly implied, other words close to the idea of anger (… jealousy), or the many metaphors such as fire … that are often associated with the concept of wrath." Bruce Baloian, "Anger," *NIDOTTE*, 4:382.

[3] More commonly the Old Testament associates wrath with the name Yahweh rather than with the general term "God" (אֱלֹהִים, *'Elowhiym*), and Scripture stresses God's personality by the use of His personal name Yahweh. In Psalms this name is mentioned in the verses about anger or in their immediate context.

anger. It is interesting that many of these terms are rich pictorially. The book of Psalms uses five main nouns to refer to God's wrath. Table 8.1 lists these with the two most common first. The most common word for anger is אַף ('aph), which also means "nose." When a human being gets angry, the emotion can cause a dilation of the nostrils and often a change in breathing, maybe even some sort of snorting; thus the connection of this emotion with a part of the body makes it possible for a language to use the same word for both. The second noun is חֵמָה (kheymah), "heat." Anger commonly makes a person feel somewhat warm. Another noun exploits this same phenomenon and refers to anger as "burning" (חָרוֹן, kharown). In three cases this noun is joined with the first to produce the literal expression "burning anger" (69:24; 78:49; 85:3). If the fifth noun is etymologically related to the Hebrew verb עבר ('avar, "to cross over"),[4] then it pictures anger as something that passes over or overflows: certain emotions grow and seem to spill over or get carried away. In Psalm 88:16a this verb (עבר) has חָרוֹן as its subject: "Your anger overwhelms me" (NET). The fourth noun (זַעַם, za'am) is a less common synonym; it has associations with "blazing fire" and cursing.[5]

Four of these nouns have related verbs that the psalmists used to express being angry or the act of angering someone else. Table 8.2 charts these as well as four additional relevant verbs along with two uncommon nouns. Two of these latter verbs add to the picture of anger as heat: בַּעַר (ba'ar), "to burn," and עָשַׁן ('ashan), "to smoke." Another verb (כַּעַס, ka'as) and its related noun (כַּעַס, ka'as) refer to the concept of provocation or vexation that incites someone to anger. Finally, there is the verb קָצַף (qatsaph) and its noun קֶצֶף (qetseph); these are basic words for angering and anger without any pictorial significance by means of metaphor or metonymy.

In the two tables, although the total of the words is 72, the verse total is only 50 because there are many verses that have more than one of these words: twelve have two words, three have three words each (2:12; 69:24; 85:3), and one has four words (78:49). In four cases one of the main nouns is the subject of one of the eight verbs: "his wrath is kindled" (2:12b); "why doth thine anger smoke" (74:1b); "shall thy wrath [חֵמָה, kheymah] burn like fire" (89:46b); "the wrath of the Lord kindled" (106:40a).

---

[4] There is uncertainty on this point. Some Hebrew scholars link this noun to a homonymous verbal root that occurs in Arabic, meaning simply "to be angry." See the discussion by K.-D. Schunck, "עֶבְרָה," TDOT, 10:426.

[5] B. Wiklander, "זַעַם," TDOT, 4:106–11.

Table 8.1 Main Nouns for the Wrath of God

Hebrew words:	אַף *'aph*	חֵמָה *kheymah*	חָרוֹן *kharown*	זַעַם *za'am*	עֶבְרָה *'evrah*
Psalm	anger	heat (wrath)	burning	indignation	fury
2:	5 12		5		
6:	1	1			
7:	6				
21:	9				
27:	9				
30:	5				
38:		1		3	
56:	7				
59:		13			
69:	24		24	24	
74:	1				
76:	7		10		
77:	9				
78:	21 31 38 49 50	38	49	49	49
79:		6			
85:	3 5		3		3
86:	15				
88:		7	16		
89:		46			
90:	7 11	7			9 11
95:	11				
102:				10	
103:	8				
106:	40	23			
110:	5				
145:	8				
totals:	27	10	5	4	4

Table 8.2 Additional Terms in Psalms for God's Wrath

Hebrew	Transliteration	English	#	References	Total in Ps.
אנף *'anap*	to be angry	4	2:12; 60:1; 79:5; 85:5	4
בער *ba'ar*	to burn	3	2:12; 79:5; 89:46	7
זעם *za'am*	to be angry	1	7:11	1
חרה *kharah*	to burn	2	18:7; 106:40	6
כעס *ka'as*	to provoke to anger	2	78:58; 106:29	3
עשן *'ashan*	to smoke	2	74:1; 80:4	4
עבר *'avar*	to become angry	4	78:21, 59, 62; 89:38	4
קצף *qatsaph*	to anger	1	106:32	1
כַּעַס *ka'as*	indignation	1	85:4	4
קֶצֶף *qetseph*	anger	2	38:1; 102:10	2

Propositions

These two tables list 50 different verses in Psalms that speak about God's wrath. Careful study of this material leads to a number of truths. First, the simple fact is that (1) *God is angry in the present*: literally, "God is being angry in every day" (7:11b).[6] In context (vv. 6–11a) David connects this fact with His justice. To stress God being in a state of anger, Asaph pictures God as being clothed with this attribute: literally, "You gird on ["put on like a belt," ESV] a remnant ["the last bit," NRSV] of wraths" (76:10b).[7] Moses notes that man lives his vain existence under God's continual wrath: "throughout all our days we experience your raging fury" (90:9, NET).

(2) *God can be angry with individuals because of their personal sin.* David experienced this situation. He pleads with God, "O LORD, rebuke me not in thine anger, neither chasten me in thy hot displeasure" (6:1; 38:1); "put not thy servant away in anger" (27:9b). Heman, another psalmist, exclaims, "Thy wrath lieth hard upon me" (88:7a), and "Thy fierce wrath goeth over me" (v. 16a). Both of these men are pleading for forgiveness because they have essentially admitted their sin and recognized that what they have done has angered the Lord. By using the verbs "rebuke" and "chasten," David is acknowledging that God has a case against him.[8] His words in 27:9

---

[6] The object of that anger is not explicitly stated, but the KJV has regarded it as obvious and added in italics "with the wicked." Alexander claims that this aspect of the truth "is even rendered more conspicuous by this omission" (p. 36).

[7] "The meaning of the statement is not entirely clear [HCSB agrees]. Perhaps the idea is that God, as he prepares for battle, girds himself with every last ounce of his anger, as if it were a weapon." *The NET Bible First Edition Notes* (n.p.: Biblical Studies Press, 2006), Ps. 76:10. Alexander says the figure of girding refers to a warrior putting a sword in his belt; then he notes that "The plural in the last clause (*wraths or angers*) seems to be an emphatic designation of abundance or success" (p. 331). In contrast, Ross understands this phrase as "the remaining expressions of human wrath" (2:621).

[8] Jennings & Lowe, however, disagree. "That the Psalmist ascribes his sufferings to God's anger (verse 1) is probably the ground on which this Psalm is numbered among the seven 'penitential Psalms' (6, 32, 38, 51, 102, 130, 143). But this view of the Psalm is incorrect, for nowhere does the Psalmist make confession of sin; on the contrary he apparently claims God's intervention on the ground that he is severed from iniquity, and from the workers of iniquity" (1:24). But Leupold argues that "Both halves of the verse taken together are in reality a plea for forgiveness and a practical admission that the wrong done is of so serious a nature that it must be disposed of, which disposal can be effected only through forgiveness" (p. 84).

indicate a feeling of guilt.[9] Heman's low estate ("lowest pit" and "in the deeps," 88:6)[10] convince him of God's anger. Much of this psalm sounds like Job speaking, but because this is an inspired poem,[11] we cannot say that the author was mistaken about his true condition under wrath.

Psalms is not alone in the Old Testament in proclaiming that (3) *the rebellion of God's covenant people incites His anger.* Psalm 78 focuses on this truth concerning the Israelites in the wilderness (vv. 21, 31, and 38) and later in the land of Canaan (vv. 58–59 and 62). Psalm 106 dwells on this fact also: "Therefore was the wrath of the LORD kindled against his people" (v. 40a); "they provoked him to anger with their inventions (v. 29a); "they angered him also at the waters of strife" (v. 32a). If it had not been for intercession, God's wrath would have destroyed His chosen people (v. 23). In several other verses the psalmists identify themselves with Israel by speaking in the plural ("we" and "us") concerning wrath (60:1; 85:4; 90:7, 9). For example, "Wilt thou be angry with us for ever? wilt thou draw out thine anger to all generations?" (85:5). Asaph asks God, "why doth thine anger smoke against the sheep of thy pasture?" (74:1b); and "how long wilt thou be angry against the prayer of thy people?" (80:4b).

It is also clear that (4) *man's injustice and cruelty rouses God's indignation.* In his monograph on anger, Bruce Edward Baloian estimates that 25 passages in Psalms indicate that God "is angrily involved if the miscarriage of justice takes place."[12] In many of these cases the psalmists refer to enemies who have cruelly oppressed them individually. An example would be Psalm 7, where we hear David pleading that he is innocent (vv. 3–5)[13] and

---

[9] "Whether all this argues for a sense of guilt on the writer's part or merely reflects the uncertainty which men feel in time of trouble cannot be easily determined." Leupold, 238.

[10] "There is no sadder prayer in the Psalter." Kidner, 2:348.

[11] "We should rather rest assured that the Spirit of God, by the mouth of Heman, has here furnished us with a form of prayer for encouraging all the afflicted who are, as it were, on the brink of despair to come to himself." Calvin, 3:407. Additional Scripture reveals to us why there can be hope for mankind, who are objects of the wrath of God (for example, Rom. 5:9).

[12] *Anger in the Old Testament* (New York: Peter Lang, 1992), 73. His chart that classifies the Psalm passages is on pp. 199–200.

[13] Concerning verse 3 Perowne writes, "With a quick turn he protests passionately his innocence, his soul surging with emotion, his words broken by the

then requesting God to respond to injustice with His anger: "Arise, O Lord, in your anger …. Awake, my God; decree justice" (v. 6, NIV). In Psalm 18 David reflects on his ungodly personal enemies (vv. 3–4) and then notes that God has responded in wrath against them (v. 7).[14] The cases of wrath against the sin of individuals support this proposition. What David did to Bathsheba and her husband was manifestly unjust. Though the two psalms that deal with this (32 and 51) do not mention wrath, we can argue that injustice is part and parcel of the individual sins that incur God's anger.

(5) *It is possible for God's wrath to cease.* Psalm 30:5a states this truth: "For his anger endureth but a moment." The author of Psalm 85 recognized this in Israel's history: "Thou hast taken away all thy wrath: thou hast turned thyself from the fierceness of thine anger" (v. 3). On this fact various psalmists base their hope and therefore request for God to terminate His anger. "O God, … thou hast been displeased; O turn thyself to us again" (60:1). "Turn us, O God of our salvation, and cause thine anger toward us to cease" (85:4). No doubt, the question in the very next verse is rhetorical, with an implied negative answer: "Wilt thou be angry with us for ever? wilt thou draw out thine anger to all generations?" Asaph's question indicates also a request[15] for cessation of wrath: "How long, LORD? wilt thou be angry for ever? shall thy jealousy burn like fire?" (79:5). Ethan's question indicates the same thing: "How long, LORD? … shall thy wrath burn like fire?" (89:46).

This truth leads to the next: (6) *it is appropriate for an individual to intercede with God to end His wrath against a large group.* This is what Moses did at Mt. Sinai: "Therefore he said that he would destroy them, had not Moses his chosen stood before him in the breach, to turn away his wrath, lest he should destroy them" (106:23). Because the Holy Spirit inspired the psalmists' prayers quoted in the previous paragraph (60:1; 79:5; 85:4–5; 89:46), such requests must be right in God's sight.

In contrast to mankind, whose wrath may irritably and quickly explode, (7) *God patiently controls His wrath.* Three times to describe God

---

vehemence of his feelings, as he thinks how *unjustly* he has been assailed" (p. 148; my emphasis).

[14] In the next verse we might be tempted to interpret the word אַף (*'aph*) to mean "anger" rather than "nose," but the parallelism with "mouth" in the next line prohibits this. See Calvin, 1:270.

[15] Concerning 79:5 & 10, Boice explains, "These questions are both actually appeals for God to help his people and punish their enemies" (2:655).

David uses the expression "slow to anger"[16] (86:15; 103:8; 145:8). In Hebrew this phrase literally says, "long of nostrils" (אֶרֶךְ אַפַּיִם, 'erek 'appayim). Since that language associates anger with the nose, this figure of speech is apparently based on the idea that it will take more time for the snort of anger to manifest itself in a person with longer nostrils. What is perfectly clear by usage, however, is that the meaning of this idiom is "longsuffering" or "patient." A historical demonstration of this principle was God's restraint in regard to Israel in the wilderness: "many a time turned he his anger away, and did not stir up all his wrath" (78:38b).

Finally, there is the truth that (8) *a time is coming in the future when God will manifest His wrath in judgment.* From ancient time Enoch prophesied that at the end time Yahweh would come to earth to judge mankind's wickedness (Jude 14). Psalm 21:8–9 informs us that Yahweh will thus deal with His enemies in wrath: "Thine hand shall find out all thine enemies …. Thou shalt make them as a fiery oven in the time of thine anger: the LORD shall swallow them up in his wrath, and the fire shall devour them."[17] Two messianic psalms describe that event of divine anger: "Then shall he speak unto them in his wrath, and vex them in his sore displeasure" (2:5); "The Lord at thy [the Messiah's] right hand shall strike through kings in the day of his wrath"[18] (110:5). Psalm 2:12 speaks of this same future day of wrath. There must be submission to the divine Messiah ("the Son"), or mankind will suffer either His anger or Yahweh's anger[19] on that day.

---

[16] KJV translates this as "longsuffering" in 86:15 but as "slow to anger" in the other two passages. NASB, ESV, and HCSB areconsistent with "slow to anger"; NET uses "patient" for all three.

[17] David is not speaking here about something that would happen in his lifetime: "but it is more probable that he here sets forth metaphorically the dreadful destruction which awaits all the adversaries of Christ" (Calvin, 1:352).

[18] Alexander regards the verb in the verse as a prophetic perfect (to be translated as future, "shall strike through," as most of the English translations do). Here we are informed of "the objects of Jehovah's wrath and the Messiah's strokes" (p. 468).

[19] "Who will be angry and destroy? The context is ambiguous. Because God requires submission to himself and to his son (vv. 11–12a) and blesses those who trust in him (v. 12c), Yahweh ("the LORD") may well be the subject of the verbs." VanGemeren, 97. This is the way NEB handles the passage.

New Testament Echoes

The Greek words that the Septuagint used to translate the main Hebrew terms for this theme occur also in the New Testament in reference to God's wrath: "anger" (ὀργή, *orgey*, 31x) and "wrath" (θυμός, *thumos*, 10x).[20] The New Testament does not explicitly refer to all eight propositions above,[21] but focuses on (a) God's present wrath and (b) His future wrath. (a) The ungodly of this world, who are "by nature the children of wrath" (Eph. 2:3) and are called "children of disobedience," are described in the present tense as being under wrath of God (Eph. 5:6; Col. 3:6). The Gospel of John confirms this truth about the unbelieving person: "the wrath of God abideth on him" (3:36b). (b) Many more passages, however, speak about a manifestation of eschatological wrath (for example, Matt. 3:7; Rom. 2:5, 8), especially in the book of Revelation (6:16–17; 11:18; 14:10; 16:19; and 19:15). Of course, the New Testament doctrine of Christ's propitiatory work (Rom. 3:25; 1 John 2:2; 4:10) involves this theme in that it addresses the subject of a divine wrath that Christ has appeased.

In conclusion let us never forget that God's wrath is a fearful matter and is central to the Biblical concept of the fear of God. The Bible sometimes refers to God's redeemed people as those that "fear God" (Neh. 5:15; Job 1:1; 2 Cor. 7:1; Eph. 5:21). "God judgeth the righteous, and God is angry with the wicked every day" (Ps. 7:11), but the psalmist addresses those that "fear God" (66:16) and announces to them what the Lord had done for him: "verily God hath heard me; he hath attended to the voice of my prayer. Blessed be God, which hath not turned away my prayer, nor his mercy from me" (vv. 19–20). No doubt a part of that prayer was a plea for deliverance from God's wrath (6:1) and a petition for God's merciful salvation: "deliver my soul: oh save me for thy mercies' sake" (6:4). This is essentially the same prayer that the gospel urges sinners to utter on the basis of the propitiation of "his Son from heaven, whom he raised from the dead, even Jesus, which delivered us from the wrath to come" (1 Thess. 1:10).

---

[20] For an analysis of this theme in the NT, see Joshua Young, "The Wrath of God : A Biblical Theology of Divine Anger Giving Special Attention to the Question of Its Reality and Function in the Experience of Believers" (Ph.D. diss., Bob Jones University, 2013), 172–212.

[21] It does refer specifically to the second proposition (the rebellion of Israel provokes wrath): "So I sware in my wrath, They shall not enter into my rest" (Heb. 3:11; also 4:3); and "wrath upon this people" (Luke 3:46b).

9

Justice

There is a moral aspect to God's holiness, and that would include His justice.[1] Furthermore, God's anger at man's injustice is natural because God Himself is just. Thus this chapter has significant connections to the last two. Although it is not unusual for angry humans to act in an unjust way toward others, of course this would never be true of God. Justice is one of the controls for His anger. God's justice is also a part of God's goodness, treated in Chapter 5 above as part of His blessing.[2]

Justice is an important attribute of God that needs to be stressed in order to counter the lie of mankind's enemy. Since the beginning Satan has been deceiving people into believing that God has treated them unfairly. He tells us that we are not experiencing justice from God or that God will not deal justly with those who have wronged us.

The Psalms frequently assert the truth of God's justice: it appears within 47 psalms in 81 distinct verses. Every one of the five Books in Psalms mentions His justice in at least six verses, with preponderance in Books I and V. Five times the psalmists boldly proclaim, צַדִּיק יהוה (*tsaddiyq Yahweh*), "Yahweh is righteous!" (11:7; 116:5; 119:137; 129:4; 145:17).[3]

---

[1] According to Augustus Strong, justice is "the transitive holiness of God, in virtue of which his treatment of his creatures conforms to the purity of his nature." *Systematic Theology* (Philadelphia: American Baptist Publication Society, 1907), 290.

[2] Millard J. Erickson discusses righteousness and justice as subheadings in his chapter on God's goodness. *Christian Theology*, 3rd ed. (Grand Rapids: Baker Academic, 2013), 255–56.

[3] Psalm 129:4 reverses the word order of the two words, but the meaning is the same. In 116:5a another attribute has been added: "Gracious is the LORD, and righteous." The psalmist says in 119:137a, "Righteous art thou, O LORD."

87

Theological Themes of Psalms

In English we often make a distinction between the concepts of *righteousness* and *justice*.[4] Biblical Hebrew and Greek, however, each employ one main word group, combining these ideas together.[5] Sometimes we also try to distinguish *fairness* from *justice*, but Scripturally we can interchange three truths: God is righteous; God is just; and God is fair. Some modern versions have translated Psalm 145:17a, "the LORD is just" (RSV, NRSV, NET, NAB); NET translates 116:5a as "The LORD is merciful and fair." When we hear the word "righteousness," we usually think about a religious concept. The Hebrew word צֶדֶק (*tsedeq*, "righteousness"), however, is broader: it refers to meeting some sort of standard,[6] whether religious, moral, covenantal, social, or legal. A study of the synonyms of צֶדֶק and its related words, verifies this.[7] The contexts of the 81 verses in Psalms indicate that most often the reference is to the standards of legal justice, truth, or keeping promises.

Vocabulary for Justice

The most significant word group in Hebrew for the concept of justice ("righteousness") contains four terms that occur 523 times in the Old Testament. There are about one fourth (139x) of these in Psalms. In this book there are four different words based on this root: two nouns (צֶדֶק, *tsedeq*, 49x; and צְדָקָה, *tsedaqah*, 34x), usually translated as "righteousness," an adjective that often serves as a substantive (צַדִּיק, *tsaddiyq*, 52x), usually translated as "righteous," and a verb (צָדַק, *tsadaq*), "to be righteous." Many of the usages of these words apply to humans; therefore, it is necessary to analyze each of the 139 occurrences of these four words in Psalms to determine which ones are describing God. Tables 9.1 and 9.2 tally 53 cases.

---

[4] For example, Erickson treats these as two distinct attributes: "The righteousness described in the preceding section is God's personal or individual righteousness. His justice is his official righteousness, his requirement that other moral agents adhere to the standards as well" (p. 259). Strong makes a similar distinction (p. 291). L. Berkhof seems to combine the two, but then he differentiates between two kinds of justice. *Systematic Theology*, 4th ed. (Grand Rapids: Eerdmans, 1949), 74–75.

[5] See Wayne Grudem, *Systematic Theology* (Grand Rapids: Zondervan, 1994), 203.

[6] Harold G. Stigers begins his analysis with "the abstract meaning of conformity to some standard." "ṣedeq," *TWOT*, 2:754.

[7] See the list of synonyms in David J. Reimer, "צדק," *NIDOTTE*, 3:768.

Examining these verses, we discover in the parallelism and in context certain synonyms and other terms concerning the concept of justice. In two verses צֶדֶק (*tsedeq*) parallels the noun מִשְׁפָּט (*mishpat*): "righteousness [translated by KJV as "justice" in the first passage] and judgment are the habitation of thy/his throne" (89:14a; 97:2). Another verse parallels the plural of this noun with צְדָקָה (*tsedaqah*): "The LORD executeth righteousness and judgment for all who are oppressed" (103:6).[8] The Hebrew noun translated here by the KJV as "judgment" actually has four distinct meanings: legal decision or judgment, custom (including the plural "ordinances"), act of judgment, and justice. This word occurs 65 times in Psalms; Table 9.1 lists the 25 cases that have been analyzed as referring to God's justice.[9]

Another parallelism makes a connection between צַדִּיק (*tsaddiyq*) and the adjective יָשָׁר (*yashar*): "Righteous art thou, O LORD, and upright are thy judgments" (119:137). This adjective occurs 119 times in the Old Testament and 25 in Psalms. The word means "straight" (describing a path) or "right" (describing a person). Table 9.1 lists the five other places in Psalms where the term describes God or His words as just or fair. A related noun, מֵישָׁרִים (*meyshariym*) is used four times as an adverb,[10] modifying two verbs that mean "to judge": literally, "judge fairly" (9:8; 75:2; 96:10; 98:9). In two other Psalms it also refers to God's justice: "let thine eyes behold the things that are equal" (17:2b), and "You have established fairness" (99:4b, HCSB). Table 19.2 also lists two related verbs on this topic (צדק, *tsadaq*, and ישר, *yashar*) and three additional terms that are used just a few times to refer to God's justice.

---

[8] Psalm 99:4 also links the two words (but here the sg of מִשְׁפָּט).

[9] In 23 of these cases at least one of the modern English versions has translated מִשְׁפָּט by "justice." For 37:28 there is general agreement: "For the Lord loves justice" (NASB, ESV, NRSV, HCSB, NAB). In the case of the exception of 17:2 ("Let my judgment come forth from Your presence," NASB), NET paraphrases the clause as "Make a just decision on my behalf." The other exception is 119:84b; this is one of six places in Psalms where God is the subject of the verb "to do" (עשה, *'sh*) and the direct object is מִשְׁפָּט (*mishpat*). In the five other cases HCSB uses "justice" or "just" to translate this term; therefore, it is possible that "justice" would be correct here also (literally, "When will You execute justice against my persecutors?"). In 14 of the 25 cases *DCH* has classified מִשְׁפָּט as meaning "justice" (5:559–61).

[10] Three times the noun is connected to the preposition בְּ (*b*), "by," and once by itself.

Theological Themes of Psalms

Table 9.1 Vocabulary for Justice

Hebrew words:	צְדָקָה tsedaqah righteousness	צֶדֶק tsedeq righteousness	צַדִּיק tsaddiyq righteous	מִשְׁפָּט mishpat justice	יָשָׁר yashar just
Psalm					
4:		1			
5:	8				
7:		17	9	6	
9:		4 8		7 16	
11:	7		7		
17:				2	
19:					8
22:	31				
25:				9	8
31:	1				
33:	5				4
35:		24 28		23	
36:	6 10			6	
37:				28	
40:	10	9			
48:		10		11	
50:		6			
51:	14				
65:		5			
69:	27				
71:	2 15 16 19 24				
72:				1 2	
85:		13			
88:	12				
89:	16	14		14	
92:					15
94:				15	
96:		13			
97:		2 6		2	
98:	2	9			
99:	4			4 [2]	
101:				1	
103:	6 17			6	
111:	3			7	8
116:			5		
119:	40 142	138 142	137	43 84 149 156	137
129:			4		
140:				12	
143:	1 11				
145:	7		17		
146:				7	
totals:	27	18	6	25	6

Table 9.2 Additional Terms in Psalms for God's Justice

Hebrew	English	#	References	Total in Ps.
מֵישָׁרִים	fairly	6	9:8; 17:2; 75:2; 96:10; 98:9; 99:4	7
תָּמִים	blameless	3	18:25, 30; 19:7	12
דִּין	legal cause	1	140:12	3
צדק	to be righteous	3	19:9; 51:4; 82:3	4
ישׁר	to make right	1	5:8	2
תמם	to prove oneself upright	1	18:25	2

Propositions

The Holy Spirit inspired the psalmists to proclaim a number of truths on this theme. Because of the challenges to this truth, it is appropriate to begin with the proposition already documented above in the introduction: (1) *God is absolutely just.* In addition to the verses listed there, in 4:1 David addresses his Lord as "O God of my righteousness." The NIV translates this as "O my righteous God."[11] David was absolutely confident in the fact of God's justice.

We are well aware that men will follow a standard of justice only for a short time, but the LORD's righteousness is not temporary. (2) *God remains constantly and eternally just:* "His righteousness endureth for ever" (111:3b). David affirmed this truth: not only is God's loving loyalty "from everlasting to everlasting," but His righteousness extends from generation to generation (103:17). We can truly announce to God, "Thy righteousness is an everlasting righteousness" (119:142a). When the psalmist said, "Thy righteousness also, O God, is very high" (71:19a), he indicated the incomprehensibility[12] of that attribute because we cannot get our minds around the concept of the infinity of eternity.[13]

All those who know the Lord understand that He is a judge sitting on His throne (Ps 9:4b). He has passed sentence on the world in the past (the

---

[11] This is the attributive genitive usage. See Alexander, 31; Steveson, 19. Others understand the phrase as indicating God's vindication of the psalmist (Anderson, 1:77; NET, HCSB).

[12] Ross, 2:524.

[13] "The righteousness of God exceeds all bounds, is infinite." Delitzsch, 2:295.

Theological Themes of Psalms

Flood, Sodom and Gomorrah), He makes judicial decisions in the present (135:14a),[14] and He will judge in the future (50:4). We understand also that judges can be unjust (Luke 18:6). Abraham asked, "Shall not the Judge of all the earth do right?" (Gen. 18:25). The psalmists affirm that (3) *God's judgment has been and will always be just and fair.* Of the 81 verses listed in the two tables above, 14 connect God's justice with His act of judging. The Psalms use two Hebrew verbs for this act: דִּין (*diyn*) and שָׁפַט (*shapat*). David uses both verbs in 9:8 to declare God's act to be just: "And he shall judge the world in righteousness, he shall minister judgment to the people in uprightness." The former verb appears two additional times for this proposition (72:1; 96:10). The latter verb is used for this truth nine times: for example, after mentioning God's act of judging in 7:8, David says in the next verse, "the righteous God trieth the hearts and reins. In another place he says, "You have sat on the throne judging righteously" (9:4b, NASB).[15] The connection of God's throne with justice occurs also in 89:14 and 97:2.

Further study of the list of verses reveals a connection between the concepts of salvation and righteousness: (4) *God delivers and saves on the basis of His justice.* When our first parents rebelled in the Garden of Eden, if Yahweh had not planned mankind's redemption, then He would undoubtedly have killed them instantly. But Genesis 3:15 (the *protevangelium*) contains a pledge of deliverance by means of a Seed. Paul informs us that God promised eternal life "long ages ago" (Tit. 1:2, NASB). Because God is just, the standard of fulfilling what He has promised must be met! In His covenants God has pledged salvation (for example, 2 Sam. 23:5 and Isa. 49:8); therefore, His righteousness and His saving acts are tied together.[16] Three times the psalmists mention these two in the same verse: "Deliver me from bloodguiltiness, O God, thou God of my salvation: and my tongue shall sing aloud of thy righteousness" (51:14); "By terrible things in righteousness wilt thou answer us, O God of our salvation" (65:5); and "The LORD hath made known his salvation: his righteousness hath he openly shewed in the sight of the heathen" (98:2).

---

[14] The NET note on this verse says, "The imperfect verbal forms here and in the next line draw attention to the LORD's characteristic actions."

[15] The other cases are 35:24; 50:6; 51:4; 75:2; 82:3; 96:24; 98:9.

[16] "When God redeems His own, ... it will always be 'in righteousness,' which leads Him to deliver His own whom He has promised to help. It is, therefore, right for Him to do so." Leupold, 475.

The need for justice in society is especially crucial when powerful persons exploit or persecute the helpless. In these cases justice demands that there be a deliverance from oppression. God has established human government to bring about such deliverance by applying justice (82:1–4). When this does not happen and the rulers themselves abuse their authoritative power and become oppressors of the weak, the psalmists appeal to God to intervene by justly delivering them from their persecutors. For example, "Deliver me in thy righteousness, and cause me to escape" (71:2a).[17] In danger of death psalmists plead for God in justice to rescue them from the enemy: "Preserve my life in your righteousness" (119:40b, NIV); Quicken me [Save my life], ... for thy righteousness' sake bring my soul out of trouble" (143:11).[18] By revelation David knew the truth that "The LORD does what is fair, and executes justice for the oppressed" (103:6, NET).

As the Lawgiver, God demonstrates His characteristic of justice by the kind of laws He makes: "Good and upright is the LORD: therefore will he teach sinners in the way" (25:8; see also v. 9). (5) *God's righteousness means that His laws are fair.* Psalm 19 proclaims this truth: "The statutes of the LORD are right" (v. 8a); "the judgments of the LORD are true and righteous altogether" (v. 9). Psalm 119 repeatedly connects the term for "ordinances" or "judicial customs" (מִשְׁפָּטִים, *mishpatiym*) with the word "righteousness" (צֶדֶק, *tsedeq*): "your just regulations" (vv. 7, 62, 75,[19] 106, 164, NET).[20] Another verse connects "just" with a different word for law: "for all thy commandments are righteousness" (v. 172b).

Because of God's enemies (Satan and the wicked), it is necessary for the faithful not only to state the fact of His justice (the first proposition) but also to declare in praise before others this attribute. (6) *Communicating to others God's absolute justice is an important and commendable activity for the godly.* We have the example of the inspired David, who praises the justice of

---

[17] "A just God would not let the wicked destroy his saints and taunt their faith." Ross, 2:517.

[18] Other examples of appeals for God to rescue on the basis of justice include 4:1; 5:8; 36:6, 10; 129:4; 143:1–3.

[19] The word order is different in this verse: "Your regulations are just."

[20] The MT has the sg in 119:160b (literally, "every ordinance of Your righteousness is for ever"), but the LXX, Syriac, Aramaic Targum, and *PiH* as well as over 20 Masoretic MSS have the plural, which has been followed by most of the English versions.

Theological Themes of Psalms

God. Two sections in particular are instructive. He says, "I have preached righteousness in the great congregation: lo, I have not refrained my lips, O LORD, thou knowest. I have not hid thy righteousness within my heart; I have declared thy faithfulness and thy salvation ..." (40:9–10). Psalm 71 repeatedly returns to this theme of praising God's justice: "My mouth shall shew forth thy righteousness" (v. 15a); "I will make mention of thy righteousness" (v. 16b); "Thy righteousness also, O God, is very high" (v. 19a); and "my tongue also shall talk of thy righteousness all day long" (v. 24a). David prophesies that someday all men will glorify Yahweh's justice: "They shall come, and shall declare his righteousness unto a people that shall be born, that he hath done this" (22:31).[21] Near the end of the Psalter, David reports that mankind will celebrate this attribute: "They shall abundantly utter the memory of thy great goodness, and shall sing of thy righteousness" (145:7). Additionally, the heavens affirm God's justice (50:6), and David exhorts us to sing about God's righteous salvation (98:2).

Finally, there is the truth that (7) *the divine Messiah will be characterized by justice.* David's prayer for his son Solomon (Ps. 72) ultimately could not really be fulfilled in any of his descendants before Christ: only the divine Messiah could accomplish some of the things here requested (for example, the submission and servitude of all rulers, v. 11). Characteristic of that divine-human Person's law court will be His justice: "He shall judge thy people with righteousness" (v. 2).[22] The verses declaring that Yahweh will come to judge and to reign in righteousness (96:13, 97:2, 98:9, 99:4) are certainly references to Christ's second coming.[23]

---

[21] "The truth that shall be thus handed down from generation to generation is "that He has executed justice." That is to say, God Himself has carried out that which was the proper thing for Him to do, namely, the saving of mankind." Leupold, 206.

[22] Because of the ancient versions, NRSV translates v. 7a as "In his days may righteousness flourish." If this is correct, then this verse augments v. 2. See Anderson, 1:522.

[23] "The only complete fulfillment of this vision [Ps. 97] must be the eventual return of Jesus Christ and the reign of Jesus in his millennial kingdom at the end of this age." Boice, 2:793.

New Testament Echoes

The Greek Septuagint commonly translated the Hebrew word family of "righteousness" (צֶדֶק, *tsedeq*) by using the δίκαιος (*dikaios*) word family. The New Testament commonly uses words in this family to speak about God's justice. Some key examples include the following from the book of Romans: "For therein [the Gospel] is the righteousness of God revealed from faith to faith" (1:17a); "the righteous judgment of God" (2:5); "But now the righteousness of God without the law is manifested, being witnessed by the law and the prophets" (3:21). Furthermore, there is the denial that God would be unfair: "For God is not unjust ..." (Heb. 6:10). A comment about Christ's reign verifies His just rule: "But unto the Son he saith, ... a sceptre of righteousness is the sceptre of thy kingdom" (Heb. 1:8).

May we not only be able to acknowledge that our God is righteous in judgment, that He will keep His promise to deliver, and that His commandments are fair; but may we also be willing to declare our God's righteousness to a lost world. Praise for the LORD's righteousness should continually be on our lips. May our hope and longing be for Messiah's return and His reign of justice, that we may flourish with Him (72:7).

10

Compassion

God's justice naturally leads Him to be compassionate for those who have experienced the bitterness of injustice. His compassion, however, is broader than this case. God feels sympathy even for those who are guilty, for wicked sinners who cry out to Him for mercy. Yes, God is angry with sinners, but He is also compassionate. When Moses wanted an in-depth knowledge of the Lord, the first characteristic adjective God mentioned was merciful (Exod. 34:6).

For this attribute in English we have the synonyms "pity," "compassion," "sympathy," and "tender-heartedness" (an older word): these all refer to a feeling of care or concern about another's misfortune or suffering, but in the first two words that feeling is accompanied by a motivation to help or to relieve. The word "mercy" is associated with compassion: it refers to action taken because of compassion, often involving a decision to withhold punishment.[1] Grace is more general than mercy. Grace refers to any favor, but mercy is a subset of grace: a favor based on compassion for the miserable state of the recipient. God may do a favor for someone with whom He is pleased even though that person is not in any kind of distress. For example, the Lord graciously chose the young man David to have the privilege of being king (1 Sam. 13:14). Furthermore, God may do a favor for a child who is not experiencing any kind of hardship because of a promise He made to the child's ancestor (for example, Abraham): that is not mercy, but it is grace. When God does a favor because of His compassion for someone in a wretched

---

[1] "In His mercy God reveals Himself as a compassionate God, who pities those who are in misery and is ever ready to relieve their distress." L. Berkhof, *Systematic Theology* (Grand Rapids: Eerdmans, 1938), 72. Note the following distinction: "If grace contemplates humans as sinful, guilty, and condemned, mercy sees them as miserable and needy." Millard J. Erickson, *Christian Theology*, 3rd ed. (Grand Rapids: Baker, 2013), 266.

condition, that is mercy; of course, it is also grace because it is undeserved. In many cases, however, grace does not involve compassion or pity.

The book of Psalms mentions God's compassion in a number of places: 54 different verses, occurring in 37 psalms. Every one of the five Books treats this subject in at least three psalms, with dominance in the first and last Books (17 verses in Book I, 19 in Book V). More than half of these psalms are Davidic, written by a man who was often in distress because of enemies and even because of his own sin. The verbs that express this concept occur as imperatives[2] (requesting mercy) 23 times, and the nouns are direct objects of imperatives eleven times; thus 32 of the 54 verses are requests for mercy (59%).[3]

Vocabulary for Compassion

There are two main word families for this concept. We start with the רחם (*rakham*) word group because it is clear that its basic meaning is "compassion." The proof for this is in a statement the Lord made to a prophet: "Call her name Lo-ruhamah: for I will no more have mercy upon the house of Israel" (Hos. 1:6). The English versions translate the verb (רחם, *rakham*) here as "have mercy," "have compassion," or "have/show/feel pity."[4] This verb is a denominative from the word that means "womb": the metaphorical development is probably based on the idea that a mother feels sympathy for her new-born.[5] Derivatives to this verb include an adjective (רחום, *rakhuwm*)[6] and a noun (רַחֲמִים, *rakhemiym*). The noun always occurs in the plural form, probably indicating an abstract idea, "compassion."[7]

---

[2] Some of these are third person jussives, grammatically used to make requests.

[3] Two of the vv. each contain two imperatives (57:1; 123:3).

[4] Exceptions are NIV ("show love") and *GOD'S WORD* ("love").

[5] The picture is in Isa. 49:15a ("Can a woman forget her sucking child, that she should not have compassion on the son of her womb?").

[6] Translated by KJV as "merciful" (8x in OT) as and "full of compassion" 5 of its 6x in Psalms.

[7] "An abstract noun is frequently expressed by a plural, which may have originally signified the diverse concrete manifestations of a quality or state." *IBHS,*

The second family includes a verb (חָנַן, *khanan*), a noun (תַּחֲנוּנִים, *takhenuwniym*), and an adjective (חַנּוּן, *khannuwn*). The basic meaning of this group involves the concept of grace, favor one person does for another. In Psalms the contexts usually indicate that these words refer more specifically to compassion or mercy and should be so translated.[8] The adjective is joined with the adjective of the first word group five times in Psalms ("gracious and merciful," in either order; 86:15; 103:8; 111:4; 112:4; and 145:8). This probably means that the words are synonyms, indicating that חַנּוּן (*khannuwn*) can have the meaning "merciful" or "compassionate."[9] What makes this idea convincing is a comment in the Law concerning the miserable estate of a poor man: "and it shall come to pass, when he crieth unto me, that I will hear; for I am gracious" (Exod. 22:27). A number of English versions translate the last two words of the sentence as "I am compassionate" (ESV, NRSV, HCSB, NIV, NAB, *GOD'S WORD*). When the psalmists use an imperative to request God's grace, the contexts usually indicate that the petitioner has sinned or is in some deep distress; thus the supplication is really for compassion and the action of mercy. For example, regarding sin, David says in Psalm 51, "Have mercy upon me [חָנֵּנִי, *khanneyniy*], O God, according to thy lovingkindness: according unto the multitude of thy tender mercies blot out my transgressions" (v. 1); regarding distress, the psalmist mentions "scorning" and "contempt" after crying out, "Have mercy upon us, O LORD" (123:3–4).

---

120 (§7.4.2a). In Psalms KJV translates this word as "tender mercies" (10x), probably understanding the plural as indicating various acts of mercy.

[8] An exception would be 119:29b. This clause (literally, "Your law be gracious to me") poses a difficulty in translation and interpretation. Many claim that the imperative must be understood adverbially and as indicating an elliptical verb ("grant," "give," or "teach"). KJV has "grant me thy law graciously," followed somewhat by a number of modern versions (for example, NASB, HCSB, NET). Basically that is how Steveson understands it ("he desires the Lord to 'graciously' ... show him the way of the 'law' "; p. 467). But it is better to follow Delitzsch (3:248) and Briggs (2:422) and recognize a verb with two accusatives (*IBHS* §10.2.3). If we invent a new word "graciate," meaning "to act with grace upon," then we can literally translate, "graciate me [by means of] Your law." In this verse God is doing a favor, but not being merciful.

[9] NET uses these two words in translation of all five of these verses. Likewise, the LXX used the Greek words οἰκτίρμων (*oiktrmōn*; "merciful" or "compassionate") and ἐλεήμων (*eleēmōn*; "merciful" or "sympathetic"), in either order.

Theological Themes of Psalms

In some of the cases in Psalms the words in these two groups refer to human pity (for example, 112:9) or graciousness (37:21). Table 10.1 lists just those instances of the five main terms that refer to God's compassion. Table 10.2 lists four verbs that refer to this theme only a few times in Psalms. The verb נָחַם (*nakham*), used twelve times in Psalms, normally means "to be sorry," but in two passages the sorrow takes the form of "being sorry for someone else" (90:13; 135:14), as indicated by the translation "have compassion" in some versions (HCSB, NIV). The noun תְּחִנָּה (*tekhinnah*), can be parallel to the word "prayer" (55:2) and usually means "supplication," but in two of the three occurrences in Psalms it refers to an "appeal for mercy," as translated by NET.

Propositions

Studying the verses on this theme, we can easily determine at least five key truths. The first is the simple proposition that (1) *God is compassionate*. Psalms makes this explicit statement four times: "The LORD is merciful and gracious" (103:8a; also 111:4b and 112:4b,[10] and 145:8a with slightly different wordings). Similarly, "Gracious is the LORD, and righteous; yea, our God is merciful" (116:5). In another place the psalmist acknowledges to his Master, "But thou, O Lord, art a God full of compassion, and gracious, longsuffering, and plenteous in mercy and truth" (86:15). The psalmist can exclaim, "Your compassion is great" (119:156, NIV). Furthermore, God feels this compassion for all His creation: "His compassion rests on all He has made" (145:9, HCSB). David uses a mundane example so that we have practical and concrete picture of this feeling: "Like as a father pitieth his children" (103:13).

The majority of the verses indicate that (2) *it is appropriate for those in distress to ask God for mercy*. In psalms that are labeled Davidic, 16 times we find the king saying under inspiration simply, "have mercy upon me"

---

[10] There is no stated subject of the last clause in this verse. Delitzsch (3:200), Anderson (2:777), and Steveson (p. 438) argue that because light can be a reference to Yahweh (Isa. 10:17) and the first two adjectives are elsewhere a description of Him, the understood subject of 4b is Yahweh (so construed by RSV and NASB). There are many, however, who disagree: commentators, Alexander (p. 464), Jennings & Lowe (2:257) Leupold (p. 787), Weiser (pp. 703–04), Kidner (16:434), VanGemeren (p. 827), Futato (p. 353–55); versions, NRSV, NIV, NET, *GOD'S WORD*, NAB. Calvin says, "For I have no doubt that the prophet intends, as applicable to God, the epithets, *gracious, merciful, and just*" (4:325).

Table 10.1 Vocabulary for Compassion or Mercy

Hebrew words:	חנן *khanan* to have mercy	תַּחֲנוּנִים *takhenuwniym* plea for mercy	חַנּוּן *khannuwn* compassionate	רַחֲמִים *rakhemiym* compassion	רחום *rakhuwm* compassionate
Psalm					
4:	1				
6:	2				
9:	13				
25:	16			6	
26:	11				
27:	7				
28:		2 6			
30:	8 10				
31:	9	22			
40:				11	
41:	4 10				
51:	1			1	
56:	1				
57:	1 [2]				
59:	5				
67:	1				
69:				16	
77:				9	
78:					38
79:				8	
86:	3 16	6	15		15
102:	13				
103:			8	4	8
111:			4		4
112:			4		4
116:		1	5		
119:	58 132			77 156	
123:	2 3 [2]				
130:		2			
140:		6			
142:	1				
143:		1			
145:			8	9	8
totals:	26	8	6	10	6

Table 10.2 Additional Terms in Psalms for God's Compassion

Hebrew	Transliteration	English	#	References	Total in Ps.
רחם	*rakham*	to take pity on	3	102:13; 103:13; 116:5	5
נחם	*nakham*	to be sorry for	2	90:13; 135:14	12
חוס	*khows*	to have pity on	1	72:13	1
חנה	*khanah*	to have compassion	1	77:9	1
תְּחִנָּה	*tekhinnah*	plea for mercy	2	6:9; 55:1	3

(חָנֵּנִי, *khanneyniy*).[11] In the anonymous 119th Psalm the author pleads with this word twice (vv. 58 and 132). There are many more of these individual petitions, using a variety of phraseology: 25:6; 28:2; 30:8; 40:11; 55:1; 86:6; 119:77; 130:2; 140:6; and 142:1. In 67:1, 79:8, 90:13, and 123:3a the psalmists plead for the group: "God be merciful unto us"; "Let Your compassion come quickly to meet us" (NASB); "Have pity on your servants" (90:13, NET); "Have mercy upon us, O LORD, have mercy upon us." These many pleas are an indication of the humility of the psalmists. A person is truly humble when he comes to God, confesses that he is a sinner, acknowledges his helpless state, and pleads for mercy. God has indicated that He is ready to help such a person (Isa. 57:17), and Christ declared that the sinner who has this attitude of humility does receive mercy (Luke 18:13). Note, however, that in one case the request is actually negative: "be not merciful to any wicked transgressors" (59:5b).[12]

A couple of times by his prayers, David informs us about a remarkable truth: (3) *God's loving compassion is part of the basis for any hope of forgiveness the sinner has.* After his heinous sin of adultery and murder, David appeals for mercy from the Judge, not because of God's justice or any other attribute,[13] but because of God's compassion and His loving loyal kindness (חֶסֶד, *khesed*) (51:1). In Psalm 69 when he is in trouble because of enemies, David appeals for help on the same basis: "thy lovingkindness" and "thy tender mercies" (v. 16).

The fact is that (4) *historically God has acted mercifully in people's lives because He is compassionate.* In Psalm 78 Asaph gives his contemporaries (v. 1) and us (vv. 4, 6) a history lesson about God's dealings with Israel and their sins in the wilderness (vv. 40–41) and in the land of Canaan (vv. 56–58). In spite of God's anger (vv. 21, 31, 58–59), history teaches that "he, being full of compassion, forgave their iniquity, and destroyed them not: yea, many a time turned he his anger away, and did not stir up all his wrath" (v. 38).

---

[11] KJV translates half of these as "be merciful unto me."

[12] This is an imprecation. Chapter 18 below will deal with this kind of statements.

[13] "We cannot come to God on the basis of his justice; justice strikes us with fear and causes us to hide from him. We are not drawn to God by his wisdom; wisdom does not embolden us, though we stand in awe of it. No more does omniscience, omnipotence, or omnipresence. The only reason we dare come to God and dare hope for a solution to our sin problem is his mercy." Boice, 2:425.

Another psalmist recognizes this pattern of God's pity in his own past: "He has heard my appeal for mercy" (116:1, HCSB).

Furthermore, we can look to the future with confidence. (5) *The saints put their hopes on God's future acts of mercy.* In two psalms where David prays for God's mercy (6:2; 31:9), the Holy Spirit suddenly reveals to him that God has heard his plea for mercy (6:9a; 31:22b).[14] Notice the past tense in these two clauses. On this basis David can now be confident in what God will do (6:10). The psalmist has presented us with a beautiful picture of how this hope works: "Behold, as the eyes of servants look unto the hand of their masters, and as the eyes of a maiden unto the hand of her mistress; so our eyes wait upon the LORD our God, until that he have mercy upon us" (123:2). Because the psalmist was inspired, we can be sure that his confidence about God in the future was not a mistake: "Thou shalt arise, and have mercy upon Zion" (102:13a). God's works of mercy will include saving (72:13), and crowning (103:4),[15] and vindicating (135:14).

New Testament Echoes

James affirms for us "that the Lord is very pitiful, and of tender mercy [οἰκτίρμων, *oiktirmōn*]" (5:11d). The last word in the verse is the Greek adjective the Septuagint used to translate the Hebrew word "compassionate" (רַחוּם, *rakhuwm*) all six times it occurred in Psalms. Christ also used this word to characterize God the Father (Luke 6:36). The Septuagint joins another Greek adjective (ἐλεήμων, *eleēmō*) with οἰκτίρμων (*oiktirmōn*) five times in Psalms,[16] and it is the word used in Hebrews 2:17 to portray Christ: "Wherefore in all things it behoved him to be made like unto his brethren, that he might be a **merciful** and faithful high priest in things pertaining to God, to make reconciliation for the sins of the people" (my emphasis). In Christ's earthly ministry He is described a number of times as having compassion on those in need (Matt. 9:36; 14:14; 15:32; 20:34; Mark 1:41; 5:19; Luke 7:13). The Greek verb used to translate חָנַן (*khanan*, "to

---

[14] Two different Hebrew words are used for this concept. See the tables above.

[15] "The figure of crowning ... suggests the idea of dignity and beauty, while the absence of merit in the object, and the sovereign freeness of the gift, are indicated by making the crown itself a crown of mercy and compassion." Alexander, 423.

[16] See the verses mentioned above where the two Hebrew adjectives are joined by a conjunction.

have mercy") is ἐλεεῖν (*eleein*), used 29 times in the New Testament. The psalmists cry out for God to have mercy on them; but significantly, in the Gospels people cry out for Christ to have mercy (Matt. 9:27; 15:22; 17:15; 20:30–31; Mark 9:22; Luke 17:13). Like the psalmists (31:22; 116:1) Paul recognized that God had been merciful to him (1 Tim. 1:13, 16).

As a fitting conclusion we look to the psalms which have the most verses on this theme. In Psalm 86 David asks for mercy three times (vv. 3, 4, 16) while at the same time acknowledging that the Lord is compassionate and merciful (v. 15). This is praying in faith with confident hope in God's character. May our prayers reflect this Scriptural pattern. Likewise in Psalm 119 there are the petitions (vv. 58, 77, 132) along with a testimony about a fact that gives us all hope: "Great are thy tender mercies" (v. 156a).

11

Love & Faithfulness

There is more to God's feeling toward mankind than compassion: the Creator loves sinful human beings. This would make sense since we expect compassion especially from those who love us, from friends, parents, spouses, and siblings. In the Old Testament it is very clear that Yahweh loves the Israelites, but actually in his writings Moses never states this fact until he writes Deuteronomy at the end of his life. In Genesis the Hebrew verb for "love" (אהב, *'ahab*) occurs fourteen times, but God is never the subject: Abraham loves his son (22:2), Isaac loves his wife (24:67) and delicious meat (27:4, 9, 14), and so forth. Later Scripture designates Abraham as God's friend, using this word "love" (Isa. 41:8; participle, literally "one loving of Me"), but Genesis does not mention this fact. In the laws of Mt. Sinai there are references to human love (Exod. 21:5; Lev. 19:18, 34), and God refers to those who love Him (Exod. 20:6), but no mention of God's love. In Deuteronomy, however, Moses informs Israel that God loved their ancestors (4:37; 10:15), and that He loved them (7:8; 23:5) and would love those who keep His commandments (7:12–13). Among the prophets, Isaiah (43:4; 48:14; 63:9) and Hosea (3:1; 11:1; 14:4) mention Yahweh's love, but this subject is rare in the rest (just Jer. 31:3; Zeph. 3:17; Mal. 1:2). All of this means it should be no surprise that in Psalms we find very few direct statements about this divine attribute and that we must wait even until the later books of the New Testament to hear a repeated emphasis on God's love (John and 1 John).

But this is not the whole story for Psalms. True love involves loyalty and faithfulness. Possibly a person can be loyal or faithful to someone (maybe a spouse) or something (like his country) without real love, but genuine love is inconceivable if faithfulness is absent. When we search the Psalms for the theme of God's faithfulness, we quickly discover scores of references to this attribute. Further contemplation of the term חֶסֶד (*khesed*, "lovingkindness") indicates the difficulty of separately treating these two attributes of God.

Hebrew Words for God's Love and Faithfulness

In Psalms the normal Hebrew verb for "love" occurs 39 times. If we use a concordance to search for the words "love" and "loving" in Psalms, we discover that the English versions have often used these words in their translation of חֶסֶד (khesed).[1] Over half of this Hebrew word's uses in the Old Testament occur in Psalms (127x). Chapter 5 ("Blessing") previously charted 37 of these as referring to God's acts of benevolence. The remaining 90 uses in Psalms probably fall into the category of covenant loyal love and faithfulness in action.[2] The evidence for this can be seen in the way various English versions have translated the term. Table 11.1 presents the main and secondary translations for nine versions. Note that eight of them use "lovingkindness"[3] or some aspect of "love"[4] (all except YLT).

One version particularly emphasizes the concept of loyalty for this word by translating the majority of its occurrences in Psalms as "loyal love" (NET, 97x), and several other versions have used "loyal" or "loyalty" a few times (CEV, NAB, NIV, NRSV, NJB). Our concept of loyalty is usually associated with governmental or communal allegiance, and that is never the case with חֶסֶד (khesed).[5] This was especially true of English in the period of the KJV translation; therefore, the KJV never uses the words "loyal"[6] or "loyalty." Furthermore, for us loyalty is a feeling or attribute, rather than the associated action. We do not say "do me a loyalty"; however, in Hebrew חֶסֶד is commonly the direct object of the verb "to do" (עָשָׂה, 'asah; for example Ps. 18:51).[7] The idea of

---

[1] This Hebrew noun has posed problems for translators ever since the LXX: for the 245x it appears in the OT the 1984 NIV translated it 24 different ways.

[2] *DCH* provides five glosses for the sg: "loyalty," "faithfulness," "kindness," "love," and "mercy" (3:277).

[3] "The word 'lovingkindness' of the KJV is archaic, but not far from the fulness of meaning of the word." R. Laird Harris, "ḥsd," *TWOT*, 1:307.

[4] Harris has presented a convincing argument "that *ḥesed* is one of the words descriptive of the love of God" (ibid.).

[5] Modern Hebrew uses this word for the concepts of grace, kindness, and charity, not loyalty.

[6] The exception is in the Apocrypha: "keep yourself loyal to the state" (2 Maccabees 11:19).

[7] The Hebrew term "always designates not just a human attitude, but also the act that emerges from this attitude." *TDOT*, 5:51.

faithfulness for חֶסֶד appears in five of the versions in the table ("unfailing love," NIV; "steadfast love," NRSV and ESV; "faithful love," HCSB; "loyal love" and "faithfulness," NET). The plural of חֶסֶד occurs eight times in Psalms (17:7; 25:6; 89:1, 49; 106:7, 45; 107:43; 119:41); NET appropriately translates four of these as "faithful deeds,"[8] clearly indicating actions based on an attribute. Eight times by using "and," the psalmists join חֶסֶד (*khesed*) with the immediately following word אֱמֶת (*'emeth*; "constancy" or "faithfulness"); in six other verses the words are in some way parallel. אֱמֶת can also mean "true": for example, "Thy word is true from the beginning" (119:160). Eight times the related word אֱמוּנָה (*'emuwnah*; "faithfulness") parallels חֶסֶד; twice they are juxtaposed with "and" (89:24; 98:3). This would be another indication of the meaning "faithfulness" for חֶסֶד.

Table 11.1 Translation of the Term חֶסֶד

Version	Main Translation	Secondary Translation	Others
KJV	mercy (89x)	lovingkindness (21x)	5 (17x)
ASV	lovingkindness (115x)	lovingkindnesses (6x)	2 (6x)
YLT	kindness (119x)	kind acts (3x)	4 (5x)
NASB	lovingkindness (121x)	lovingkindnesses (4x)	2 (2x)
NIV	love (81x)	unfailing love (33x)	7 (13x)
NRSV	steadfast love (120x)	kindness (2x)	4 (4x)
ESV	steadfast love (123x)	kindness (3x)	1 (1x)
HCSB	faithful love (88x)	love (30x)	5 (9x)
NET	loyal love (97x)	faithfulness (14x)	7 (16x)

At this point we are dealing with two attributes: love and faithfulness. The columns of Table 11.2 list four Hebrew words: the first (אהב, *'ahav*) refers to love; the second (חֶסֶד, *khesed*) to love/faithfulness (or loyalty); the third and fourth (אֱמוּנָה, *'emuwnah*; אֱמֶת, *'emeth*) to faithfulness. Each of these terms sometimes refers to a human attribute. In fact, אהב ("to love") usually refers in Psalms to humans: God is the subject of this verb just eight times. In half of these cases the object of His love is justice. The other objects are Jacob (47:4), the righteous ones (146:8), Zion (78:68), and Zion's gates (87:2). On the other hand, חֶסֶד usually refers to God in this book rather than to man, 87 times out of 90. For אֱמוּנָה the ratio is 20 out of 22; for אֱמֶת it is 18 out of 37. Table 11.2 lists just the verses that refer to God's attributes.

---

[8] KJV, ASV, and NASB use the words "lovingkindnesses" and "mercies" for some of the eight.

Theological Themes of Psalms

Table 11.2 Vocabulary for Love and Faithfulness

Hebrew words:	אהב 'ahav	חֶסֶד khesed	אֱמוּנָה 'emuwnah	אֱמֶת 'emeth
Psalm	to love	lovingkindness	faithfulness	constancy
6:		4		
11:	7			
13:		6		
18:		50		
21:		7		
25:		10		10
26:		3		3
30:				9
31:		16		6
33:	5	5 18 22	4	
36:		5 7 10	5	
37:	28			
40:		10 11	10	10 11
44:		26		
47:	4			
48:		9		
54:				5
57:		3 10		4 10
59:		10		
61:		7		7
62:		12		
69:		13		13
71:				22
78:	68			
85:		7 10		10 11
86:		13		15
87:	2			
88:		11	11	
89:		1 2 14 24 28 33 49	1 2 5 8 24 33 49	14
91:				4
92:		2	2	
96:			13	
98:		3	3	
99:	4			
100:		5	5	
101:		1		
103:		17		
106:		45		
107:		1 8 15 21 31 43		
108:		4		4
109:		21 26		
115:		1		1
117:		2		
119:		41 76 88 124 149 159	75 86 90 138	
130:		7		
136:		vv. 2–26 (25x)		
138:		2 8		
141:				
143:		8 12	1	
146:	8			
totals:	8 (3/1/2/0/1)	87 (15/8/11/6/47)	20 (3/0/8/4/5)	19 (6/6/4/1/2)

Thus these two attributes of God occur in 114 verses within 50 different psalms, in all five Psalm Books, with predominance in Book V.

Propositions

Since the word חֶסֶד (*khesed*) includes both love and faithfulness, the propositions in this section will focus on this term. This is appropriate also because the two other words for faithfulness occur in the same or adjoining verse where חֶסֶד occurs 26 out of the 39 times they are used. But for the first proposition we will start with the normal word אָהַב ('*ahav*, "to love"). (1) *God loves those with whom He has made a covenant*: "the excellency of Jacob whom he loved [אָהֵב]" (47:4b).[9] In the midst of three verses describing what God does for the afflicted (literally, "the hungry," "prisoners," "blind ones," "the ones bowed down,"[10] "aliens," "orphan and widow"), the psalmist proclaims, "the LORD loveth the righteous" (146:8c). Since this passage is millennial (see v. 10, "The Lord shall reign for ever"), "the righteous" must be those in His kingdom who have a covenant relation with Christ.[11]

The psalmists also proclaim that (2) *God's loyal love is plentiful*. They use the following expressions: "the abundance of His faithful love" (106:45b, HCSB), "For great is thy lovingkindness" (86:13a, ASV), and "For his loyal love towers over us" (117:2a, NET). The psalmists present other vivid images of this abundance: "the earth is full of the steadfast love of the LORD" (33:5b, ESV; also 119:64). Four times David declares that its range extends to the clouds of the sky (36:5; 57:10; 103:11; 108:4). He also indicates its extension in time: "The lovingkindness of God endures all day long" (52:1, NASB).[12]

(3) *God's loyal love delivers His saints from their enemies and from death*. "My God in his steadfast love will meet me;[13] God will let me look in

---

[9] It would be difficult to read this verse without thinking of "Jacob have I loved" (Rom. 9:13 quoting Mal. 1:2). "The excellency of Jacob" refers to the land of Israel's inheritance (Broyles, 214), but the object of "love" is Jacob.

[10] That is, the discouraged. This should be given "the broadest application. God has at numberless times lifted up the discouraged and those who were physically bowed down and given them fresh hope." Leupold, 986.

[11] Notice what Christ says in Luke 4:18–19 as He quotes Isaiah 61:1–2.

[12] Michael L. Brown has developed this proposition in more detail by including many additional verses from other OT books. "חסד," *NIDOTTE*, 2:217.

[13] "The idea here is that of coming to meet one in a friendly manner." Alexander, 261.

triumph on my enemies" (59:10); "And in Your lovingkindness, cut off my enemies" (143:12a, NASB). Three times in Psalm 119 the author asks his Lord to rescue him from approaching death: "Quicken me after thy loving-kindness" (v. 88a; similarly vv. 149 and 159). David asks the Lord to rescue his life "for the sake of your steadfast love" (6:4, ESV).

In Chapter 8 above we noted the fact of God's wrath, but (4) *God's loyal love can counter wrath*. David sets wrath and love side by side in a contrast: "But you, O Lord, are ... slow to anger and abounding in lovingkindness and faithfulness" (86:15, ESV). In other words, love can trump wrath! In at least seven psalms there is the mention of wrath and then the request or claim that love has offset that divine emotion. For example, David pleads, "O LORD, rebuke me not in thine anger, neither chasten me in thy hot displeasure" (6:1); then a few verses later he makes another request "for thy mercies' sake" (v. 4). In Psalm 88 the author says, "Thy wrath lieth hard upon me" (v. 7a); then a few verses later he mentions "lovingkindness" and "faithfulness" (v. 11). In Psalm 106 the author speaks of God's wrath against the idolatry of Israel that resulted in their captivity (vv. 40–43), but God "relented"[14] (NASB, NIV, ESV, HCSB) because of His covenant, "according to the multitude of his mercies [חֲסָדָיו, *khesadayw*]" (v. 45). The other cases are Psalm 30 (v. 5 compared with v. 9), Psalm 78 (v. 59 compared with v. 68), Psalm 85 (vv. 3–5 compared with vv. 7 & 10), Psalm 89 (v. 46 compared with v. 49).

One reason love triumphs over wrath is that (5) *God's loyal love is perpetual*. Psalm 136 has the refrain "For his lovingkindness endureth for ever" (ASV) at the end of each of its 26 verses. Psalm 118 affirms this truth five times (vv. 1–4, 28). Psalms 106 and 107 each contain this statement at the end of the first verse after the clause "for he is good." The psalmists sometimes state this fact more emphatically: "Lovingkindness will be built up forever; In the heavens You will establish Your faithfulness" (89:2, NASB); "the steadfast love of the LORD is from everlasting to everlasting" (103:17, ESV). God Himself promised David that His love would be unending: "I will always preserve My faithful love for him" (89:28a, HCSB); "... my

---

[14] The Hebrew verb behind this translation means "to be sorry" or "to repent." When God is the subject of this verb (*niphal* & *hithpael*), KJV translates it as "repent" 35x. This does not deny God's immutability. Rather this language indicates God's personhood in that God "relents or changes his dealings with men according to his sovereign purposes." Marvin R. Wilson, "*nāḥam*," *TWOT*, 2:571.

lovingkindness will I not utterly take from him, nor suffer my faithfulness to fail" (89:33).[15]

Each of these five propositions can be a basis for the fact that (6) *the great hope of God's saints is His loving faithfulness*. In the difficulties of life the saints fix their confidence on remembering this faithful love.[16] When David's enemies bragged about their victory over him (13:5), he could say, "I have trusted in thy lovingkindness" (v. 6a). When he called on God, he was sure of an answer (17:6) because of God's "marvellous lovingkindness," and he could say to his Lord, "O thou that savest by thy right hand them which put their trust in thee from those that rise up against them" (v. 7). David had confidence that should he stand before God as his judge (26:2), he could count on[17] "lovingkindness" (חֶסֶד, *khesed*) as he lived on the basis of God's "faithfulness" (אֱמֶת, *'emeth*) (v. 3). Here is how one psalmist stated this sixth proposition: "Behold, the eye of the LORD is upon them that fear him, upon them that hope in his mercy [חֶסֶד]" (33:18). The last verse of this same psalm again ties hope to lovingkindness: "Let thy mercy, O LORD, be upon us, according as we hope in thee" (v. 22). The hope that looks for refuge and that trusts in God's action based on His love is mentioned in three more places on the table above: 36:7; 143:8; 147:11.

New Testament Echoes

It is common knowledge for Christians that the New Testament proclaims God's love, not just for His children (Rom. 5:8; Eph. 2:4; 2 Thess. 2:16) but for all mankind (John 3:16; Titus 3:4). After all, "God is love" (1 John 4:8b). Christ's love for the redeemed is also evident. Paul knew that His Lord personally loved him (Gal. 2:20). "Christ also loved the church" (Eph. 5:25b), and He loves "us" (Eph. 5:2; Rev. 1:5). This love is permanent: "Who shall separate us from the love of Christ?" (Rom. 8:35a); nothing can "separate us from the love of God, which is in Christ Jesus our Lord" (vv. 38–39).

---

[15] Brown has also developed this point further with many more OT Scriptures (2:215).

[16] Ibid., 2:216–17.

[17] This is what it means to have חֶסֶד "before my eyes." "The clause [in v. 3a] emphasizes a fixed and enduring condition. It indicates that this has been his permanent state of mind—his focus is continually on the LORD's faithful covenant love." Ross, 1:613.

Theological Themes of Psalms

The Lord's faithfulness to His promises (Heb. 10:23b; 11:11b) and to His children is a common New Testament theme as well: "God is faithful" (1 Cor. 1:9a; 10:13b); "But the Lord is faithful" (2 Thess. 3:3a). That faithfulness transfers into actions: "Faithful is he that calleth you, who also will do it" (1 Thess. 5:24). Peter refers to God as "a faithful Creator" (1 Pet. 4:19). Hebrews describes Christ as "a merciful and faithful high priest (2:17). Christ Himself claims to be "the faithful and true witness" (Rev. 3:14b). We know that God's faithfulness is permanent since even man's unbelief and unfaithfulness cannot cancel it (Rom. 3:3; 2 Tim. 2:13). Indeed, "If we confess our sins, he is faithful and just to forgive us our sins" (1 John 1:9a).

David sums up God's love and faithfulness for us in Psalm 40:10–11. He acknowledges that Yahweh's compassion is always there for him (v. 11a). He affirms his hope that his Lord's kind act of blessing will constantly protect him (v. 11b). These facts have previously driven him to proclaim to others four benevolent attributes of God (v. 10): His justice (צְדָקָה, tsedaqah), His faithfulness (אֱמוּנָה, 'emuwnah), His loyal love (חֶסֶד, khesed), and His constancy (אֱמֶת, 'emeth). Tucked in the middle of these four is the mention of God's beneficent work of salvation.[18] May we be as grateful[19] and dependable as David to announce our Lord's virtues to other believers and to an unbelieving world.

---

[18] "Here it is necessary to observe the accumulation of terms which are employed to denote the same thing. To the righteousness of God the Psalmist adds his truth, his salvation, and his mercy. And what is the design of this, but to magnify and set forth the goodness of God by many terms or expressions of praise? We must, however, notice in what respects these terms differ; for in this way we may be able to ascertain in what respects they apply to the deliverance of which David here discourses. If these four things should be taken in their proper order, *mercy* will hold the first place, as it is that by which alone God is induced to vouchsafe to regard us. *His righteousness* is the protection by which he constantly defends his own people, and the goodness by which … he preserves them. And, lest any should doubt that it will flow in a constant and uninterrupted course, David adds in the third place *truth*; by which we are taught that God continues always the same, and is never wearied of helping us, nor at any time withdraws his hand…. *Salvation* is the effect of righteousness, for God continues to manifest his free favour to his people, daily affording them aid and assistance, until he has completely saved them." Calvin, 2:106.

[19] Calvin warns that "our perverse and ungrateful silence very often closes the gate" to God's additional favors (ibid.).

12

Protection

The Fall and the curse on mankind has made this world a dangerous place for humans. Because of God's covenant love and His faithfulness to keep His promises, He is zealous to protect His people from disasters and from enemies. The psalmists were well aware of this fact, and they celebrated it in their praise of Yahweh. As they found themselves in those dangerous situations, they based their petitions on this truth. David was particularly sensitive to his need for protection because of his experiences of being pursued by King Saul and by his son Absalom. The theme of Yahweh's protection has a close connection to His deliverance or redemption (2 Sam. 21:1), but that theme will be the subject of a later chapter. The notable distinction for this theme is that David and the other psalmists use a number of metaphors to communicate the kind of safety that this defense from harm provides.

Imagery for God's Protecting Power

In Psalm 18:2 David uses five military images to communicate how his God provided defensive protection for him.[1] By searching in a concordance for other passages in Psalms that use these same words, we are able to discover in the other verses five additional military defensive terms. Table 12.1 charts these ten metaphors in three groups: (1) rock, (2) fortification, and (3) shield. The ten Hebrew nouns, except for the last (סֹחֵרָה, *sowkheyrah*; a hapax legomenon), occur frequently in the Old Testament; therefore, we have at our disposal a number of illustrative passages to help us understand the images. The table indicates how many times each of these words occurs in the Old Testament and just in Psalms. Since sometimes the psalmists use these words non-figuratively or to describe

---

[1] For David these "were all emblems of Him who had been throughout his true Refuge and Deliverer." Kirkpatrick, 87.

human events, the table's last column indicates just the cases in Psalms describing God's protection. The rock imagery (צוּר, *tsuwr*; and סֶלַע, *sela'*) refers to natural refuges that offer a place to hide from an enemy or to be unreachable: rocky mountain areas or cliffs such as provide security for wild goats (1 Sam. 24:2) or hyraxes (Prov. 30:26).

Five terms fall into the second group, humanly built fortifications: (a) the מִשְׂגָּב (*misgav*) is the high, inaccessible structure built for defending a city's walls (Isa. 25:12); (b) in a storm one needs some sort of shelter (מַחְסֶה, *makhseh*) to use as a refuge (Isa. 25:4); (c) the noun מָעוֹז (*ma'owz*) means "a place of strength,"[2] thus a "stronghold," like the fortress entered by a conquering king (Dan. 11:7); (d) a מְצוּדָה (*metsuwdah*) is a fortress, like Zion that was captured by David from the Jebusites (2 Sam. 5:7); (e) in times of war ancient peoples would enter a tower (מִגְדָּל, *migdal*) for protection (Judg. 9:51). Many times our English translations cause us to lose sight of these metaphors by simply translating these various words as "refuge."

The third group has three words that mean "shield," a protective armament for an individual. The מָגֵן (*mageyn*) is a small shield held with one hand while the other hand held a spear or sword (Neh. 4:16). The צִנָּה (*tsinnah*) is a large shield used to cover the whole body: Goliath had one of these that someone carried for him (1 Sam. 17:7). The word סֹחֵרָה (*sowkheyrah*) occurs just once in the Bible; some ancient witnesses (Targum, *PiH*) point to a small shield or some form of protection. Two occurrences of מָגֵן (*mageyn*) in Psalms present us with translation problems. When the psalmist says, "our shield, see, O God" (84:9a, literal translation), is he addressing God as his Shield, or is he asking God to notice His anointed king, the nation's shield? KJV, A V, and some ancient translations (LXX, *PiH*) take the first position, but many modern English versions (for example, NASB, ESV, HCSB) follow the second. Because Yahweh is called "shield" in verse eleven, the vocative is more likely correct for this verse.[3] There is a similar issue in 89:18 concerning "shield": is "shield" parallel to "our king," the one belonging to Yahweh; or should the verse be translated "Truly the LORD is

---

[2] It is derived from a verb (עָזַז, *'azaz*) that means "to be strong." Because of an Arabic cognate many of the Hebrew dictionaries (BDB, *HALOT*, *DCH*) want to connect this noun to a verb (עוּז, *'uwz*) that means "to seek refuge," but the spelling of some forms of this noun clearly indicate its relationship to עָזַז. A stronghold would of course be used as a refuge.

[3] This is the argument Alexander uses (p. 365).

114

our shield, the Holy One of Israel, our king!" (NAB; similarly, KJV). Table 12.1 regards the first verse as an image for God, but not the second.

Table 12.1 Imagery in Psalms for Divine Security

Hebrew Terms	Transliteration	English Translation	# OT/Ps.	Relevant References	Total
צוּר	tsuwr	rock	73/24	18:2, 31, 46; 19:14; 28:1; 31:2; 61:2; 62:2, 6, 7; 71:3; 73:26; 78:35; 89:26; 92:15; 94:22; 95:1; 144:1	18
סֶלַע	sela'	rock	63/9	18:2; 31:3; 42:9; 71:3	4
מִשְׂגָּב	misgav	high tower	17/13	9:9[2]; 18:2; 46:7, 11; 48:3; 59:9, 16, 17; 62:2, 6; 94:22; 144:2	13
מַחְסֶה	makhseh	shelter	20/12	14:6; 46:1; 61:3; 62:7, 8; 71:7; 73:28; 91:2, 9; 94:22; 142:5	11
מָעוֹז	ma'owz	stronghold	36/9	27:1; 28:8; 31:2, 4; 37:39; 43:2; 52:7	7
מְצוּדָה	metsuwdah	fortress	18/6	18:2; 31:2, 3; 71:3; 91:2; 144:2	6
מִגְדָּל	migdal	tower	45/2	61:3	1
מָגֵן	mageyn	shield	60/19	3:3; 7:10; 18:2, 30, 35; 28:7; 33:20; 59:11; 84:9, 11; 115:9, 10, 11; 119:114; 144:2	15
צִנָּה	tsinnah	shield	20/3	91:4	1
סֹחֵרָה	sowkheyrah	buckler	1/1	91:4	1

The psalmists also use a number of verbs that indicate the action of God's protection. Table 12.2 lists the occurrences of two synonymous verbs that are so used in Psalms thirty times. Used frequently in Psalms (71x), שׁמר (*shamar*) means "to guard" or "to watch." David asks God to guard him from harm (using the imperative 6x): for example, he says, "O keep my soul" (25:20a), and "Keep me from the snares which they have laid for me" (141:9a). Eight times the psalmists use the participle of this verb to describe God: "One who protects" (34:20; 97:10; 116:6; 121:3, 4, 5; 145:20; 146:9). The second verb (נצר, *natsar*) appears twice after the first in the same verse: "Thou shalt keep them, O LORD, thou shalt preserve them from this generation for ever" (12:7); "Keep me, O LORD, from the hands of the wicked; preserve me from the violent man ..." (140:4).

If from God's perspective, He guards His own; then from man's viewpoint, the saints take refuge (חסה, *khasah*) in Him. The connection between the metaphors and the verb occurs in 18:2, when in the midst of his list of five military images, David says, "in whom I take refuge" (NASB). This verb the KJV usually translates as "put [pronoun: their/my] trust," but in

57:1 it translates the second usage of the verb as, "in the shadow of thy wings will I make my refuge ...."

The table also lists three nouns (each used 6x) that add more metaphors. (1) A bird uses its wings (כְּנָפַיִם, *kenaphayim*) to protect its young. (2) A shadow (צֵל, *tseyl*) protects from the sun's heat. (3) A hiding place (סֵתֶר, *seyther*), provides safety from nature's storms (Isa. 32:2).

Table 12.2 Hebrew Verbs and Additional Nouns in Psalms for Protection

Hebrew words:	שמר	נצר	חסה	כְּנָפַיִם	צֵל	סֵתֶר
	shamar	*natsar*	*khasah*	*kenaphayim*	*tseyl*	*seyther*
Psalm	to guard	to protect	to take refuge	wings	shadow	hiding place
2:			12			
5:			11			
7:			1			
11:			1			
12:	7	7				
16:	1		1			
17:	8		7	8	8	
18:			2 30			
25:	20		20	8	8	
27:						5
31:		23	1 19			20
32:		7				7
34:	20		8 22			
36:			7	7	7	
37:	28		40			
40:		11				
41:	2					
57:			1 [2]	1	1	
61:		7	4	4		4
63:				7	7	
64:		1	10			
71:			1			
86:	2					
91:	11		4	4	1	1
97:	10					
116:	6					
118:			8 9			
119:						114
121:	3 4 5 7[2] 8				5	
127:	1					
140:	4	1 4				
141:	9		8			
144:			2			
145:	20					
146:	9					
totals:	22	8	25	6	6	6

Table 12.3 lists six less common verbs that describe God's protecting actions, adding four more pictures to the list of images. One way to protect

someone is (1) to make him inaccessible by putting him in a high place. This is what the Lord has done: "Yet setteth he the poor on high from affliction" (107:41). The verb here is שׂגב (*sagav*), used five of its seven times for this action.[4] Another way is (2) to hide the person from the sight of enemies: "Keep me as the apple of the eye, hide [סתר, *sathar*] me under the shadow of thy wings" (17:8). Related to this act is treasuring or keeping something valuable secure by hiding: "For He will conceal[5] me in His shelter in the day of adversity" (27:5, HCSB). Next, (3) the verb כסה (*kasa*) presents us with an interesting image clarified by a literal translation: "Near Thee I am covered" (143:9, YLT). Finally, there is protection by (4) surrounding (עטר, *'atar*) the one threatened: "with favour wilt thou compass him as with a shield" (5:12). This verb has a common synonym (סבב, *savav*; 162x in OT, 23x in Ps.) that David used twice to indicate God's defense: "thou shalt compass me about" (32:7b; also v. 10). Related to this latter verb is another word in the table, a noun functioning as a preposition: סָבִיב (*saviyv*; "surroundings," "around"). In two of its 19 uses in Psalms it refers to a protection around someone: "The angel of the LORD [the pre-incarnate Christ] encampeth round about them that fear him ..." (34:7); "As the mountains are round about Jerusalem, so the LORD is round about his people from henceforth even for ever" (125:2). The two other nouns in this table picture a shelter that would protect from the sun (27:5a; 31:20b), such as the prophet built for himself outside of Nineveh (Jon. 4:5). The last noun refers to a place of fleeing (59:16), where one runs for safety. David expressed that desire to get away from danger in 55:6–8, flying away like a bird wandering in the wilderness or hurrying to shelter from a gale.

Categories of Sentences

Examining the 118 verses listed in the three tables above, we notice that the vast majority of the verses in the tables above fall into two categories.

---

[4] Ross says that the verb "has a military connotation": "just as someone might place something inaccessibly high, so should God make the king safe and secure in battle [in 20:1], out of reach, so to speak, of his enemies" (1:494). In English versions the metaphor is often lost because the word is usually translated as "protect" (NRSV, 4x; ESV, 3x; NIV, 3x; HCSB, 3x; NET, 3x) or "defend" (KJV in 20:1; 59:1). NASB, however, renders the verb as "set securely on high" in all five passages.

[5] "The word here used means to hide; to secrete; and then, to defend or protect." Barnes, 1:239. It "may also mean hide in the sense of treasure, store up, or reserve ...." Andrew E. Hill, "צפן," *NIDOTTE*, 3:840.

Theological Themes of Psalms

(1) The first group are those that contain sentences that simply state the fact that God is the Protector of the saints. Some of these are in the past tense: for example, 59:16b ("For thou hast been my defence and refuge in the day of my trouble"); 94:22 ("But the LORD is my defence; and my God is the rock of my refuge"). Many of these refer to the future: for example, 12:7 ("Thou shalt keep them, O LORD, thou shalt preserve them from this generation for ever"); 57:1b ("Yea, in the shadow of thy wings will I make my refuge"); 121:7 ("The LORD shall preserve thee from all evil: he shall preserve thy soul"). Most of these, however, are statements about the present truth: 3:3; 5:12; 9:9; 18:2, 30–31; 27:1; 28:8; 31:3; 32:7; 34:20; 41:2; 46:1, 7, 11; 62:8; 84:11; 115:9–11, and many more. In many cases the fact of protection is indicated by an apposition (almost like a title) rather than a clausal statement: for example, "Unto thee will I cry, O LORD my rock" (28:1a); "I will say unto God my rock" (42:9); "and bring them down, O Lord our shield" (59:11c).

Table 12.3 Additional Terms in Psalms for God's Protection

Hebrew	Transliteration	English	#	References	Total in Ps.
שׂגב	sagav	to make inaccessible	5	20:1; 59:1; 69:29; 91:14; 107:41	7
סתר	sathar	to hide	4	17:8; 27:5; 31:20; 64:2	23
צפן	tsaphan	to treasure (hide)	3	27:5; 31:20; 83:3	9
כסה	kasah	to cover oneself	1	143:9	17
עטר	'atar	to surround	1	5:12	4
סבב	savav	to surround	2	32:7, 10	23
סָבִיב	saviyv	around	2	34:7; 125:2	19
סֹךְ	sowk	shelter	1	27:5	3
סֻכָּה	sukkah	shelter	1	31:20	2
מָנוֹס	manows	refuge	1	59:16	2

(2) The second group of verses contains requests for God's protection. The fact expressed in the first group does not negate what happens in the second: it is appropriate and even needful to ask God for something He has promised.[6] Four times the psalmists use imperatives of שׁמר (shamar)

---

[6] "The insensible transition from direct prayer to confident anticipation is characteristic of the psalms of David." Alexander, 551. In 140:1 an imperative ("Deliver") is followed by an imperfect ("Thou keepest," YLT). Starting with the

with "me" as the direct object: "Preserve [once]/Keep [3x] me" (16:1; 17:8; 140:4; 141:9). In 17:8a the request is particularly bold: "Keep me as the apple of the eye."[7] Twice David asks to have security for his soul or life (25:20; 86:2). Sometimes the psalmists provide a basis for such requests by reminding God that they have taken refuge (חסה, *khasah*) in Him: for example, "O keep my soul … and deliver me: Let me not be ashamed; for I put my trust in thee" (25:20); "Be merciful unto me, O God …, for my soul trusteth in thee: Yea, in the shadow of thy wings will I make my refuge …" (57:1). In many of the verses in both groups the psalmists personalize the statements: "my Rock" (12x), "my Stronghold" (8x), "my Refuge" (6x), "my Fortress" (5x), "my Shield" (5x), "my Hiding Place" (2x).

New Testament Echoes

The New Testament does not exploit the many metaphors for God's protecting power the way Psalms does, but it clearly expresses this fact. At the end of the first missionary trip, Paul and Barnabas "entrusted [their converts] to the protection of the Lord" (Acts 14:23, NET).[8] Paul tells the Thessalonians, "But the Lord is faithful, who shall … keep you from evil" (2 Thess. 3:3), using the same Greek verb (φυλάσσω, *phulassō*) that translated שמר (*shamar*, "guard") in Psalms (for example, 16:1; 17:8) in the Septuagint. Two other passages use this verb to indicate God's protection of the saints (2 Tim. 1:12; Jude 24). Peter and John use synonyms of this Greek verb to express the same truth: "who [the elect] are kept by the power of God through faith unto salvation ready to be revealed in the last time" (1 Pet. 1:5); "but God protects the one he has fathered" (1 John 5:18, NET).[9] In Christ's high priestly prayer we find two of these Greek terms (τηρέω, *tēreō*; φυλάσσω, *phulassō*): "Holy Father, keep … those whom thou hast given me"

LXX it has been common for translators incorrectly to treat both verbs as imperatives ("Deliver," "preserve"). This kind of transition happens also in 59:1 and 71:3. Concerning 64:1–2 Alexander notes that "the expression of confidence insinuates itself into the prayer itself," translating the clauses as "from fear of the enemy thou wilt preserve my life," and "Thou wilt hide me from the secret of evil doers" (p. 281).

[7] "The request is that God's protective care should never let him out of his sight (an anthropomorphic way of speaking)." Ross, 1:425.

[8] The NET note on this clause points out that in a context like this the Greek verb "to place beside" (παρατίθημι, *paratithēmi*) implies that the purpose of this act is for care or protection.

[9] See the study note on this verse in NET.

(John 17:11); "I kept them in thy name: those that thou gavest me I have kept" (v. 12); "but that thou shouldest keep them from the evil" (v. 15).

In conclusion let us consider an interesting Christological picture that comes from the New Testament and has a connection with Psalms. In Hebrew there is a synonym for the two words translated as "rock" listed in Table 12.1 above: אֶבֶן (*'even*, "stone"; used 270x in OT), used just three times in Psalms, but not to picture Yahweh as Guardian. Psalm 118:22 says, "The stone [אֶבֶן] which the builders refused is become the head stone of the corner." 1 Peter 2:6–8 indicates that this Stone is Christ. Now a "stone" is usually small and a "rock" large, such as offers protection, but could there not still be a connection?[10] The Israelites got water from the Rock in the wilderness (Deut. 8:15), and Moses claims that Yahweh is "The Rock" (Deut. 32:4), the same Rock David speaks about (Ps. 18:2) and that Paul identifies as Christ (1 Cor. 10:4). Christ is the Great Protector of the believer! Indeed, we can say to Him, "He is my refuge and my fortress: My God; in him will I trust" (91:2). "Blessed are all they that put their trust [or take refuge] in him" (2:12b).

---

[10] The two Hebrew words are used in parallelism in Isa. 8:14 ("for stone of stumbling and for a rock of offence"), quoted in 1 Pet. 2:8.

13

Iniquity

In contrast to all God's goodness and His beneficent attributes, mankind has rebelled against the Creator. Iniquity is one of the three or four main themes of God's revelation to mankind in both testaments. The Lord began speaking to our first parents about this issue in the Garden of Eden. When Moses led the Israelites into the wilderness, God's laws and ceremonies focused on the matter of sin. The messages of the prophets concentrated on this topic. Christ took on Himself human flesh so that He could accomplish His work of terminating rebellion, making "an end of sins" and atoning "for iniquity" (Dan. 9:24). When He returned to heaven, He sent the Holy Spirit, "and when he is come, he will reprove the world of sin, ... of sin, because they believe not on me" (John 16:8–9).

The topic of sin surfaces frequently in Psalms. In fact, it begins in the first verse of the Psalter, which mentions those who are "ungodly," "sinners," and "scornful" and continues until the next to last psalm with its reference to "vengeance," "punishments," and "judgment" on sinners (149:7–9). The theme is prominent enough to require four chapters in this book: Chapter 15 focuses on the persons who sin, the "Wicked"; Chapter 16 ("Enemy") discusses the sinners' relationship to God and His saints; this chapter deals with the numerous general terms for sin and specific sins that are mentioned in Psalms; and Chapter 14 considers the particularly heinous sin of pride.

Of course, the psalmists have much to say about the iniquity of the ungodly, but often even God's own people revolt against the will of their covenant Lord and commit sin. In fact iniquity exists in the lives of even the godly psalmists who wrote their poems under inspiration. Additionally, iniquity distressed their lives because they were frequently the offended object of someone else's sin. At least 83 psalms say something about sin, the subject occurring in 248 different verses (10% of the book's verses).

Vocabulary for Iniquity

The book of Psalms uses 26 general terms for the subject of iniquity and 34 different words for specific sins (not counting pride). The most common general words appear below in Table 13.1. Five are general nouns used for the concept of iniquity. Two words are usually translated "iniquity": (1) עָוֹן ('awown; over 200x in the OT and 31x in Ps.) and (2) אָוֶן ('awen; over 70x in the OT and 27x in Ps.).[1] The third word is (3) רָעָה (ra'ah; about 300x in the OT and 31x in Ps.), a general word for something bad or evil: about half of the usages in Psalms refer to disaster or misfortune (for example, 27:5) and the rest to something evil or sinful (17x).[2] In Hebrew the familiar word for sin is (4) חַטָּאת (khatta'th; almost 300x in the OT but only 13x in Ps.); since "sin is the transgression of the law" (1 John 3:4b), this term is semantically equivalent to "iniquity" (a word borrowed from Latin into English whereas "sin" is a Middle English word). Another synonym for iniquity is the common noun (5) פֶּשַׁע (pesha'; 93x in the OT including 14x in Ps.). Some modern translations have rendered this word as "rebellion" (for example, HCSB and NET),[3] but several times the term parallels "sin" (25:7; 51:3; 59:3) or "iniquity" (89:32; 107:17). Thus "transgression" or "crime" would be an appropriate translation since these English words are close synonyms for "sin" and "iniquity." The one general adjective is (6) רַע (ra'; over 350x in the OT and 33x in Ps.), related to the noun רָעָה (ra'ah); it is

---

[1] The word occurs two additional times (55:3; 90:10) for the concept "trouble," a metonymy of the cause ("iniquity") substituted for the effect ("problem"). See Ross, 2:248.

[2] Six times David refers to enemies who wish for "my hurt" (רְעָתִי: 35:26; 38:12; 40:14; 70:2; 71:13; 71:24), meaning that trouble should befall him; however, in 35:4 because the accompanying verb is "devise" the reference is to some evil act committed against him.

[3] R. Knierim (in *TLOT*, 2:1033) seems to hold L. Köhler responsible for this term being usually translated as "dispute, rebellion." In the nineteenth century, however, Robert Baker Girdlestone had categorized פֶּשַׁע as "rebellion." *Synonyms of the Old Testament* (1897; reprint, Grand Rapids: Eerdmans, n.d.), 81. Furthermore, the Geneva Bible and KJV had sometimes translated it as "rebellion" (see 25:7 and Job 34:37). Knierim has presented a credible argument that the word is a comprehensive term basically meaning "crime" (2:1034–37). The LXX reflects both the difficulty of precisely defining this Hebrew word and its general nature by translating it eighteen different ways.

Table 13.1 Common General Words for Iniquity in Psalms

Hebrew words:	עָוֹן 'awown	אָוֶן 'awen	רָעָה ra'ah	חַטָּאת khatta'th	פֶּשַׁע pesha'	רַע ra'
Psalm	iniquity	iniquity	evil	sin	transgression	bad
5:		5			10	4
6:		8				
7:		14				4 9
10:		7				
14:		4				
15:			3			
18:	23					
19:					13	
21:			11			
25:	11			7 18	7	
28:		3	3			
31:	10					
32:	2 5[2]			5[2]	1 5	
34:			21			13 14 16
35:			4 12			
36:	2	3 4 12			1	4
37:						27
38:	4 18		20	3 18		
39:	11				8	
40:	12		12			
41:		6	7			5
49:	6					
50:			19			
51:	2 5 9			2 3	1 3	4
52:			1			3
53:		4				
54:						5
55:		10	15			
56:		7				5
59:	4	2 5		3 12	3	
64:		2				5
65:	3				3	
66:		18				
69:	27[2]					
73:						8
78:	38					
79:	8			9		
85:	2			2		
89:	32				32	
90:	8					
92:		7 9				
94:		4 16 23	23			
97:						10
101:		8				4
103:	3 10				12	
106:	43					
107:	17		34		17	
109:	14		5	14		20
119:		133				101

Hebrew words:	עָוֹן	אָוֶן	רָעָה	חַטָּאת	פֶּשַׁע	רַע
	'awown	'awen	ra'ah	khatta'th	pesha'	ra'
Psalm	iniquity	iniquity	evil	sin	transgression	bad
125:		5				
130:	3 8					
140:			2			
141:		4 9	5			4
totals:	31	26	17	13	14	20

used 20 times for the evil of iniquity.[4] Usually it functions as a substantive (an adjective used like a noun, "a bad *thing*"), for example, "neither shall evil dwell with thee" (5:4).

The psalmists additionally mention many specific sins. Table 13.2 lists the six most common terms. In one sense when a person disobeys God by sinning or committing iniquity, it is an act of rebellion against his sovereign. (1) The verb מרה (*marah*; "to rebel") occurs ten times in Psalms. Mankind's sinful nature most naturally manifests itself also in his propensity to lie. Two common terms for this sin are (2) שֶׁקֶר (*sheqer*, "falsehood"; 19x in Ps.) and (3) מִרְמָה (*mirmah*, "deceit"; 14x in Ps.). The psalmists use (4) a noun (חֶרְפָּה, *kherpah*; 18x) and (5) a verb (חרף, *kharaph*; 11x) to express mankind's verbal violence against others. Their term for physical violence is (6) חָמָס (*khamas*; 14x).

Less frequent general words for iniquity include twelve nouns and eight verbs listed below respectively in Table 13.3 and Table 13.4. Some of these terms in Psalms refer both to the sin and the consequence. For example, the word for "trouble" (עָמָל, *'amal*) can refer to the trouble a sinner causes or the trouble that comes upon a person as punishment or because of the evil someone else has done. The table lists the seven references in Psalms where עָמָל is a sin: for example, concerning the wicked "under his tongue is mischief and vanity" (10:7b), a reference to sinful speech. Six other references in Psalms refer to the consequences: for example, the psalmist thinks that the wicked "are not in trouble as other men" (73:5a). The term הַוָּה (*hawwah*; 13x in the OT) usually means "destruction," an aftereffect of sin, but in at least three of its eight occurrences in Psalms it is a metonymy, where the effect (ruin) stands in place of the cause (wickedness): "very wickedness" (5:9), "in

---

[4] Eleven times the adjective refers to something that is bad (like trouble, danger, or news), but in cases where iniquity is not the issue. Twice it refers to a bad man (treated below in Chapter 15).

Table 13.2 Common Words for Specific Sins in Psalms

Hebrew words: Psalm	מרה *marah* to rebel	שֶׁקֶר *sheqer* falsehood	מִרְמָה *mirmah* deceit	חֶרְפָּה *kherpah* reproach	חרף *kharaph* to reproach	חָמָס *khamas* violence
5:	10		6			
7:		14				16
10:			7			
11:						5
15:				3		
17:			1			
18:						48
22:				6		
24:			4			
25:						19
27:		12				12
31:		18		11		
34:			13			
35:			20			11
36:			3			
38:			12			
39:				8		
42:					10	
43:			1			
44:				13		
50:			19			
52:		3	4			
55:			11 23		12	9
57:					3	
58:						2
63:		11				
69:		4		7 9 10 19 20	9	
72:						14
73:						6
74:				22	10 18	20
78:	8 17 40 56					
79:				4 12	12	
89:				41 50	51 [2]	
101:		7				
102:					8	
105:	28					
106:	7 33 43					
107:	11					
109:		2	2	25		
119:		[8x]†		22 39	42	
120:		2				
140:						1 4 11
144:		8 11				
totals:	10	19	14	18	11	14

† Verses 29, 69, 78, 86, 104, 118, 128, 163.

his wickedness" (52:7), and "throne of wickedness" (94:20).⁵ In the lists below two of the nouns (חֵטְא, *kheyt*; חֲטָאָה, *kheta'ah*) and one verb (חטא, *khata'*) are word forms closely related to the normal word for sin (חַטָּאת, *khatta'th*). Another family of words would be אָשָׁם (*'asham*) and אַשְׁמָה (*'ashmah*), referring to the condition of guilt or a sinful act, translated as "guilty ways" (ESV, HCSB) or "sins" (NIV) in 68:21 and as "wrongs" (NASB, ESV) or "sins" (KJV, ASV) in 69:5. An appropriate English word would be "fault."⁶ These two families of words are somewhat difficult to distinguish, but clearly they both refer to the general concept of iniquity.⁷

Table 13.3 Additional General Nouns in Psalms for Iniquity

Hebrew	Trans-literation	English	#	References	Total in Ps.
שָׁוְא	*shaw'*	worthlessness	9	12:2; 24:4; 26:4; 31:6; 41:6; 119:37; 139:20; 144:8,11	15
עוֹלָה	*'awlah*	wickedness	8	37:1; 43:1; 58:2; 64:6; 92:15; 107:42; 119:3; 125:3	9
עָמָל	*'amal*	trouble	7	7:14, 16; 10:7, 14; 55:10; 94:20; 140:9	13
רֶשַׁע	*resha'*	wickedness	6	5:4; 10:15; 45:7; 84:10; 125:3; 141:4	6
חֵטְא	*kheyt'*	sin	3	51:5, 9; 103:10	3
הַוָּה	*hawwah*	wickedness	3	5:9; 52:7; 94:20	8
חֲטָאָה	*kheta'ah*	sin	2	32:1; 109:7	3
עָוֶל	*'awel*	iniquity	2	53:1; 82:2	3
אִוֶּלֶת	*'iwweleth*	foolishness	2	38:5; 69:5	2
אָשָׁם	*'asham*	fault	1	68:21	1
אַשְׁמָה	*'ashmah*	fault	1	69:5	1
זֻלּוּת	*zulluwth*	baseness	1	12:8	1

Each of the verbs in Table 13.4 requires some explanation. In one of its nine uses in Psalms חטא (*khata'*, "to sin") refers to a purification from

---

⁵ Possibly 52:2 is another case ("Thy tongue deviseth mischiefs"), but here many translations correctly have in view the desired result of the scheming (NASB, NRSV, ESV, HCSB, NET). Alexander, however, understands some uses of the word as a metonymy in the opposite way: concerning 94:20 he says, "Both this word and its parallel [עָמָל] translated *mischief* are applied in usage to the sufferings brought upon one person by the misconduct of another" (p. 401).

⁶ See BDB's entry on אָשָׁם.

⁷ See D. Kellermann, "אָשָׁם *āshām*," *TDOT*, 1:431–32.

sin:[8] "Purge me with hyssop" (51:7a); thus the table does not include this reference. The verbs סוג (*suwg*) and שָׁגַג (*shagag*) literally mean "to turn back" and "to go astray." Metaphorically, these words refer to deviation from moral standards or unfaithfulness to personal commitment, in other words, sin. For סוג (*suwg*) four of its usages in Psalms refer to God's act of thwarting (turning back) someone who intends to do evil (35:4; 40:14; 70:2; 129:5); the remaining references are to cases of apostasy or failing to remain in God's ways. The psalmist confesses his sin by saying that he had gone astray (שָׁגַג, *shagag*; 119:67). The verb רעע (*ra'a*) appears fifteen times in Psalms. Nine times the participle occurs, meaning "evildoer": these will be covered below in Chapter 15. In three cases the reference is to hurting someone, not to a sin (15:4; 44:2; 106:32). The remaining three cases are relevant to this chapter. The verb רשע (*rasha'*, "act wickedly") occurs four times, but twice it means "to declare guilty" (37:33; 94:21). The term meaning "to fornicate" (זנה, *zanah*) occurs in Psalms only in the metaphorical sense of spiritual unfaithfulness; thus this is being classified as a general term, although it could be regarded as the specific sin of idolatry.[9] In the *niphal* theme the verb עוה ('*awah*) literally means "to be bent" (38:6), but the *hiphil* means "commit iniquity" (106:6), a general term. Another general reference to iniquity is the concept of abomination: the verb form for this act is תעב (*ta'av*; OT 22x including 6x in Ps.). Sometimes the verb expresses a person's abhorrence of something: either God's (5:6; 106:40) or man's (107:18; 119:163), but twice the Hebrew refers to abominable acts of mankind (14:1; 53:1).

Less frequent words indicating specific sins include twelve nouns (Table 13.5) and seventeen verbs (Table 13.6). The nouns fall into six categories (indicated in the table by the solid lines between the groups). Four terms (בּוּז, *buwz*; כְּלִמָּה, *kelimmah*; לַעַג, *la'ag*; קֶלֶס, *qeles*) refer to the sin of abusive speech, which is sometimes slander but not necessarily. The second category involves sins of falsehood: lying (כָּזָב, *kazav*; כַּחַשׁ, *kakhash*) and

---

[8] This is the privative usage of the piel theme on a denominative verb. GKC § 52h. An example of a privative in English would be the verb "dust" in the sentence "she dusted her living room."

[9] The expression "commonly refers to idolatrous practices, but is used sometimes of other kinds of declension and alienation from God" (Rawlinson, 2:72–73). An example would be Num. 14:33, where the specific sin was Israel's unbelief and rebellion about entering Canaan, not idolatry.

Theological Themes of Psalms

Table 13.4 Verbs in Psalms for General Acts of Iniquity

Hebrew	Trans-literation	English	#	References	Total in Ps.
חטא	khata'	to sin	8	4:4; 39:1; 41:4; 51:4; 78:17, 32; 106:6; 119:11	9
סוג	suwg	to deviate	4	44:18; 53:3; 78:57; 80:18	8
רעע	ra'a'	to do evil	3	37:8; 74:3; 105:15	15
זנה	zanah	to fornicate	2	73:27; 106:39	2
רשע	rasha'	to act wickedly	2	18:21; 106:6	4
שגג	shagag	to go astray	2	119:21, 67	3
תעב	ta'av	to act abominably	2	14:1; 53:1	6
עוה	'awah	to pervert	1	106:6	2

deceit (רְמִיָּה, remiyyah; תַּרְמִית, tarmiyth). The remaining four are oppression (תֹּךְ, towk), hatred (שִׂנְאָה, sin'ah), cursing (אָלָה, 'alah), and vexation (כַּעַס, ka'as), a malice that seeks to annoy, but not necessarily with words.

Table 13.5 Additional Nouns for Specific Sins in Psalms

Hebrew	Trans-literation	English	#	References	Total in Ps.
בּוּז	buwz	contempt	4	31:18; 119:22; 123:3, 4	5
כְּלִמָּה	kelimmah	insult	4	4:2; 44:15; 69:7, 19	7
לַעַג	la'ag	derision	3	44:13; 79:4; 123:4	3
קֶלֶס	qeles	derision	2	44:13; 79:4	2
כָּזָב	kazav	lie	5	4:2; 5:6; 40:4; 58:3; 62:4	6
רְמִיָּה	remiyyah	deceit	5	32:2; 52:2; 101:7; 120:2, 3	6
כַּחַשׁ	kakhash	lying	1	59:12	1
תַּרְמִית	tarmiyth	deceit	1	119:118	1
תֹּךְ	towk	oppression	3	10:7; 55:11; 72:14	3
שִׂנְאָה	sin'ah	hatred	3	25:19; 109:3, 5	4
אָלָה	'alah	cursing	2	10:7; 59:12	2
כַּעַס	ka'as	vexation	1	10:14	4

The verb list includes nine categories, four of which parallel noun categories: falsehood with four different words (כזב, kazav; נבל, nakal; שוא, shawa'; שקר, shaqar), hatred with two synonyms (שנא, sana'; שטם, satam), oppression (צרר, tsarar), and vexation (כעס, ka'as). The main word for hatred (שנא) occurs 41 times in Psalms, but only three of these refer to sinful hatred of mankind for others (25:19; 105:25) or for discipline (50:17); many are participles which will be treated below in Chapter 16 (Enemy), and some refer

Table 13.6 Additional Verbs for Specific Sins in Psalms

Hebrew	Trans-literation	English	#	References	Total in Ps.
נאץ	na'ats	to despise	5	10:3, 13; 74:10, 18; 107:11	5
בזה	bazah	to despise	2	22:6; 119:141	8
מאס	ma'as	to reject	2	106:24; 118:22	8
כזב	kazav	to lie	1	78:36	3
נכל	nakal	to act deceitfully	1	105:25	1
שוא	shawa'	to deceive	1	89:22	2
שקר	shaqar	to treat falsely	1	44:17	2
בגד	bagad	to commit treachery	2	73:15; 78:57	5
צרר	tsarar	to oppress	2	129:1, 2	2
הרג	harag	to murder	3	10:8; 44:22; 94:6	9
רצח	ratsakh	to murder	2	62:3; 94:6	2
שנא	sana'	to hate	3	25:19; 50:17; 105:25	41
שטם	satam	to hate	1	55:3	1
שסס	shasas	to plunder	1	89:41	1
שסה	shasah	to plunder	1	44:10	1
שחת	shakhath	to corrupt	2	14:1; 53:1	5
כעס	ka'as	to irritate	2	78:58; 106:29	3

to a proper hatred (for example, "I hate every false way"; 109:104). Three of the remaining categories contain multiple verbs: plundering (שסס, *shasas*; שסה, *shasah*), contempt (נאץ, *na'ats*; בזה, *bazah*; מאס, *ma'as*),[10] an intense variety of hatred with outward indications, and murder (הרג, *harag*; רצח, *ratsakh*). The first word for murder (הרג) occurs nine times, but most of these refer to God's execution of sinners (for example, 78:31). The remaining sins are treachery (בגד, *bagad*) and corruption (שחת, *shakhath*). This last verb (שחת) occurs five times in the text of Psalms (not counting

---

[10] The last two (מאס & בזה) each occur six more times without indicating mankind's sin: e.g., "a broken and a contrite heart, O God, thou wilt not despise" (51:17b); in judgment God "greatly abhorred Israel" (78:59b).

titles), three times to refer to destruction (78:38, 45; 106:23). In 14:1 and 53:1 the term describes the sin of spoiling or ruining oneself.[11]

Propositions

Under inspiration the psalmists proclaimed a number of truths about iniquity. To begin with, they affirm that (1) *God is totally without sin.* "For thou art not a God that hath pleasure in wickedness: neither shall evil dwell with thee" (5:4). In fact, God hates "all workers of iniquity" (v. 5b) and personally[12] hates "the wicked and him that loveth violence" (11:5b). The stronger word "abhor" is used in the next verse. Abraham had asked the question "Shall not the Judge of all the earth do right?" (Gen. 18:25c). The psalmists answer this question by saying, "Good and upright is the LORD" (25:8a); "... the LORD is upright: ... and there is no unrighteousness in him" (92:15); and "The LORD is righteous in all his ways" (145:17a). Iniquity is an opposite of uprightness and righteousness!

In contrast, there is the familiar fact that (2) *sin is universal for mankind.* David proclaimed, "There is none that doeth good" (14:1), and "They are all gone aside, they are all together become filthy: there is none that doeth good, no, not one) (v. 3). In a later psalm he told the Lord, "For in Your sight no man living is righteous" (143:2, NASB). Another psalmist said, "If thou, LORD, shouldest mark iniquities, O Lord, who shall stand?" (130:3).

Since all men are sinners, that must include those that Psalms refers to as "the righteous": (3) *the saints experience the awfulness of personal sin.* David said about himself, "For I acknowledge my transgressions: and my sin is ever before me" (51:3). Referring to the same incident, David later wrote,[13] "I acknowledged my sin unto thee, and mine iniquity have I not hid. I said, I will confess my transgressions unto the LORD" (32:5). In a more general sense David exclaims, "For mine iniquities are gone over mine head: as an heavy burden they are too heavy for me" (38:4); and "For I will declare mine iniquity; I will be sorry for my sin" (v. 18). David was conscious not only

---

[11] "Sinfulness is described as corruption and perversion with this word" (Ross, 1:376). See Gen. 6:12 and Isa. 1:4.

[12] "This is not simply equivalent to *he hates*, but denotes a cordial [heartfelt] hatred. ... He hates with all his heart." Alexander, 62. I understand the word נֶפֶשׁ here to mean "person," thus "personally."

[13] See Perowne (1:298) and Steveson (p. 126) for the idea that this psalm was later than 51.

about the great number of his sins (רָעוֹת, *ra'owth*) but also about their dominant presence (אָפְפוּ־עָלַי, *'aphephuw-'alay*): "For innumerable evils have compassed me about" (40:12). Because of the parallel ("mine iniquities"), the word "evils" here probably refers to his sins rather than the troubles he suffered because of iniquity.[14] Further confession of sin occurs in 41:4b and 64:3a. Another psalmist said, "If thou, LORD, shouldest mark iniquities, O Lord, who shall stand?" (130:3). In other words, "for in thy sight shall no man living be justified" (143:2b). Moses wrote, "Thou hast set our iniquities before thee, our secret sins in the light of thy countenance" (90:8).

The distinguishing characteristic of the righteous in contrast to the wicked, however, is that (4) *the saints grieve over the fact of their sin against God.* Here again, David is exemplary: "When I kept silence, my bones waxed old through my roaring all the day long" (32:3). David is just sick[15] about his sin: "my strength faileth because of mine iniquity,[16] and my bones are consumed" (31:10b). "There is no soundness in my flesh because of thine anger; neither is there any rest in my bones because of my sin" (38:3); "My wounds stink and are corrupt because of my foolishness" (v. 5).

Because of this grief that leads to confession, the saints cry out to God for mercy (51:1) and deliverance (39:8a; 51:14; 79:9b). One of the prayers is "let not any iniquity have dominion over me" (119:133b). Another one is "forgive all my sins" (25:18b).[17] As a result (5) *the saints receive from God*

---

[14] Most commentators, however, understand that David is talking about the punishments he has received and also that "iniquities" is a metonymy of the cause for the effect. Calvin points out that David "does not now complain of being punished unjustly, or above his desert, but rather confesses plainly that it is the just recompense of his sins which is rendered to him. ... Accordingly, since David calls the afflictions which he endures the fruit or effect of his transgressions, there is implied in this a humble confession, from which we may ascertain with what reverence and meekness he submitted to the judgments of God, seeing that, when overwhelmed with an accumulation of miseries, he sets forth his sins in all their magnitude and aggravation" (2:108).

[15] "The language is that of illness occasioned by sin" (Futato, 125).

[16] On this word NIV follows the ancient Greek translation of Symmachus, which understood different vowels from what the MT supplied later; thus NIV has "affliction" instead of "iniquity."

[17] The psalmist's isolation from God is "a consequence of the awareness of sin within (v 18b) which, if not removed, would bar him from the divine friendship." Craigie, 221.

forgiveness for sins. David acknowledged this fact to God: "thou forgavest the iniquity of my sin" (32:5d); "as for our transgressions, thou shalt purge them away" (65:3b); "For thou, Lord, art good, and ready to forgive; and plenteous in mercy unto all them that call upon thee" (86:5). There is the recognition that God has forgiven the true Israel: "Thou hast forgiven the iniquity of thy people, thou hast covered all their sin" (85:2); "As far as the east is from the west, so far hath he removed our transgressions from us" (103:12).

An examination of the verses on iniquity give us insight into the nature of sin. Sin is first a matter of the heart. The evil of the mind then finds expression in what the sinner says, the words of the mouth venting maliciousness: lies, abusive language, and cursing. Next come actions, but sometimes what is in the mind skips directly to evil deeds, bypassing words. The next three propositions reflect these three stages: the mind, the mouth, and the act.[18] (6) *The sinful nature of the wicked is manifested in their attitudes.* David complains about his foes that "they plan ways to harm me" (41:7b, NET), and "Every day they wrest my words: all their thoughts are against me for evil" (56:6). The wicked "search out iniquities; they accomplish a diligent search: both the inward thought of every one of them, and the heart, is deep" (64:6). They have what they think is a perfect plan.[19] "Transgression speaks to the wicked deep in his[20] heart" (36:1a, ESV), indicating that sin is controlling his thoughts.[21] This truth about wicked thinking is plainly evident to the one Person that matters: "The LORD knoweth the thoughts of man" (94:11a).

Human thoughts have an outlet. (7) *Sinfulness emerges in mankind's speech.* Psalm 5:9, that points out that the wicked's "inward part is very wickedness," mentions also their mouth, throat, and tongue, various organs

---

[18] Psalm 36:1-4 indicates this process in "the character of the ungodly: first, the sin of his heart (ver. 1, 2); then the sin of his lips (ver. 3); lastly, the sin of his hands, the evil schemes which he devises and executes (ver. 4): thought, word, and deed, as in 17:3, 4." Perowne, 1:320.

[19] "It is evidently David's meaning that his enemies practised secret stratagem ... and showed themselves to be possessed of the deepest penetration in discovering dark and unimagined methods of doing mischief." Calvin, 2:448.

[20] MT has "my," but ancient witnesses indicate that the correct text has "his." See Kraus, 1:396.

[21] That is, the sinner "possesses this inspiration of iniquity as the contents of his heart." Delitzsch, 2:4.

of speech. Another psalm connects the mouth and tongue to five specific and general sin terms that are listed in the tables above: "His mouth is full of **cursing** and **deceit** and **fraud**: under his tongue is **mischief** and **vanity**" (10:7, my emphasis). Psalm140 connects the heart of "evil man" (v. 2) with his tongue and lips (v. 3). In the lists of specific sins above, there are sixteen different Hebrew words that refer to speech. These terms fall into the categories of **deceit** (including lying), **reproach** (including insult and derision), **contempt**, **cursing**, and **vexation**.

Thoughts and talk usually lead to deeds. It is no surprise, therefore, that wickedness in the mind and mouth of humans means that (8) *sinfulness is prevalent in the actions of mankind.* Concerning the wicked, David says, "they have done abominable **works**, there is none that **doeth** good" (14:1b, my emphasis). In 53:1 David substituted the word "iniquity" (עָוֶל, *'awel*) for "works" (עֲלִילָה, *'eliylah*). David asks the Lord to "Give them according to their **deeds**, and according to the **wickedness** of their **endeavours**: give them after the **work** of their hands; render to them their desert" (28:4, my emphasis). The word "endeavours" (מַעַלְלִים, *ma'elaliym*) is usually translated "deeds" (NRSV, ESV, HCSB, NET). David prays that God would not permit his heart to turn aside "to practice wicked works with men that work iniquity" (141:4b). He recognized that God's enemy is one "who goes on in his guilty deeds [plural of אָשָׁם, *'asham*]" (68:21, NASB). The tables above list various specific sins involving acts of brutality (violence, oppression, murder, and plunder).

New Testament Echoes

Romans 3:23a reaffirms the theme of iniquity in Psalms by summing up the Biblical truth about sinfulness and mankind: "For all have sinned." Earlier in that same chapter (vv. 10–18) Paul backs up his statement "that they [Jews and Greeks] are all under sin" (v. 9) by quoting six different verses from Psalms (14:3; 14:2; 5:9; 140:3; 10:7; 36:1). Reflecting the many different words for sin in the tables above, the New Testament contains 23 vice lists[22] (Matt. 15:19; Mark 7:21-22; Rom. 1:29–31; 13:13; 1 Cor. 5:10–11; 6:9–10; 2 Cor. 12:20; Gal. 5:19–21; Eph. 4:31; 5:3–5; Col. 3:5–9; 1

---

[22]For bibliography and discussion of these, see J. D. Charles, "Vice and Virtue Lists," *Dictionary of New Testament Background: A Compendium of Contemporary Biblical Scholarship,* ed. Craig A. Evans and Stanley E. Porter (Downers Grove: InterVarsity Press, 2000), 1252–57.

Theological Themes of Psalms

Tim. 1:9–10; 6:4–5; 2 Tim. 3:2–5; Tit. 3:3; 1 Pet. 2:1; 4:3, 15; Jude 8, 16; Rev. 9:20–21; 21:8; 22:15). There are about a hundred different Greek terms in these lists. Additionally, the writers refer to sins not included in the 23 catalogues (for example, κλέπτω, *kleptō*, "stealing").[23] Consequently, the New Testament, like the Psalms, confronts the humanity with their sin, holding up a mirror so that we can recognize the truth about ourselves and do something about it (Jam. 1:23–25)

Truly the theme of man's iniquity abounds in Psalms. Most prominent on the topic is Psalm 51, David's prayer concerning his sin in the Bathsheba case. In the first five verses of this psalm, four of the six common general words occur seven times. Verses 4–5 include two additional terms. Two words in verse 9 make the total eleven occurrences. Concerning his depravity from birth (v. 5), David later reaffirmed as a general truth about mankind: "The wicked are estranged from the womb: they go astray as soon as they be born, speaking lies" (58:3). Fortunately, Paul tells us that "where sin abounded, grace did much more abound" (Rom. 5:20).

---

[23] See also Jam. 4:17.

14

Pride

We know that the greatest commandment is to love God (Matt. 22:37); thus the love of God must be the greatest virtue. But what is the greatest vice or sin?[1] At the root of mankind's sinful rebellion is the sin of pride, where man selfishly loves himself and exalts himself into God's place. Commenting on Psalm 16:11, Augustine claimed that man fell from his original condition because of pride.[2] Commenting on sins in Psalm 19:13, he quotes from the Jewish sage: "The beginning of human pride is to forsake the Lord" (Sirach 10:12, NRSV).[3] There are 24 psalms[4] that touch on the subject of pride. If we distinguish falsehood from deceit, then more verses mention the sin of pride than any of the other specific sins listed above in Chapter 13. This particular sin, therefore, requires special attention.

Hebrew Words for Pride

In Psalms there are 17 different Hebrew words used to indicate the concept of pride. These occur 44 times in 37 different verses, as charted in

---

[1] "Love to God is the essence of all virtue. The opposite to this, the choice of self as the supreme end, must therefore be the essence of sin." Augustus Hopkins Strong, *Systematic Theology* (Philadelphia: American Baptist Publication Society, 1907), 567.

[2] *Expositions on the Book of Psalms*, ed. Philip Schaff, trans. A. Cleveland Coxe, vol. 8 of A Select Library of the Nicene and Post-Nicene Fathers of the Christian Church, 1st series (New York: Christian Literature Company, 1888), 49.

[3] Ibid., 56.

[4] Some commentators (Kraus, 1:513; Futato, 190; Kidner, 15:215; Mays, 206) and versions (NEB, NRSV, NJB, NIV) follow a textual variant in 54:3, substituting the "insolent" or "arrogant" (זֵדִים, *zeydiym*) for "strangers" (זָרִים, *zariym*). For arguments against accepting this reading, see Ross (2:227–28, n. 2; 231–32) and Dahood (17:24). This psalm, therefore, was not included in the pride list.

Theological Themes of Psalms

Table 14.1 below. A good place to begin is with the manifestation of pride in thinking or speech. The Hebrew verb הלל (*halal*)[5] occurs frequently in Psalms to indicate praise for Yahweh (for example, "hallelujah"),[6] but in some forms and contexts it refers to the sinful boasting of those who are proud: for example, "the boastful" (5:5, NASB) and "that boast themselves of idols" (97:7). Seven verses fall into this category, with one verse containing two uses of this verb: "I said to the boastful [a plural participle], 'Do not boast [a jussive]'" (75:4a, NASB). Psalm 119 uses an adjective meaning "insolent" (זֵד, *zeyd*) six times. There is also in Psalms a noun used adverbially that means "arrogant" (עָתָק, *'athaq*): for example, "speak grievous things proudly" (31:18b). Another noun meaning "a proud person" (רָהָב, *rahav*; only once in the OT) occurs in 40:4.[7]

Usually, the psalmists express the idea of pride by using words that refer to height or exaltation: they use 11 terms that fall into three groups based on their roots. (1) The first root is רום (*ruwm*), "to be high": Psalms uses the verb 50 times, sometimes in the causative sense ("make high," "exalt"); some of these are literal (for example, "the rock that is higher," 61:2), many refer to exalting God (for example, 107:32). The psalmists used the verb figuratively six times for the concept of arrogance (for example, "nor my eyes haughty," 131:1a, NASB). They used the related noun (מָרוֹם, *marowm*), three times:[8] for example, "they speak loftily" (73:8). (2) A second

---

[5] It actually is three different verbs: (I) "to shine"; (II) "to praise"; and (III) "to be senseless." See *TWOT*, 1: 217–19. Strong's concordance combines these into one verb that occurs 94x in Psalms. The Table 14.1 follows that analysis for its data.

[6] In some contexts the verb refers to boasting about God (34:2; 44:8); of course, this is not sinful pride. This falls into the category of what Paul mentions as glorying in the cross of Christ (Gal. 6:14).

[7] The MT of 90:10 contains the word רֹהַב (*rowhav*), used only once in the OT and probably related to רַהַב (*rahav*). KJV translated it as "strength," but other translations have used the word "pride" (ASV, NASB). Dahood (with a repointing of the word, 17:321, 25) and Kraus (2:213) also prefer "arrogance" or "pageantry" in the sense of pride. NLT, HCSB, NET, and NIV take this to mean "the best of them [years]." If "pride" is correct, it is not sinful pride, the subject of this chapter. Ancient translations, however, have translated this term by words that mean something like "span" (followed by NRSV, ESV, and Ross, 3:22) or "greater part."

[8] In 56:2 the KJV understood this word as a vocative addressing God as "most High"; NRSV, NAB, and NET followed suit. ASV, RSV, NASB, NIV, ESV, and HCSB all understand it as being used adverbially to describe the adjectival

Table 14.1 Terms for Pride in Psalms

Hebrew	Trans-literation	English	#	References	Total in Ps.	Total in OT
הלל	halal	to boast	8	5:5; 10:3; 49:6; 52:1; 73:3; 75:4[2]; 97:7	94	165
זֵד	zeyd	insolent	7	86:14; 119:21, 51, 69, 78, 85, 122	8	13
רוּם	ruwm	to be high	6	18:27; 66:7; 75:4, 5; 131:1; 140:8	50	197
גַּאֲוָה	ga'ewah	haughtiness	5	10:2; 31:18, 23; 36:11; 73:6	7	19
מָרוֹם	marowm	height	3	56:2; 73:8; 75:5	13	54
עָתָק	'athaq	arrogant	3	31:18; 75:5; 94:4	3	4
גֵּאֶה	gey'eh	haughty	2	94:2; 140:5	2	8
גָּאוֹן	ga'own	haughtiness	1	59:12	2	49
גֵּאוּת	gey'uwth	haughtiness	1	17:10	3	8
גַּאֲיוֹן	ga'eyown	haughtiness	1	123:4	1	1
גבה	gavah	to be lofty	1	131:1	3	34
גָּבֵהַּ	gaveyah	lofty	1	101:5	1	4
גָּבֹהַּ	gavowah	lofty	1	138:6	2	37
גֹּבַהּ	gowvah	loftiness	1	10:4	1	17
עָלַז	'alaz	to exult	1	94:3	7	16
רָהַב	rahav	pride	1	40:4	1	1
רָחָב	rakhav	arrogant	1	101:5	4	26

root is גאה (ga'ah), which also means "to be high," but to distinguish this from the first, we can use the English synonym "to be haughty." To indicate pride the psalmists employ an adjective (גֵּאֶה, gey'eh), "haughty," twice (94:2; 140:5) and four nouns (גַּאֲוָה, ga'ewah; גָּאוֹן, ga'own; גֵּאוּת, gey'uwth; and גַּאֲיוֹן, ga'eyown), "haughtiness." The first noun (גַּאֲוָה) occurs seven times in the book, once literally for the rising up or swelling of the sea (46:3) and once figuratively for God's majesty (68:34), but five times for the haughtiness of pride (10:2; 31:18, 23; 36:11; 73:6). The other three occur just once each. (3) The third root is גבה (gavah), which we will gloss as "to be lofty." In speaking of arrogance, the psalmists employ a verb (גבה, gavah), two adjectives (גָּבֵהַּ, gaveyah; גָּבֹהַּ, gavowah), and a noun (גֵּאֶה, gey'eh), just one time each.

---

participle "the ones fighting." The NET note explains what is happening here. See also Steveson, 219, for additional details.

Finally, there is the normal Hebrew adjective that means "wide" (רָחָב, *rakhav*; used in the OT 26x). Usually its uses are literal: for example, concerning the broadness of the promise land (Exod. 3:8) and "this great and wide sea" (Ps. 104:25). The psalmists, however, use it three other times in a figurative sense: representing freedom (119:45), concerning the unlimited nature of God's law (119:96), and in reference to "an arrogant heart" (101:5, HCSB).

Besides the verses with these terms there are several additional ways to speak of the sin of pride.[9] In Psalm 75, which speaks of pride in verses 4–5, part of Asaph's conclusion says, "All the horns of the wicked also will I cut off" (v. 10a). This last verse is actually a quotation, an announcement from God Himself.[10] Verses 4–5 had already connected pride in the expression "lift up the horn"; therefore, we should understand this as a reference to self-exaltation, a key aspect of pride. When God metaphorically cuts off the horns, He is destroying this kind of arrogance. Of course, if God Himself exalts "the horns of the righteous" (v. 10b), that is a different matter: this exaltation is what God brought about for His anointed servant David (89:16–17, 19, 24).

In Psalm 12 there is a reference to "flattering lips" (vv. 2–3), insincere speech intended to deceive.[11] In verse 3 David connects God's judgment of this kind of lie with His punishment of "the tongue that speaketh proud things," literally, "great things" (גְּדֹלוֹת, *gedowlowth*). The self-centered person will flatter and brag in order to get what he wants for himself.[12] Then

---

[9] In Psalm 20:7 some translate the verb as "boast" (RSV, NEB, NASB, NLT; see also *GOD'S WORD*); some as "take pride in" (NRSV, HCSB); but others translate it as "trust" (NIV, CEV, ESV; see also NET). Literally, the verb (hiphil of זכר, *zakar*) means "cause to remember" in the sense of reminding, mentioning, acknowledging, or even praising (71:16). Since the context does not necessitate boasting, this verse was not included as a pride text.

[10] "Verse 10 again is an oracle [vv. 2–3 also] from the LORD, for it is he who brings down and raises others up" (Ross, 2:606). NET adds the words "God says" to the beginning of the verse to make this clear. Notice, however, that other commentators understand the "I" to refer to the psalmist as God's servant cooperating with Him in judgment (for example, Leupold, 547).

[11] "Instead of the truth, what is agreeable and flattering to the hearer is spoken although not sincerely meant" (Cohen, 29).

[12] "Flattering lips and a vaunting tongue are one, insofar as the braggart becomes a flatterer when it serves his own selfish interest" (Delitzsch, 1:194–95).

near the end of the psalm David says "the wicked walk on every side," literally "walk about all around" (v. 8a). Some translations understand this to mean "strut about" (NASB, NIV; "parade around," *GOD'S WORD*);[13] thus in context this is a comment about the pride of sinners.[14]

Propositions

The Holy Spirit inspired the psalmists to proclaim a number of truths about pride. In the first place, (1) *there is a definite connection between wickedness and pride.* This is clearly seen in Psalm 94:2–4. The psalmist addresses God as an avenger (v. 1), then mentions the proud (v. 2) and links them to the wicked (v. 3). Finally, he says, "All who do wickedness vaunt themselves" (v. 4a, NASB).[15] Nine additional Psalms passages connect the wicked with the attribute of pride: 10:2–4; 12:8; 17:9–10; 31:17–18; 36:11; 73:3; 75:4–5; 140:4–5, 8.

(2) *Because pride leads the wicked into misplaced trust, they ignore God.* Psalm 40 praises the man who puts his trust in Yahweh (v. 4), but Psalm 97 speaks of those that "boast themselves of idols" (v. 7). Another passage speaks of those who "trust in their wealth, and boast themselves in the multitude of their riches" (49:6). It is evident, therefore, that "the wicked, through the pride of his countenance, will not seek after God: God is not in all his thoughts" (10:4). In fact, the previous verse indicates that in pride a wicked person actually "spurns" (NASB, NJB) God![16] This contemptuous attitude is actually what precedes his leaving God out of his life.

(3) *Pride leads to a contemptuous attitude about other people.* If pride produces in a person a wrong relationship with God, on the manward side, there are also evil consequences. A proud person denigrates God's image as well. The psalmist says, "The proud have had me greatly in derision"

---

[13] See also CEV, "But all who are wicked will keep on strutting."

[14] Delitzsch says that the verb here is "used of going about unopposed with an arrogant and vaunting mien" (1:197).

[15] Alexander, following the KJV, claims that this verse is a continuation of the question "how long" in the previous verse (p. 399). It is better, however, to follow Delitzsch (3:80) and to regard verse 4 as the beginning of a second strophe that provides a description of the wicked.

[16] KJV in contrast understands God, not as the object, but as the subject of this verb: "whom the LORD abhorreth," but very few other translations or interpreters follow this.

Theological Themes of Psalms

(119:51a). In fact, "The proud have forged a lie against me" (119:69a). They "speak wickedly *concerning* oppression: they speak loftily" (73:8). Another psalmist describes what the righteous feel: "Our soul is exceedingly filled with the scorning of those that are at ease, and with the contempt of the proud" (123:4).

But pride goes beyond having a bad attitude and speaking contemptuously about mankind. (4) *In pride the wicked attack others.* David says, "The wicked in his pride doth persecute the poor" (10:2a), "For they are many who fight proudly against me" (56:2b, NASB), and "O God, the proud are risen against me, and the assemblies of violent men have sought after my soul" (86:14). They dig pits (119:85a) and set traps (140:5).

The book of Psalms describes, but it also instructs. (5) *The Holy Spirit exhorts mankind not to be proud.* The inspired psalmist admonishes the wicked, "let not the rebellious exalt themselves" (66:7). "I say to the boastful, 'Do not boast,' and to the wicked, 'Do not lift up your horn. Do not lift up your horn against heaven or speak arrogantly'" (75:4–5).

In Psalms the encouraging matter for afflicted righteous persons is that (6) *God opposes and actually fights against, the proud.* "The proud he knoweth afar off" (138:6c).[17] "Thou hast rebuked the proud that are cursed" (119:21a). David stated this truth clearly: "The foolish shall not stand in thy sight: thou hatest all workers of iniquity" (5:5). He says to God, "you bring down those who have a proud look" (18:27b, NET), and he tells us that the Lord "plentifully rewardeth the proud doer" (31:23b). Another psalmist acknowledges that those proud horns of the wicked will be "cut off" (75:10a).

New Testament Echoes

The Septuagint uses the noun ὑπερήφανος (*huperēphanos*) to translate three of the pride terms (גֵּאֶה, *gey'eh*; גָּבֵהַ, *gaveyah*; זֵד, *zeyd*) in Table 14.1 above. New Testament writers use this word in five passages (Luke

---

[17] Perowne offers four possible explanations for this clause (2:437), but Delitzsch is probably correct in saying, "even from afar ... He sees through ... the lofty one who thinks himself unobserved and conducts himself as if he were answerable to no higher being" (3:340). Spurgeon expounds it as follows: "He has no fellowship with them, but views them from a distance; he is not deceived, but knows the truth about them, despite their blustering; he has no respect unto them, but utterly abhors them" (6:246). Ross appropriately rejects the attempt to apply a different meaning (NEB, "humbles") for the verb יָדַע (*yada'*) in this clause (3:807, n. 23).

140

1:51; Rom. 1:30; 2 Tim. 3:2; James 4:6; 1 Pet. 5:5). The last two verses contain the well-known statement that "God resisteth the proud," a quote from Proverbs 3:34, that echoes the last proposition above. Particularly significant is the Romans passage that uses three different words to describe this kind of sinner: "despiteful [insolent], proud, boasters." Paul instructed Timothy "that in the last days" people would be among other things "boasters, proud" as well as conceited (v. 4).

In conclusion notice how the truths about pride and about those who are arrogant affect the prayer requests of the righteous psalmists. "May the Lord cut off all flattering lips, the tongue that makes great boasts" (12:3, ESV). "Let the lying lips be put to silence; which speak grievous things proudly and contemptuously against the righteous" (31:18). "For the sin of their mouth and the words of their lips let them even be taken in their pride" (59:12a). "Lift up thyself, thou judge of the earth: render a reward to the proud" (94:2). "Let the proud be ashamed" (119:78a); "let not the proud oppress me" (v. 122b). These prayers are imprecatory, the subject of Chapter 18 below.

15

The Wicked

The last two chapters focused on the topic of sin; this chapter takes up the theme concerning the sinner. Those who persist in their iniquity and who refuse to submit to God because of their pride are called in Biblical language "the wicked." The first verse of Psalms introduces us to this kind of person, successively referred to in the plural as "the ungodly,"[1] "sinners," and "the scornful." References to this person using 22 different Hebrew words or phrases (like "bloody men," 59:2) occur in 60 different psalms. Every one of the five Books in Psalms mentions the theme in at least eight verses, with special emphasis in Books I (58 vv.) and V (30 vv.). The total of distinct verses is 125, about 5% of the verses in the book.

Key Passage about the Wicked

The Psalter contains one main passage that describes the character of the wicked. The first line of 36:1–4 presents several difficulties for translators and interpreters.[2] A literal translation of the Hebrew could be, "An oracle: the wicked possesses a transgression in the middle of his heart."[3] The first word, נְאֻם (ne'um), occurs 376 times in the Old Testament, almost all in some variety of the expression "the declaration of Yahweh";[4] in all of its uses

---

[1] In Psalms the KJV translates the term as "ungodly" 6x (4x in Ps. 1) and as "wicked" 75x. NASB, ESV, and HCSB consistently translate it as "wicked." The exceptions are in 36:1 for NASB ("ungodly") and 109:7 for all three.

[2] Alexander says, "This is one of the most difficult and doubtful verses in the whole book of Psalms" (p. 163).

[3] Broyles translates it as "An oracle. Transgression belongs to the wicked; it is in the midst of his heart"(p. 174). He regards "an oracle" as part of the title.

[4] KJV usually translates these as "saith the LORD"; other translations use "declares the LORD" (NASB, NIV, ESV) or "the LORD's declaration" (HCSB). I

143

it refers to a divine oracle, sometimes mentioning a prophet: "the oracle of Balaam" (Num. 24:3, NASB) or "the oracle of David" (2 Sam. 23:1, ESV). The term can appear alone without indicating whose oracle it is: the false prophets "use their own tongues to make a declaration" (Jer. 23:31, HCSB).[5] In Psalm 36:1 נְאֻם (ne'um) should not be grammatically connected with the following word ("transgression");[6] we should understand that it is a nominative absolute[7] that introduces a topic, "An oracle: ...."

A second issue in 36:1 is how to translate the two words after "oracle": "the transgression of the wicked"; "transgression ... to the ungodly" (NASB). KJV understands the Hebrew one-letter preposition לְ (le) as indicating a genitive ("of"); NASB interprets it as indicating the person addressed. It is better to recognize this particle as indicating possession (like the verb "have");[8] thus "the wicked has a transgression." Third, there is a textual variant: "my heart" or "his heart." The problem with the first reading is that if "my" is correct, who is speaking?[9] A few Hebrew manuscripts and the Syriac Peshitta (and probably LXX) indicate that this should be "his."[10] Thus the oracle reveals that right in the middle of the fallen, depraved man's heart lies a crime against God, a grievous sin.

---

prefer the HCSB translation since the Hebrew word is really a noun, as indicated by the vowel pointing (see GK § 84^{a}m). The related verb occurs just once (Jer. 23:31, where it means "declare"); the noun would mean "that which has been declared."

[5] Literally, "the ones taking their tongue and they say, 'an oracle!'"

[6] It could not be "an utterance of transgression" (as proposed by VanGemeren, 337) because a genitive after נְאֻם (ne'um) does not indicate the topic but always names the speaker (Delitzsch, 2:2–3).

[7] Williams defines this as "a word or phrase at the beginning of a sentence that does not play a grammatical role in the rest of the sentence." Other names for this are "topic-comment construction" and "focus marker." WHS §35.

[8] Hebrew has no verb "to have," expressing this idea by joining the possession (or experience) to the owner (or actor) by the preposition "to" (לְ): for example, "the LORD hath a controversy with the nations" (Jer. 25:31), literally, "to Yahweh a controversy"; "who hath babbling?" (Prov. 23:29), literally, "to whom babbling?"

[9] Ross says the answer is the psalmist, who "has received a deep understanding of the nature of the wicked" (1:779). Steveson says, "David knows in his heart what transgression says to the wicked" (p. 145).

[10] Among the commentaries that accept this reading are Kirkpatrick, 183; Perowne, 1:320; Jennings & Lowe, 1:157; and Broyles, 174.

What is this crime? The second half of verse 1 reveals that it is the fact "that there is no fear of God before his eyes." In other words, he is a practical atheist, one who leaves God out of his thinking and thus lives his life independently from God. If Adam had really believed what God had said about death, he would have been afraid to disobey his Creator. The Bible teaches that Adam's fallen nature has been passed on to all his descendants (Rom. 5:19a). God's revelation, therefore, informs us about mankind's basic evil nature rooted deep in his heart.

The remaining verses of this passage (2–4) reveal additional truths about the wicked.[11] Verse 2 is also difficult for translation and interpretation, but it provides the contrast[12] to fearing God: in self-deceptive pride ("flattereth himself in his own eyes")[13] the wicked encounters[14] his iniquity of hatred. His speech is iniquitous because of deceit (v. 3a). He is neither wise nor good (v. 3b). He plots evil (v. 4a), chooses an evil way of life (v. 4b), and refuses to reject evil (v. 4c).

Vocabulary for the Wicked

The Hebrew word for "wicked" (רָשָׁע, *rasha'*) occurs 82 times in the book of Psalms. In one case it is a predicate adjective: "When he is judged, let him come forth **guilty**" (109:7a, NASB; my emphasis).[15] The adjective used as a substantive (a noun equivalent) for the person, "the wicked one," occurs in 79 different verses, charted in Table 15.1 below. Usually the word is plural (52x), "wicked persons" (רְשָׁעִים, *resha'iym*); in the 29 cases of the singular, some are collective: for example, "thou hast destroyed the wicked, thou hast put out **their** name for ever and ever" (Psalm 9:5b). This term appears frequently in Proverbs as the antonym of "righteous" (צַדִּיק, *tsaddiyq*; over 40x): for example, "The LORD is far from the wicked: but he

---

[11] "Such an intense portrayal of the arrogant wicked is as severe as any found in the psalms." Waltner, 189.

[12] After a negative ("no fear") the Hebrew particle כִּ (*kiy*) can be translated "rather" or "but instead" (*WHS* §447).

[13] The Hebrew verb here is literally "make smooth" (הֶחֱלִיק, *hekheliyq*), "speaking or acting in a flattering matter" (Alexander, 164).

[14] The infinitive "to find" (לִמְצֹא, *limtsow*) here means "to discover" or "to meet accidentally."

[15] The KJV translation in 109:7 is "let him be condemned."

heareth the prayer of the righteous" (Proverbs 15:29). Since צַדִּיק refers to the adherence of a some sort of standard,[16] mundane or spiritual, רָשָׁע necessarily indicates that a requirement or standard has been broken. In other words, the רָשָׁע is a criminal, a guilty person.[17]

By noticing parallel terms in the verses that mention רָשָׁע (rasha') we discover eight synonymous phrases or words. The two most common are listed below in Table 15.1. The expression "workers of iniquity" (פֹּעֲלֵי אָוֶן, pow'eley 'awen) is parallel to the plural of רָשָׁע three times (28:3; 92:7; 101:8). The term "evildoers" (מְרֵעִים, merey'iym) parallels רָשָׁע in 26:5 and "workers of iniquity" in 64:2 and 94:16 ("Who will rise up for me against the **evildoers**? or who will stand up for me against the **workers of iniquity?**"). The word the KJV translates as "evildoers" is a participle from a causative verb: literally, "ones causing evil." Table 15:1 lists occurrences of another participle that fits into the category of nefarious adversaries:[18] those whom David called "my persecutors" (רֹדְפַי, rowdephay) (142:6) or "them that persecute me" (7:1; 31:15; 35:3). The author of Psalm 119 refers to these persons in this way three times (vv. 84, 150, and 157).[19]

In Psalm 1:1 the two synonyms of רָשָׁע (rasha') are "sinners" (חַטָּא, khatta') and "scorners" (לֵץ, leyts). Table 15.2 lists the six references where the former appears; the latter occurs only here in Psalms. The expression "bloody men" is parallel to רָשָׁע in 139:19, occurring four other times in Psalms with the word "man" as singular (5:6) or plural (26:9; 55:23; 59:3). The Hebrew is literally, "man of bloods" (אִישׁ־דָּמִים, 'iysh-damiym): the

---

[16] See, for example, Harold G. Stigers, "ṣādēq," TWOT, 2:754 ("conformity to some standard").

[17] "The use of rš' always includes the idea of wickedness, evil intent, and injustice against God or persons." Eugene Carpenter and Michael A. Grisanti, "רשע," NIDOTTE, 3:1201.

[18] Hans-Joachim Kraus notes the connection between the four terms in the table. The Theology of the Psalms, trans. Keith Crim (Minneapolis: Augsburg, 1986), 129–31.

[19] There is a textual issue about the vowel pointing in v. 150. On the basis of how the LXX and PiH rendered this verse, ESV, NRSV, and NJB have "persecute me" or "my pursuers"; thus they read the vowels as רֹדְפַי (rowdephay) instead of MT's רֹדְפֵי (rowdephey), literally, "ones pursuing of ...." There are even some Masoretic MSS that back up the translation "my persecutors." See Allen, 180; Hossfeld & Zenger, 15C:256.

Table 15.1 Vocabulary for the Wicked

Hebrew words: Psalm	רָשָׁע *rasha'* wicked	פֹּעֲלֵי אָוֶן *pow'eley 'awen* worker of iniquity	מְרֵעִים *merey'iym* evildoers	רֹדְפַי *rowdephay* my persecutors
1:	1 4 5 6			
3:	7			
5:		5		
6:		8		
7:	9			1
9:	5 16 17			
10:	2 3 4 13 15			
11:	2 5 6			
12:	8			
14:		4		
17:	9 13			
22:			16	
26:	5		5	
27:			2	
28:	3	3		
31:	17			15
32:	10			
34:	21			
35:				3
36:	1 11	12		
37:	[13x]†		1 9	
39:	1			
50:	16			
53:		4		
55:	3			
58:	3 10			
59:		2		
64:		2	2	
68:	2			
71:	4			
73:	3 12			
75:	4 8 10			
82:	2 4			
91:	8			
92:	7	7 9	11	
94:	3 [2] 13	4 16	16	
97:	10			
101:	8	8		
104:	35			
106:	18			
109:	2 6			
112:	10 [2]			
119:	[6x]*		115	84 150 157
125:		5		
129:	4			
139:	19			
140:	4 8			
141:	10	4 9		
142:				6
145:	20			
146:	9			
147:	6			
totals:	81	16	9	7

† Verses 10, 12, 14, 16, 17, 20, 21, 28, 32, 34, 35, 38, 40.   * Verses 53, 61, 95, 110, 119, 155.

147

plural of "blood" indicates bloodshed. Another synonym is "evil person" (רַע, *ra'*): "Break thou the arm of the wicked and the evil man" (10:15a). The noun "thief" (גַּנָּב, *gannav*) in 50:18 belongs also in this table.

Table 15.2 Other Nouns or Phrases Describing the Wicked

Hebrew	Trans-literation	English	#	References
חַטָּא	*khatta'*	sinner	6	1:1, 5; 25:8; 26:9; 51:13; 104:35
אִישׁ־דָּמִים	*'iysh-damiym*	the bloodthirsty	5	5:6; 26:9; 55:23; 59:2; 139:19
רַע	*ra'*	evil person	2	10:15; 140:1
גַּנָּב	*gannav*	thief	1	50:18
לֵץ	*leyts*	scorner	1	1:1

Three additional participles (besides those in Table 15.1) parallel רָשָׁע (*rasha'*). In 71:4 we have "wrongdoer" (NASB; עוֹל, *'uwl*) and "oppressor" (NET; חָמָץ, *khamats*), each used only once in Psalms; 37:38 proclaims the judgment awaiting "transgressors" (פֹּשֵׁעַ, *pasha'*) and "the wicked," the former being mentioned alongside of "sinners" in 51:13. Table 15.3 lists these and nine additional relevant participles. The psalmists describe the wicked as "rebellious" (סָרַר, *sarar*) four times (66:7; 68:6, 18; 78:8)[20] and as "treacherous" (בָּגַד, *bagad*) three times (25:3; 59:5; 119:158). They are also "them that err" (119:21, 118) or those straying (שָׁגָה, *shagah*) from God's requirements.[21] In 44:16 we find "reproacher" (חָרַף, *kharaph*), "reviler" (ESV; גָּדַף, *gadaph*), and "avenger" (נָקַם, *naqam*; also in 8:2).[22] Three more participles are used just once each: "reprobate" (NASB, 15:4), "adulterers" (50:18), and "liars" (116:11).

Propositions

Many of the 125 verses in Psalms that mention the wicked describe what God will do to them in time and in eternity. For example, "the wicked

---

[20] The synonymous participle מָרָה (*marah*), "rebellious," in 78:8 was listed in Chapter 13 with its other verb forms.

[21] "Let it be carefully observed that, by wandering from his commandments, is not meant all kinds of transgression indiscriminately, but that unbridled licentiousness which proceeds from impious contempt of God." Calvin, 4:415–416.

[22] A fourth participle, "enemy," occurs in 44:16, but it the subject of the next chapter since it does not describe so much of an action as a position (animosity).

Table 15.3 Participles in Psalms Describing the Wicked

Hebrew	Trans-literation	English	#	References
סרר	sarar	the rebellious	4	66:7; 68:6, 18; 78:8
בגד	bagad	the treacherous	3	25:3; 59:5; 119:158
נקם	naqam	avenger	2	8:2; 44:16
פשע	pasha'	transgressor	2	37:38; 51:13
שגה	shagah	those straying	2	119:21, 118
גדף	gadaph	reviler	1	44:16
חמץ	khamats	oppressor	1	71:4
חרף	kharaph	reproacher	1	44:16
כזב	kazav	liar	1	116:11
מאס	ma'as	the reprobate	1	15:4
נאף	na'ap	adulterer	1	50:18
עול	'uwl	wrongdoer	1	71:4

shall perish" (37:20a). This punishment will be the topic of Chapter 17 later. Many other verses are actually prayers by the godly requesting God to punish His enemies and theirs ("let the wicked be no more," 104:35b), in other words, imprecations, the subject of Chapter 18. Apart from those verses the inspired psalmists have proclaimed several truths about the wicked. To begin with, they affirm that (1) *the wicked have an animosity toward God.* After mentioning the boasting of the wicked man in 10:3a, David says, "the greedy man curses and spurns the LORD" (10:3b, NASB).[23] Later in the same psalm he asks, "Wherefore doth the wicked contemn God?" (v. 13a). The Hebrew verb used in these two verses (נאץ, na'ats) means "treat disrespectfully" or "revile" and can be paralleled to "hate" (Prov. 5:12). Asaph used it twice in Psalm 74 in regard to God's enemies' speaking against His name (vv. 10, 18) and parallels it both times to the verb "reproach" (חרף, kharaph), clearly

---

[23] There are just four Hebrew words (participle, verb/verb proper noun) in this line, but three interpretation issues: two grammatical questions and one word meaning. The first verb ברך (barak) can mean "bless" (usually) or "curse" (for example, Job 2:9). Grammatically, is "the greedy man" the subject or object of the verb; is Yahweh the subject or object of the second verb? Translations have used four possible combinations, but by far the majority has the greedy person (the wicked) cursing and disdaining Yahweh (NASB, NJB, NAB, NRSV, CEV, NET, HCSB, ESV, and others). This is confirmed partly by 10:13.

verbal animosity. Later in the psalm Asaph says, "Arise, O God, plead thine own cause: remember how the foolish man reproacheth thee daily" (v. 22).[24]

The truth about animosity links with another truth: (2) *the wicked endeavor to dismiss God from their lives.* "The wicked, through the pride of his countenance, will not seek after God: God is not in all his thoughts" (10:4). That last line could be translated "All his thoughts are, 'There is no God'" (NASB, ESV). As a practical atheist his thinks that God will not call him into accountability: "He hath said in his heart, God hath forgotten: he hideth his face; he will never see it" (10:11). Sinners ask, "How doth God know? and is there knowledge in the most High?" (73:11). He has no interest in praying (14:4c).[25] In his mind he is confident that he is in a secure state, not threatened by coming judgment (10:6).[26] He does not submit himself to God's authority (12:4);[27] hence he does not strive to know God's word (119:155), thus forsaking (v. 53) and wandering away from God's ways (vv. 21, 118).

Alienation from God leads to something else: (3) *the wicked conspire against the righteous.* "The wicked plotteth against the just" (37:12a). David knew about "the secret counsel of evildoers" (64:2a, NASB). Sinners pretend one thing by their speech (they "speak peace to their neighbours," 28:3; also 55:21 & 12:2b) but plan something else: "but they devise deceitful matters against them that are quiet in the land" (35:20b).[28] There is an appropriate action from God about such plotting: "let them be taken in the devices that they have imagined" (10:2b).

Scheming, of course, leads to action: (4) *the wicked persecute the powerless righteous.* "The wicked in his pride doth persecute the poor" (10:2a).

---

[24] This verse thus connects "the wicked" with the fool (נָבָל, *naval*) who is a practical atheist (14:1; 53:2). Verse 18 had also connected foolishness with reproaching and reviling. Reproach and foolishness are linked also in 39:8.

[25] "This last phrase [of v. 4] can be used … in the sense of proclaiming the Lord …, but it also means, as here, to use God's name in prayer (Gen. 4:26)." Harman, 167.

[26] "The wicked man, who has always prospered, expects to prosper in the future; he has no anticipation of coming change …." Rawlinson, 1:66.

[27] "They do not tolerate authority but prefer autonomy and anarchy." VanGemeren, 166.

[28] "The implication of this is that they may appear to speak peace …, but as the psalmist rightly discerns they are not speaking peace because they are planning (not speaking) deceit (or deceitful things)." Ross, 1:773–74.

The godly psalmist concedes that "Many are my persecutors and mine enemies" (119:157). It appears to the godly that they are surrounded by evildoers (17:9; 27:2a; 119:61a), who are like vicious dogs (22:16). They are ready to use their weapons with deadly effect (11:2; 37:14). The psalmist says, "The wicked have laid a snare for me" (119:110a; see also 141:9). They have set nets (141:10a).[29]

A fact so distressing to the righteous is that (5) *the wicked in the present enjoy prosperity.* "Behold, these are the ungodly, who prosper in the world; they increase in riches" (73:12). Earlier in this psalm Asaph had confessed, "For I was envious of the arrogant, as I saw the prosperity of the wicked" (v. 3, NASB). Using an apt picture, David said, "I have seen a wicked and ruthless man flourishing like a luxuriant native tree" (37:35, NIV).[30] Actually, a more appropriate picture would be the grass that quickly sprouts and flourishes (92:7). This is because Scripture reveals that such prosperity is short-lived: "For they shall soon be cut down like the grass, and wither as the green herb" (37:2). The godless are "men of the world, which have their portion in this life" (17:14). "For when he dieth he shall carry nothing away: his glory shall not descend after him" (49:17).

New Testament Echoes

The Septuagint basically used two Greek words to translate the Hebrew term for "wicked" (רָשָׁע, *rasha*') in Psalms: ἀσεβής (*asebēs*; "ungodly"; 16x) and ἁμαρτωλός (*hamartōlos*; "sinner"; 62x). The New Testament uses the first word nine times: for example, "Christ died for the ungodly" (Rom. 5:6b). The second word occurs frequently (47x); for example, "For as by one man's disobedience many were made sinners" (Rom. 5:19a). These two Greek words appear together once: "for the ungodly and for sinners" (1 Tim. 1:9). Paul gave us a description of the wicked man's depraved mind in Romans 1:21–25 that echoes Psalm 36:1–4. In Romans 3:10–18 he quoted from key psalms that had described the wicked (14, 5, 140, and 10), finishing up with "There is no fear of God before their eyes"

---

[29] "The insidious procedure is illustrated by means of images from hunting." Kraus, 2:528.

[30] Alexander notes, "a vigorous tree, rooted in its native soil, and seemingly immoveable" (p. 166). The LXX translated a Hebrew text that read "like a cedar of Lebanon," but this is six consonants different from the MT and not likely correct. The NRSV, however, chose this reading.

Theological Themes of Psalms

(from Ps. 36:1b). The New Testament reaffirmed the animosity of evildoers toward God, specifically Christ: "For every one that doeth evil hateth the light, neither cometh to the light, lest his deeds should be reproved" (John 3:20). Jesus is this Light that entered the world (v. 19). Christ affirmed to His disciples, "If the world hate you, ye know that it hated me before it hated you" (15:18). Jesus recognized also the persecution of the righteous: "Blessed are they which are persecuted for righteousness sake" (Matt. 5:10a). He mentions even the reviling and evil speaking (v. 11).

In conclusion, we note that Psalm 1, that introduced us to the wicked sinners, also announced their demise: "like the chaff which the wind driveth away" (v. 4b) and "the way of the ungodly shall perish" (v. 6b). The godly can take great comfort in knowing that God is completely aware of the nature and actions of the wicked, even their thoughts: "He knoweth the secrets of the heart" (44:21).

16

The Enemies

The last chapter focused on the sinful character of the ungodly; this chapter examines their hostility. The wicked are not content to sin only against God Himself and to become His enemy. They egregiously proceed in their iniquity to become the enemy of the righteous. The first psalm introduced us to the wicked; in the second psalm we see opposition and hostility against Yahweh and the Messiah (2:1–3), although the text does not mention the word "enemies." In the third psalm David begins by immediately mentioning "adversaries" (צָרַי, *tsaray*, "my foes") and later identifies "the wicked" as his enemies (3:7). References to enemies (plural or singular) occur in 65 different psalms. Every one of the five Books in Psalms mentions the theme in at least nine verses, with special prominence in Books I (48 vv.) and II (33 vv.). The total of distinct verses is 132, almost 5½% of the verses in the book.

Hebrew Terms for Enemies

The common Hebrew word for enemy is אֹיֵב (*'owyeyv*; 282x in OT), occurring 73 times in Psalms.[1] Table 16.1 charts these along with three frequent synonyms the psalmists use: "hater" (שׂוֹנֵא, *sowney*),[2] "adversary" (צֹרֵר, *tsowreyr*), and "foe" (צַר, *tsar*). Poetic parallelism links אֹיֵב with each of these: "hater" ten times (for example, 18:17, 40), "adversary" in 8:2 and 143:12, and "foe" four times (for example, 13:4 and 74:10). In 44:7, 10 the

---

[1] Not counting the one occurrence in a psalm title (18:1).

[2] In English versions it is a little difficult for the reader to detect the occurrences of this term because of the different ways the participle is translated. For example, in the KJV only once do we find "haters" (81:15); there are ten additional renderings: for example, "them that hate" (5x), "they that hate" (4x), "they which hate" (2x), "they that hated" (106:41). NASB is more consistent, translating the plural participle as "those who hate" 16x out of 21 cases.

Theological Themes of Psalms

Table 16.1 Terms for the Enemies

Hebrew words: Psalm	אֹיֵב 'owyeyv enemy	שׂוֹנֵא sowney' hater	צֹרֵר tsowreyr adversary	צַר tsar foe
3:	7			1
6:	10		7	
7:	5		4 6	
8:	2		2	
9:	3 6	13		
10:			5	
13:	2 4			4
17:	9			
18:	3 17 37 40 48	17 40		
21:	8	8		
23:			5	
25:	2 19			
27:	2 6			2 12
30:	1			
31:	8 15		11	
34:		21		
35:	19	19		
37:	20			
38:	19	19		
41:	2 5 11	7		
42:	9		10	
43:	2			
44:	16	7 10		5 7 10
45:	5			
54:	7			
55:	3 12	12		
56:	9			
59:	1			
60:				11 12
61:	3			
64:	1			
66:	3			
68:	1 21 23	1		
69:	4 18	4 14	19	
71:	10			
72:	9			
74:	3 10 18		4 23	10
78:	53			42 61 66
80:	6			
81:	14	15		14
83:	2	2		
86:		17		
89:	10 22 42 51	23		23 42
92:	9 [2]			
97:				3
102:	8			
105:				24
106:	10 42	10 41		11
107:				2

Hebrew words:	אֵיב *'owyeyv* **enemy**	שׂוֹנֵא *sowney'* **hater**	צֹרֵר *tsowreyr* **adversary**	צַר *tsar* **foe**
Psalm				
108:				12 13
110:	1 2			
112:				8
118:		7		
119:	98			139 157
127:	5			
129:		5		
132:	18			
136:				24
138:	7			
139:	22	21		
143:	3 9 12		12	
totals:	73	23	12	26

psalmist parallels foes and haters; and there is another case of this identification: "And I will beat down his foes before his face, and plague them that hate him" (89:23). The term "foe" (צַר, *tsar*) has a homonym that sometimes is difficult to distinguish. The homonym means "distress": for example, in "In my distress, I called ..." (18:6). In two of the 26 occurrences listed in the table for צַר, the KJV has "trouble" (60:11; 108:12); it was following the Septuagint and the Vulgate (which have "tribulation").

Most of the 134 terms listed in the table are plural. The singular ("enemy," "foe," etc.) occurs 32 times. Usually David and the other psalmists are struggling with multiple adversaries. There are 18 verses where the Lord's enemies are in view, always in the plural.[3] These include Messianic passages that mention Christ's enemies (72:9 & 110:1–2).[4] The bold type in the table identifies these verses.

In addition to the common synonyms that refer to foes, the psalmists use eight other expressions, listed in Table 16.2. Parallel to David's "foes" in 3:1 is the expression "they that rise up against me." The Hebrew (קָמִים, *qamiym*) is a participle followed by a preposition that means "against." Although not always followed by this preposition, the plural participle appears

---

[3] In 8:2 and 74:3 "the enemy" (אֹיֵב) is sg, but he is not identified as specifically the Lord's enemy as in all the other cases. The context would indicate that as a generic enemy he is the people's foe as well as the Lord's.

[4] In 72:9 a few translations capitalize the pronouns ("Him" and "His") to indicate a reference to Christ (Amplified Bible, New King James Version, and New Life Version).

Table 16.2 Additional Expressions for Enemies

Hebrew	English	#	References
רָעָתִי ...	... my ruin	7	35:4, 26; 38:12; 40:14; 70:2; 71:13, 24
קָמִים ...	ones rising ...	6	3:1; 18:39, 48; 44:5; 74:23; 92:11
מִתְקוֹמְמִים	ones raising themselves ...	2	17:7; 59:1
תְּקוֹמֵם	a raising of oneself	1	139:21
שׁוֹרְרִים	enemies	5	5:8; 27:11; 54:5; 56:2; 59:10
שׁוּרִים	enemies	1	92:11
שֹׂטְנִים	adversaries	5	38:20; 71:13; 109:4, 20, 29
שֹׂטֵם	to be antagonistic	1	55:3

five more times in Psalms to indicate foes. Related to this verbal is another plural participle from the same root (קוּם, *quwm*) that means "the ones who raise themselves":[5] the text that has the parallelism says, "Deliver me from **mine enemies**, O my God: defend me from **them that rise up against me**" (59:1, my emphasis). Related to this verb, the noun תְּקוֹמֵם (*teqowmeym*) occurs just once in Scripture (139:21): literally, "an act of raising oneself."[6]

Another way that David refers to his foes is to describe them as those who desire to effect his ruin. He prays, "let them be turned back and brought to confusion that devise my hurt" (Psalm 35:4b). The Hebrew word for "my hurt" is רָעָתִי (*ra'athiy*); this is the common noun that means "evil" or "disaster." In total there are seven verses where we see such expressions as "them ... that rejoice at mine hurt" (35:26), "they that seek my hurt" (38:12), and "them ... that wish me evil" (40:14).

Another noun that means "enemies" is (שׁוֹרְרִים, *showreriym*), occurring five times in the book: for example, "Mine enemies would daily swallow me up" (56:2a). A related noun is שׁוּרִים (*shuwriym*), occurring just once in the Bible (92:11).[7] Five times the book also uses a verb that means

---

[5] The Hebrew verbal form is a causative-reflexive (*hithpael*).

[6] On the basis of a few Hebrew MSS, some want to amend the text to read the *hithpael* participle (מִתְקוֹמְמִים, *mithqowmemiym*), used earlier in Psalms (17:7 & 59:1): Kraus, 2:511; Allen, 320; NET. Alexander says, "The Hebrew word is a noun formed from the participle" (p. 550). The meaning of the verse remains the same either way.

[7] Some understand this word to mean "them that lie in wait for me" (Cohen, 306). NET follows this course. Alexander mentions this possibility (p. 396).

"to be an adversary": three times we find the plural participle, "adversaries" (שֹׂטְנִים, *sowteniym*) and the verb twice (literally, "they are my adversaries," in 38:20; 109:4).[8] Finally, there is the verb שָׂטַם (*satam*), occurring in Genesis (3x) and Job (2x) and meaning "to nourish animosity toward"; in Psalms we find, "and in wrath they hate me" (55:3d).

Observations

A perusal of the 132 verses allows us to make several observations. (1) *The wicked become God's enemies.* We know from Genesis 4:5 that when Cain's offering was not acceptable to God, Cain became angry with God. The opposition to God expressed in Psalm 2:1–3 appears again in Psalm 8, where there is an explicit reference to "adversaries" (pl. of צֹרֵר, *tsowreyr*) and "the enemy" (v. 2). The bold type in Table 16.1 above indicates the verses that refer to the Lord's enemies.

As Psalm 2 makes clear, (2) *enmity toward God means a hostility toward His anointed ruler (David and the Messiah) as well as those who have a right standing with God (the righteous).* Just as Cain attacked righteous Abel without any real cause (What had Abel done to him?), so the wicked become the adversaries of the righteous, and "without cause" (35:19; 109:3–4). David expressed this with a statement that Paul applies to Christ (Rom. 15:3): "the reproaches of them that reproached thee are fallen upon me" (69:9). That the Messiah has enemies is clear from 110:1–2. Related to this is the fact that (3) *the righteous identify with God by regarding His enemies as theirs.* David said, "Do not I hate them, O LORD, that hate thee? And am not I grieved with those that rise up against thee? I hate them with perfect hatred: I count them mine enemies" (139:21–22).

(4) *The psalmists have used three word pictures to describe how the enemies of the righteous attack them.*[9] (a) Their foes are like a powerful and aggressive army (3:6–7; 27:2–3; 56:1–2; 61:3). (b) They are hunters or fishermen. "Consider my trouble which I suffer of them that hate me .... The heathen are sunk down in the pit that they made: in the net which they hid is their own foot taken" (9:13b, 15); "Pull me out of the net that they have

---

[8] Cognate to the verb is the noun שָׂטָן (*satan*), "adversary," in 109:6, but here he is not God's or the psalmist's foe. Of course, this noun is used elsewhere in the OT for the devil (for example, Job 1:6).

[9] These are noted and developed by Hans-Joachim Kraus, *The Theology of the Psalms*, trans. Keith Crim (Minneapolis: Augsburg, 1986), 130–31.

laid privily for me" (Psalm 31:4a). The net and pit appear also in 35:7–8. In Psalm 64 "the enemy" (v. 1) "shoot in secret at the perfect" (v. 4a). (c) The enemy have the nature of wild animals that assail the helpless: a lion (7:2; 22:13)[10] and fierce bulls (22:12).

(5) *The foes have a tenacity in their animosity that manifests itself in the persistence of pursuit.* "Many are my persecutors and mine enemies" (119:157a). "For the enemy hath persecuted [pursued] my soul" (143:3a; also 119:84b, 86b). Other verses are 7:1; 31:15; 35:3; 69:26; 109:16. Similar to Satan's accusation of Job, (6) *the enemies falsely accuse the godly.* David says, "In return for my love they accuse me" (109:4a, ESV). Another psalmist says, "For mine enemies speak against me; and they that lay wait for my soul take counsel together" (Psalm 71:10).[11]

(7) *It is common for the psalmists to pray for deliverance from their enemies.* David cries out, "Arise, O LORD, in thine anger, lift up thyself because of the rage of mine enemies" (7:6a), and "let me be delivered from them that hate me" (69:14b). Sometimes it is "consider my trouble" (9:13), "hide me" (17:8–9), "give us help" (60:11; 108:12), "preserve my life" (64:1), or "deliver me" (143:9).

What is remarkable is that (8) *the psalmists have complete confidence that God will accomplish the victory for them over their enemies.* Note the future tenses: "All my enemies will be ashamed and shake with terror; they will turn back and suddenly be disgraced" (6:10, HCSB); "Through God we shall do valiantly: for he it is that shall tread down our enemies" (60:12; 108:13). That confidence is well placed because (9) *the psalmists recognize that in the past God has provided victory over the enemies of the godly.* In Psalm 18 David celebrated how God had rescued him from his enemy Saul and other foes (vv.

---

[10] "By the figure of a lion, [David] represents in a stronger light the cruelty of Saul" (Calvin, 1:77). Kidner remarks that in Psalm 22 "the crowd is pictured as bestial (bulls, lions, dogs, wild oxen), but it is all too human" (15:124).

[11] There is another verse that falls into this category. The ESV translation of 69:4 has the phrase "those who attack me with lies." The Hebrew is difficult here: אֹיְבַי שֶׁקֶר (*'owyevay sheqer*), literally, "my enemies falsehood." NEB has "those who accuse me falsely." These translations understand the noun "enemies" as a verbal ("attack" or "accuse") and the noun "lie" as adverbial (modifying the verb), but the same phrase in 35:19 is translated "who are wrongfully my foes" and "treacherous enemy," respectively. Alexander says the phrase "may either mean in general perfidious, treacherous, or more specifically, using calumny and falsehood as a means for the attainment of their wicked ends" (p. 300).

3, 17, 39, 40, 47–48).[12] The psalmists said, "But thou hast saved us from our enemies, and hast put them to shame that hated us" (44:7), and "For thou hast been a shelter for me, and a strong tower from the enemy" (61:3). There is the clear recognition that God has delivered the Israelites from their enemies (106:10; 107:2–3).

New Testament Echoes

For the Hebrew word אֹיֵב (*'owyeyv*) the Septuagint usually employed ἐχθρὸς (*ekhthros*)[13] in its translation, a term that occurs 32 times in the New Testament. Notably, Christ identified a key enemy as Satan (Matt. 13:39). By employing a Greek word (ἀντίδικος, *antidikos*) not used in Psalms, the Apostle informs us that the devil is our adversary as well (1 Pet. 5:8). Associated with Satan are the enemies of the message of Christ's redemption: Paul noted that he had an open door for preaching, but faced "many adversaries" (1 Cor. 16:9), including Elymas, the "child of the devil, ... enemy of all righteousness" (Acts 13:10). Furthermore, Paul informs us that evil works alienate mankind from God, making them enemies (Col. 1:21). The one who is "a friend of the world is the enemy of God" (Jam. 4:4). In His ministry Christ faced many adversaries (Lk. 13:17), but we are told that Christ "must reign, till he hath put all enemies under his feet" (1 Cor. 15:25). Christ called attention to this fact by quoting Psalm 110:1 (Matt. 22:44). Then Paul tells Christians that "the last enemy that shall be destroyed is death" (15:26).

If we add together the verses in Psalms that mention iniquity (including those on pride) with the verses about the wicked and the enemies, we get a total of 449 verses (18% of Psalm vv.). In many cases the verses adjoining these provide additional information about wickedness without

---

[12] Some of the verbs in these verses are imperfects or participles, which in context indicate continuing action in the past. NAB and ESV translate these verbs as past. Concerning vv. 47–48, Goldingay explains that "one might initially take the opening participles in each verse ... as statements of Yhwh's ongoing activity, but the wayyiqtol [waw-consecutive imperfect] in v. 47b and the psalm's characteristic yiqtols [imperfects] in the second and third cola suggest that vv. 47–48 is all retrospective summary" (1:277–78). Note also his comments about the general characteristics of a psalm of thanksgiving concerning past events (1:258).

[13] This Greek word was also used a number of times in Psalms to translate the three main Hebrew synonyms listed above in Table 16.1.

using any of the terms: for example, 12:3 mentions pride; then verses 4–5a continue on this topic to tell us what sinners have said and done. Truly, it must be disconcerting for the wicked to realize how much God knows about their sinful nature and acts and that He has revealed this information in Scripture. On the other hand, the righteous can take comfort in knowing that God is cognizant of all the sins of mankind and that He is well aware of His enemies and theirs. David acknowledged to the Lord, "And in your steadfast love you will cut off my enemies, and you will destroy all the adversaries of my soul, for I am your servant" (143:12, ESV).[14]

---

[14] The verb tenses in this verse should be translated as futures, not imperatives. The *waw* perfect in the second clause usually indicates the future tense, not an imperative idea. See Paul Joüon, *A Grammar of Biblical Hebrew*, trans. and rev. T. Muraoka (Rome: Pontificio Istituto Biblico, 1991), 2:396 (§ 119 c). The LXX and *PiH* both translate the two verbs as futures.

17

Punishment

God, being holy, is angry about sin and takes action against sinners. God in justice must punish iniquity. From the beginning (1:6) to near the end of the book (149:9a) the psalmists express this truth about God's judgment. Furthermore, acts of judgment are interrelated with God's sovereignty. The theme under discussion here is punishment rather than judgment for two reasons. The Hebrew verb for judging (שָׁפַט, *shapat*) and the noun judgment (מִשְׁפָּט, *mishpat*) often refer to other matters: vindicating (for example, 10:18; 26:1), condemning (109:31), justice (119:121), ordinance (18:22), and custom (119:132). Secondly, the actions of a judge include much more than sentencing punishment. In God's sovereign reign He vindicates (72:4), arbitrates,[1] and governs (67:4). Psalms contains a number of verses that are imprecatory, where the psalmists request for God to punish the wicked: these will be the subject of Chapter 18. There are over 100 remaining passages in 55 Psalms that in some way affirm (as distinct from requesting) God's punishing of sin in the past, present, or future. These verses occur in all five Books with prominence in Book I (34 references).

The Vocabulary of Punishment

The English word "punishment" occurs just one time in Psalms: "punishments upon the people" (149:7b). Most English versions render this plural Hebrew term as singular (NASB, NIV, NRSV, NAB, HCSB), treating it as an abstract plural.[2] Even the word for vengeance (נְקָמָה, *neqamah*) appears just five times in the book (18:47; 94:1 [2]; 79:10; 149:7). The noun "judgment" (מִשְׁפָּט, *mishpat*) has the general sense of punishment in just

---

[1] When a man wanted Jesus to intervene in his case against his brother, Jesus said, "who made me a judge or a divider [arbitrator] over you?" (Luke 12:14).

[2] *IBHS* § 7.4.2a; GKC § 124d–f.

five of its 65 occurrences (7:6; 119:84, 120; 146:7; 149:9); the verb "judge" (שפט, *shapat*) means generally "punish" in only eight of 32 uses (7:8; 9:8, 19; 51:4; 75:7; 82:8; 94:2; 109:7).

The psalmists normally treat the theme by using a large number of verbs and nouns that indicate specific acts of punishment (such as casting down, smiting, sword, coals). The seven main verbs are listed in Table 17.1 below. Two of these indicate the shame that God inflicts upon the sinner. The other five refer to the destruction that is the consequence of sin. Of course, many of the references above and those below in the table occur in the imprecatory passages treated in the next chapter.

Table 17.1 Main Hebrew Verbs for Types of Punishment

Hebrew	Translit-eration	English	#	References	Total in Ps.
בוש *bowsh*	shame	18	6:10 [2]; 25:3; 31:17; 35:4, 26; 40:14; 44:7; 53:5; 70:2; 71:13, 24; 83:17; 86:17; 97:7; 109:28; 119:78; 129:5	34
אבד *'avad*	perish *causative:* destroy	17	1:6; 2:12; 9:3, 6; 10:16; 37:20; 49:10; 68:2; 73:27; 80:16; 83:17; 92:9; 112:10 *causative:* 5:6; 9:5; 21:10; 143:12	26
כלה *kalah*	end	10	37:20 [2]; 39:10–11; 59:13 [2]; 71:13; 74:11; 78:33; 90:7	23
כרת *karath*	cut off	9	12:3; 34:16; 37:9, 22, 28, 34, 38; 109:13, 15	14
צמת *tsamath*	annihilate	7	54:5; 73:27; 88:16; 94:23 [2]; 143:12	11
חפר *khaphar*	be ashamed	6	35:4, 26; 40:14; 70:2; 71:24; 83:17	7
שמד *shamad*	exterminate	5	37:38; 83:10; 92:7; 106:23; 145:20	6

Key Punishment Passages

Psalms contains three long passages about punishment: 44:9–16; 78:43–51; and 88:4–9. These describe God's judgment on three distinct objects. Psalm 78 is about God's punishment of the Egyptians at the time of the exodus. It mentions six of the plagues, using two different Hebrew verbs for destroying: שחת (*shakhat*) in verse 45 and הרג (*harag*) in verse 47. The Egyptians experienced "trouble" from God's agents of punishment (v. 49).[3]

---

[3] The term "evil angels" does not describe character but the disastrous work of the holy angels; "those who to the heirs of salvation are ministers of grace, are to the heirs of wrath executioners of judgment. ... See how sin sets all the powers of heaven in array against man." Spurgeon, 3:342.

Specifically, they suffered "pestilence" and "death" (v. 50), including the death of the firstborn (v. 51).

Psalm 44 is a report on how God, after giving Israel their land, has now afflicted them.[4] He has "cast off," "put to shame" (v. 9), made Israel "turn back," made them "spoil" (v. 10), "scattered" them (v. 11), sold them into slavery (v. 12), made them "a reproach," "a scorn and a derision" (v. 13), "a byword,"[5] and "a shaking of the head" (v. 14). Psalm 88 is an individual lament, where the psalmist feels as though God is punishing him like the wicked who "go down into the pit" (v. 4). He mentions "the dead" and "the grave" and being "cut off" (v. 5). He pictures himself as being "in darkness" in the depths of the sea (v. 6) with God's "waves" battering him (v. 7), somewhat like what Jonah experienced for his sin. He has been "afflicted" (vv. 7 & 9). He is "an abomination," "shut up" (כָּלֻא, *kalu*) or restrained by imprisonment (v. 8).

Types of Punishment

The large number of shorter passages are listed below in Table 17.2, each with some key words that describe the punishment. The list contains 144 verses or parts of verses. The specific instances of punishment can be grouped into eight categories. What the psalmists have done is to give us a terrifying picture of what God's judgment looks like. Indeed, "It is a fearful thing to fall into the hands of the living God" (Heb. 10:31).

(1) Removal of Blessing

When our first parents sinned, they lost the blessing of God's presence. God removed them from the blessing of the paradise of the Garden of Eden. When Israel provoked God in the wilderness, there was a first consequence: they lost the blessing of the promise land. God said, "Unto whom I sware in my wrath that they should not enter into my rest" (95:11). Psalm 107 describes how God changes the blessing of a fruitful and productive land

---

[4] The psalmist does not mention the cause behind the disaster: Israel's sin. He looks for an additional cause and says, "Yea, for thy sake are we killed all the day long; we are counted as sheep for the slaughter" (v. 22). The psalm "sees that God's people are caught up in a war that is more than local: the struggle of 'the kings of the earth ... against the Lord and his Anointed' (2:2)." Kidner, 15:168.

[5] The Hebrew term (מָשָׁל, *mashal*) means "proverb" and in this context "a well-known example of reproach." We speak of a well-known case or example of something as being "proverbial."

Theological Themes of Psalms

Table 17.2 Psalms Passages about Punishment

Reference	Key Words (KJV)
1:4–6	drive away, not stand, perish
2:9b	dash
2:12a	perish
3:7bc	smite, broken
5:6	destroy
7:12–13	instruments of death
7:15b–16	return, come down,
9:3	fall, perish
9:5–6	destroyed, put out, perpetual end, perished
9:15–17	sunk down, judgment, snared, hell
10:13	require
11:5b–6	snares, fire, brimstone, tempest
12:3	cut off
16:4	sorrows
18:39b–42	subdue, destroy, beat, none to save, dust, cast out
18:47	subdue
21:8–10	find out, fiery oven, swallow, fire, destroy
21:12	turn their back
25:3b	ashamed
32:10a	sorrows
34:16	turned against, cut off
34:21	slay, desolate
37:2	cut down, wither
37:9a	cut off
37:10	not be
37:13	laugh at
37:15	sword, broken
37:17a	broken
37:20	perish, consume
37:22b	cursed, cut off
37:28b	cut off
37:36	passed away, not be
37:38	destroyed, cut off
39:11	consume
44:7b	shame
49:10	die, perish
49:12	perish
49:14	grave, death, consume
49:17	die
49:19	never see light
49:20b	perish
50:22b	tear in pieces
52:5	destroy, take away, pluck out, root out
53:5	fear, scatter, shame
55:19a	afflict
55:23	bring down, pit of destruction, not live
58:11b	judge

Reference	Key Words (KJV)
59:8	laugh at, derision
62:12b	render according
63:9–10	lower parts, fall, sword, portion for foxes
63:11b	stopped
64:7–8	shoot at, arrow, wounded, fall
68:21	wound
68:23	blood
71:24b	confounded, shame
73:17–20	end, cast down, destruction, desolation, terrors
73:27	perish, destroy
74:3	perpetual desolations
75:7–8	put down, cup, dregs
75:10a	cut off
76:5–6	spoiled, cast, dead sleep
78:21	fire, come up against
78:31	slay, smite
78:33–34	consume, trouble, slay
78:61–64	captivity, sword, fire
78:66	smite, perpetual reproach
79:1–4	defiled, dead, blood, reproach, scorn, derision
81:12	give them up
82:7	die, fall
88:15–18	afflicted, die, terrors, distracted, cut off, darkness
89:10	break, scatter
89:23	beat down, plague
89:48	death, grave
90:7	consumed, troubled
92:7c	destroyed
92:9	perish, scatter
94:13	pit
94:23	cut off
95:11	not enter into rest
97:7	confounded
101:8	destroy, cut off
106:15	leanness
106:23	destroy
106:26–27	lift up hand against, overthrow, scatter
106:29	plague
106:40–43c	kindled, into the hand, oppressed, subjection
106:43c	brought low
107:10	darkness, death, bound, affliction
107:12	bring down, labour, fall
107:17–18	afflicted, death
107:33–34	wilderness, dry ground, barrenness
107:39–40	oppression, affliction, sorrow, contempt, wander
109:28b	ashamed
112:10	grieve, gnash teeth, melt away, perish
119:21	rebuke

Reference	Key Words (KJV)
119:78a	ashamed
119:118a	tread down
119:119a	put away, dross
119:120b	judgments
119:155a	salvation far away
120:4	arrows, coals
145:20b	destroy
146:4	return to earth, perish
149:6b–9a	sword, vengeance, punishments, bind, judgment

into a dry wilderness (vv. 33–34), basically by withholding the rain. Another indication of this loss is the statement, "Salvation is far from the wicked" (119:155a).

(2) Giving Over

God often punishes sin with sin, an expression used by Milton and John Donne. That is, He delivers the sinner over to his own sinful desires. He gives him what he wants as a punishment. Since Israel would not listen, God says, "So I gave them up unto their own hearts' lust: and they walked in their own counsels" (81:12). In the wilderness they desired sinfully, "and he gave them their request; but sent leanness into their soul" (106:14–15).

(3) Recompensing

Then there is the principle of sowing and reaping. It is justice that the harm the sinner does to others comes back to him on the rebound. God has "a pattern of punishment":[6] "the wicked is snared in the work of his own hands" (9:16). David affirmed that pay-back time was coming from God: "He shall reward [שוב, shuwv, "return"][7] evil unto mine enemies" (54:5a). David acknowledged before his Lord, "You recompense a man according to his work" (62:12b, NASB). Yahweh "plentifully rewardeth the proud doer" (31:23b). As for the wicked, "he made a pit, and digged it, and is fallen into the ditch which he made. His mischief shall return upon his own head, and his violent dealing shall come down upon his own pate" (7:15–16). God "shall bring upon them their own iniquity" (94:23a).

---

[6] Leupold, 114.

[7] NASB translates this verb here as "recompense"; HCSB translates as "repay."

(4) Shaming

When our first parents sinned, they hid from God because they were ashamed (Gen. 2:25, 3:10). The fact is that sin brings shame as part of God's punishment. The psalmist recognizes God's justice in that the wicked "are confounded" and "they are brought into shame" (71:24b). The first verb (בוש, *bowsh*) in this clause is used repeatedly by the psalmists to describe how God punishes wrongdoers: "those who act treacherously without cause will be disgraced" (25:3b, HCSB); "thou hast put them to shame" (53:5c). Other references are 44:7; 109:28b (NASB); and 119:78a.[8] Involved in this shame is the fact that God "laughs at" His enemies (2:4; 37:13; 59:8). The last reference even adds the stronger word "ridicule" (HCSB).[9] The noun "reproach" (חֶרְפָּה, *kherpah*) falls into this category: God gave over His enemies into "a perpetual reproach" (78:66). When God punished Israel, they confessed, "We are become a reproach to our neighbours, a scorn and derision to them that are round about us" (79:4).

(5) Scattering

Another punishment for the wicked is their dispersal. When God punished Israel, He scattered them among the heathen nations (44:11). Deportations were acts of judgment: God lifted His hand against Israel "to scatter them in the lands" (106:27b). The psalmist could say to his Lord, "thou hast scattered thine enemies with thy strong arm" (89:10b). Victory in war often begins with the enemy fleeing and dispersing. The psalmist proclaims, "For, lo, thine enemies, O LORD, for, lo, thine enemies shall perish; all the workers of iniquity shall be scattered" (92:9).

(6) Destroying

By far the greatest focus of God's punishment is on its destructive nature. Frequently we find the statement in Psalms that the wicked will "perish" (אבד, *'avad*): 1:6; 2:12; 9:3; 37:20; 49:10; and others. The causative

---

[8] I understand this verb as a future ("the proud will be ashamed") instead of as a jussive ("let the proud …") because that parallels the future at the end of the verse ("I will meditate …").

[9] "The greatest, cleverest, and most malicious of the enemies of the church are only objects of ridicule to the Lord …. In the end of all things it will be seen how utterly contemptible and despicable are all the enemies of the cause and kingdom of God." Spurgeon, 3:16.

of this verb means "destroy," and God is the agent of this action (5:6; 9:5; 21:10). The psalmists employ a number of major synonyms for this act: "cut off" (כרת, *karath*) (for example, 12:3; 34:16), "annihilate" (צמת, *tsamath*) (for example, twice in 94:23), "exterminate" (שמד, *shamad*) (for example, 37:38), and "be consumed" (כלה, *kalah*) (for example, 90:7). The synonyms are close enough to each other that the English versions often interchange their translations with little consistency. For example, the KJV in Psalms sometimes translates three of these five as "destroy." NASB uses "cut off" to translate two of these as well as two of the infrequent verbs (גדע, *gada'*, in 75:10; and גזר, *gazar*, in 88:5). There are about six other infrequent verbs in Psalms for this concept: בצר, *batsar*, in 76:12; דמה, *damah*, in 49:12, 20; הרס, *haras*, in 28:5; מחה, *makhah*, in 9:5; and נתץ, *nathats*, in 52:5.[10] The nouns that express this punishment include חָרְבָּה (*khorbah*; "destruction" in 9:6), מַשּׁוּאָה (*mashshuw'ah*; "destruction" in 73:18 & 74:3), and שַׁמָּה (*shammah*; "desolation" in 73:19).

(7) Killing the Body

The warning to Adam was "thou shalt surely die" (Gen. 2:17), and when God passed sentence on him, He said, "unto dust shalt thou return" (Gen. 3:19). In various passages in Psalms the killing of the body is a punishment. The word for "death" (מָוֶת, *maweth*) occurs in several judgment passages: 7:13 ("instruments of death"); 49:14, 17; 89:48; and 107:18. The corresponding verb, "die" (מות, *mowth*), refers to punishment in 34:21 and 82:7. Another verb that means "die" or "expire" (גוע, *guw'*) appears in 88:15. The term "grave" (קֶבֶר, *qever*) also appears in 49:11[11] and 88:5. Several passages mention the dust (עָפָר, *'aphar*) of death (18:42; 22:15, 29; 30:9).[12] The deadly weapons of warfare allude to the penalty of death: sword (37:25; 63:10; 78:62; 149:6) and arrows (64:7; 120:4). The mention of bloodshed points to death (68:23; 79:2). Relevant to this theme is the word צַלְמָוֶת

---

[10] Table 17:2 indicates how the KJV translates three of these verbs. In the case of 28:5, an imprecatory verse, the translation is "destroy"; in 76:12 it is "cut off."

[11] "Their graves are their eternal homes" (HCSB). The MT has קֶרֶב (*qerev*; "inward thought"), but there is strong evidence from the ancient versions (LXX, Syriac, and Targum) that this is a scribal error for the similar word קֶבֶר (*qever*).

[12] In 90:3a Moses alludes to God's verdict for Adam: "You turn man back into dust [דַּכָּא, *dakka*]." There is an issue about the meaning of the Hebrew word. See Goldingay, 3:26.

(*tsalmaweth*),[13] "shadow of death": the rebels punished in Psalm 107 "sit in darkness and in the shadow of death" (v. 10). The words that indicate killing are הרג (*harag*), "slay" (78:31, 34), נכה (*nakah*), "smite" (3:7; 78:66), and the causative of כרע (*kara'*), "subdue" or "smite down" (18:39; 78:31).

(8) Condemning to Hell

Finally, we come to the most fearful of all the types of punishment. Christ said, "And fear not them which kill the body, but are not able to kill the soul: but rather fear him which is able to destroy both soul and body in hell" (Matt. 10:28). Hell is the ultimate judgment for the wicked (Rev. 20:15). Psalms presents this truth clearly: "The wicked shall be turned into hell, and all the nations that forget God" (9:17). Since hell is a fiery place, it is possible that references in Psalms to judgment by fire may point to the ultimate punishment: "Upon the wicked he shall rain snares, fire and brimstone, and an horrible tempest: this shall be the portion of their cup" (11:6).[14] Another reference could be "a fiery oven" and "the fire" (21:9).[15] A synonym in Psalms for "hell" is "the pit"[16] (the English translation for three Hebrew terms: בְּאֵר, *be'eyr*; בּוֹר, *bowr*; and שַׁחַת, *shakhath*). Literally, these words refer to a well or a hole in the ground that can be used as a trap or a prison (for example, 7:15 and 35:7). These are appropriate terms, therefore, to use for God's prison house of hell.[17] That sense appears in 28:1; 55:23;

---

[13] Many modern scholars have argued that since Hebrew does not use compound words this word should be repointed (צַלְמוּת, *tsalmuwth*) and translated as "deep darkness" (NIV & NRSV in 44:19). See Briggs, 1:211–12. The rabbis who translated the LXX from the Hebrew, however, used two Greek words (shadow & death), and the inspired NT quoted the Greek expression (σκιᾷ θανάτου) from Isa. 9:2 in the LXX (Matt. 4:16). See Kidner, 15:111.

[14] Calvin's comments that David is alluding to what happened to Sodom and Gomorrah; then he mentions that Jude in the NT tells us that these cities "are set forth for an example, suffering the vengeance of eternal fire" (v. 7). 1:166–67.

[15] Spurgeon makes this comment on the verse: "Reader, never tolerate slight thoughts of hell, or you will soon have low thoughts of sin. The hell of sinners must be fearful beyond all conception, or such language as the present would not be used" (1:316).

[16] " 'Pit' is merely another word for Sheol or the afterlife." Leupold, 241.

[17] "*The Pit* … may also suggest the deepest confines of [Sheol], like a dungeon for the worst offenders." Kidner, 15:122.

88:4; and 94:13. In some other places the terms serve as metaphors for the grave (30:3, 9; 69:15; 88:6; 143:7). These references would fit above into type of punishment number 7.

New Testament Echoes

The various types of punishment clearly appear in the New Testament. (1) Esau experienced the loss of blessing (Heb. 2:17). (2) Paul mentions God's giving over sinners to their evil desires (Rom. 1:24, 26, 28). (3) Peter announces that God will recompense the false teachers with "the reward of unrighteousness" (2 Pet. 2:13). The sowing and reaping principle occurs in the statement "he that doeth wrong shall receive for the wrong which he hath done" (Col. 3: 5).

(4) Paul refers to the shame that comes to opponents when they have "no evil thing to say" about believers (Tit. 2:8). Peter encourages his readers with this statement: "Having a good conscience; that, whereas they speak evil of you, as of evildoers, they may be ashamed that falsely accuse your good conversation in Christ" (1 Pet. 3:16). By using the Greek word (καταισχύνω, kataiskhunō) found in the Septuagint translation of Psalms 35:4 and 40:14, Paul says, "God hath chosen the foolish things of the world to **confound** the wise; and God hath chosen the weak things of the world to **confound** the things which are mighty" (1 Cor. 1:27, my emphasis).

(5) Mary refers to the punishment of scattering in the Magnificat: "he hath scattered the proud" (Luke 1:51). (6) Christ warns that God is able to destroy both soul and body in hell" (Matt. 10:28). Paul refers to this destruction as a cutting off (Rom. 11:22), and Peter speaks of the destruction of the unjust, who "shall utterly perish in their own corruption" (2 Pet. 2:12). Jude points to those who "perished in the rebellion of Korah" (v. 11, NASB).

(7) In His discourse about light Jesus told the Jews three times, "ye shall die in your sins" (John 8:21, 25). "For the wages of sin is death" (Rom. 3:23a). (8) Concerning hell, Christ prophesied, "Then shall he say also unto them on the left hand, Depart from me, ye cursed, into everlasting fire, prepared for the devil and his angels," and "these shall go away into everlasting punishment" (Matt. 25:41 & 46a). Paul referred to those "who shall be punished with everlasting destruction from the presence of the Lord, and from the glory of his power" (1 Thess. 1:9). And that hell is a terrifying fiery place: "But a certain fearful looking for of judgment and fiery indignation, which shall devour the adversaries" (Heb. 10:27).

After the introductory psalm that mentions the wicked and their perishing, Psalm 2 begins with the transgression of the nations (Gentiles) and the people (Israel). Corresponding to this at the end of the book before the final doxology of Psalm 150, the psalmist culminates by mentioning God's vengeance and punishment of "the nations" and "the peoples" (149:7) and speaking about "the judgment written" (v. 9a). Where was it written? One place is clearly the book of Psalms.[18] As God says in another place, "Behold, it is written before me: I will not keep silence, but will recompense" (Isa. 65:6). Once God has completed His decreed punishment of the wicked, the saints will glorify Him for His justice and praise Him (literally, "He is the glory belonging to all His saints; praise Ya!" 149:9b).[19]

---

[18] Some say this phrase refers to the law. "But the best view is that which goes beyond the Pentateuch, and ... understands in the expression of ver. 9a. the judgments registered in the Sacred Books generally ...." Moll, 676.

[19] The pronoun הוא (*huw*) could be translated as "that." "But perhaps it is better to take the pronoun as referring to God: 'He is a glory to all,' ... *i.e.* He is the glorious object of their praise." Perowne, 2:485.

18

Imprecation

Knowing that God punishes sin, the psalmists in various prayers simply implore God to do what He has already said that He would. Theological books refer to these as imprecatory psalms.[1] Actually, no psalm is entirely imprecatory. It would be more accurate to refer to psalms with imprecatory verses. The English adjective "imprecatory" is related etymologically to a Latin verb that simply means "to pray for [something]." The noun "imprecation" in English has come to mean "a prayer for disaster on an enemy." Such psalms occur in every one of the five Books of Psalms; Book I has the most with ten; and Book II has three major ones.

The Problem

The presence of imprecatory verses in Psalms has been a difficulty for interpreters since the time of the church fathers. Augustine noted that a couple of these passages seem to contradict Christ's exhortation to love our enemies (Matt. 5:44).[2] Furthermore, there is the instance when James and John wanted to call fire from heaven to fall on the Samaritans (Luke 9:52–54). Christ rebuked them, saying, "Ye know not what manner of spirit ye are of" (v. 55).[3] In contrast to what the psalmists prayed for, Christ's objective

---

[1] Chalmers Martin notes that this label "seems to imply that there is a body of psalms in which imprecation forms a chief element." It is better "to speak of 'imprecations in the psalms" than of "imprecatory psalms." "Imprecations in the Psalms," in *Classical Evangelical Essays in Old Testament Interpretation*, ed. W. C. Kaiser, Jr. (Grand Rapids: Baker, 1972), 113.

[2] *Our Lord's Sermon on the Mount According to Matthew*, Book 1, chapter 21, section 71.

[3] There is a textual issue about this verse. See the note in NET. It is probable that if there is a scribal gloss here, the gloss reflects an oral tradition about what Christ

Theological Themes of Psalms

in His first coming was reconciliation rather than judgment: "For the Son of man is come to seek and to save that which was lost" (Luke 19:10). Another aspect of the problem is that these imprecations can properly be called curses, and Paul admonished believers to "bless them that persecute you; bless, and curse not" (Rom. 12:14). Some have said, therefore, that this is the most difficult problem in Psalms.[4]

Identification of Imprecatory Verses

Before discussing solutions to the problem, we should attempt to identify how many verses fall into this category. Although it has been easy to identify some key examples of imprecatory psalms (such as 109 and 137), there has not been general agreement about a complete listing of imprecatory verses. Writers on the subject have differed on the number of major imprecatory psalms[5] and on the complete list of verses.[6]

Table 18.1 below represents another attempt at cataloging the imprecatory elements. It groups the verses by psalm (column 1) and thus recognizes 33 psalms as containing imprecatory elements. The total number of verses in these psalms is 563 (column 7);[7] the number of imprecatory verses

actually said. See R. C. H. Lenski, *The Interpretation of St. Luke's Gospel* (Columbus: The Wartburg Press, 1946), 556.

[4] For example, "perhaps there is no part of the Bible that gives more perplexity and pain to its readers than this; perhaps nothing that constitutes a more plausible objection to the belief that the psalms are the productions of inspired men than the spirit of revenge which they sometimes seem to breathe, and the spirit of cherished malice and implacableness ...." Barnes, 1:xxv–xxvi.

[5] VanGemeren lists Psalms 35, 58, 69, 83, 109, and 137 (p. 954). Alex Luc has the same list. "Interpreting the Curses in the Psalms," *JETS* 42 (1999): 410. Johannes G. Vos also lists six major psalms, but he substitutes 55, 59, and 79 for 35, 58, and 83. "Ethical Problem of the Imprecatory Psalms," *Westminster Theological Journal* 4 (1942): 123. J. Carl Laney identifies nine where "the imprecatory element is a leading feature of each psalm and is crucial to the psalmist's argument." He adds Psalms 7, 59, and 139 to VanGemeren's list. "A Fresh Look at the Imprecatory Psalms," *BibSac* 138 (1981): 36.

[6] VanGemeren adds 17 psalms to his list of six major ones (p. 954). James E. Adams includes an index of 104 verses from 36 psalms. *War Psalms of the Prince of Peace* (Phillipsburg, NJ: Presbyterian and Reformed, 1991), 116. Alex Luc includes a table that charts 75 verses from 28 psalms (42: 410).

[7] Just the section (8 vv.) of Psalm 119 that contained an imprecatory element was figured into the number of psalm verses (last column).

174

is 101 (columns 2 & 6), only about 18% of the total. The table itemizes passages based on the presence of Hebrew imperatives or jussives[8] (listed in the 3rd and 4th columns) that request God to punish someone. There are two exceptions. In the first case the psalmist asks God a question that implies that he wants God to punish his enemies: "when wilt thou execute judgment on them that persecute me?" (119:84b). The second exception involves a wish when David says, literally, "If you would kill the wicked, O God," without finishing his sentence (139:19a);[9] then the passage goes on to state what they have done (vv. 19b–20) and to declare David's hatred for those that rebel against his Lord (vv. 21–22).

Some verses listed by others as imprecatory have been omitted because the key verbs were classified not as jussives but as futures[10] that indicated what would eventually happen to the wicked. For example, in 63:9–11[11] David uses four imperfect verbs that refer to the future (for example, "the mouth of them that speak lies shall be stopped," v. 11). Most English translations render 119:78a as a request: "Let the proud be ashamed." Since, however, the second half is a contrast and clearly future ("but I will meditate in thy precepts"), the first half should be translated as "the proud will be ashamed."[12]

The table identifies seven major imprecatory psalms with a bullet (•) in the first column. These are the psalms that contain five or more verses with imprecations. Psalm 137 with only three imprecatory verses, however, is an

---

[8] A jussive is a Hebrew modal verb form that indicates a wish or request. It functions very much like an imperative: for example, "Let their table become a snare before them" (69:22).

[9] Calvin, however, has another way of understanding the passage. He regards the imperative in 19b as the completion of the sentence. His translation would be, "If thou shalt slay, O God! the wicked, then depart from me, ye bloody men" (5:220).

[10] Jussives often differ from imperfect futures in form, but in numerous cases there is no distinction, and the context must determine the meaning.

[11] A passage that VanGemeren lists as imprecatory (p. 953). Adams lists vv. 9 & 10 from this psalm.

[12] Calvin admits, "it would not be unsuitable to explain the meaning thus: As the proud have dealt mischievously with me, and molested me without a cause, the Lord will give them their reward" (4:458). He decides, however, to treat the verse as a request.

Table 18.1 List of Psalms with Imprecation

Psalm	Verses	Imperatives	Jussives	Author	# vv.	Ps. vv.
5:	10	2	1	David	1	12
6:	10		4	David	1	10
7:	6 9		1	David	2	17
9:	19–20	1	2	David	2	20
10:	2b 15	1	1	anon.	2	18
17:	13	2		David	1	15
28:	4–5	3		David	2	9
31:	17–18		3	David	2	24
•35:	1 3–6 8 26	3	11	David	7	28
40:	14–15		5	David	2	17
54:	5	1	1	David	1	7
55:	9a 15	3	2	David	2	23
56:	7	1		David	1	13
•58:	6–10	2	2	David	5	11
•59:	5 11–15	4	1	David	6	17
68:	1–2 30	1	4	David	3	35
•69:	22–25 27–28	3	8	David	6	36
70:	2–3		5	David	2	5
71:	13		3	anon.	1	24
74:	22b–23	1	1	Asaph	2	10
79:	6 10b 12	2	1	Asaph	3	13
82:	8	1		Asaph	1	8
•83:	9–17	4	4	Asaph	9	18
94:	1–2	1		anon.	2	23
97:	7a		1	anon.	1	12
104:	35		1	anon.	1	35
•109:	6–20 29	1	19	David	16	31
119:	84			anon.	1	8
129:	5–8		3	anon.	4	8
•137:	7–9	1		anon.	3	9
139:	19–22			David	4	24
140:	8–11		7	David	4	13
141:	10		1	David	1	10
33	101	38	92	21 David	101	563

exception, but it is included because of its universal recognition in this category. The "Author" column indicates that eight psalms in the list are anonymous; however, the Septuagint identifies four of these as Davidic.[13] David is the stated author by the Hebrew texts for 21 in the list and for five of the major imprecatory psalms. On the basis of an evaluation of the Septuagint

---

[13] These are 71, 97, 104, & 137. Actually, Psalm 10 should be added to this list since the LXX regarded it as a continuation of Psalm 9, which is Davidic. We can not put too much confidence, however, in these additional identifications because the LXX regards Psalm 137 as Davidic when its content indicates an exilic author.

data (omit 137, include Psalm 10), we could say that David wrote 25 psalms with imprecatory elements. Asaph wrote one major and three others.

Proposed Solutions for the Imprecations

Some say simply that the psalmists are wrong to pray in this fashion and argue that the New Testament presents a contrasting ethic.[14] C. S. Lewis is notorious for this position: "The reaction of the Psalmists to injury, though profoundly natural, is profoundly wrong."[15] Another writer is even more specific: "But these psalms are not the oracles of God; … their expressions of vindictiveness and hatred are not 'purified' or 'holy' simply by virtue of being present in Scripture."[16] This position would deny that the Holy Spirit inspired the psalmists,[17] and particularly David, to say these things. The New Testament makes it clear that David wrote as a prophet: "the Holy Ghost by the mouth of David spake" (Acts 1:16); "Therefore being a prophet … spake" (Acts 2:30–31). Psalm 69:22–24 is quoted in the New Testament as Scripture (Rom. 11:9–10), and Peter refers to 69:25 and 109:8 as prophetic concerning Judas (Acts 1:20).[18]

Another way to handle this problem is to argue that these imprecations belong to another dispensation. The Old Testament saints needed a confirmation of God's justice by witnessing His punishment of sinners, but we can now look back to what God did in the sacrifice of His Son to understand that there is indeed punishment for sin.[19] What David

---

[14] "In substance, the imprecations of the Psalter are normal and valid; in their external form and modes of expression they belong to an age of religion which has been displaced by Christianity." "It is the form and general character of these imprecations which are most obnoxious to the modern mind …." Briggs, 1:c–ci.

[15] *Reflections on the Psalms* (New York: Harcourt, Brace, and Company, 1958), 26.

[16] Craigie, 41.

[17] In some cases those taking this position might argue that inspired Scripture is simply quoting what some man has said (like Job's friends), and the man was in error, not the author. But David, who voiced these curses, is also the author who writes under inspiration.

[18] Luc discusses this solution further (42:397–98).

[19] "It is not quite so necessary now as it was before the coming of the Lord Jesus that God vindicate His righteousness and justice by spectacular strokes of retributive justice." "It is less appropriate for New Testament believers to offer up the

prayed was appropriate for him, but Christians do not need to pray for vengeance now. The problem with this solution is that these many verses in Psalms would not really be relevant for Christians though we are told that "All scripture ... is profitable for doctrine, for reproof, for correction, for instruction in righteousness" (2 Tim. 3:16).[20]

Observations

A careful study of these psalms leads to three observations that are significant to explaining how to handle the problem. First, (1) *the imprecations are not examples of personal vengeance.* The precept in the law that said, "eye for eye" (Exod. 21:24) was not calling for personal vengeance but was a matter of judicial justice in court from judges (Deut. 19:18–21). When Paul told Christians not to avenge themselves (Rom. 12:19), he backed up his admonition by quoting the Old Testament (Deut. 32:35; Prov. 25:21–22). The imprecations do not reflect a vengeful heart but are examples of committing the issue of someone else's wickedness to the Judge, who said, "Vengeance belongeth unto me, I will recompense" (Heb. 10:30).

(2) *The historical Davidic background indicates that David is exemplary in not seeking personal vengeance.* The fact is that the great majority of imprecatory verses (at least 74 out of 104) were written by David. Another fact is that David was not a vindictive person. He had two opportunities to avenge himself against Saul and refused to act (1 Sam. 24:4–15; 26:8–12). At one point David planned to seek revenge against Nabal, but Abigail talked him out of doing so, and David praised her for preventing him from an act of vengeance (25:21–39). When David was king, he was not vengeful toward Shimei (2 Sam. 16:5–13; 19:18–23) or Absalom (18:5, 32–33). There is a significant connection between these two facts. David's heartfelt prayers that asked for and committed to God the punishment of evildoers made it possible for him to be such a good example of one who avoided seeking personal vengeance.

(3) *There is a close connection between these requests and the decreed and prophesied punishments for the wicked.* A study of the verses on punishment covered in Chapter 17 and a comparison to imprecatory verses

---

same call for vengeance ...." Gleason L. Archer, *Encyclopedia of Bible Difficulties* (Grand Rapids: Zondervan, 1982), 245–46.

[20] Laney evaluates a number of other solutions that have been offered (138:37–40).

indicate this.[21] Table 18.2 lists verbs describing punishment for sinners which were discussed in that chapter. The last column provides the references where these verbs are imperatives or jussives that request punishment; column four indicates the ratio of imprecatory uses to the total occurrences concerning punishment. The shame and destruction that the psalmists record as past punishment and that they prophesy for the wicked are the same shame and destruction they request from the Judge of all the earth. In the notorious Psalm 137 there is only one imperative: "Remember, O LORD" (v. 7). The anonymous psalmist[22] asks God to remember (to call to mind and to act on that basis) what He had prophesied against Edom through Amos, Obadiah, Joel, Ezekiel, and Isaiah. Then in verses 8–9 there is no request but merely comments about what God had said would surely happen to Babylon: "Because the spoiler is come upon her, even upon Babylon, and her mighty men are taken, every one of their bows is broken: for the LORD God of recompences shall surely requite" (Jer. 51:56). Verse 8 of Psalm 137 uses some of the same wording as the prophecy: שׁדד, *shadad*, "destroyed" and "spoiler"; שׁלם, *shalam*, "rewardeth" and "requite"; and גּמוּל, *gemuwl*, "recompense" (NASB). Isaiah 13:16a had prophesied the very same shocking thing mentioned in 137:9 ("dasheth thy little ones against the stones").[23]

New Testament Echoes

Imprecations are not absent from the New Testament. If these verses in Psalms are curses, the opposite of the blessings in the book, then what are Christ's "woes" (Matt. 23:13–33; Luke 6:24–26), which are opposite His

---

[21] This is basically the thesis of Luc's article: "A study of the prophetic role of the psalmists, the imprecatory parallels in prophetic speeches, and the prior Biblical bases of the curses suggest that the psalmic curses are quite similar to the prophetic proclamations of judgment in the other parts of the OT" (42:409). He provides two tables comparing the imprecations in Psalms with the book's predictions of punishment (42:410).

[22] Possibly this is the request of the exiles who had spoken in verse 4 and possibly had individually expressed themselves in verses 5–6. See Alexander, 543.

[23] "The writer of the psalm may have known of this prediction and may have here sought to express the thought that what the Almighty has decreed he on his part would also like to see executed. If a man takes such an attitude, is he more cruel than the Lord?" Leupold, 936–37.

Theological Themes of Psalms

Table 18.2 Hebrew Verbs in Imprecatory Verses

Hebrew	Transliteration	English	Ratio	References
בּוֹשׁ	bowsh	shame	11/18	6:10 [2]; 31:17; 35:4, 26; 40:14; 70:2; 71:13; 83:17; 97:7; 129:5
אבד	'avad	perish *causative:* destroy	3/17	68:2; 83:17 *causative:* 143:12
כלה	kalah	end	3/10	59:13 [2]; 71:13
כרת	karath	cut off	2/9	109:13, 15
צמת	tsamath	annihilate	1/7	54:5
חפר	khaphar	be ashamed	5/6	35:4, 26; 40:14; 70:2; 83:17
בהל	bahal	be dismayed	2/6	6:10; 83:17
כלם	kalam	be humiliated	3/4	35:4; 40:14; 70:2
סוג	suwg	turn back	4/4	35:4; 40:14; 70:2; 129:5

blessings?[24] Peter approvingly quotes imprecatory passages from Psalms in Acts 1:20. Paul uses the strong language of cursing against Bar-Jesus in Acts 13:10–11. Paul ends one of his letters with "If any man love not the Lord Jesus Christ, let him be Anathema [accursed] …" (1 Cor. 16:22). Paul sounds like David in Psalms: "let him be accursed"; "I would they were even cut off which trouble you" (Gal. 1:8–9; 5:12). Although Paul interceded for those who had forsaken him ("may it not be counted against them!" NASB), he had another attitude about Alexander the coppersmith (2 Tim. 4:16, 14). Most telling of all, however, is the cry of the glorified saints in heaven: "How long, O Lord, holy and true, dost thou not judge and avenge our blood on them that dwell on the earth?" (Rev. 6:10).

In conclusion, the imprecatory passages are relevant for believers in this age. They serve to lay before God all our frustrations concerning the wickedness around us and the sin that brings harm into our lives and the lives of the ones we love. Praying in this fashion removes any temptation we may have to take things into our own hands and to seek revenge. David's identification with most of these imprecatory verses can lead to the conclusion that these words also express the desires of the Lord Jesus, who said, "I have come to cast fire upon the earth; and how I wish it were already

---

[24] "Jesus uses an expression somewhat similar to Ps 137:9 when he rebukes Jerusalem, saying that the enemies 'will dash you to the ground, you and the children within your walls' (Luke 19:44)." Luc, 42:398.

kindled!" (Luke 12:49, NASB).[25] We must, however, keep in mind that at the present we have a ministry of reconciliation and that we have a duty of intercessory prayer that sinners would be saved. Like Abraham (Gen. 18:23–32) and Moses (Exod. 32:30–32), we cry to God for mercy and a temperance of judgment.

---

[25] "We conclude, then, that the Psalms are ultimately the prayers of Jesus Christ, Son of God. He alone is worthy to pray the ideal vision of a king suffering for righteousness and emerging victorious over the hosts of evil. As the corporate head of the church, he represents the believers in these prayers. Moreover, Christians, as sons of God and as royal priests, can rightly pray these prayers along with their representative Head." Bruce K. Waltke, "A Canonical Process Approach to the Psalms," in *Tradition and Testament: Essays in Honor of Charles Lee Feinberg,* ed. Paul Feinberg and John Feinberg (Chicago: Moody Press, 1981), 16.

19

Affliction

One's own iniquity and the sin of others result in suffering or affliction. Because of the wicked and especially because of enemies, the psalmists frequently bring before God the fact of their affliction; thus Psalms presents a doctrine of suffering.[1] Affliction is something that is common to mankind. Eliphaz said, "man is born unto trouble, as the sparks fly upward" (Job 5:7). The psalmists certainly recognized this and addressed the one Person who could do something about it.

It is difficult catalogue all the verses on this subject because in one sense all the passages about enemies (Chapter 16) and about God's punishment (Chapter 17) are speaking about someone's affliction. Working on the list of terms for trouble, I constantly discovered other ways the psalmists could mention the subject. For example, a key term (עֳנִי, *tserah*; "affliction") occurs in 25:18 joined with the word עָמָל (*'amal*), that normally refers to labor or toil, but in this context does it mean "trouble" (NASB, ESV, HCSB)?[2] What is clear is that there are at least 126 verses (about 5% of the verses in the book) occurring in 60 different psalms that mention this theme. Prominence belongs to Book I, which contains 34 of these verses in 19 psalms, but Book V uses the most words for the concept (41). Of the 48 individual lament psalms (see Appendix B), 30 touch on the

---

[1] Grogan says, "There is certainly material here for a doctrine of suffering." He then presents four propositions on this theme (pp. 335–39).

[2] It was not included in the tables below. This word occurs 13x in Psalms. In 73:5 it could certainly mean "trouble," and it is parallel to a verb (translated as "are plagued") that occurs also in v. 14, leading to a parallel noun that means "correction" (3x in Psalms) and leads to 39:11 with a term ("consume away") that refers to punishment. Where does it end?

theme of affliction. Of the 74 psalms attributed to David, 31 mention affliction.

Vocabulary for Affliction

The psalmists use five principal words for the concept of affliction, charted in Table 19.1 below. Two of the key words for this theme are related to each other: צַר (*tsar*) and צָרָה (*tsarah*). The first word is translated in the KJV as "trouble" eleven times ("distress" twice; "affliction" once). The second word appears as "trouble" in the KJV for 20 of its 22 occurrences in Psalms.[3] Often the affliction to which the psalmists refer is a mental or emotional condition brought about by the mockery of enemies. This is affliction of a social nature rather than physical. The word חֶרְפָּה (*kherpah*), "reproach," occurs 18 times for this kind of distress.[4] Five of these occur in Psalm 69 (vv. 7, 9, 10, 19, 20). Two more words that are related to each other are עֳנִי (*'eniy*), a noun meaning "affliction," and עָנָה (*'anah*), its cognate verb meaning "to afflict."[5]

The psalmists utilize a number of synonyms for "trouble" that occur seven or fewer times, listed below in Table 19.2. The general word (רָעָה, *ra'ah*) for evil (whether ethical or otherwise) occurs 31 times in Psalms, seven of which refer to disasters or misfortunes the righteous are experiencing. Some of the words in the list concern not physical but emotional distress: יָגוֹן

---

[3] The difficulty in determining the vocabulary for this theme is that both of these words have homonyms. The homonym for צַר (*tsar*) means "enemy." In some of the verses in Psalms, translations do not agree: for example, in 60:11 the KJV has "trouble," following the LXX and *PiH* (or Vulgate), but other English translations have "enemy" (NIV, NET) or "foe" (ESV, HCSB). The NEB translates 138:7a as "Though I walk among foes," regarding צָרָה (*tsarah*) as a homonym, but almost everyone else rejects this.

[4] Many of these NET translates with some form of the word "insult." "In contexts where an adversary reproaches with scorn or insults, 'taunt' is an acceptable translation (Jud 8:15; Ps 119:42)." Thomas E. McComiskey, "749 חָרַף," *TWOT*, 1:326.

[5] This verb has an homonym that means "to answer." The MT pointed the verb in Psalm 55:19 as a *qal*, "and answer them" (NASB; Leupold, 425; Ross, 2:242), but the ancient translators (LXX, *PiH*, Syriac Peshitta, and Targum), who were looking at an unpointed text, analyzed it as a piel and thus understood it to mean "afflict" or "humble." This is followed correctly by the KJV and most modern English translations.

Table 19.1 Main Vocabulary for Affliction

Hebrew words:	צַר *tsar*	צָרָה *tsarah*	חֶרְפָּה *kherpah*	עֳנִי *'eniy*	ענה *'anah*
Psalm	trouble	trouble	reproach	affliction	to afflict
4:	1				
9:				13	
18:	6				
20:		1			
22:		11	6		
25:		17 22		18	
31:	9	7	11	7	
32:	7				
34:		6 17			
37:		39			
39:			8		
44:			13	24	
46:		1			
50:		15			
54:		7			
55:					19
59:	16				
66:	14				
69:	17		7 9 10 19 20		
71:		20	13		
77:		2			
78:		49	66		
79:			4 12		
81:		7			
86:		7			
88:				9	7
89:			41 50		22
90:					15
91:		15			
94:					5
102:	2				
106:	44				
107:	6 13 19 28			10 41	17
109:			25		
116:		3			10
119:	143		22 39	50 92 153	67 71 75 107
120:		1			
132:					1
138:		7			
142:		2			
143:		11			
totals:	14	22	18	10	12

(*yagown*), "grief" or "sorrow"; אֵימָה (*'eymah*), "terror"; מֵצַר (*meytsar*), "torment"; פַּחַד (*pakhad*), "fear"; אָוֶן (*'awen*), "sorrow"; and עֹצֶר (*'owtser*), "anguish." The rest are probably more of a general nature, referring to any kind of affliction.

Table 19.2 Additional Terms in Psalms for Affliction

Hebrew	Transliteration	English	#	References
רָעָה	ra'ah	disaster	7	27:5; 34:19; 35:26; 40:12; 41:1; 88:3; 107:39
מְצוּקָה	metsuwqah	distress	5	25:17; 107:6, 13, 19, 28
יָגוֹן	yagown	grief	4	13:2; 31:10; 107:39; 116:3
נֶגַע	nega'	affliction	4	38:11; 39:10; 89:32; 91:10
דַּךְ	dak	oppressed	3	9:9; 10:18; 74:21
לַחַץ	lakhats	oppression	3	42:9; 43:2; 44:24
אֵימָה	'eymah	terror	2	55:4; 88:15
בַּצָּרָה	batsarah	trouble	2	9:9; 10:1
מֵצַר	meytsar	torment	2	116:3; 118:5
פַּחַד	pakhad	fear	2	64:1; 91:5
אָוֶן	'awen	sorrow	1	90:10
אֵיד	'eyd	calamity	1	18:18
מוּעָקָה	muw'aqah	affliction	1	66:11
מָצוֹק	matsowq	anguish	1	119:143
עֱנוּת	'enuwth	affliction	1	22:24
עֹצֶר	'owtser	oppression	1	107:39
עָקָה	'aqah	pressure	1	55:3

Table 19.3 charts three verbs in Psalms that are used to indicate oppressive action that results in affliction: עָשַׁק ('ashaq); לָחַץ (lakhats); and יָנָה (yanah). Three other verbs in this list specify emotional states of grief: הָמָה (hamah), "being upset"; שָׁחַח (shakhakh), "despairing"; and בָּהַל (bahal), "being dismayed." Two other verbs refer to the common way that oppressors bring dismay to their victims: בָּעַת (ba'ath), "terrorize"; and עָרַץ ('arats), "terrify." Indicating more specific actions, two other verbs are צָרַר (tsarar), "harass"; and כָּנַע (kana'), "humble."[6]

---

[6] This last verb appears in 106:42 and is often translated "brought into subjection" (KJV, ASV, NRSV, ESV), but "most often in the historical books the vb. refers to humiliation imposed by political force, often upon arrogant national assertion." W. J. Dumbrell, "כנע," *NIDOTTE*, 2:667. See also Alexander, 450.

Table 19.3 Some Verbs in Psalms for Acts or States of Affliction

Hebrew	Transliteration	English	#	References
עשק	'ashaq	to oppress	6	72:4; 103:6; 105:14; 119:121, 122; 146:7
המה	hamah	to be upset	5	42:5, 11; 43:5; 55:17; 77:3
שחח	shakhakh	to despair	5	42:5, 6, 11; 43:5; 44:25
בהל	bahal	to be dismayed	3	6:3, 4; 90:7
לחץ	lakhats	to oppress	2	56:1; 106:42
צרר	tsarar	to harass	2	129:1, 2
בעת	ba'ath	to terrorize	1	18:4
ינה	yanah	to oppress	1	74:8
כנע	kana'	to humble	1	106:42
ערץ	'arats	to terrify	1	10:18

Propositions

Pondering the 126 verses where these words appear in Psalms, we are able to assert several theological truths. (1) *The affliction the psalmists describe includes a wide variety of both physical suffering and emotional grief.* Mental suffering is indicated by various words such as "reproach," "grief," and "terror." It is not unusual to experience mental distress apart from any physical pain. It is, however, not likely that bodily pain can occur without producing any emotional effects. Psalm 107 describes four scenarios of trouble: lost voyagers without food and water (vv. 4–9), guilty prisoners (vv. 10–15), ailing sinners (vv. 17–22), and mariners in a storm, trouble from nature's force (vv. 23–30). The Davidic psalms that mention affliction sometimes contain material in the title describing the various historical incidents that led to the distress: danger from the Philistines (34 & 56), treachery of the Ziphites (54), and Saul's deadly stalking (59 & 142). The title of Psalm 18 groups together Saul with David's many other enemies. The non-specific nature of so many of the affliction verses in Psalms (for example, 40:12a) has the effect of making these passages applicable to whatever kind of affliction we may face.

(2) *The variety of suffering includes those cases where the psalmists recognize that their trouble has a connection to their sin.* David ties the two together in the same verse: "Look upon mine affliction and my pain; and forgive all my sins" (25:18); "Deliver me from all my transgressions: make me not the reproach of the foolish" (39:8). In other cases he mentions his sin

and trouble within a few verses: "acknowledged my sin" (32:5) and "trouble" (v. 7); "my sins are not hid from thee" (69:5) and "shame hath covered my face" (v. 7). He can reverse the order: "I am in trouble" (31:9) and "because of my iniquity" (v. 10). In the Davidic covenant God announced this correlation: "Then will I visit their transgression with the rod, and their iniquity with stripes" (89:32). Moses also correlates the two: "For we are consumed by thine anger, and by thy wrath are we troubled. Thou hast set our iniquities before thee, our secret sins in the light of thy countenance" (90:7–8).

(3) *The fact that the psalmists bring before God their afflictions and ask for His help indicates their awareness that God not only knows what is happening, but that He is in control and has the power to remedy the situation.*[7] David says, "I poured out my complaint before him; I shewed before him my trouble" (142:2). He declares, "Thou hast known my reproach, and my shame, and my dishonour: mine adversaries are all before thee" (69:19). The psalmists' questions indicate they assume God knows and has some responsibility for their condition. For example, one psalmist declares, "I will say unto God my rock, Why hast thou forgotten me? why go I mourning because of the oppression of the enemy?" (42:9). Other questions include 43:2; 44:24; and 88:14–15. We find bold statements declaring that God is the agent of affliction: "thou hast afflicted us" (90:15b); "thou hast afflicted me with all thy waves" (88:7b). The terror distressing the psalmist is God's terror (88:15). The implication is that since God is in control, He can alleviate the situation.

(4) *In their prayers the psalmists often reflect on how God has responded to their suffering in the past.* David recognizes that God has seen and known what has happened (31:7). His reflection on the past is evident when he says, "Thou hast enlarged me when I was in distress" (4:1b).[8] In another place he says, "This poor man cried, and the LORD heard him, and saved him out of all his troubles" (34:6). Additional examples of this type of thinking include 18:6; 54:7; 59:16b; and 120:1. This fact of past action becomes a basis for

---

[7] "The prayers for help are a *theological interpretation of suffering.* They place the troubles of life in a context of meaning. They provide the way to move affliction out of the realm of merely accidental, fortuitous meaninglessness into the comprehension of a view of self, world, and God" (his emphasis). James Luther Mays, *The Lord Reigns: A Theological Handbook to the Psalms* (Louisville: Westminster John Knox, 1994), 43.

[8] The NIV treats the 2MS verb here as a precative perfect ("Give me relief"), but a present perfect is the normal way to translate it. David "recalls how the LORD has set him free from distress before." Ross, 1:233.

further requests: the deliverance asked for in 22:19–21 is grounded on the history mentioned in 22:24.

(5) *The psalmists indicate their confidence in God by proclaiming what He will do in the future about their affliction.* David affirms, "The LORD also will be a refuge for the oppressed, a refuge in times of trouble" (9:9). Personally, he can say, "For in the time of trouble he shall hide me in his pavilion ..." (27:5a). The imperfect verb in the well-known statement, "Many are the afflictions of the righteous: but the LORD delivereth him out of them all" (34:19), can be translated as a future ("will deliver"), as the Septuagint did.[9] The same thought appears in another verse in the future tense: "the LORD will deliver him in time of trouble" (41:1b). David tells the Lord, "Though I walk in the midst of trouble, thou wilt revive me" (138:7a).

This confidence has its basis on promises God has already made. For example, "And call upon me in the day of trouble: I will deliver thee, and thou shalt glorify me" (50:15). Psalm 91 contains several promises: "Thou shalt not be afraid for the terror by night; nor for the arrow that flieth by day" (v. 5); "There shall no evil befall thee, neither shall any plague come nigh thy dwelling" (v. 10); and "He shall call upon me, and I will answer him: I will be with him in trouble; I will deliver him, and honour him" (v. 15).

(6) *God uses affliction to accomplish something good for the righteous.* After acknowledging the affliction of God's people in 94:5, the psalmist proclaims, "Blessed is the man whom thou chastenest, O Lord" (v. 12a). Another psalmist in faith declares "It is good for me that I have been afflicted" (119:71a).[10] He confesses that "Before I was afflicted I went astray" (v. 67a).

New Testament Echoes

The Septuagint commonly translated the Hebrew synonyms for affliction by using θλῖψις (*thlipsis*), often translated as "tribulation" in the New Testament (21x). Some key examples include the following from the book of Romans: "And not only so, but we glory in tribulations also: knowing that tribulation worketh patience" (5:3); "Who shall separate us from the love of Christ? shall tribulation, or distress ...?" (8:35a); "Rejoicing in hope; patient in tribulation" (12:12a). Barnabas and Paul announced to the new

---

[9] Alexander translated it as future in his commentary (p. 156). *PiH* also has a future.

[10] "A thousand benefits have come to us through our pains and griefs." Spurgeon, 5:273.

Christians what they would face: "that we must through much tribulation enter into the kingdom of God" (Acts 14:22b). Paul realized that his own afflictions promoted the cause of Christ: "And whether we be afflicted, it is for your consolation and salvation" (2 Cor. 1:6a); "But in all things approving ourselves as the ministers of God, in much patience, in afflictions, in necessities, in distresses" (6:4); "Who now rejoice in my sufferings for you, and fill up that which is behind of the afflictions of Christ in my flesh for his body's sake, which is the church" (Col. 1:24).[11]

It was prophesied that Christ would be "a man of sorrows, and acquainted with grief" (Isa. 53:3b). The Lord indicated to His disciples that "he must go unto Jerusalem, and suffer many things of the elders and chief priests and scribes" (Matt. 16:21b), affirming that this would fulfill Scripture: "it is written of the Son of man, that he must suffer many things, and be set at nought" (Mark 9:12b). There were other aspects of Christ's afflictions. For example, when Jesus saw Mary weeping after the death of her brother, "he groaned in the spirit, and was troubled" (John 11:33). Just anticipating what He would suffer on the Passover, He said, "Now is my soul troubled; and what shall I say? Father, save me from this hour: but for this cause came I unto this hour" (John 12:27). In the Garden of Gethsemane Jesus said, "My soul is exceeding sorrowful,[12] even unto death" (Matt. 26:38a).

As long as we Christians are in this world, we will face troubles. "Yea, and all that will live godly in Christ Jesus shall suffer persecution" (2 Tim. 3:12). "Beloved, think it not strange concerning the fiery trial which is to try you, as though some strange thing happened unto you" (1 Pet. 4:12). Let us follow the example of the psalmists, recognizing that God is in control, and say to Him, "thou in faithfulness hast afflicted me" (119:75b). We know as they knew that we can go to the Lord in prayer: "In my distress I cried unto the Lord" (120:1a). Additionally, what encouragement we have from the refrain in Psalm 107! "Then they cried unto the LORD in their trouble, and he delivered them out of their distresses" (vv. 6, 13, 19, 28; with variations).

---

[11] Paul's sufferings were not redemptive. Redemption is Christ's completed work alone. To accomplish his missionary work, however, it was necessary for Paul to endure hardships in order to proclaim the gospel. See Richard R. Melick, *Philippians, Colossians, Philemon*, vol. 32 of NAC (Nashville: Broadman & Holman Publishers, 1991), 240.

[12] The Greek word here is περίλυπος (*perilupos*), the same word the LXX used in Psalms 42:5, 11; 43:5 ("Why art thou cast down, O my soul?")

20

Prayer

When affliction comes to the godly, they naturally pray to God for deliverance. By definition a prayer is a petition to deity. Accordingly, we expect to discover many prayers in Psalms. The titles, however, label just five psalms as prayers: Psalms 17, 86, and 142 are David's prayers; 90 is a prayer of Moses; and 102 is "A Prayer of the afflicted, when he is overwhelmed, and poureth out his complaint before the LORD." Of course, there are various indications that many more than five psalms are prayers. If we notice the characteristics of these labeled prayers, it will become evident that these same traits occur in a number of other psalms. For example, Psalm 86 contains 15 masculine singular imperatives that address God (for example, "bow down," "hear," "preserve," and "save" in vv. 1–2). It also uses the verb "cry" or "call" (קרא, qara'; vv. 3, 5, and 7) to indicate praying and the particle "for" (כִּי, kiy; vv. 1–5, 7, 10, and 13) to introduce the grounds for the petitions.[1]

On the basis of such characteristics, many of the laments would therefore be prayers, at least 56 of the 64 (see Appendix B for the types). The other laments may not be classified as prayers for various reasons. What makes categorization difficult is that in many cases only a part of a psalm is a prayer while the rest of it can be testimony or instruction. For example, in Psalm 6 David addresses the Lord in prayer in verses 1–6, but in verses 8–10 he speaks to his enemies.[2] Sometimes the prayer is just one verse of the psalm: "Unto thee, O God, do we give thanks, unto thee do we give thanks: for that thy name is near thy wondrous works declare" (75:1); then there is an oracle from God followed by praise from Asaph, the psalmist. Psalm 14 can be called a

---

[1] See W. L. Liefeld, "Prayer," *ISBEr*, 3:933.

[2] "The psalmist turns immediately away from the lament over his suffering at the hand of his enemies to warn those very enemies that they are now in mortal danger," showing that he believes the Lord will answer his petition. Ross, 1:269–70.

Theological Themes of Psalms

lament because of the wish expressed in verse 7 ("Oh that the salvation of Israel were come out of Zion!"),[3] but it contains no prayer. Psalm 42 is a lament because of a complaint about troubles; it does not seem to be a prayer since there are no petitions,[4] but the psalmist addresses God three times (vv. 1b, 6–7, and 9) in what could be called short prayers.

Certain psalms of the remaining types could be classed as prayers. In addition to Psalm 75 other thanksgiving psalms that include prayers are 116 (vv. 4b, 8, 16–17) and 118 (21, 25, 28). Some wisdom psalms contain petitions (impv) that make them also prayers: Psalm 19:12–14 and Psalm 119 (59 impv). In the royal Psalm 89 Ethan twice petitions God to "remember" (vv. 47 & 50). In a psalm of trust we find David speaking directly to God in prayer (23:4–5). Among the hymn types it is not unusual to find prayers. Psalm 106 ends with "Save us, O Lord our God, and gather us …" (v. 47). Psalms 65 and 66 address God directly with affirmations (for example, 65:5–8 & 66:9–12) and promises (for example, 65:1 & 66:13–15). David makes promises to his Lord in the hymns of Psalms 138 and 145 (for example, 138:1–2a & 145:1–2). The Zion Psalm 84 contains a petitionary prayer (vv. 8–9). Certainly, at least half of the 150 psalms are in some sense prayers. The first prayer in the book is Psalm 3 and the last one is Psalm 145, both by David.

Vocabulary for Prayer

The words the psalmists use for the concept of prayer do not occur only in the prayers themselves, such as "give ear to my prayer" (17:1). In some psalms that are not prayers, these terms appear in statements about the doctrine: for example, God says, "Thou calledst in trouble, and I delivered you" (81:7). The key word in the book for prayer turns out not to be the noun "prayer" (תְּפִלָּה, *tephillah*; 27x apart from the titles, listed below in Table 20.1) or the verb (פלל, *palal*; just 3x). The common way the psalmists speak about prayer is by using verbs that mean "call." The most common is קרא (*qara'*), parallel to the word "prayer" in 4:1; it refers to invoking the Lord 49 times. Its close synonym is רִנָּה (*rinnah*), used a total of 15 times in

---

[3] Ross says, "The psalm cannot be easily classified according to the standard types that we have…. [It] seems to be a unique composition that draws on many features of different types of psalms" (1:373).

[4] Ross argues that Psalms 42 and 43 were originally one and that the petition is now in Psalm 43 (2:15–16).

192

Table 20.1 Vocabulary for Prayer

Hebrew words: Psalm	קרא *qara'* to call	תְּפִלָּה *tephillah* prayer	תַּחֲנוּן *takhenuwn* supplication	רִנָּה *rinnah* cry	קוֹלִי *qowliy* my voice
3:	4				
4:	1 3	1			
5:					3
6:		9			
14:	4				
17:	6	1		1	
18:	3 6				6
20:	9				
22:	2				
27:	7				7
28:	1		2 6		
30:	8				
31:	17		22		
34:	6				
35:		13			
37:		12			
40:					
42:		8		4	
47:				1	
50:	15				
53:	4				
54:		2			
55:	16	1			17
56:	9				
57:	2				
61:	2	1		1	
64:					1
65:		2			
66:	17	19 20			
69:	3	13			
72:		20			
79:	6				
77:					1 [2]
80:	18	4			
81:	7				
84:		8			
86:	3 5 7	6	6		
88:	9	2 13		2	
89:	26				
91:	15				
99:	6 [2]				
102:	2	1 17 [2]			
105:	1				
106:				44	
109:		4 7			
116:	2 4 13 17		1		1
118:	5				
119:	145 146			169	149
120:	1				

Hebrew words:	קרא qara' to call	תְּפִלָּה tephillah prayer	תַּחֲנוּן takhenuwn supplication	רִנָּה rinnah cry	קוֹלִי qowliy my voice
Psalm					
130:	1		2		2
138:	3				
140:			6		1
141:	1 [2]	2 5			1
142:				6	
143:		1	1		
145:	18 [2]				
totals:	49	27	8	8	11

Psalms, sometimes meaning "a shout of joy" (107:22, HCSB) but several times paralleling the word "prayer": for example, "attend unto my cry, give ear unto my prayer" (17:1). Thus the term can refer to a prayerful cry: "let my cry come near before thee" (119:169; also 106:44 & 142:6).[5] Parallel to "prayer" in 86:6, another term is תַּחֲנוּן (takhenuwn), often translated as "supplication": for example, "give ear to my supplications" (143:1b). Another way to refer to prayer is with the simple expression "my voice" (קוֹלִי, qowliy). David joins the verb "cry" with the expression "my voice" when he refers to prayer (3:4; 27:7); he also says, "Hearken unto the voice of my cry" (5:2). Then he can use the term "my voice" alone as "a metonymy for what he says"[6] in prayer: "hear my voice" (55:17; 64:1) being equivalent to "hear my prayer." This leads us to understand the difficult syntax of 77:1 (literally, "my voice to God" twice)[7] as a reference to prayer. There are eleven of these cases for "my voice" by itself (apart from "cry") in Psalms.

Less common nouns and verbs for praying are listed below in Table 20.2. Catalogued there are three different nouns meaning "cry" used as

---

[5] In 42:4 and 47:1 the psalmist mentions "the voice of joy" (NASB), which could refer to singing. The connection with thanksgiving, which must be addressed to God, in 42:4, however, suggests that this may be a communal prayer at a temple festival.

[6] Ross, 2:253.

[7] "This utterance is rather abrupt because in the Hebrew the verb is missing, and thus the opening words read: 'My voice to God.' That may be one of those ellipses in which the verb is quite naturally supplied from the context and would then read something like, 'I will raise my voice.'" Leupold, 555. Alexander translates the verse as "My voice unto God (I will raise) and will cry; my voice unto God (I will raise), and he will give ear to me," and then comments, "He would not pray if he despaired of being heard" (p. 332).

synonyms for "pray" in Psalms: שַׁוְעָה (*shaw'ah*), צְעָקָה (*tse'aqah*), and שֶׁוַע (*shewa'*). Two additional verbs are synonymous with קְרָא (*qara'*), "to cry": זְעַק (*za'aq*) and צְעַק (*tsa'aq*). The verb חנן (*khanan*) in the *hithpael* theme (30:8; 142:1) means "to make supplication"; its cognate noun תְּחִנָּה (*tekhinnah*), synonymous with the more common תַּחֲנוּן (*takhenuwn*), "supplication," occurs three times in the book (6:9; 55:1; 119:170), though it is common in the Old Testament (a total of 26x). The verb שִׂיחַ (*siykh*) and its cognate noun שִׂיחַ (*siyakh*) refer in certain contexts to meditation or to complaints that one presents to God. The title of Psalm 102 connects the noun with the word "prayer"; the verb occurs in Psalms 14 times, but just in Psalms 55 and 77 does it refer to prayer: "Evening, and morning, and at noon, will I pray [שִׂיחַ] and cry aloud: and he shall hear my voice" (55:17);

Table 20.2 Additional Terms in Psalms for Prayer

Hebrew	Translit-eration	English	#	References
שַׁוְעָה	*shaw'ah*	cry	6	18:6; 34:15; 39:12; 40:1; 102:1; 145:19
זְעַק	*za'aq*	to cry	5	22:5; 107:13, 19; 142:1, 6
צְעַק	*tsa'aq*	to cry	5	34:17; 77:1; 88:1; 107:6, 28
אֲנָחָה	*'enakhah*	groaning	4	6:6; 31:10; 38:9; 102:5
שִׂיחַ	*siykh*	to complain	4	55:17; 77:3, 6, 12
פלל	*palal*	to pray	3	5:2; 32:6; 72:15
שִׂיחַ	*siyakh*	complaint	3	55:2; 64:1; 142:2
תְּחִנָּה	*tekhinnah*	supplication	3	6:9; 55:1; 119:170
חנן	*khanan*	to make supplication	2	30:8; 142:1
צְעָקָה	*tse'aqah*	cry	1	9:12
שֶׁוַע	*shewa'*	cry	1	5:2

in the context of remembering God, being overwhelmed in spirit, and contemplating God's actions, Asaph's meditation in 77:3, 6, and 12 is probably prayer.[8] Another noun is אֲנָחָה (*'enakhah*), "groan," occurring in four individual laments, where the psalmist is telling God about weeping in the night, bodily suffering, and depression, acknowledging that God knows

---

[8] The verb "has the idea of communing, reflecting, and even lamenting in prayer to God." Ross, 2:633.

about his "groaning" (6:6; 31:10; 38:9; 102:5). Are these not the groans of distressed prayer?[9]

The Petitions and Content of Psalm Prayers

By studying the inspired prayers in Psalms, we can learn much about what we should talk about as we address our Lord in prayer. In order to be brief, I have chosen ten psalms to analyze, all of them laments. Five of them are the ones identified in their titles as prayers: four individual laments and one community lament (Psalm 90 by Moses). Two of the ten are penitential psalms (6 & 51), one imprecatory (109), a lament with praise (57), and a very short community lament (123). In content all ten psalms, of course, contain petitions because they are prayers.

There are six categories of petitions. (1) *The psalmists often ask God to listen to them.* Sometimes this occurs in the beginning of the prayer: for example, 17:1; 86:1; and 102:1. Why is it necessary to ask this of God? First, it indicates that the psalmists are fervent about their prayers;[10] second, the request for a hearing implies their expectation that God will act, and that is what they are asking. Further on, the psalmists repeat this petition: "incline thine ear unto me, and hear my speech" (17:6b; also 86:6 & 102:2b).

(2) *They also request for God to be gracious.* In 6:2, 51:1, 57:1, 86:3, and 123:3, the Hebrew word they use is חָנַן (*khanan*), translated in the KJV as "be merciful." The desire is that God would grant an undeserved favor. This indicates that men like David recognized they had not earned God's help.[11] The request of Moses is for sympathy: "Turn and have compassion on Your servants" (90:13, HCSB).

(3) *The psalmists need some kind of assistance.* They express this using various imperatives: "deliver" (6:4; 17:13; 51:14; 109:21; 143:6), "save" (6:4; 57:3; 86:2, 16; 109:26), "keep" or "preserve" (17:8; 86:2), "help" (109:26),

---

[9] Calvin says that 38:9 "may be explained in a twofold sense, either as denoting his confident assurance that his prayers and groanings were heard by the Lord, or a simple declaration that he had poured out before God all his cares and troubles" (2:61). Clearly, Calvin understands that David is talking about praying "with groanings which cannot be uttered" (Rom. 8:26).

[10] Since David "asks twice to be heard, in this there is expressed to us both the vehemence of his grief and the earnestness of his prayers." Ibid., 1:39.

[11] "All the deliverances of saints, as well as the pardons of sinners, are the free gifts of heavenly grace." Spurgeon, 1:35.

and "bring out" (142:7). This petition occurs in seven of the ten psalms being studied. The psalmists do not specify the action associated with the mercy and compassion they request in Psalms 90, 102, and 123.

(4) *They also plead for protection from their enemies.* Sometimes these are "the wicked" (17:9, 13; 109:2) or "persecutors" (142:6). David uses the metaphors of "lions" (57:7) and hunters (57: 6) to describe his enemies. The enemy can be death (6:4). And there are various other ways to refer to the foes: "those that rise up" (17:7), "the proud" (86:14; 123:4), and "they which hate" (86:17).

(5) *The request can be for God to work in the life of the godly.* David asks God to change him internally: "Create in me a clean heart, O God; and renew a right spirit within me" (51:10), and "Restore unto me the joy of thy salvation; and uphold me with thy free spirit" (v. 12). In another psalm his petition is "Rejoice the soul of thy servant" (86:4a). Furthermore, he wants the Lord to teach him and to give him an undivided heart that fears God (v. 11).[12] He also wants God's strength in his life (v. 16).[13] Moses makes three requests for God's internal spiritual working: wisdom (90:12), satisfaction (v. 14), and gladness (v. 15). A fourth request is for the labors of the godly to endure: "Make our endeavors successful!" (v. 17b, NET).

(6) *The request can be for God to do good to others.* Since Psalm 90 is a communal lament, the petitions of Moses mentioned above would be for the benefit of others and not just focused on himself. In his penitential prayer David requests prosperity for others: "Do good in thy good pleasure unto Zion: build thou the walls of Jerusalem" (51:18). In his prayer concerning his distress, he also speaks of Zion's need of grace and mercy (102:13).[14]

These prayers contain additional content besides petitions. (7) *The psalmists confess their insignificance.* Moses acknowledges human frailty: we are subject to death according to God's desire (90:3). We are as ephemeral as a dream or the grass that thrives only briefly (vv. 5–6). Our lifetime "is soon cut off, and we fly away" (v. 10d). David says that his "days are consumed

---

[12] "David's request, 'unite my heart,' asks God … to keep [his heart] from having divided loyalties." Steveson, 336.

[13] "When the Lord gives us his own strength we are sufficient for all emergencies, and have no cause to fear any adversaries." Spurgeon, 3:468.

[14] "Now the writer's mind is turned away from his personal and relative troubles to the true source of all consolation, namely, the Lord himself, and his gracious purposes towards his own people." Spurgeon, 4:254.

like smoke" (102:3). We live in a temporal universe that will soon pass away (v. 26). He admits, "I am gone like the shadow when it declineth: I am tossed up and down as the locust" (109:23).

(8) *They also express their confidence in the Lord.* Contrasted with a humble opinion of themselves is the psalmists' declared trust in Yahweh. David in his talk with God is confident: "The LORD hath heard my supplication; the LORD will receive my prayer" (6:9). The verbs in the next verse need to be translated as futures, not jussives: "my enemies will be ashamed ..." (v. 10).[15] David ends Psalm 17 with the statement, "As for me, I will behold thy face in righteousness: I shall be satisfied, when I awake, with thy likeness" (v. 15). Toward the beginning of his prayer also, David can express his confidence: "He shall send from heaven, and save me .... God shall send forth his mercy and his truth" (57:3).

(9) *Then there is thanksgiving.* Three of the ten prayers include expressions of thanks. David, after lamenting what his enemies are doing, takes time to reflect in anticipation of God's deliverance and to say, "I will give thanks to you, O Lord" (57:9a, ESV).[16] In another psalm after promising faithfulness, David says the same thing (86:12). Toward the end of an imprecatory psalm, he promises, "I will fervently thank the Lord with my mouth" (109:30a, HCSB). Again he pledges, "Bring my soul out of prison, so that I may give thanks to Your name" (142:7a).

(10) *The psalmists spend time in their prayers exalting the Lord.* In a lament David uses a refrain the magnify his Lord: "Be thou exalted, O God, above the heavens; let thy glory be above all the earth" (57:5, 11). In another psalm he says, "For thou art great, and doest wondrous things: thou art God alone" (86:10). Another psalmist praises the Lord by saying, "But thou, O LORD, shalt endure for ever; and thy remembrance unto all generations" (102:12), and "But thou art the same, and thy years shall have no end" (v. 27). Even in the very short prayer of Psalm 123 there is room for the acknowledgment that Yahweh gloriously dwells in heaven (v. 1).

---

[15] "But just as certain as he is that his prayers have been accepted, just so assured is he of the complete overthrow of his enemies." Leupold, 89.

[16] Ross analyzes verses 7–10 as the "thanksgiving of the psalmist for deliverance" (2:280).

New Testament Echoes

The Septuagint commonly translated the Hebrew nouns for prayer and supplication as προσευχή (*proseukhē*) and δέησις (*deēsis*). These are the first two words in the list where Paul makes prayer a priority: "I exhort therefore, that, first of all, supplications, prayers, intercessions, and giving of thanks, be made for all men" (1 Timothy 2:1). The subject of prayer permeates the New Testament. Jesus taught on the subject in His Sermon on the Mount, in parables, and elsewhere. Prayer characterized His personal life. Luke emphasized prayer both in his Gospel and in the book of Acts. The Epistles and Revelation contain many references to prayer.[17]

Our lives should be characterized by prayer just as the psalmists' lives were. Our God has provided patterns of prayer for us in both testaments, but Psalms provides the most extensive collection of prayers in the Bible. May it be said about us that "they cried unto the LORD in their trouble" (107:6, 13, 19, 28). Individually, I should be able to say with the psalmist, "I cried with my whole heart" (119:145). Surely, "The LORD is nigh unto all them that call upon him, to all that call upon him in truth" (145:18).

---

[17] For extensive data, see W. L. Liefeld, "Prayer," *ISBEr*, 3:934–37.

21

Redemption

When the godly experience affliction, they pray to God for help, and He provides deliverance. The pages of Psalms are full of examples of this scenario. The refrain of Psalm 107 expresses it well: "they cried unto the LORD in their trouble, and he delivered them out of their distresses" (vv. 6, 13, 19, 28). Those three words, "distresses," "cried," and "delivered" sum up the themes of Chapters 19–21 (Affliction, Prayer, and Redemption). Salvation is certainly one of the dominant themes of the book: as many as 97 psalms touch on this topic; at least 269 verses make some mention of the concept (about 11% of the book's verses). The theme starts in Psalm 3 and continues until 149:4. For the concept of salvation, English has a number of synonyms: deliverance, rescue, help, preservation, and redemption. Redemption was chosen as the title of this chapter because the term includes the idea of some price being paid for the deliverance. Biblically, God's deliverance of mankind from Satan's domain of sin required a ransom because of God's justice. The connection of a payment with salvation is indicated in several Psalm verses: the key passage says, "Help us, O God of our salvation, for the glory of thy name: and deliver us, and purge away our sins, for thy name's sake" (79:9). The word "purge" (KJV)[1] translates the Hebrew כפר (kaphar), the verb related to the noun that means "ransom" (כֹּפֶר, kowpher).[2] Two English translations appropriately render the phrase as "atone for our sins"

---

[1] Other translations have "forgive our sins" (ASV, NASB, NIV, NRSV, NET, TEV).

[2] "It seems clear that this word aptly illustrates the theology of reconciliation in the OT. The life of the sacrificial animal specifically symbolized by its blood was required in exchange for the life of the worshipper. Sacrifice of animals in OT theology … was the symbolic expression of innocent life given for guilty life." R. Laird Harris, "1023 כָּפַר," TWOT, 1:453.

(ESV, HCSB). Since the English definition of "atonement" is reparation or amends for some wrong, the idea of a payment is present. The other verses mentioning atonement are 65:3 ("You can atone for our rebellions," HCSB) and 78:38 ("Yet He was compassionate; He atoned for their guilt," HCSB).

The topic of redemption is prominent in all five Books of Psalms. Even Book IV, the shortest, has 22 verses. Book I has 92 verses on the subject, almost 15% of its verses. All types of psalms touch on the subject: lament (for example, 69), hymn (20), thanksgiving (40), royal (18), Zion (76), wisdom (119), trust (62), and liturgy (50). The main Hebrew root for this concept of salvation (יָשַׁע, *yasha'*) occurs 136 times in Psalms, more that 38% of its occurrences in the Old Testament. This topic relates closely to Psalms' focus on God and His works. In the past He redeemed Israel from Egypt (77:15; 106:10, 21), now He is there to help (22:19; 33:20; 54:4), and He will save the godly from eternal damnation ("the pit," 103:4; 130:8).

Vocabulary for Redemption

There are seven key verbs in the book that refer to the event of redemption. Table 21.1 charts the 159 occurrences, all seven of them appearing in Books I. III, and V. The verb יָשַׁע (*yasha'*), "to save," occurs 178 times in the Old Testament, 53 of them in Psalms. Two of the other verbs are usually translated as "deliver": נָצַל (*natsal*)[3] and מָלַט (*malat*). Two others mean "rescue": פָלַט (*palat*) and חָלַץ (*khalats*). The verb פָדָה (*padah*) expresses the concept of redemption. Its synonym גָּאַל (*ga'al*) connotes that the act of redemption is performed by a family member.[4]

In addition to the verbs there are three key nouns that mean "salvation" in Psalms. Each of these is related to the verb יָשַׁע (*yasha'*). Table 21.2 lists these as well as two nouns meaning "help" that are used in the sense of salvation. Four verses parallel the first of these two nouns with nouns for

---

[3] This verb occurs 45x in Psalms, but the table lists just 43 verses because in 119:43 it refers not to the deliverance of salvation but to the snatching away of a word ("take not the word of truth utterly out of my mouth"). In Psalm 18 נָצַל (*natsal*) appears in the title, not the text.

[4] "The primary meaning of this root is to do the part of a kinsman and thus to redeem his kin from difficulty or danger." R. Laird Harris, "300 גָּאַל," *TWOT*, 1:144. "OT texts of various genres portray Yahweh as the divine *gō'ēl* who, like his familial counterpart, helps those who have fallen into need." Robert L. Hubbard, Jr., "גאל," *NIDOTTE*, 1:792.

Table 21.1 Seven Verbs for Redemption

Hebrew words:	ישע *yasha'* save	נצל *natsal* deliver	פלט *palat* rescue	פדה *padah* redeem	חלץ *khalats* rescue	גאל *ga'al* redeem	מלט *malat* deliver
Psalm							
3:	7						
6:	4				5		
7:	1	1 2					
12:	1						
17:				13			
18:	3 27	17 48	2 43 48		19		
19:						14	
20:	6 9						
22:	21	8 20	4 8				5
25:		20		22			
26:				11			
28:	9						
31:	2 16	2 15	1	5			
32:			7				
33:	16	16 19					17
34:	6 18	4 17 19		22	7		
35:		10					
36:	6						
37:	40		40[2]				
39:		8					
40:		13	17				
41:							1
43:			1				
44:	3 6 7			26			
49:				7[2] 15			
50:		22			15		
51:		14					
54:	1	7					
55:	16			18			
56:		13	7				
57:	3						
59:	2	1 2					
60:	5				5		
69:	1 35	14[2]		18		18	
70:		1	5				
71:	2 3	2 11	2 4	23			
72:	4 13	12				14	
74:						2	
76:	9						
77:						15	
78:				42		35	
79:		9					
80:	3 7 19						
81:					7		

Theological Themes of Psalms

Hebrew words:	ישע yasha' save	נצל natsal deliver	פלט palat rescue	פדה padah redeem	חלץ khalats rescue	גאל ga'al redeem	מלט malat deliver
Psalm							
82:		4	4				
86:	2 16	13					
89:							48
91:		3	14		15		
97:		10					
98:	1						
103:						4	
106:	8 10 47	43				10	
107:	13 19	6				2[2]	20
108:	6				6		
109:	26 31	21					
116:	6				8		4
118:	25						
119:	94 117 146	170		134	153	154	
120:		2					
124:							7[2]
130:				8			
138:	7						
140:					2		
142:		6					
143:		9					
144:		7 11	2				
145:	19						
totals:	53	43	19	14	11	11	8

salvation: עֶזְרָה ('ezrah) and יֵשַׁע (yeysha') in 27:9; עֶזְרָה ('ezrah) and תְּשׁוּעָה (teshuw'ah) in 38:22, 60:11, and 108:12. For example, we find, "Make haste to help me, O Lord my salvation" (38:22). Thus we can associate Yahweh's helping with His acts of deliverance. The verb for helping (עָזַר, 'azar) occurs 17 times in Psalms, four times as an imperative; two of these are connected with the act of salvation: "Help us, O God of our salvation" (79:9a), and "Help me, O LORD my God: O save me according to thy mercy" (109:26). If we are correct in connecting the act of helping with redemption, then עָזַר leads us to another verb that could be a synonym: "Behold, God is mine helper [עֹזֵר, 'owzeyr]: the Lord is with them that uphold my soul" (54:4).[5] The verb translated "uphold" is סָמַךְ (samak), sometimes rendered

---

[5] The Hebrew of this verse is difficult to interpret because of the plural participle. The LXX translated it with the sg word ἀντιλήμπτωρ (antilēmptōr), which means helper or protector. Ross believes the LXX understood the term "as a plural of

Table 21.2 Additional Vocabulary for Salvation

Hebrew words: Psalm	יְשׁוּעָה yeshuw'ah salvation	יֵשַׁע yeysha' salvation	תְּשׁוּעָה teshuw'ah salvation	עֶזְרָה 'ezrah help	עֵזֶר 'eyzer help	עָזַר 'azar to help	סָמַךְ samak to sustain
3:	2 8						5
9:	14						
7:	1						
10:						14	
12:		5					
13:	5						
14:	7						
18:	50		2 35 46				
20:	5		6		2		
21:	1 5						
22:	1			19		11	
24:			5				
25:			5				
27:			1 9	9			
28:	8					7	
30:						10	
33:			17		20		
35:	3 9			2			
37:			39			40	17 24
38:			22	22			
40:			10 16	13 17			
41:							
42:	5 11						
43:	5						
44:	4			26			
46:				1		5	
50:		23					
51:		12	14				12
53:	6						
54:						4	4
60:			11	11			
62:	1 2 6	7					
63:				7			
65:		5					
68:	19 29						
69:		13					
70:	4			1	5		
71:			15	12			6
72:						12	
74:	12						
78:	22						
79:		9				9	
80:	2						
85:			4 7 9				
86:						17	

---

majesty," and he suggests translating the preposition בְּ (*be*) with "in the capacity of" (2:233–34).

Hebrew words: Psalm	יְשׁוּעָה yeshuw'ah salvation	יֵשַׁע yeysha' salvation	תְּשׁוּעָה teshuw'ah salvation	עֶזְרָה 'ezrah help	עֵזֶר 'eyzer help	עֹזֵר 'azar to help	סָמַךְ samak to sustain
88:	1						
89:	26				19		
91:	16						
94:				17			
95:		1					
96:	2						
98:	2 3						
106:	4						
107:						12	
108:			12	12			
109:						26	
112:							8
115:					9 10 11		
116:	13						
118:	14 15 21					7 13	
119:	123 155 166 174		41 81			86 173 175	116
121:					1 2		
124:					8		
132:		16					
140:	7						
144:			10				
145:							14
146:			3		5		
149:	4						
totals:	45	20	13	14	11	17	9

as "sustain" (3:5).[6] When this act keeps someone from falling or perishing, it is equivalent to deliverance. This is confirmed by 51:12, where David says, "Restore unto me the joy of thy salvation; and uphold me with thy free spirit," thus connecting salvation and upholding. Also in 145:14 David associates upholding with raising up, another way to describe the divine rescue.

Less common verbs and other terms for salvation are listed below in Table 21.3. Catalogued there are four different synonyms that refer to pardon for sin: נשׂא (nasa'), כפר (kaphar), כסה (kasah); and סלח (salakh). The first verb literally means "lift up" (49x in Psalms); when used with "sin" or "iniquity" as its direct object, it can refer to forgiveness, as in 25:18 ("forgive all my sins"). The second verb is the normal term for atoning: for example, "He atoned for their guilt" (78:38, HCSB). The third literally means "to cover" (17x in Psalms). Covered sins are either hidden (as in 32:5) or forgiven: "Blessed is he whose transgression is forgiven [נשׂא], whose sin is

---

[6] In Psalms the NIV translates this verb as "sustain" three additional times (51:12; 54:4; and 119:116).

Table 21.3 Additional Terms in Psalms for Salvation

Hebrew	Translit-eration	English	#	References
סעד	*sa'ad*	to uphold	6	18:35; 20:2; 41:3; 94:18; 104:5; 119:117
נשׂא	*nasa'*	to forgive	5	25:18; 32:1, 5; 85:2; 99:8
כפר	*kaphar*	to atone	3	65:3; 78:38; 79:9
זקף	*zaqaph*	to raise up	2	145:14; 146:8
כסה	*kasah*	to cover	2	32:1; 85:2
סלח	*salakh*	to pardon	2	25:11; 103:3
מוֹשִׁיעַ	*mowshiya'*	Savior	4	7:10; 17:7; 18:41; 106:21
מוֹשָׁעָה	*mowsha'ah*	salvation	1	68:20
סַלָּח	*sallakh*	forgiving	1	86:5
סְלִיחָה	*seliykhah*	forgiveness	1	130:4

covered" (32:1). There are also two more cognate nouns of the verb for salvation: מוֹשִׁיעַ (*mowshiya'*), "Savior" (4x in Psalms), and מוֹשָׁעָה (*mowsha'ah*), "salvation" (68:20). For the concept of the pardon necessary in God's saving act, we find an adjective (סַלָּח, *sallakh*), "forgiving," and a noun (סְלִיחָה, *seliykhah*), "forgiveness," each used just one time in the book. A synonym of the verb סמך (*samak*), "to sustain," סעד (*sa'ad*), "to uphold," occurs six times. Its connection to salvation is confirmed by 18:35, where, after mentioning God's salvation shield, David says, "thy right hand upholds me." Further confirmation occurs in 20:2, where it is parallel to a noun that means "help." Another verb used to indicate Yahweh's help is זקף (*zaqaph*), "to raise up" (145:14; 146:8).

Observations

By studying the many verses about redemption in Psalms, we naturally notice certain details. It would be appropriate to begin with a negative observation. (1) *People often seek help from sources that fail them.* Military strength is no guarantee for deliverance from trouble: the psalmists can say, "I will not trust in my bow, neither shall my sword save me" (44:6), and "There is no king saved by the multitude of an host: a mighty man is not delivered by much strength. An horse is a vain thing for safety: neither shall he deliver any by his great strength" (33:16–17). Indeed, "vain is the help of man" (60:11b; 108:12b). In the face of God's wrath, human redemption is impossible (49:7). The advice of the psalmist is "Put not your trust in princes, nor in the son of man, in whom there is no help" (146:3).

Theological Themes of Psalms

In contrast, (2) *the psalmists describe the Lord as the one agent of salvation*. Yahweh is the "Helper" (10:14; 30:10; 54:4; 118:7), "Redeemer" (19:14; 78:35), "Saviour" (17:7; 106:21), "Sustainer" (54:4, HCSB), and "Deliverer" (18:2). David affirms, "Salvation belongeth unto the LORD" (3:8a), and "But the salvation of the righteous is of the LORD: he is their strength in the time of trouble" (37:39).

(3) *The psalmists frequently request salvation from the Lord*. Addressing Yahweh, they use imperatives of the verbs for redemption: "save" (21x), "deliver" (19x), "deliver [מלט, *malat*]" (4x), "redeem" (5x), "rescue" (3x, NASB), "help" (3x), "uphold" (119:116),[7] "hold up" (119:117), "forgive" (25:18), "purge away our sins" (79:9), and "pardon" (25:11). Thus those who pray employ imperatives for 11 of the 14 verbs in the three tables above. Their requests are urgent: "Make haste to help me" (38:22a; also 40:13b), and "haste thee to help me" (22:19).

(4) *The psalmists desire deliverance not just from their enemies and the distresses of mundane life, but from sin and its consequences*. They recognized that they were in the greatest danger from a holy God and that they needed redemption because of the sin problem. The psalmist speaks of Yahweh redeeming Israel from iniquity (130:8). Mentioning salvation and deliverance, Asaph prays for God to "purge away our sins" (79:9). David pleads for forgiveness of sin (25:18) and pronounces the man blessed "whose transgression is forgiven, whose sin is covered" (32:1). He also says, "Deliver me from all my transgressions" (39:8a).

(5) *God has a history of redeeming work and characteristically practices delivering those in distress*. The past tense of some of the verbs indicates historical facts. For example, David exclaims, "You forgave the guilt of my sin" (32:5b, NASB). Asaph tells us that God "being full of compassion, forgave [Israel's] iniquity" (78:38a). Indeed, the psalmist can say to God, "Thou hast forgiven the iniquity of thy people, thou hast covered all their sin" (Psalm 85:2). Present participles in Hebrew grammar indicate characteristic conduct. For example, we note David's description: "LORD, who is like unto thee, which deliverest the poor from him that is too strong for him?" (35:10b). Other examples include, "The LORD upholdeth all that fall, and raiseth up all those that be bowed down" (145:14), and "the LORD raiseth them that are bowed down" (146:8b).

---

[7] In 51:12 David used a jussive form of the verb "uphold" to express his request; both the LXX and English versions translate it as an imperative.

(6) *The psalmists express thanks to God and praise Him for their redemption.* David blessed the Lord and boasted about God's action because "This poor man cried, and the LORD heard him, and saved him out of all his troubles" (34:6). In Psalm 116 the author reviews God's deliverance (vv. 4, 8) and salvation (vv. 6, 13), then he pledges a "sacrifice of thanksgiving" (v. 17). David begins Psalm 138 by praising the Lord (vv. 1–2) and toward the psalm's end he indicates his reason. He has absolute confidence in God's future work of redemption in his life: "Though I walk in the midst of trouble, thou wilt revive me: thou shalt stretch forth thine hand against the wrath of mine enemies, and thy right hand shall save me" (138:7).

New Testament Echoes

The two most common Greek verbs used in the Septuagint for salvation and deliverance are σώζω (*sōdzō*) and ῥύομαι (*ruomai*). These verbs and their cognate nouns occur frequently in the New Testament (almost 200x). The first chapter announces that Jesus "shall save his people from their sins" (Matt. 1:21). A key text reflects the main proposition in Psalms: "the Lord knows how to rescue [ῥύεσθαι] the godly from trials" (2 Peter 2:9a). In Psalms Yahweh is the Deliverer (18:2) and Savior (17:7, NASB; 106:21); the New Testament proclaims Jesus as the Deliverer (Rom. 11:26)[8] and Savior (Luke 2:11; Acts 5:31; and many more times).

In conclusion on this theme in Psalms, we can probably do no better than to consider the many times Psalm 119 refers to redemption (17 vv.). The psalmist is not reluctant to ask the Lord for personal ("me") deliverance (using 9 impv): "help thou me," "save me," "uphold me," "hold thou me up," "redeem me" (NASB), "rescue me" (NASB), and "deliver me." He bases his request on the Lord's promise (5x in HCSB). His hope (v. 166) and his longing (v. 174) is for that salvation. Five times the psalmist refers to "thy salvation" (vv. 41, 81, 123, 166, and 174), thus attributing the work of redemption to Yahweh. May our prayers reflect his prayers.

---

[8] "The reference is to a manifestation to Israel of her divine Redeemer—a manifestation which Paul may well identify in his mind with the parousia of Christ." F. F. Bruce, *Romans: An Introduction and Commentary*, vol. 6 of Tyndale New Testament Commentaries (Downers Grove, IL: InterVarsity Press, 1985), 218.

22

Hope

When the psalmists ask God for deliverance, they have the confidence that He is able to save and that He will do what He has promised. We generally call that confidence "hope." Hope is a person's expectation that something beneficial will happen. The hope that the Scripture usually speaks about is not identical to the way contemporary man views the concept. When we mention hope, often we are thinking about something possible that we would like to see happen but that we believe is unlikely or at best only probable. Biblically, hope is associated with trust, a faith that God is reliable. God has made specific promises in Scripture. When we trust God, believing those promises, then we are certain about what will happen. At that point we possess Biblical hope, and we then wait for God to act.

The concept of hope begins in Psalm 2, which pronounces a blessing on those who trust in God. It extends all the way to 147:11 ("those that hope in his mercy"). We find this theme in laments (for example, Psalm 25), hymns (for example, 106), thanksgiving songs (for example, 18), wisdom psalms (for example, 119), and, of course, poems expressing trust (for example, 62). The theme appears in every one of the Psalm Books with Book I dominating. There are over 60 psalms that have at least one verse on the subject for a total of around 118 verses. It is somewhat difficult to tabulate all these because the theme can appear in places even though none of the words for the concept are in the passage.[1] For example, the psalmist asks about the source of his "help" (121:1); his answer is "from the LORD" (v. 2), indicating his hope. The passage, therefore, concerns the subject of trust or

---

[1] "Although hope is clearly associated with various Hebrew roots, the concept is present in many OT texts even when these roots are absent. For this reason, it is important to look beyond the distribution of specific vocabulary when assessing the importance of hope in the OT." M. W. Elliott, "Hope," *NDBT*, 559.

hope without using any of the vocabulary listed in the tables below. Another example would be 20:7, which says literally, "These in chariotry and these in horses, but we in the name of Yahweh our God will cause to remember," meaning that they will mention or acknowledge the Lord. This clearly indicates where their trust is in contrast to those who trust in military might.[2]

Vocabulary for Hope

The main verb for the concept of hope in Psalms is יחל (*yakhal*), occurring 19 times,[3] as tallied in Table 22.1 below. Because of hope's connection with trust and faith, the vocabulary for this theme must also include the verbs "to trust" (בטח, *batakh*; 45x in Psalms) and "to believe" (אמן, *'aman*). The latter root occurs 15 times in Psalms, but about half of these mean "to be sure"; however, the verb used in the *hiphil* theme means "believe" (7x in Psalms): for example, "I had fainted, unless I had believed to see the goodness of the LORD in the land of the living" (27:13). Another way of indicating hope is the verb "to wait" (קוה, *qawah*; 17x in Psalms, 14x relevant to the theme); if a person expects something good in the future, he waits for that benefit. For example, "Let not them that wait on thee, O Lord GOD of hosts, be ashamed for my sake" (69:6). In 130:5 we see the connection clearly between waiting and hoping: "I wait for the LORD, my soul doth wait, and in his word do I hope." Another synonym was covered in Chapter 12 above as a term for God's protection: חסה (*khasah*), "take refuge." Because this verb often refers to a hope for protection and confidence that God will provide such, it is appropriate to include it again as part of the key vocabulary for hope. David connects trusting with refuge: "Trust in him at all times; ye people, ... God is a refuge for us" (62:8). The Septuagint's usual translation of three of these Hebrew verbs (בטח, 36x; יחל, 12x; and חסה 20x) with one Greek verb (ἐλπίζω, *elpidzō*), "to trust," confirms that these verbs are indeed synonyms.

---

[2] Some English versions supply the verb "trust" at the beginning of the verse (KJV, ASV, NIV, ESV, NET): "Some trust ...." Note Gerald H. Wilson's explanation of the verse: "The assembled people affirm their trust and dependence on Yahweh in a set of opposingly parallel lines contrasting the fate of those who trust in their own strength with those who hope in Yahweh." *Psalms*, NIVAC

[3] Translated as "hope" 18x in the KJV. The exception is 69:3, "while I wait for my God."

Table 22.1 Verbs for Hope

Hebrew words:	בטח *batakh* trust	יחל *yakhal* hope	קוה *qawah* wait	אמן *'aman* believe	חסה *khasah* take refuge
Psalm					
2:					12
4:	5				
5:					11
7:					1
9:	10				
11:					1
13:	5				
16:					1
17:					7
18:					2 30
21:	7				
22:	4[2] 5 9				
25:	2		3 5 21		20
26:	1				
27:	3		14[2]	13	
28:	7				
31:	6 14	24			1 19
32:	10				
33:	21	18 22			
34:					8 22
36:					7
37:	3 5		9 34		40
38:		15			
39:			7		
40:	3		1[2]		
41:	9				
42:		5 11			
43:		5			
44:	6				
49:	6				
52:	7 8		9		
55:	23				
56:	3 4 11				
57:					1[2]
61:					4
62:	8 10				
64:					10
69:		3	6		
71:		14			1
78:	22			22 32	
84:	12				
86:	2				
91:	2				4
106:				12 24	
115:	8 9 10 11				
116:				10	
118:	8 9				8 9
119:	42	43 49 74 81 114 147		66	
125:	1				

Hebrew words:	בטח *batakh*	יחל *yakhal*	קוה *qawah*	אמן *'aman*	חסה *khasah*
Psalm	trust	hope	wait	believe	take refuge
130:		5 7	5[2]		
131:		3			
135:	18				
141:					8
143:	8				
144:					2
146:	3				
147:		11			
totals:	45	19	14	7	25

Some additional words for hope appear a few times in Psalms. Four verbs[4] synonymous with those above are charted below in Table 22.2 according to how many times each occurs in the book. Two cognate nouns are also listed there: מִבְטָח (*mivtakh*), "trust," and תִּקְוָה (*tiqwah*), "hope." Two additional nouns are synonyms: שֵׂבֶר (*seyver*), "hope," and כֶּסֶל (*kesel*), "confidence." Three other terms in the chart are relevant for the theme: an adjective, "trusting" (בָּטוּחַ, *batuwakh*), an adverbial accusative, "in silence" (דוּמִיָּה, *duwmiyyah*),[5] and one more noun, "approach" (קִרְבָה, *qirevah*). This last word indicates the act of moving near. In 73:28a (literally, "As for me, coming close of God is good for me") that approach is toward the Lord,

---

[4] The verb גלל (*galal*) normally means "to roll," but in 22:8 it has a special meaning: "The literal meaning of the first clause is, *roll to* (or *on) Jehovah*, which would be unintelligible but for the parallel expressions in Ps. xxxvii. 5, *roll thy way upon Jehovah*, and in Prov. xvi. 3, *roll thy work upon Jehovah*, where the idea is evidently that of a burden cast upon another by one who is unable to sustain it himself. This burden, in the first case, is his *way, i.e.* his course of life, his fortune, his destiny, and in the other case, his *work, i.e.* his business, his affairs, his interest. In evident allusion to these places, the apostle Peter says, *casting all your care upon him, for he careth for you* (1 Pet. 5:7). By these three parallels light is thrown on the elliptical expression now before us, *roll, i.e.* thy burden or thy care *upon Jehovah*." Alexander, 108. Thus various English versions have translated this verb as "trust" (KJV, NIV, NJB, CEV, ESV).

[5] This word occurs 4x in Psalms, but only in 62:1 is it relevant for the hope theme. In this passage NASB supplies the verb "waits": "My soul waits in silence for God only." Alexander explains the phrase as a reference to hope: "This trust, and this alone, can set his mind at rest, and free him from the natural disquietude of man when alienated from his God" (p. 276).

thus indicating that Asaph trusts Him. The context ("I have made the Lord God my refuge") confirms that this is what Asaph was thinking.[6]

Table 22.2 Additional Terms in Psalms for Hope

Hebrew	Transliteration	English	#	References
מִבְטָח	*mivtakh*	trust	3	40:4; 65:5; 71:5
שׂבר	*savar*	to wait	3	104:27; 119:166; 145:15
תִּקְוָה	*tiqwah*	hope	3	9:18; 62:5; 71:5
שֵׂבֶר	*seyver*	hope	2	119:116; 146:5
בָּטוּחַ	*batuwakh*	trusting	1	112:7
גָּלַל	*galal*	to roll (commit)	1	22:8
דּוּמִיָּה	*duwmiyyah*	in silence	1	62:1
חוּל	*khuwl*	to wait	1	37:7
חכה	*khakah*	to wait	1	33:20
כֶּסֶל	*kesel*	confidence	1	78:7
קִרְבָה	*qirevah*	approach	1	73:28

Propositions

A study of the verses in the two tables leads us to several statements of truth. We begin with negative observation. (1) *There are certain things that persons must not trust.* The psalmists warn their readers about four areas of misplaced trust. (a) Some trust in military might: "Some trust in chariots, and some in horses" (20:7a). Such hope will bring disappointment: "An horse is a vain thing for safety: neither shall he deliver any by his great strength" (33:17). A psalmist gives his personal testimony: "For I will not trust in my bow, neither shall my sword save me" (44:6). (b) Others trust in wealth. David gives this advice: "if riches increase, set not your heart upon them" (62:10b). The first half of this verse indicates that people often sin to get the wealth that they think offers them security.[7] (c) Still others trust in idols

---

[6] "In the subsequent clause he informs us that we draw near to God in a right manner when our confidence continues firmly fixed in him." Calvin, 3:158. See also Alexander, 319–20.

[7] "The Psalmist bids us ... purge ourselves of every vicious desire that would usurp the place of God in our hearts. One or two kinds of sin only are mentioned, but these are to be understood as representing a part for the whole ...." Calvin, 2:427.

(31:6; 115:8; 135:18), but that is vain as well. (d) A trust in man for deliverance, even the powerful rulers, is also vain (118:8–9; 146:3).

(2) *God is the proper object of trust.* The psalmists repeatedly testify that they are trusting the Lord: David says, "O my God, I trust in thee" (25:2a; 31:14a), "I put my trust [חסה, *khasah*] in thee" (25:20c; 31:1), "For in thee, O LORD, do I hope [יחל, *yakhal*]" (38:15), and "I will trust in thee" (55:23c; 56:3b). Another passage says, "Our soul waiteth [חכה, *khakah*] for the LORD" (33:20a). Asaph affirms, "I have put my trust in the Lord GOD" (73:28b). Another psalmist announces, "I will say of the LORD, He is my refuge and my fortress: my God; in him will I trust" (91:2). Sometimes God's word is connected with this hope: "I wait for the LORD, my soul doth wait, and in his word do I hope" (130:5).

(3) *God commands us to hope.* Several times the Holy Spirit through the mouth of David instructs the reader to "wait [קוה, *qawah*] on the LORD" (27:14; 37:34), to "trust in the LORD" (4:5; 37:3; 62:8), and to "commit" one's activities[8] to God (37:5a; also 55:22a with "cast"). Other psalmists as well as David exhort Israel to trust the Lord (115:9; 130:7; 131:3). The duty falls to Aaron as well as and to those who fear Yahweh (115:10–11).

(4) *Abundant reward awaits those who trust God.* The word that expresses the benefits that God gives (אַשְׁרֵי, *'asherey*) occurs five times in reference to those whose hope is in Yahweh: (a) "Blessed are all they that put their trust in him" (2:12c); (b) "blessed is the man that trusteth in him" (34:8b); (c) "Blessed is that man that maketh the LORD his trust" (40:41); (d) "Blessed is the man that trusteth in thee" (84:12b); and (e) "Happy is he that hath the God of Jacob for his help, whose hope is in the LORD his God" (146:5). David accurately expresses this proposition by saying, "Oh how great is thy goodness, which thou hast laid up for them that fear thee; which thou hast wrought for them that trust in thee before the sons of men!" (31:19). These servants receive the benefit of redemption (34:22). They obtain an inheritance (37:9b, 34b). Their faith in God's protection provides them with the stability of ultimate safety (125:1–2).

(5) *Trust eliminates fear.* An additional benefit is that the mental attitude of confidence in God eradicates fear from the mind. Psalm 112:7 expresses the promise for the godly: "He shall not be afraid of evil tidings: his heart is fixed, trusting in the LORD." David says, "What time I am afraid, I

---

8 "There can be no doubt, that by the term *ways* we are here to understand all *affairs* or *businesses*." Ibid., 2:21.

will trust in thee" (56:3), and "In God have I put my trust: I will not be afraid what man can do unto me" (v. 11). That trust allowed him to write "I will fear no evil: for thou art with me" (23:4b), and "I sought the LORD, and he heard me, and delivered me from all my fears" (34:4).

(6) *Hope leads to praise.* Because the saints trust God for their salvation, it is natural for them to rejoice in anticipation and thus praise the Lord. David connects rejoicing, trust, and praise together in 64:10. The godly can identify with his testimony: "The LORD is my strength and my shield; my heart trusted in him, and I am helped: therefore my heart greatly rejoiceth; and with my song will I praise him" (28:7). Another psalmist tells the Lord, "But as for me, I will hope continually, And will praise You yet more and more" (71:14, NASB).

(7) *The hope for God's salvation often requires patience.* The key word that communicates this truth is קוה (*qawah*), "to wait."[9] David precisely expresses this proposition when he says, "Rest in the LORD, and wait patiently for him: fret not thyself ..." (37:7a).[10] David tells the Lord, "on thee do I wait all the day" (25:5c). In spite of difficulties and tears, he continues to trust: "I am weary of my crying: my throat is dried: mine eyes fail while I wait for my God" (69:3). Patience is indicated in cases where one must encourage himself to continue trusting: "My soul, wait thou only upon God; for my expectation is from him" (62:5).[11] Patience is evident when David speaks of trust "without wavering" (26:1) and when he expresses his faith about the future:

---

[9] This word "seems to capture something of the tension of waiting. In all the Semitic languages the word and its related forms have meanings that suggest some tension, such as twisting in knots.... The positive uses of the verb 'hope, wait for' simply emphasize the idea of eagerly waiting for something, hoping for it." Ross, 1:598, n.

[10] This passage expresses "the point of view of quiet submission and patient waiting." Leupold, 301.

[11] "It is not without a struggle that the saint can compose his mind; and we can very well understand how David should enjoin more perfect submission upon a spirit which was already submissive, urging upon himself farther advancement in this grace of silence, till he had mortified every carnal inclination, and thoroughly subjected himself to the will of God.... The danger is, that when new winds of troubles spring up, we lose that inward tranquillity which we enjoyed, and hence the necessity of improving the example of David, by establishing ourselves in it more and more." Calvin, 2:423.

"I believe that I shall look upon the goodness of the LORD in the land of the living" (27:13, ESV).

New Testament Echoes

The Septuagint translated four of the Hebrew verbs in Psalms for this theme of hope (בטח, יחל, חסה, and שבר) with the word ἐλπίζω (*elpidzō*). This Greek verb occurs in the New Testament 31 times. The noun ἐλπὶς (*elpis*) occurs even more often (53x). Many of these usages have nothing to do with our theme: for example, Felix "hoped also that money should have been given him of Paul" (Acts 24:26). Some, however, reflect the hope the psalmists expressed, such as Acts 26:6–7. Paul says, "For we are saved by hope" (Rom. 8:24a). In Psalms it was Yahweh that was the hope of the saints. The New Testament reaffirms that fact: "we trust in the living God" (1 Tim. 4:10), and "your faith and hope might be in God" (1 Pet. 1:21). Holy women (1 Pet. 3:5) and godly widows (1 Tim. 5:5) have had this hope. But now Christ becomes the hope of the believer: "we have hope in Christ" (1 Cor. 15:19). Paul refers to "Christ in you, the hope of glory" (Col. 1:27) and "Christ Jesus, our hope" (1 Tim. 1:1). Indeed, Christ is the hope of the nations (Matt. 12:21; Rom. 15:12). The concept of waiting in faith also appears:[12] "even we ourselves groan within ourselves, waiting for the adoption, to wit, the redemption of our body" (Rom. 8:23b), and regarding salvation "we with patience wait for it" (v. 25b). We also wait "for the coming of our Lord Jesus Christ" (1 Cor. 1:7; also Phil. 3:20; Heb. 9:28).

To sum up, we notice that Psalm 119 touches on this theme in at least ten verses. The psalmist's hope is in God's word (vv. 42–43, 49, 66, 74, 81, 114, 116, 147). Verse 81 connects God's word with His salvation: the psalmist thus trusts God to do what He has promised. He says explicitly, "I have hoped for thy salvation" (v. 166a). Would that we could give this same testimony: that we have complete confidence in God's word, which has promised us eternal salvation; and while we wait, we practice obedience (v. 166b).

---

[12] The Greek verb used in the NT (ἀπεκδέχομαι, *apekdekhomai*), however, is not the one the LXX employed in Psalms.

23

The Righteous

The redemption that God has provided for the afflicted that have cried out to him for deliverance has filled their hearts with hope. In faith they wait for what God has promised. This group the psalmists generally refer to as the righteous, but there are many ways of labeling them: they are the "saints," the "just," the "meek" and the "needy"; they are God's servants, His people. The book of Psalms begins talking about them in the very first verse, and they are the ones being told to praise the Lord in every verse of the last psalm. They are mentioned in 110 different psalms; over 300 verses refer to them in some way. Every one of the 17 psalms in Book III mentions them; Book V contains 32 psalms with some reference to the godly.

Identification of the Righteous

The authors of Psalms make great use of related words sharing the root צדק (*tsadaq*, 139x). These include a verb, two nouns, and an adjective. Involved in these words is the concept of some kind of standard.[1] The adjective, that often serves as a substantive (צַדִּיק, *tsaddiyq*, 52x), is usually translated as "righteous." Seven times in Psalms it refers to God's trait of justice: for example, "for the righteous God trieth the hearts and reigns" (7:9c), and "God is a righteous judge" (7:11a, NASB). The other 45 times the psalmists use the term (sometimes plural but mostly singular[2]) for a certain group of humans, specifically for those who have met a specific

---

[1] "It will be seen that *ṣdq* terms regularly deal with behavior that, usually by implication, accord with some standard. The standard might be the law, but often this is not the case or, at least, revealed law is not to be understood but rather some natural law or assumed standard." David J. Reimer, "צדק," *NIDOTTE*, 3:746.

[2] Some of the singulars, however, are actually collective: for example, "God is with those who are righteous" (14:5, HCSB).

standard in God's view. These usages are listed below in Table 23.1. In one sense, "There is none righteous" (Rom. 3:10a), reflecting Psalm 14:1 ("there is none that doeth good"): the standard here is sinlessness, and Psalms affirms that "in Your sight no man living is righteous" (143:2).

If not sinlessness, then what is the standard for the persons that Psalms refers to as "the righteous"? Psalm 112 provides us with the answer. The acrostic Psalm 111 enumerates God's attributes, including His right- eousness (v. 3). The companion acrostic that follows then describes the godly righteous person.[3] The psalmist begins by identifying him as one "that feareth the LORD and that delighteth greatly in his commandments" (112:1). The previous psalm had ended by declaring that "The fear of the LORD is the beginning of wisdom" (111:10). Thus true insight starts when a person believes God's pronouncements about sin and judgment and is truly afraid of the punishment from God.[4] Furthermore, this godly fear is associated with the faith that has an enthusiasm for what God has said in His word.[5] Then the psalmist specifically refers to the righteousness of this person: "his right- eousness endureth for ever" (112:3), and "he is gracious, and full of compas- sion, and righteous" (v. 4).[6] Finally, the Holy Spirit pinpoints the righteous

---

[3] Psalm 112 "is the second of a closely linked pair, both of them acrostics … : the first about God and his ways, and the second about the man of God." Kidner, 16:433. Mays says, "Psalm 112 makes an astonishing list of claims for [the godly]. The claims are even more astonishing when they are compared to what is said about the LORD in Psalm 111. … The correlation is not a presumptuous claim that the upright independently and autonomously realize goodness. Rather, by their fear of the Lord, they enter into the works of the Lord, who works on and in and through their lives. Their goodness is godliness" (p. 360).

[4] "The deep taproot of godly living is the fear of the Lord, which … is almost the equivalent of faith and trust in God." Leupold, 785.

[5] "To this man God's word is as fascinating as are his works to the naturalist; and the term used for it, *his commandments*, implies that his interest is practical. What grips him is God's will and call." Kidner, 16:434.

[6] In this verse there is an interpretational issue as to the reference of the pronoun "he": Calvin says, "For I have no doubt that the prophet intends, as applicable to God, the epithets, gracious, merciful, and just" (4:325). Delitzsch argues that "The three adjectives … are a mention of God according to His attributes" (3:200). Steveson agrees (p. 438). The RSV follows this interpretation in its translation of the verse, adding "LORD" before the adjectives. But most commentators disagree: Rawlinson says, "It is a very forced interpretation to

Table 23.1 Vocabulary for the Righteous

Hebrew words:	צַדִּיק tsaddiyq	חָסִיד khasiyd	יָשָׁר yashar	עָנִי 'aniy	עָנָו 'anaw	אֶבְיוֹן 'evyown
Psalm	righteous	godly	just	humble	meek	needy
1:	5 6					
4:		3				
5:	12					
7:	9		10			
9:				12 18		18
10:				2 9[2] 12	17	
11:	3 5		2 7			
12:		1		5		5
14:	5			6		
16:		10				
18:		25		27		
22:				24	26	
25:				16	9[2]	
30:		4				
31:	18	23				
32:	11	6	11			
33:	1		1			
34:	15 19 21			6	2	
35:				10[2]		10
36:			10			
37:	[9x]†	28	14 37	14	11	14
40:				17		17
43:		1				
49:			14			2
50:		5				
52:	6	9				
55:	22					
58:	10 11					
64:	10		10			
68:	3			10		
69:	28			29	32	33
70:				5		5
72:	7			2 4 12		4 12 13[2]
74:				19 21		21
75:	10					
76:					9	
79:		2				
82:				3		4
85:		8				
86:		2		1		1

understand this as said of Jehovah. The entire subject of the psalm is the righteous, God-like man. In him are reflected shadows of all the Divine qualities" (p. 43). Spurgeon concurs (5:17), as do Alexander, 464; Barnes, 3:147; Murphy, 588; Kirkpatrick, 675; Kidner, 16:434; Allen, 131; Futato, 355; and Kraus, 2:364. Various English translations render the verse in a way that indicates its subject is the godly man (NIV, NLT, ESV, and NET).

Hebrew words:	צַדִּיק	חָסִיד	יָשָׁר	עָנִי	עָנָו	אֶבְיוֹן
	tsaddiyq	khasiyd	yashar	'aniy	'anaw	'evyown
Psalm	righteous	godly	just	humble	meek	needy
88:				15		
89:		19				
92:	12					
94:	21		15			
97:	11 12	10	11			
102:				1		
107:			42			41
109:				16 22		16 22 31
111:			1			
112:	4 6		2 4			9
113:						7
116:		15				
118:	15 20					
125:	3[2]		4			
132:		9 16				15
140:	13		13	12		12
141:	5					
142:	7					
145:		10				
146:	8					
147:					6	
148:		14				
149:		1 5 9			4	
totals:	45	24	18	31	10	23

† Verses 12, 16, 17, 21, 25, 29, 30, 32, 39.

person as the one whose "heart is fixed, trusting in the LORD" (v. 7).[7] This point is confirmed in other psalms: "The righteous shall be glad in the LORD, and shall trust in him" (64:10ab); "none of [his servants] that trust in him shall be desolate" (34:22b); "the LORD shall help [the righteous], and deliver them ... because they trust in him" (37:40). Consequently, the three standards that the godly person meets are (1) fearing God, (2) relishing God's word, and (3) having true faith in God. We recognize that for a person with a sinful nature to be able to meet these standards, God must circumcise his heart or, in New Testament terminology, regenerate him.

Synonymous Terms for the Righteous

An examination of the verses mentioning the righteous (צַדִּיק, tsaddiyq) reveals that there are a number of alternative ways of referring to

---

[7] "The epithets 'established,' 'trusting,' 'upheld,' are all strikingly descriptive of the true attitude of faith, as that which leans upon and is supported by God." Perowne, 2:321.

these persons. Psalm 97 ends with three verses commenting about the righteous, referring to them with a singular form (צַדִּיק, *tsaddiyq*), which is collective, in verse 11 and with a plural (צַדִּיקִים, *tsaddiyqiym*) in verse 12. Verse 10 uses the word חָסִיד (*khasiyd*) to describe them: "he [Yahweh] preserveth the souls of his saints"; verse 11 parallels the term יָשָׁר (*yashar*), "the upright." The former word is related to חֶסֶד (*khesed*), "loyal love" or "loyal kindness." This word חָסִיד is a passive form: it indicates that the person is an object of God's covenant love and of His gracious kindness.[8] The word יָשָׁר is parallel four more times to צַדִּיק (32:11; 33:1; 64:10; 140:13) and means "right" or "correct," referring to conformity with a standard.[9] In 37:14 יָשָׁר is parallel to עָנִי (*'aniy*), "the poor," and אֶבְיוֹן (*'evyown*), "the needy." These synonyms characterize the righteous as suffering at the hands of the wicked. This oppression, whether from Satan or his ungodly seed, occurs because of the connection of the righteous with their Lord (John 15:19–20).[10] Another synonym is עָנָו (*'anaw*), "meek," used ten times in Psalms for the godly, mostly in Book I.

Table 23.2 charts four other ways of referring to the righteous individual or persons. He is God's servant (עֶבֶד, *'eved*): for example, "Make thy face to shine upon thy servant" (31:16). As a group they are called God's people (עַם, *'am*), "Israel" (יִשְׂרָאֵל, *Yisra'eyl*), or Jacob (יַעֲקֹב, *Ya'eqowv*), all included in a covenant relationship with Yahweh.

The psalmists use a handful of additional adjectives to characterize the righteous, listed below in Table 23.3. Some of these describe the state of

---

[8] "The devout are the people who are in covenant with God, who desire to love and serve the LORD, but who often find that they need forgiveness in order to maintain a proper relationship with the LORD." Ross, 1:715. The covenant relationship appears clearly in 50:5 ("Gather my saints together unto me; those that have made a covenant with me by sacrifice"). The LXX usually translates the Hebrew word with a form of ὅσιος (*hosios*), "saint" or "holy one." The Israelites in the wilderness after the exodus were "holy" because God had made a covenant with them, setting them apart (Deut. 7:6), not because they were sinless or even very godly.

[9] What is the standard the psalmists refer to in these passages? "I answer, that none others are received into favour but those who are dissatisfied with themselves for their sins, and repent with their whole heart." Calvin, 1:536.

[10] "The 'needy' and 'meek' here mentioned, together with the 'poor' of v. 12, are the same, namely, the persons who are in reality the godly but suffer oppression for the Lord's sake." Leupold, 114.

Theological Themes of Psalms

Table 23.2 Additional References to the Righteous

Hebrew words:	עֶבֶד	עַם	יִשְׂרָאֵל	יַעֲקֹב
	'eved	*'am*	*Yisra'eyl*	*Ya'eqowv*
Psalm	servant	people	Israel	Jacob
3:		8		
14:		4 7	7[2]	7
18:		27		
19:	11 13			
20:				1
22:			3 23	23
24:				6
25:			22	
27:	9			
28:		9		
29:		11[2]		
31:	16			
33:		12		
34:	22			
35:	27			
41:			13	
44:		12		4
46:				7 11
47:		9[2]		4
50:		4 7	7	
53:		4 6	6[2]	6
59:			5	13
60:		3		
62:		8		
68:		7 35	8 26 34 35	
69:	17 36		6	
71:			22	
72:		2 3 4	18	
73:			1	
75:				9
76:			1	6
77:		15 20		15
78:	70	1 20 52 62 71	[7x]†	5 21 71
79:	2 10	13		7
80:		4	1	
81:		8 11 13	4 8 11 13	1 4
83:		3	4	
84:				8
85:		2 6 8		1
86:	2 4 16			
87:				2
89:	3 20 39 50	15 19	18	
90:	13 16			
94:		5 14		7
95:		7		
98:			3	
99:				4
100:			3	
102:	14 28	18		

Hebrew words:	עֶבֶד *'eved*	עַם *'am*	יִשְׂרָאֵל *Yisra'eyl*	יַעֲקֹב *Ya'eqowv*
Psalm	servant	people	Israel	Jacob
103:			7	
105:	6 25 26 42	24 25 43	10 23	6 10 23
106:		4 40 48		
107:		32		
109:	28			
110:		3		
111:		6 9		
113:	1	8		
114:			1 2	1 7
115:			9 12	
116:	16[2]	14 18		
118:			2	
119:	[13x]*			
121:			4	
122:			4	
124:			1	
125:			5	
128:			6	
129:			1	
130:			7 8	
131:			3	
132:	10			2 5
134:	1			
135:	1 14	12 14	4 12 19	4
136:	22	16	11 14 22	
143:	2 12			
144:	10	15[2]		
146:				5
147:			2 19	19
148:		14[2]	14	
149:		4	2	
totals:	51	65	63	34

† 5, 21, 31, 41, 55, 59, 71   * 17, 23, 38, 49, 65, 76, 84, 122, 124, 125, 135, 140, 176

Table 23.3 Additional Terms in Psalms for the Righteous

Hebrew	Transliteration	English	#	References
דַּל	*dal*	poor	5	41:1; 72:13; 82:3, 4; 113:7
קָדוֹשׁ	*qadowsh*	holy	5	16:3; 34:9; 89:5, 7; 106:16
חֵלְכָה	*kheylekah*	helpless	3	10:8, 10, 14
שָׁבַר + לֵב	*shavar + leyv*	brokenhearted	3	34:18; 51:17; 147:3
תָּמִים	*tamiym*	blameless	3	18:23, 25; 37:18
כָּאָה + לֵב	*ka'ah + leyv*	brokenhearted	1	109:16
רָשׁ	*rash*	destitute	1	82:3

oppression the righteous often endure: "poor" (דַּל, *dal*), "helpless" (חֶלְכָּה, *kheylekah*), "brokenhearted" (שָׁבַר + לֵב, *shavar* + *leyv*; and כָּאָה + לֵב, *ka'ah* + *leyv*), and the participle "destitute" (רָשׁ, *rash*). Other terms are more positive: "holy" (קָדוֹשׁ, *qadowsh*) and "blameless" (תָּמִים, *tamiym*; KJV has "upright").

Propositions

In the hundreds of verses listed in the three tables above, the Holy Spirit proclaimed several truths about the righteous. (1) *It is normal for the righteous to suffer at the hands of enemies.* The godly Israel says, "Many a time have they afflicted me from my youth" (129:1). It is the regular activity of the wicked to oppress God's people: "The wicked in his pride doth persecute the poor" (10:2a; also 109:16), plotting (37:12) and ambushing (10:8–9). The psalmist reports to his Master, "They break in pieces thy people ... and afflict thine heritage" (94:5). It is evident that God allows all this to happen, for David tells the Lord, "Thou hast shewed thy people hard things: thou hast made us to drink the wine of astonishment" (60:3).

(2) *God is well aware of their circumstances and cares immensely about their suffering.* He "knoweth the way of the righteous" (1:6a; also 37:18). "The eyes of the LORD are upon the righteous, and his ears are open unto their cry" (34:15). He is sympathetic about the condition of "the poor and needy" ("He will have compassion," 72:13a, NASB). "For Yahweh will ... have compassion on His servants" (135:14, HCSB). The fact that He loves Jacob (47:4) is an indication of care. The references to Yahweh as a shepherd (23:1–2; 95:7; 100:3) are further indications of care. The fact that God hears the cries of the righteous is further evidence of His care: "This poor man cried, and the LORD heard him, and saved him out of all his troubles" (34:6); "LORD, thou hast heard the desire of the humble: ... thou wilt cause thine ear to hear" (10:17); "For he hath not despised nor abhorred the affliction of the afflicted; neither hath he hid his face from him; but when he cried unto him, he heard" (22:24).

(3) *In fact, God identifies Himself with the righteous.* The Lord calls them "my people" (50:7; 81:8, 11, 13). He has personally selected them ("the people whom he hath chosen for his own inheritance, 33:12a). God has shown the godly person "distinguishing grace":[11] "But know that the LORD

---

[11] Spurgeon, 1: 35. David uses the verb (פלה, *palah*) that signifies "the segregation of Israel from the rest of men (Ex. 8:18, 9:4, 11:7, 33:16), here applied

hath set apart him that is godly for himself" (4:3a). He is not ashamed to be called "the God of Jacob," as the inspired psalmists refer to Him ten times (for example, 20:1; 46:7; 81:1). The psalmists depict God as a shepherd who owns a flock: Asaph says, "Oh, give ear, Shepherd of Israel, You who lead Joseph like a flock" (80:1, NASB); for the people David requests, "Be their shepherd also, and carry them forever" (28:9b, NASB).

(4) *God has provided deliverance for them in the past and will continue to rescue them from their enemies.* "Then they cried out to the LORD in their trouble; He delivered them out of their distresses" (107:6, 13, 19, & 28, NASB); "... God arose to judgment, to save all the meek of the earth" (76:9). In numerous statements David uses present and future tenses in confidence about God's actions: for example, "My defence is of God, which saveth the upright in heart" (7:10); "For thou wilt save the afflicted people" (18:27a); "The LORD is nigh unto them that are of a broken heart; and saveth such as be of a contrite spirit" (34:18); "The LORD redeemeth the soul of his servants" (v. 22a).

(5) *It is appropriate, however, for the righteous to pray for this deliverance.* David encourages the godly man to pray to God "in a time when [He may] be found" (32:6a). Though David is confident that God will rescue those who trust Him (25:3a), he prays, "Turn thee unto me, and have mercy upon me; for I am desolate and afflicted. The troubles of my heart are enlarged: O bring thou me out of my distresses" (vv. 16–17). Later he prays for God's people: "Redeem Israel, O God, out of all his troubles" (v. 22). Recognizing past experience ("thou hast been my help") and in faith (recognizing the "God of [his] salvation"), David pleads, "Hide not thy face far from me; ... leave me not, neither forsake me" (27:9). The requests may even express urgency: "I am in trouble: hear me speedily" (69:17b); "But I am poor and needy: make haste unto me, O God: thou art my help and my deliverer; O LORD, make no tarrying" (70:5).

(6) *God has promised the righteous a glorious future.* The righteous are certain to flourish (like the palm tree or cedar, 92:12). They will be well established, like a tree planted in a good place (1:3; 52:8; 92:13). They can expect His blessing: "For thou, LORD, wilt bless the righteous; with favour wilt thou compass him as with a shield" (5:12); "the LORD will bless his people with peace" (29:11b). His servants can confidently say, "Thou hast

---

to the designation of an individual to the highest theocratical dignity." Alexander, 23–24.

dealt well … according unto thy word" (119:65). Eventually, "The upright will see His face" (11:7b, HCSB). God has laid up for them a glorious and everlasting inheritance (37:11, 18, 29; 69:36; 111:6).

(7) *The righteous, therefore, are thankful: they rejoice and praise God.* In Psalms expressions of thanksgiving are common, coming from the godly (30:4), the righteous (97:12; 140:13), and the just (111:1), as well as from God's people (79:13) and Israel (122:4). We notice the righteous and the godly rejoicing (58:10a; 68:3; 118:15a; 149:5). David says to the Lord, "let thy servant rejoice" (109:28c). Praise is even more frequent: from the godly (30:4; 148:14; 149:1b, 9b), the righteous (33:1), the just (33:1; 111:1), the humble (74:21), God's people (79:13; 106:48; 107:32; 148:14), and His servants (113:1; 135:1).

From a negative standpoint (8) *God can be angry with His people and punish them.* Though God shepherded Israel in the wilderness after the exodus (78:52), calling them "Jacob his people" (v. 71), because of their rebellion "he was wroth, and greatly abhorred Israel" (v. 59; also v. 62). The people's rebellion in Canaan led to the same wrath and abhorrence (106:40). Asaph asks the Lord, "how long wilt thou be angry against the prayer of thy people?" (80:4).[12] This is why an intercessor is necessary (106:23), making possible the forgiveness of sins (32:1; 78:38; 85:2).

New Testament Echoes

The Septuagint commonly translated the Hebrew substantive "the righteous" (צַדִּיק, *tsaddiyq*) by using the δίκαιος (*dikaios*). The New Testament writers use this Greek word in the same way. Thus we find the same contrast between "the wicked" and "the righteous" that occurs in Psalms and Proverbs: for example, someday the angels will remove "the wicked from among the just" (Matt. 13;49); Paul speaks about "a resurrection of both the righteous and the wicked" (Acts 24:15, NASB); and Revelation indicates the eventual eternal state of the wicked and the righteous (22:11). Luke refers to certain individuals as righteous: Zacharias and Elizabeth (1:6), Simeon (2:25), and Joseph of Arimathea (23:50). Of course, Christ Himself is the Righteous One (Acts 3:14; 7:52; 1 John 2:1). Christians are the righteous who are "scarcely" (with difficulty) saved (1 Pet. 4:18). Affirming what

---

[12] Rawlinson notes that "Ordinarily, God forgives, and ceases from his anger, as soon as the afflicted one makes earnest prayer to him. But this is not always so" (2:156).

Psalms teaches, Paul explains how a person can become righteous in God's sight: the gospel provides mankind with God's way of righteousness, which is "from faith to faith" (Rom. 1:17). This righteousness is "apart from the law" "through faith in Jesus Christ" (3:21–22, ESV, HCSB). The righteous, therefore, are those who trust Jesus Christ and call upon Him for salvation (10:11–13).

Christ exhorted us to "strive to enter in at the strait gate" (Luke 13:24). To enter one must be righteous in God's sight. The book of Psalms begins by describing the righteous as those who delight in God's word (1:2), who "serve the Lord with fear," and who "put their trust in him" (2:11–12), calling upon Yahweh the Savior (4:3; 6:4; 7:1). The book assures them that "the salvation of the righteous is of the LORD: … the LORD shall help them, and deliver them …, and save them, because they trust in him" (37:39–40).

24

Joy

When one who is suffering affliction laments and prays in hope to the Lord, God is faithful to bring His deliverance into the life of His saint. Sometimes the rescue is immediate, but often the Lord simply assures the saints that salvation is definitely in their future. The natural reaction to the act or to the promise of salvation that fulfills the saints' expectation is the emotion of joy! As Leupold succinctly put it, God's "goodness to us calls for appropriate response."[1] The heart rejoices when its hopes are realized. The greater the agony experienced, the greater is the ecstasy that follows. For example, the psalmist groans about "sorrow in my heart daily" but then ends his poem with "I will sing unto the LORD, because he hath dealt bountifully with me" (13:2b, 6). Almost half of the Psalms (72) touch on this theme in 147 verses (6% of the verses in the book). These words and verses are distributed most heavily in Books II and IV, and least in Book III. Naturally connected to the emotion is the immediate reaction of a shout; then after the cry of victory some contemplation results in a musical response. For example, when God delivered the Hebrews at the Red Sea, Moses, Miriam, and the people sang (Exod. 15:1, 20-21).

Vocabulary of Joy

Table 24.1 charts the five main words the psalmists use to express this elation over salvation. There are 149 occurrences of these verbs for this particular theme. The totals at the bottom of the table indicate the distribution of each verb according to the five Books of Psalms. Table 24.2 lists the occurrences of an additional dozen terms with a cumulative total of 69 for this concept.

---

[1] Page 991.

Theological Themes of Psalms

Table 24.1 Key Terms for Rejoicing

Hebrew words: Psalm	שמח samakh be glad	זמר zamar sing	רנן ranan shout for joy	שיר shiyr sing	גיל giyl rejoice
2:					11
5:	11		11		
7:		17			
9:	2	2, 11			14
13:				6	5
14:	7				7
16:	9				9
18:		49			
20:			5		
21:	1	13		13	1
27:		6		6	
30:	1	4, 12			
31:	7				7
32:	11		11		11
33:	21	2	1	3	
34:	2				
35:	27		27		9
40:	16				
47:		6[4], 7			
48:	11				11
51:			14		8
53:	6				6
57:		7, 9		7	
58:	10				
59:		17	16	16	
61:		8			
63:	11		7		
64:	10				
65:			8	13	
66:	6	2, 4[2]			
67:	4		4		
68:	3	4, 32		4, 32	
69:	32				
70:	4				
71:		22, 23	23		
75:		9			
81:			1		
84:			2		
85:	6				
86:	4				
89:			12	1	16
90:	14, 15		14		
92:	4	1	4		
95:			1		
96:	11		12	1[2], 2	11
97:	1, 8, 12				1, 8
98:		4 5	4 8	1	
101:		1		1	
104:	34	33		33	

Hebrew words:	שמח *samakh*	זמר *zamar*	רנן *ranan*	שיר *shiyr*	גיל *giyl*
Psalm	be glad	sing	shout for joy	sing	rejoice
105:	3	2		2	
106:	5			12	
107:	30, 42				
108:		1, 3		1	
109:	28				
118:	24				24
119:	74				
122:	1				
126:	3				
132:			9, 16		
135:		3			
137:				3, 4	
138:		1		5	
144:		9		9	
145:			7		
146:		2			
147:		1, 7			
149:	2	3	5	1	2
totals:	**42** (12/10/2/10/8)	**41** (9/16/1/6/9)	**24** (5/6/3/6/4)	**24** (4/5/1/8/6)	**18** (9/3/1/3/2)

Table 24.2 Additional Terms in Psalms for Rejoicing

Hebrew	English	#	References	Totals: Ps./all
גִּיל	rejoicing	2	43:4; 65:12	3/9
זִמְרָה	song	2	81:3; 98:5	2/4
זָמִיר	song	2	95:2; 119:54	2/7
עָלַז	exult	4	28:7; 68:4; 96:12; 149:5	7/17
עָלַץ	rejoice	3	5:11; 9:2; 68:3	4/8
עָנָה	sing	2	119:172; 147:7	3/14
רוּעַ	shout	9	47:1; 65:13; 66:1; 81:1; 95:1, 2; 98:4, 6; 100:1	12/44
רִנָּה	shout of joy	9	30:5; 42:4; 47:1; 105:43; 107:22; 118:15; 126:2, 5, 6	15/34
רְנָנָה	shout of joy	2	63:5; 100:2	2/4
שׂוּשׂ	rejoice	6	35:9; 40:16; 68:3; 70:4; 119:14, 162	7/27
שִׂמְחָה	gladness	9	4:7; 16:11; 21:6; 30:11; 43:4; 68:3; 97:11; 100:2; 106:5	13/94
שָׂשׂוֹן	joy	3	51:12; 105:43; 119:111	5/22
שִׁיר	song	12	28:7; 33:3; 40:3; 42:8; 69:30; 96:1; 98:1; 137:3[2], 4; 144:9; 149:1	12/47
תְּרוּעָה	shout of joy	4	27:6; 33:3; 47:5; 89:15	5/36

The most frequent in the first group is שמח (*samakh*), a common verb (used 156x in the OT) occurring 52 times in Psalms, 41 times to indicate specifically the rejoicing over Yahweh's deliverance.[2] Table 24.1 includes an adjective ("glad" in 126:3) to make the total 42.The related noun שִׂמְחָה (simkhah), "gladness," occurs nine more times for this idea. Psalms uses three less common synonymous verbs that express this same emotional feeling: שׂוּשׂ (suws; 6x), עָלַז ('alaz; 4x), and עָלַץ ('alats; 3x). In fact, the first of these appears twice before שָׂמַח (samakh) in the same verse: "Let all those that seek thee rejoice and be glad in thee" (40:16; 70:4). The related noun שָׂשׂוֹן (sasown), "joy," refers to this specific theme in three of its five occurrences (for example, "the joy of thy salvation," 51:12).

Of the remaining four key words, two designate the immediate outward response of a joyful shout (a combined total of 42x). The verbs רנן (ranan; 53x in the OT, 25x total in Psalms) and גִּיל (giyl; 47x in the OT, 25x in Psalms) can each be used for any kind of shout, not necessarily of rejoicing over salvation. The first verb refers to a cry of despair in 17:1, and the cognate noun גִּיל (giyl) related to the second verb describes a wedding shout of joy in 45:15.[3] Cognate with the first verb are the nouns רִנָּה (rinnah; 9 of its 15 occurrences in Psalms for rejoicing in the Lord) and רְנָנָה (renanah; 63:5; 100:2). Another word for shouting, רוּע (ruw'), in nine of its twelve occurrences signifies this joyful shout; it is the Hebrew behind the familiar "make a joyful noise" (100:1). In three cases it appears in the same verse as רנן (ranan) (81:1; 95:1; 98:4). The connections between these terms is clear when we consider that שָׂמַח (samakh) and גִּיל (giyl) appear in the same verse twelve times, five times with שָׂמַח first and seven times with גִּיל first. In fact, שָׂמַח occurs in close context, often in the same verse, with all of the other main verbs and with six of the additional ones. There are numerous other cases of the eighteen terms listed in the two tables being joined with one another in pairs or triads in the same verse, sometimes in poetic parallelism. In the first five verses of Psalm 149 all five of the main verbs occur as well as עָלַז ('alaz; v. 5) and שִׁיר (shiyr; v. 1).

---

[2] In other cases the term refers to the joy of enemies over the plight of the righteous (35:15, 19, 24; 38:16; 89:42), a bridegroom over music (45:8), and the city of God over its streams (46:4). God's precepts can gladden the heart (19:8); so can wine (104:15). Egypt was glad when the tribes left (105:38). In other contexts it is Yahweh Himself that rejoices over something (for example, 60:6; 104:31; 108:7, 9). Of course, all such verses are **not** included in the data of the tables below.

[3] Its two other occurrences in Psalms fit our theme here (43:4; 65:13). Michael A. Grisanti has aptly defined this word as "a spontaneous, vocal outburst of rejoicing." "גיל," *NIDOTTE*, 1:855.

After the shout of joy comes the celebration by music. In contrast, the Jewish exiles question the possibility of singing and playing musical instruments while in distress (137:2-4). The two main verbs, זמר (*zamar*) and שִׁיר (*shiyr*), referring to the musical reaction to God's deliverance appear 41 and 24 times, respectively. They are almost always translated as "sing." There are cognate nouns related to these verbs: appearing twice each are זָמִיר (*zamiyr*), "song," and זִמְרָה (*zimrah*), "song" or "melody";[4] שִׁיר (*shiyr*), "song," occurs a dozen times.[5] There is one more possible term: the verb עָנָה (*'anah*; 119:172; 147:7), that has not always been recognized because translators have confused it with its common homonym (*to answer*).

Closely associated with the singing response are various musical instruments. This would further indicate that some amount of planning was necessary for this activity. Table 24.3 lists four instruments[6] that occur in contexts of joy. Psalm 150:3-5 mentions all four of them as well as three others that are used only once in the book: מִנִּים (*minniym*),[7] "stringed instruments," עוּגָב (*'uwgav*), "flute," צְלְצְלִים (*tseltseliym*), "cymbals." Two more terms occur just once in Psalms: עָשׂוֹר (*'asowr*), "ten-stringed instrument" (92:3), and חֲצֹצְרָה (*khetsowtserah*), "trumpet" (98:6; 28x elsewhere in the

Table 24.3 Musical Instruments Connected with Rejoicing

Hebrew	transliteration	English	References	Totals: Ps./all
כִּנּוֹר *kinnowr*		lyre	33:2; 43:4; 57:8; 71:22; 81:2; 92:3; 98:5[2]; 108:2; 147:7; 149:3; 150:3 (+ two more not related to joy)	14/42
נֵבֶל *neval*		harp	33:2; 57:8; 71:22; 81:2; 92:3; 108:2; 144:9; 150:3	8/38
שׁוֹפָר *showpher*		horn	47:5; 81:3; 98:6; 150:3	4/72
תֹּף *towph*		tambourine	81:2; 149:3; 150:4	3/17

---

[4] Possibly 118:14 contains a third usage, but some scholars have argued that the word there is a homonym that means "protection." See Allen, 162.

[5] This noun occurs an additional 30x in the psalm titles, not counted in the statistics of the table.

[6] For a discussion of the identification of these instruments based on documentary data as well as details from archaeology about the their nature, see D. A. Foxvog and A. D. Kilmer, "Music," *ISBEr*, 3:438-44.

[7] This term may occur also in 45:8, where it would be connected to joy. Note the following translations: ASV, NASB, ESV, HCSB, and NET. See the explanation in Delitzsch, 2:85.

OT). Possibly connected to the instruments is the practice of hand-clapping, though this may relate simply to the shout of joy, as 47:1 indicates.

Propositions

The Holy Spirit teaches us seven truths on this theme of joy. Many of the verses on this theme present an exhortation, indeed the command, to rejoice. In propositional form, (1) *God requires all His creatures to react joyfully.* Of the 216 instances of the vocabulary for joy, 41 are plural imperatives:[8] someone is telling a group to rejoice, even with shouting and singing. When we ask the question, who is speaking? we naturally think of the psalmist. The first instance appears in 2:11, "rejoice with trembling." In this Davidic psalm many think of David both as the Anointed in verse two and the author; however, more careful contemplation backed up by New Testament revelation results in significant insight. The one speaking in verses 10-12 would seem to be distinct from the Son (v. 12), Himself the Anointed. Since the New Testament identifies David as a prophet who speaks about his Son, the Anointed (Acts 2:30), we are warranted in viewing the ultimate speaker in these verses as the Holy Spirit Himself. Thus it would make sense that throughout the book the Holy Spirit is commanding the responses of rejoicing, shouting, and singing. The one exception is 137:3, where the Babylonian captors order the Jews to sing a song of Zion. The psalmist himself may complain, pray, and vow to God, but how can he command others to rejoice? Who gives him that authority? He can voice these imperatives only by inspiration as the spokesman of the Holy Spirit, as God's ambassador, just as Paul said, "as though God did beseech you by us: we pray you in Christ's stead" (2 Cor. 5:20). Indeed, rejoicing and festivals are statutes or ordinances from God for His people (81:4). Who are the groups that are being directed to respond in joy? First, it is Israel, God's people (81:1, 4, 8). This is a specific requirement for the "saints" (חֲסִידִים, *khesiydim*; 30:4; 149:1), the righteous or upright (צַדִּיקִים, *tsaddiyqiym*; יְשָׁרִים, *yeshariym*; 32:11; 33:1; 68:4–5; 97:12), God's servants (עֲבָדִים, *'evadiym*; 135:1, 3). But the Holy Spirit extends this obligation far beyond Israel to the "kingdoms of the earth" (68:32) and literally, "all the peoples" (47:1), indeed, "all the earth" (66:1; 96:1; 98:4; 100:1).[9]

---

[8] This includes all the verbs from the two tables except for עָלַץ (*'alats*).

[9] Kidner has discerned the significance of Psalm 47: "The opening summons to *all peoples* sets the scene truly: the vision is world-wide." (15:194).

Related to these imperatives are two other groups of verbs. Many Hebrew jussives[10] are a type of third person imperatives; to express this idea in English we have to use an auxiliary verb like "let" or "may." These can indicate commands, exhortations, or just invitations. First-person plural cohortatives (forms that require the English translation "let us") are ways for someone to encourage, prompt, or invite others to do something. In these cases it would make sense to say that the psalmists are trying to instigate others to rejoice, but the jussives could be interpreted as commands from the Holy Spirit. The presence of a few plural cohortatives, however, would lead us to interpret many of the jussives also as urgings. Thus we arrive at a second proposition: (2) *The saints have a duty to encourage one another and to invite the whole world to rejoice.* The statistics for this point are impressive: 19 verses[11] contain 32 jussives; every one of the nine verbs except רוע (*ruw'*, "shout") occurs; usually these verses contain two jussives. In one case the text says that the rescued ones should "declare his works with rejoicing" (107:22), with the key word being the last noun. The cohortatives of six different verbs appear nine times in six verses (20:5; 21:13; 66:6; 95:1, 2; 118:24). The groups being urged include "all those that put their trust" in God (5:11), those "that favour [the saint's] righteous cause" (35:27), "those that seek" God (40:16; 70:4; 105:3), the people of "mount Zion" (48:11), Jacob (53:6), "the nations" (67:4), "the righteous" (68:3), those whom God has healed (107:20, 22), the ones fearing God (119:74); priests (132:9), "the children of Zion" (147:2–3), and "the saints" (חֲסִידִים, *khesiydim*).

What is the reason for the joy? The "why" of rejoicing is the third proposition: (3) *God has already done great things that the saints and all mankind should celebrate.* The most obvious of these works is the Lord's provision of the deliverance for which the saint has pleaded. For example, David proclaimed that the Lord "inclined unto me, and heard my cry. He brought me up also out of an horrible pit, out of the miry clay, and set my feet upon a rock, and established my goings"; then there was "a new song" in

---

[10] A jussive is a shortened form of the Hebrew verb that expresses a subjunctive idea. For concise explanation of jussives and cohortatives, see *WHS*, 78–80.

[11] One verse (68:3) is particularly controversial: some commentaries and translations (NET, ESV, HCSB, NAB) regard the three verbs in the verse as present or future tenses whereas others analyze them as jussives (KJV, NASB, NIV, NRSV). In these cases the two forms are the same. Because of the imperatives in the next verse, these are most likely jussives.

Theological Themes of Psalms

David's mouth (40:1–3). Psalm 18 reports, "In my distress I called upon the LORD, and cried unto my God: he heard my voice out of his temple …" (v. 6). Later in this psalm we read, "Therefore will I give thanks unto thee, O LORD, among the heathen, and sing praises unto thy name" (v. 49). In Psalm 34, which mentions rejoicing in verse 2, David reports that Yahweh has already "delivered" (vv. 4, 17) and "saved" (v. 6).

What is not so obvious, however, is the call for rejoicing concerning what God has done in the distant past, His acts in history that have significance for the saints in the present. In a number of cases the same psalm that mentions rejoicing refers to God's historical acts recorded in the Pentateuch. Psalm 66 begins with the imperative for all to "make a joyful noise unto God" (v. 1) and continues by commanding singing, testimony, and worship (vv. 2–4). After mentioning what God did at the Red Sea for Israel, the psalmist says, "There let us rejoice in Him!" (NASB). This is surprising: in context, what we expect is "there did we rejoice in him" (KJV, AV, RSV, ESV). But the Hebrew grammar is clear:[12] the saints are to rejoice about what happened long ago. Broyles has had the insight to understand and to state succinctly what this verse is teaching: "the individual worshipers are … to align their *present* experience of God not only with humanity in general and with corporate Israel in particular but also with past history. Individual worshipers are invited to see their own experience of deliverance in light of the nation's exodus, and vice versa."[13] Psalm 81 begins with Asaph calling for rejoicing; then God recounts His deliverance of Israel from slavery in Egypt (vv. 6, 10). Additional psalms tie together present rejoicing with the past exodus and conquest events (105, 106, and 135).

Sometimes the psalmists connect the theme of joy with God's long-past creative acts. The premier creation psalm ends with Yahweh rejoicing

---

[12] The grammatical form is clearly cohortative: נִשְׂמְחָה (*nismekhah*). What some of the commentators claim is that this is a special usage: "since the cohortative form of the future can also … be referred to the past, and does sometimes at least occur where the writer throws himself back into the past (2 Sam. 22:38), the rendering: Then did we rejoice in Him, cannot be assailed on syntactical grounds." Delitzsch, 2:234–35. Waltke regards this form as a "pseudo-cohortative … used to refer to past time." *IBHS*, 576 (§34.5.3b2). See also GKC, §108g. The LXX translated it as a future.

[13] Page 275. Harmon confirms this: "The recollection of past divine actions is meant to form the basis of continuing praise" (1:483).

over His works (104:31) and a twofold mention of the psalmist's joy (vv. 33–34). In Psalm 33, which uses five different terms for joy (vv. 1–3, 21), we are told, "By the word of the LORD were the heavens made; and all the host of them by the breath of his mouth" (v. 6), and that God "spake, and it was done; he commanded, and it stood fast" (v. 9). The saints can rejoice because what God says always happens, just as it did in creation. Psalms 95 and 96 each begin with the theme of joy and then declare that God made sea, dry land, hills (95:4–5), and heaven, firmly establishing the world (96:5, 10). Psalm 146 promises singing in joy (v. 2) then states that the Lord "made heaven, and earth, the sea, and all that therein is" (v. 6). In the next psalm after beginning with joy (147:1, 7), the poet moves to a long list of the created elements: clouds, rain, grass, food for animals, wheat, snow, frost, ice, and wind (vv. 8–9, 14, 16–19). Indeed, connected with rejoicing over God's past act of creation is the rejoicing over what we presently observe in nature. For example, Psalm 65 speaks of the shout of joy (vv. 8, 13) in reference to mountains, waves, dawn, sunset, rivers, showers, pastures, hills, meadows, and valleys as well as their abundant production of grain and flocks (vv. 7–13). Furthermore, fourteen (9, 31, 40, 71, 75, 86, 96, 98, 105, 106, 107, 118, 119, 145) of the 72 psalms that mention joy also refer to God's wonders (פלא, *pala'*), which can be either His works in nature or history. For example, David says, "I will shew forth all thy marvellous works. I will be glad and rejoice in thee: I will sing praise to thy name" (9:1b–2a).

The saints have cause to rejoice not only in what God has already done but also in what God has said He will do. This leads to another proposition: (4) *on the basis of faith and hope the saints rejoice about what God has promised to do in the future.* In several of the laments, after the psalmist prays, in some way God assures him deliverance; then the psalmist rejoices in anticipation.[14] For example, in Psalm 13 David cries out in sorrow to God (vv. 1–4), then expresses his faith (v. 5a), and finally celebrates: "my heart shall rejoice in thy salvation. I will sing unto the LORD, because he hath dealt bountifully[15] with me" (vv. 5b–6). In Psalm 27 David perceives the danger

---

[14] Kidner describes this phenomenon as follows: "This sudden access of confidence, found in almost every suppliant psalm, is most telling evidence of an answering touch from God, almost as if we saw the singer's face light up in recognition" (15:79).

[15] Ross understands the verb here as a future perfect: "because he shall have dealt bountifully with me" (1:370).

his enemies intend (vv. 2–3), but he clearly has confidence in the Lord (v. 5) because of God's message for him to trust, perhaps reflected in the last verse: "Wait for the LORD; Be strong and let your heart take courage; Yes, wait for the LORD" (NASB); then he speaks of joy and singing (v. 6). On another occasion David describes the wicked (58:2–4), asks God to punish them (vv. 6–8), confidently affirms that indeed He will judge (vv. 9b, 10a, 11b), and anticipates joy (v. 10). Another example is Psalm 59, where David expresses his present joy (v. 16) before making his vow (v. 17). It is not just in laments that we see this rejoicing in hope. In Psalm 75, a thanksgiving, after hearing God's promise to judge the wicked (vv. 2-5), the psalmist expresses his joy in what God will do in the future.[16]

It is perfectly understandable that the psalmists would mention joy as they write hymns of praise and thanksgiving songs (27 out of 43 or 63% contain this element), but significantly almost half (31 out of 63 or 49%) of the psalms of lament contain some reference to rejoicing or song. In fact, every category of psalm contains some cases of joy.[17] This is the "when" of rejoicing. Thus the following proposition is apparent: (5) *joy for God's people is appropriate in all circumstances, even in difficult times.* In situations of distress (4:1; 18:6; 66:14, NASB) and ridicule (4:6) or reproach (31:11; 109:25), in the presence of boastful (5:5; 13:4) and lying enemies (vv. 8–9), facing deadly plots (7:14–15; 9:15) and enduring sickness (69:20, NASB), expecting persecution (119:157) and death (18:4–5; 107:18), the righteous can be glad (4:7; 5:11; 9:2; 14:7; 31:7), rejoice (9:14; 13:5; 14:7; 109:28; 119:162), and sing (5:11; 7:17; 9:11; 13:6; 18:49; 66:2; 69:30; 107:22)! Note that the same psalms that contain the negative circumstances also include the references to joy.

In what way do the saints express their joy? This is the "how" of rejoicing. (6) *It is suitable to express one's joy in an outward manner by shouting, singing, or playing a musical instrument.* The discussion earlier in this chapter about the Hebrew terms demonstrates how often the words for rejoicing are associated with shouting, singing, and playing instruments. The grammatical meaning indicated by the imperatives, jussives, and cohortatives makes the sixth proposition perfectly clear: we see requirements and encouragements for

---

[16] As Futato recognized: "whereas psalms of thanksgiving typically thank God for deliverance from some trouble in the past, Psalm 75 gives thanks for what God will do at some point in the future" (p. 249).

[17] Appendix B lists six main categories and two minor ones.

the saints to convey outwardly their inward gladness. For example, Psalm 98:4 says "Make a joyful noise unto the LORD, all the earth: make a loud noise, and rejoice, and sing praise." Four times rejoicing (שָׂמַח, *samakh*) is followed in the same verse by the term "shout for joy" (רָנַן, *ranan*): 5:11; 32:11; 67:4; 92:4. Psalm 27:6 connects "shouts of joy" (NASB) with singing. In Psalm 13 we find, "my heart shall rejoice in thy salvation. I will sing unto the LORD" (vv. 5b-6a). Additional examples of connections between joy and song include the following: "I will be glad and rejoice in thee: I will sing praise to thy name, O thou most High" (9:2); "my heart greatly rejoiceth; and with my song will I praise him" (28:7); "Sing unto God, sing praises to his name: extol him that rideth upon the heavens by his name JAH, and rejoice before him" (68:4). Psalm 98 illustrates the linking of joyfulness with instrumental music: "Sing unto the LORD with the harp; with the harp, and the voice of a psalm with trumpets and sound of cornet make a joyful noise before the LORD (vv. 5–6).

Another way of expressing of joy is to make promises about the future. When someone experiences something wonderful, often the on-the-spot reaction is to resolve to celebrate further. Sometimes the person pledges, even takes an oath, to plan a special occasion for festivity. And this is what we find in Psalms: vows of celebration. (7) *It is appropriate for the person rescued to vow the response of rejoicing before the Lord.* The psalmists often use first-person singular (1CS) cohortatives to express their determination to sing for joy in God's presence. Grammatically, this particular verb form indicates a request, a desire, uncertainty, or resolve.[18] Only the last nuance fits the context of the eight occurrences of the verb שִׁיר (*shayar*), "sing" (13:6; 27:6; 57:7; 89:1; 101:1; 104:33; 108:1; 144:9). Thus the psalmists were making a promise, in fact, a vow. In Psalm 61:8 David says, "So will I sing praise [a cohortative] unto thy name for ever, that I may daily perform my vows," clearly linking the act of vowing with that particular grammatical form.

The five other verbs (not counting "sing") in the two tables above occur as 1CS cohortatives 20 times in 15 different psalms: 7:17; 9:2 (3x), 14; 18:49; 27:6; 31:7 (2x); 57:7; 59:17; 61:8; 71:22–23; 75:9; 101:1; 104:33; 108:1; 144:9; 146:2. Fifteen of these are the verb זָמַר (*zamar*): "I will sing praise," a resolution or vow. For example, Psalm 7 ends "with a vow to praise

---

[18] "In cases where the speaker has the ability to carry out an inclination it takes on the coloring of resolve …." Bruce K. Waltke and M. O'Connor, *An Introduction to Biblical Hebrew Syntax* (Winona Lake: Eisenbrauns, 1990), 573.

Theological Themes of Psalms

God for his justice"[19] (v. 17). In Psalm 71 the aging author, possibly David in his declining years, trustingly (vv. 1a, 3, 5, 14a) pleads with God not to abandon him (vv. 9–11, 18), reminding the Lord about His past occasions of deliverance (vv. 15–17, 19–20); then at the end of the prayer (vv. 22–23) he uses three cohortatives in his vows:[20] "I will also praise thee with the psaltery," "unto thee will I sing with the harp," and "Yes, I will sing your praises" (NET), the last two clauses using זמר (*zamar*). Psalm 75 "ends with the individual vowing to proclaim what God has done"[21] and to sing in approval. In Psalm 144:9 "the king [David] makes a vow to sing and play … a song of thanksgiving, newly composed for the occasion, in commemoration of God's newly coming to his aid."[22] Furthermore, there are psalms that indicate a vow without using the 1CS cohortative. David ends Psalm 30 with a promise to sing and praise God eternally (v. 12).[23] Psalm 35:28 is a similar example, though mentioning praise rather than joy.

New Testament Echoes

In the New Testament joy is a common theme, even venerated as a fruit of the Spirit (Gal. 5:22). There are two key verbs: χαίρω (*khairō*), used 74 times in 68 different verses, and ἀγαλλιάω (*agalliaō*), used eleven times.[24] The noun related to the former is χαρά (*khara*), used 59 times in 57 verses. Many of these uses, however, are not relevant to our theme, referring rather to mundane joy unrelated to God (for example, Mk. 14:11) and as a means of greeting (for example, Acts 23:26) or farewell (2 Cor. 13:11).

---

[19] Futato, 51.

[20] As VanGemeren recognizes: "The Psalm concludes on a vow to praise Yahweh publicly for his fidelity" (p. 543). Leupold says, "From this point onward resolution to praise the Lord occupies all the singer's thoughts …. He is resolved …" (p. 515).

[21] Futato, 250.

[22] Allen, 364. Futato agrees with the vow classification (p. 425).

[23] Ross recognized the vow here: "The psalmist, restored to his life in God's favor, vows to praise him forever" (1:678). So did Futato here and in 35:28 (pp. 123, 138).

[24] Some additional verbs are used, for example, in OT quotations because of the wording in the LXX (Acts 2:26; Rom. 15:10; Gal. 4:27).

The New Testament reaffirms each of the first six propositions. (1) First, the "who" that God commands to rejoice would be Christians, yes and even the whole universe. With apostolic authority Paul uses the plural imperative from χαίρω (*khairō*) to tell the saints what God expects from them: "Finally, my brethren, rejoice in the Lord"; "Rejoice in the Lord always: and again I say, Rejoice" (Phil. 3:1; 4:4). The apostle John writes, "Therefore rejoice, *ye* heavens, and ye that dwell in them" (Rev. 12:12a), and "Rejoice over her, *thou* heaven, and *ye* holy apostles and prophets ..." (18:20). (2) Encouraging and inviting others to rejoice occurs in Revelation 19:7, when a great multitude says, "Let us be glad and rejoice, and give honour to him: for the marriage of the Lamb is come ...." In another passage we find, "let us offer the sacrifice of praise to God continually ..." (Heb. 13:15). This is related to the admonition to "consider one another to provoke unto love and to good works" in the context of assembling together (Heb. 10:24–25).

(3) The New Testament mentions various occasions of joy over what God has already accomplished. There was rejoicing over the birth of John the Baptist, the miracle God performed for a childless couple in order to prepare for the Messiah (Lk. 1:14). Jesus tells the disciples that they will have continuous joy when they see Him again and realize that His resurrection has happened (John 16:22). The women at the tomb, learning that the resurrection of Jesus had occurred, returned to the city in "great joy" (Matt. 28:8). The Philippian jailer rejoiced that God had just saved him (Acts 16:34). Paul rejoiced that God was bringing about the propagation of the Gospel in the world (Phil. 1:18). John "rejoiced greatly" as he recognized what God had done in the sanctification of those he had evangelized (2 John 4; 3 John 3). (4) The "why" of rejoicing shows up also in the indications that Christians "rejoice in hope" (Rom. 5:2). Christ tells his disciples that when they experience persecution, they are to "rejoice, and be exceeding glad: for great is your reward in heaven" (Matt. 5:12), a clear case of looking to the future in faith. Peter writes to believers to instruct them to rejoice as they look forward to Christ's second coming (1 Pet. 4:13). Earlier in the epistle the apostle noted that "though now ye see him not, yet believing, ye rejoice with joy unspeakable and full of glory" (1:8).

(5) The "when" of rejoicing surfaces as the New Testament indicates that joy is appropriate for all occasions. Paul rejoiced in all his circumstances, even paradoxically in his times of sorrow (2 Cor. 6:10). Peter writes to persecuted believers concerning their salvation: "Wherein ye greatly rejoice, though now for a season, if need be, ye are in heaviness through manifold

temptations" (1 Pet. 1:6). (6) Concerning the "how" of rejoicing, the topic of music and song appears seldom in the New Testament,[25] with no direct connections between joy and music. Possibly the reason for this is the fact that there is no additional book of hymns in the New Testament. The Old Testament book sufficed for the church, and Christians have always read it and applied its theological themes to their lives.[26] We know from a few passages that song was a part of the early church services: Jesus and the disciples sang at the Last Supper (Matt. 26:30), Paul and Silas sang in jail (Acts 16:25), and Paul refers to sacred edification in the church by means of "psalms and hymns and spiritual songs, singing and making melody in your heart to the Lord" (Eph. 5:19; also Col. 3:16). No doubt this singing was a reflection of the inward spiritual fruit of joy.

Finally, "Rejoice in the LORD, O ye righteous: for praise is comely for the upright" (33:1).

---

[25] "Superficially the NT appears almost to disregard music. Outside of the Book of Revelation, in which music is part of a rich eschatological drama, there are not more than a dozen passages in the entire canon ...." H. M. Best and D. Huttar, "Music; Musical Instruments," *ZPEB*, 4:316.

[26] Furthermore, vowing is mentioned infrequently in the New Testament, mainly in the book of Acts. A very negative case appears as Herod takes an oath before his dinner guests to grant the daughter of Herodias any wish, resulting in the beheading of John the Baptist (Mk. 6:22–28).

25

Praise

Joy over deliverance leads naturally to praise for the person who effected the deliverance. Joy is an emotion that can express itself in the actions of shouting, singing, playing musical instruments, and making vows. Although it is an item that belongs in this list of expressions, praise can occur independent of joy since it is a verbal response that is more closely related to the creature's rational nature than to his emotional. As human beings made in God's image, we are capable of thinking, reasoning, and evaluating ourselves and others. When we observe attributes or actions that we approve, we voice our admiration. If we vent self-admiration, that is called boasting. For example, the Lord warns, "Let not the wise man glory [boast] in his wisdom, neither let the mighty man glory in his might, let not the rich man glory in his riches" (Jer. 9:23). When we articulate high regard for someone else, that is praise. For example, when the Egyptians noticed Sarah's beauty, they "praised her to Pharaoh" (Gen. 12:15, NASB). Of course, in this chapter we focus on the praise of God. Theological praise is doxological;[1] that is, it gives glory to God. The classic hymn that begins the long list of Scriptural poems of praise for God is Exodus 15:1-19, the Song of Moses, that exalts Yahweh (v. 2). The book of Psalms picks up on that theme and by employing a wealth of vocabulary greatly expands it.

---

[1] "The psalms voice and lead praise that is *doxological*. The hymns are composed and sung to give God the glory—or, better stated, to recognize and testify that the glory belongs to God." James Luther Mays, *The Lord Reigns: A Theological Handbook to the Psalms* (Louisville: Westminster John Knox, 1994), 63. In Scripture praise for God is first mentioned when Noah said, "Praise the LORD, the God of Shem" (Gen. 9:26a, HCSB). Melchizedek praised the most High God (Gen. 14:20), and Leah said, "Now will I praise the LORD: therefore she called his name Judah" (from the Hebrew root יָדָה [*yadah*], which is often translated "thank").

245

Theological Themes of Psalms

The ancient Jewish name for the book is *Tihillim* (תְּהִלִּים),[2] a noun meaning "praises," a clear indication of the importance of this theme for this book. Although Psalms refers both to boasting (10:3; 12:3; 49:6; 52:1; 75:4; 94:4) and to praise of other people (49:18; 97:7), over half of the psalms (82) touch on this doxological theme in 198 different verses (8% of the verses in the book).[3] Of course, this theme is at the center of mankind's worship of God. In proper worship God must be the focus, not man, nor how he feels. It is difficult to imagine a positive emphasis on God in the absence of praise.

Vocabulary of Praise

Table 25.1 charts the four main words for the theme of praise, three verbs and one noun. There are 223 occurrences of these terms concerning praising God or the Messiah. The totals at the bottom of the table indicate the distribution of each word according to the five Books of Psalms. Notice the dominance of this theme in Book V (109 cases). Table 25.2 lists the occurrences of an additional six terms with a cumulative total of 32 for this concept in Psalms.

The most frequent in the first group is הלל (*halal*), a common verb (used 165x in the OT) occurring 89 times in Psalms,[4] 84 times for glorifying God. In three of the other five times the word occurs, it is grammatically marked (parsed as *hithpael*) and refers to praising oneself for something, which is boasting (49:6, concerning riches; 52:1, evil acts; 97:7, idols of pagan

---

[2] The form of this word (masculine plural) does not occur in Biblical Hebrew, possibly this was a special term used only for this book. See Kraus, 1:11. The usual plural form in the Bible is feminine.

[3] "The praise of God is a golden thread that runs through the fabric of the book." Mark D. Futato, *Transformed by Praise: The Purpose and Message of the Psalms* (Phillipsburg, N. J.: P&R Publishing, 2002), 3.

[4] A homonym of הלל (*halal*) occurs five times in Psalms: 5:5; 73:3; 75:4 [2]; 102:8. The KJV has used "foolish," "fool," "foolishly," or "mad" as translations. The modern translations use "boastful" or "arrogant" (for example, NASB, ESV, HCSB, NIV, and RSV). Poetic parallelism in the first two verses makes clear that we are speaking about the wicked; thus "the foolish" or the "arrogant" would fit well. In 75:4, however, the parallel "lift not up the horn" would seem to favor the translation "boastful." I prefer the idea that this verbal root refers to being or acting crazy (as indicated in 1 Sam. 21:14). For a discussion of the possible meanings of this term, see Chou-Wee Pan, "הלל (*hll* III)," *NIDOTTE*, 1:1038–40; Leonard J. Coppes, "הָלַל (*hālal*) III," *TWOT*, 1:218–19.

Table 25.1 Key Terms for Praise

Hebrew words: Psalm	הלל *halal* praise	ידה *yadah* praise	ברך *barak* bless	תְּהִלָּה *tehillah* praise
6:		5		
7:		17		
9:		1		14
16:			7	
18:	3	49	46	
22:	22, 23, 26			3, 25
26:			12	
28:		7	6	
30:		4, 9, 12		
31:			21	
33:		2		1
34:	2		1	1
35:	18	18		28
40:				3
41:			13	
42:		5, 11		
43:		4, 5		
44:	8	8		
45:		17		
48:	1			10
51:				15
52:		9		
54:		6		
56:	4, 10[2]			
57:		9		
63:	5, 11		4	
64:	10			
65:				1
66:			8, 20	2, 8
67:		3[2], 5[2]		
68:			19, 26, 35	
69:	30, 34			
71:		22		6, 8, 14
72:			15, 18, 19	
74:	21			
75:		1[2]		
76:		10		
78:				4
79:		13		13
84:	4			
86:		12		
88:		10		
89:		5	52	
92:		1		
96:	4		2	
97:		12		
99:		3		
100:		4	4	4
102:	18			21

Theological Themes of Psalms

Hebrew words:	הלל	ידה	ברך	תְּהִלָּה
	halal	yadah	barak	tehillah
Psalm	praise	praise	bless	praise
103:			1, 2, 20, 21, 22[2]	
104:	35		1, 35	
105:	3, 45	1		
106:	1, 5, 48	1, 47	48	2, 12, 47
107:	32	1, 8, 15, 21, 31		
108:		3		
109:	30	30		1
111:	1	1		10
112:	1			
113:	1[3], 3, 9		2	
115:	17, 18		18	
116:	19			
117:	1, 2			
118:		1, 19, 21, 28, 29	26	
119:	164, 175	7, 62	12	171
122:		4		
124:			6	
134:			1 2	
135:	1[3], 3, 21		19[2], 20[2], 21	
136:		1, 2, 3, 26		
138:		1, 2, 4		
139:		14		
140:		13		
142:		7		
144:			1	
145:	2, 3	10	1, 2, 10, 21	21
146:	1[2], 2, 10			
147:	1, 12, 20			1
148:	1[3], 2[2], 3[2], 4, 5, 7, 13, 14			14
149:	1, 3, 9			1
150:	1[3], 2[2], 3[2], 4[2], 5[2], 6[2]			
totals:	84 (6/10/2/8/58)	65 (10/14/7/7/27)	45 (7/9/1/11/17)	29 (7/8/2/5/7)

Table 25.2 Additional Terms in Psalms for Praise

Hebrew	English	#	References	Totals: Ps./all
גּדל	magnify	2	34:3; 69:30	2/25
כבד	glorify	5	22:23; 50:15, 23; 86:9, 12	7/38
רום	exalt	7	30:1; 34:3; 99:5, 9; 107:32; 118:28; 145:1	14/27
רוֹמֵם	praise	2	66:17; 149:6	2/2
שבח	praise	5	63:3; 106:47; 117:1; 145:4; 147:12	5/8
תּוֹדָה	thanksgiving	11	26:7; 42:4; 50:14, 23; 56:12; 69:30; 95:2; 100:4; 107:22; 116:17; 147:7	12/32

gods).[5] In the two other cases (10:3; 78:63) the praising is directed toward humans, not God. In addition the related noun תְּהִלָּה (*tihillah*), "praise," occurs 29 times.[6]

Psalms uses six other verbs that express this same idea. The verb יָדָה (*yadah*) presents somewhat of a difficulty: in Psalms the KJV translates this verb as "praise" 43 times and as "give thanks" 23 times[7] whereas NASB uses "praise" only 15 times and "give thanks" 50 times.[8] So, does this word refer to praise or thanksgiving? We normally think of praise as something we express about someone (the object of praise) to another person and thanksgiving as what we express directly to the person himself. Of course, we are capable also of addressing praise directly to the person we highly esteem. In Hebrew the word יָדָה (*yadah*) clearly has a usage as a synonym for הלל (*halal*),[9] as indicated in the following verses: 109:30 and 111:1. Basically, יָדָה communicates the idea of acknowledging some fact. If that fact is one's sin, then it means "confess," for example Psalm 32:5 ("I will confess my transgressions unto the LORD"). On the other hand, if someone in gratitude acknowledges what someone else has done for him in answering a request, then it is thanksgiving (for example, "I thank you that you have answered me," 118:21a, ESV). If a person acknowledges someone else's desirable attributes or wonderful deeds, then it is praise (for example, 107:8). If those

---

[5] The *hithpael* occurs five other times in reference to praising God (34:2; 63:11; 64:10; 105:3; 106:5), raising the question of why the reflexive form. Ross thinks that it "emphasizes the intensive, iterative nature of the word. He [the psalmist] will praise regularly and repeatedly ..." (1:748). But a better idea comes from Alexander, who suggests that this indicates "glorying": this is a verbal "form ... denoting a more permanent affection of the mind, to *glory, i.e.* to exult in the possession and enjoyment of some admired and beloved object" (p. 153). He elaborated further in later comments, saying that a saint will "felicitate himself on the possession of these glorious distinctions and advantages" (p. 281); the psalmist says, "congratulate yourselves that you possess a right and interest in the favour of so glorious a Being" (p. 437).

[6] The term occurs an additional time in the title of Psalm 145:1 ("David's Psalm of praise").

[7] In one of these cases (100:4) the KJV has "be thankful." In one case (49:18) men are praising other men, not God.

[8] One additional case is 28:7, where the translation is "shall thank."

[9] To translate these Hebrew verbs in Psalms, the LXX usually uses the verbs ἐξομολογέω (*exomologeō*) and αἰνέω (*aineō*), both of which mean "praise."

249

deeds were done for someone's benefit, the acknowledgement could include thankfulness; therefore, thanksgiving can be one part of praise.[10] The related noun תּוֹדָה (*towdah*) appears eleven times in Psalms.[11] This is the word Leviticus uses for a thank offering (7:12–15). A check of seven English translations (KJV, NASB, ASV, RSV, NRSV, ESV, and HCSB) reveals that they have rendered this noun as "thanksgiving" 90% of the time.[12]

Another difficulty concerns the term בָרַךְ (*barak*), usually translated "bless." There is, however, a clear distinction between God's blessing a man and a creature blessing God. When God blesses someone, He prospers that person or makes him successful. For example, "So the LORD blessed the latter end of Job more than his beginning" (Job 42:12a). When men bless God, however, they are not empowering Him but actually praising Him: "God blesses people by conferring good on them; we bless God by praising the good in him."[13] This happens in any case where the an inferior blesses a superior; for example, Joab blessing David (2 Sam. 14:22), the people blessing Solomon (1 Kings 8:66), and the afflicted blessing Job (29:13). The verbal

---

[10] The distinction that Claus Westermann makes between "descriptive praise," which appreciates "God for his actions and his being as a whole," and "declarative praise," which focuses on something specific that God has done for the person, may be helpful; however, his attempt to identify the former with הלל (*halal*) and the latter with ידה (*yadah*) misses the strong indications of synonymy. *Praise and Lament in the Psalms,* trans. Keith R. Crim and Richard N. Soulen (Atlanta: John Knox, 1981), 31f. Furthermore, his claim that ידה never refers to thanksgiving as we understand the concept (p. 27) goes too far. He claims that "for primitive man [who speaks in the OT] an attitude does not exist except in its expression," but for us moderns we can have "the thankful attitude" that "can then be expressed in a variety of ways" (pp. 28–29). The New Testament makes clear that this notion of gratitude exists in the nature of mankind (though it can be suppressed): Paul speaks of man owing God both praise ("glorified") and thanks (Rom. 1:21). We may note, however, that in the NT the Greek words εὐχαριστία (*eukharistia*) and εὐχαριστέω (*eukharisteow*) used for thanksgiving do not occur in the LXX translation of Psalms. Westermann does admit, however, that "The expression of thanks to God is included in praise, *it is a way of praising*" [his emphasis] (p. 27).

[11] An additional time occurs in the title of Psalm 100:1 ("A Psalm of praise").

[12] The KJV uses "praise" three times (42:4; 50:23; 56:12) and HCSB "thank offering" twice (50:14, 23). Only in 42:4 NASB, RSV, and NRSV use the word "thanksgiving."

[13] Michael L. Brown, "בָרַךְ (*brk* II)," *NIDOTTE,* 1:764.

root בָרַך (*barak*) actually occurs in Psalms 74 times.[14] Table 25.1 records just those 45 cases where the word refers to praising God. The Geneva Bible translated בָּרוּך (*baruwk*; "blessed") with "praysed" a few times (66:20; 68:19; 124:6), but the KJV did not follow suit.[15]

Five other words occur in Psalms to express praise for God. The verb שָׁבַח (*shavakh*) occurs in Aramaic and Arabic as well as in Hebrew, but only eight times in the Old Testament, five times in Psalms. The verbal root גָּדַל (*gadal*) means "to be great"; when it occurs in the *piel* theme, it is causative: "to make great" or "to magnify." In this latter usage it is a synonym for "praise": "O magnify the LORD with me" (34:3a); "I will praise the name of God with a song, and will magnify him with thanksgiving" (69:30). Two other verbs work basically the same way: כָבַד (*kavad*) means "to be honored" or "to be glorified" with its causative carrying the sense "to glorify or honor" (8x in Psalms, five in reference to God); and רוּם (*ruwm*) means "to be high" with its causative conveying exalting or extoling (14x in our book, seven for the Lord). Related to the latter is the noun רוֹמַם (*rowmam*), "praise," occurring twice in Psalms (66:17; 149:6).

A careful examination of the two tables will reveal that the ten terms listed are connected in the same verse in 22 different combinations. Psalm

---

[14] The homonym בָרַך (*brk* I), "to kneel," occurs once in 95:6 ("let us kneel before the Lord our maker").

[15] The NIV reflects this distinction between "bless" and "praise" by different translations for the two categories. For the 45 cases of בָרַך (*barak*) in the table, it uses "praise" 40x and "extol" 3x (34:1; 115:18; 145:1). The two other cases are somewhat controversial. Is 72:15 part of a prayer by the people for God to bless a Davidic king, or is this a messianic passage where the King, the Lord Jesus, Yahweh Himself, is blessed by mankind? Steveson says, "The remainder of the psalm [after v. 1] deals with various aspects of the kingdom of the Lord" (p. 273). See also Alexander's comments on this passage (pp. 310–12). In the second case 118:26a is the passage ("Blessed be he that cometh in the name of the LORD") the crowd quoted at Christ's triumphal entry (Matt. 21:9). Many of the people in Jerusalem may not have realized that the psalmist wrote this verse as praise for the divine Messiah, the One coming to save His people. The NIV has treated this clause as someone's wish for God's blessing to be on someone important. Despite the distinction between blessing and praise, it is best to maintain the translation "bless" for בָרַך (*barak*) to preserve the verbal connection between the two senses; besides, the expression "God be blessed" has become standard in Hebrew, Greek, English, and any number of other languages, where people understand it as an formula for divine praise, basically equivalent to "Praise the Lord."

Theological Themes of Psalms

106:47b combines three terms: "Then we will **give thanks** to your holy name, and **boast** about your **praiseworthy** deeds" (NET). In 100:4 two nouns and two verbs all occur together: "Enter into his gates with **thanksgiving**, and into his courts with **praise**: **be thankful** unto him, and **bless** his name."

Propositions

Thorough contemplation of the 198 praise verses and their contexts leads us to at least seven truths about this theme of praising God. (1) *Praise of God is a duty for all creatures.* The evidence for this is abundantly clear since the verb הלל (*halal*) occurs 49 times in the plural imperative.[16] A total of thirty more plural imperatives for five of the other six verbs occur in the book: thirteen times each for ברך (*barak*) and ידה (*yadah*); שבח (*shavakh*) twice (117:1; 147:12); and once each for גדל (*gadal*) ("O magnify the LORD with me," 34:3a) and כבד (*kavad*) ("all ye the seed of Jacob, glorify him," 22:23b). Clearly, the psalmist under inspiration by the Holy Spirit is commanding various groups.[17]

Who are these groups? Obviously, Israel is one: "Bless the LORD, O house of Israel" (135:19a); "O give thanks [ידה (*yadah*)] .... Let Israel now say ..." (118:1–2). The psalmists can refer to the nation as "the congregation" (68:26;[18] 149:1). The instruction is for the "seed of Abraham" or "children of Jacob" as in 105:1, 6, and for "Jerusalem" or "Zion" in 147:12. More

---

[16] Some of these imperatives could be understood as interjections rather than commands. In English "we typically use the words 'praise the Lord' as an exclamation. 'Praise the Lord' is also used in the Book of Psalms as an exclamation.... With one exception (Ps. 135:3), 'hallelujah' occurs only at the beginning or end of a number of psalms .... In these cases 'hallelujah' or 'praise the Lord' serves as a kind of introductory and concluding exclamation of praise." Futato, 7. A good example is 106:48, where the psalmist asks the people to say "Amen," and then ends with the interjection "Praise the LORD!" NASB, ESV, HCSB, NET all end with an exclamation point.

[17] Apparently, this is not evident to everyone. Westermann says, "Freedom and spontaneity belong to the essence of praise; giving thanks can become a duty.... Praise can never, but thanks must often, be commanded" (p. 27). Futato, however, recognized that " 'Praise the Lord' is a command like 'Open the door' " (p. 8).

[18] In this verse several versions interpret the plural ("congregations") as indicating "the great congregation" (NRSV, ESV, NIV, TEV), a superlative usage, but it probably indicates the different choirs and tribes that make up the congregation.

252

specifically Yahweh's servants receive this directive (113:1; 134:1–2; 135:1). This group is also called "the saints" (30:4; 149:1) or "the righteous" (97:12). They are those who "seek the LORD" (105:3) and those "that fear the LORD" (22:23; 135:20). Yes, they are "the redeemed" (107:1–2).

But the charge to praise extends beyond God's chosen people: for "peoples" (66:8; 117:1), for "all the earth" (96:1; 100:1, 4). The exhortation extends beyond the earth: "Bless the LORD, ye his angels .... Bless ye the LORD, all ye his hosts" (103:20–21). Truly, we know from Isaiah 6:3 that angelic beings acknowledge God's attribute of holiness and thus praise Him.

With its ten imperatives and two jussives (used as third-person imperatives), Psalm 148 progresses from an obligation for angels to the requirement of praise from all kinds of inanimate objects (sun, moon, stars, heavens, waters, deeps, fire, hail, snow, vapours, wind, mountains, hills, trees, cedars) and lower forms of life (dragons, beasts, cattle, creeping things, fowl). In this passage the author is employing the poetic device of metonymy of the cause for the effect. These inanimate objects and living organisms attest to the Creator's glory and thus prompt mankind to praise, as indicated by the reason clause ("for") in verse 5b: "for he commanded, and they were created."[19] In fact, the command to praise is for "all his works in all places" (103:22). Indeed, the last verse of the Psalter says, "Let every thing that hath breath praise the LORD" (150:6). Yes, "It is a good thing to give thanks unto the LORD" (92:1a), an excellent requirement!

(2) *Praise includes gratitude.* The Psalms indicate, furthermore, that one of the aspects of praise is the attitude of thankfulness that expresses itself in verbally giving thanks. First, there are the numerous cases where the

---

[19] Steveson recognized this figurative language: "All of these give praise by their existence. Just as a work of art testifies to the creativity of its maker and a symphony to the talent of its composer, so these inanimate objects praise the God Whose wisdom and power brought them into being" (p. 556). Calvin evidently recognized this also, saying about the stars that the psalmist "merely intimates that the glory of God is everywhere to be seen, as if they sang his praises with an audible voice. And here he tacitly reproves the ingratitude of man; for all would hear this symphony, were they at all attent upon considering the works of God. For doth not the sun by his light, and heat, and other marvelous effects, praise his Maker?" The heavenly bodies are "witnesses to reprove our indolence.... And he [the psalmist] asks no other praise than that which may teach us that the stars did not make themselves, nor the rains spring from chance; for notwithstanding the signal proofs we constantly have before our eyes of the divine power, we with shameful carelessness overlook the great author" (5:304–06).

psalmist cries out for help in a specific crisis, receives God's deliverance, and then praises Him in a way that clearly indicates gratitude. In Psalm 30 mentioning that his life was in danger (v. 3), David says, "I cried to thee, O LORD; and unto the LORD I made supplication" (v. 8); he acknowledged that God delivered him (v. 1) and that his weeping has become rejoicing (v. 11); then he ends with "O LORD my God, I will give thanks unto thee for ever" (v. 12). In 35:10 David describes himself as "the poor and the needy," requests that God "rescue my soul from their destructions" (v. 17), and promises, "I will give thee thanks [יָדָה, *yadah*] in the great congregation" (v. 18). In 44:7a the psalmist says, "But thou hast saved us from our enemies," and in the next verse he proclaims, "we will give thanks to your name forever." In 138:3 David remembers that "in the day when I cried thou answeredst me"; therefore, he says, "I will praise [יָדָה, *yadah*; "give thanks," ESV, HCSB] thee with my whole heart" (v. 1). Confirmation for the presence of this attitude comes from the mention of sacrificing a thank offering (תּוֹדָה, *towdah*). For example, in Psalm 50 Asaph talks about this kind of sacrifice twice (vv. 14, 23); notice also 107:22 and 116:17.

Second, the fact that commentaries regularly speak of gratitude in their analysis of psalms that contain praise verses indicates that this aspect is present. For example, Kraus notes that in Psalm 109 when the psalmist experiences deliverance, he will "in gratitude praise his God."[20] Kidner says that in Psalm 105 one aspect of worship is "to show gratitude for past mercies by coming back for more."[21] Futato says that "Psalm 136 is a psalm that expresses gratitude to God for the abundant manifestations of his unfailing love," and he labels the verses into five categories of gratitude, such as "Gratitude for the Faithful Love of the God of Heaven (136:1–3, 26)."[22]

A third indication would be how the word for "bless" (בָּרַךְ, *barak*) is used. Westermann has argued that for the ancient Hebrews where one person wanted to thank another human, this is the verb that did that service (for example, 2 Sam. 14:22).[23] In Psalm 66 after the psalmist recounts his cry (v. 17) and the Lord's answer (v. 19), he says, "Blessed be God" (v. 20), what

---

[20] 2:339.

[21] 2:407. In this same psalm Futato speaks of "the gratitude of the first verse" and "Worship characterized by grateful praise" (p. 336).

[22] Page 406.

[23] Page 27.

we would expect a grateful person to say. Earlier in the passage, the psalmist requests others to express thanks: "O bless our God, ye people" (v. 8a).

The reason it is necessary to command praise and its associated gratitude provides the next proposition. (3) *Praise is contrary to fallen human nature.* The problem is that mankind in a fallen state of rebellion does not care about praising his Creator, and gratitude is generally lacking in the heart. That sinful state is from birth, as David acknowledges about himself (51:5). We know that "The wicked are estranged from the womb: they go astray as soon as they be born, speaking lies" (58:3). Notice from this verse the effect of sin on one's speech, and praise is a matter of communication. Psalms teaches us also that "The wicked, through the pride of his countenance, will not seek after God: God is not in all his thoughts"[24] (10:4). He does not try to find God to make peace with Him because he does not bother even to think about his Creator; therefore, divine praise cannot be present in his heart, much less in his mouth. Since the wicked hold God in contempt (v. 13, פְאָֽן, *na'ats*, "disdain"), they will not glorify Him. God addresses the wicked in Psalm 50:16 and identifies them as those "that forget God" (v. 22).[25] There will not be any praise from them, for the next verse says, "Whoso offereth praise glorifieth me" (v. 23a). Men in their sinful state do not contemplate God's works (28:5a); therefore, they do not praise Him for His creation. They have no interest in seeking or investigating God statutes (119:155b), which instruct us to offer Him honor and glory. Because we all still have this old nature, David says to the Lord, "Search me, O God, and know my heart: try me, and know my thoughts: And see if there be any wicked way in me, and lead me in the way everlasting" (139:23–24).

There are two groups of thoughts that motivate us to praise our God. These are the basis for the next two propositions. We discover these by

---

[24] Most modern English translations render 10:4b as "all his thoughts are, 'There is no God'" (ASV, NASB, RSV, ESV) or with some equivalent (for example, "'There is no God,' sums up his thoughts," NAB). But later verses indicate that this wicked person knows of God's existence (he says, "God hath forgotten," v. 11, and "Thou wilt not requite *it*," v. 13). The Hebrew says very literally, "not God in all his considerations," in other words, he does not ponder God, as the NIV says, "in all his thoughts there is no room for God." In fact, the whole verse can be variously construed. Calvin's comments and the NET Bible note on this verse are very helpful in understanding the different possibilities.

[25] Calvin says, God "also charges them with base ingratitude, in having forgotten God" (2:279).

noticing two phenomena in the text: (a) the mention of praise followed by a causal clause;[26] (b) the connection of praise terms with information about God. The first group would be facts about God's character or nature. (4) *Praise springs from recognizing God's attributes.* As God's rational creatures properly consider God's person, that contemplation drives them to glorify their Lord. Psalms connects numerous attributes of God with our duty to praise, but generally these fall into two main categories: God's goodness and His greatness.[27] The summary statement for the former occurs in 135:3a: "Praise the LORD; for the LORD is good." Several other verses connect His **goodness** to praise: 100:4–5; 145:9–10. Furthermore, His name is good (54:6). Additionally, the expression "O give thanks unto the Lord; for he is good" occurs five times (106:1; 107:1; 118:1, 29; 136:1). All five of these verses tie this goodness to the Lord's **loyal love**[28] (חֶסֶד, *khesed*; translated as "mercy" by the KJV 86x in Psalms): "for his mercy endureth for ever." This attribute appears repeatedly linked with the various terms expressing praise or joy: for example, 13:5; 59:16–17; 63:3; 90:14; 101:1; 117:2; 136:1. Often joined to the attribute of loyal love is God's **faithfulness** (אֱמֶת, *'emeth*, or אֱמוּנָה, *'emunah*): for example, 57:9–10; 92:1–3; 108:4; 138:2. We praise God also for His attribute of **righteousness** (צֶדֶק, *tsedek*, or צְדָקָה, *tsedakah*): 7:17; 35:28; 48:10; 71:14–16, 22–24; 88:10–12; 111:1–3. A causal clause in 99:9 ties **holiness** to praise: "Exalt the LORD our God, and worship at his holy hill; for the LORD our God is holy." Other passages that connect this attribute with praise include 22:3; 30:4; 71:22; 99:5. Frequently the psalmists direct praise to God's "holy name" (33:21; 103:1; 105:3; 106:47; 145:21), in 99:3 saying, "Let them praise thy great and terrible name; for it is holy."

(5) *Praise arises from recognizing God's works.* Psalm 13:6 is the summary statement for basing the Lord's praise on what He has done: "I will

---

[26] In Hebrew the most significant particle that introduces such clauses is כִּי (*kiy*), "for," or "because," a word that occurs 443x in Psalms (but not all of these are used as causals).

[27] "Although the Psalms contain many 'messages' of a historical, theological, and practical nature, their primary message is that God is great and God is good." Terry C. Muck, "General Editor's Preface," in Gerald H. Wilson, *Psalms: Volume 1*, NIVAC (Grand Rapids: Zondervan, 2002), 12.

[28] When this term is plural or when it is connected to the verb meaning "do" (עָשָׂה, *'asah*), it refers to acts or deeds of loyal kindness.

sing unto the LORD, because he hath dealt bountifully with me." Also important is 103:2, "Bless the LORD, O my soul, and forget not all his benefits." The psalmists in praising God focus on three categories of His works. Most generally they speak of His **wonders**, extraordinary, unusual, or spectacular acts.[29] "I will praise thee, O LORD, with my whole heart; I will shew forth all thy marvellous works" (9:1). Usually the term is the direct object of the common verb for "do" (עֲשָׂה, *'asah*): "Blessed be the LORD God, the God of Israel, who only doeth wondrous things" (72:18). Other cases include 40:3–5b; 78:4; 86:10–12; 98:1; 111:1–4; 136:3–4. In Psalm 107 the psalmist repeatedly exclaims, "Oh that men would praise the LORD for his goodness, and for his wonderful works to the children of men!" (vv. 8, 15, 21, and 31). Some other passages that connect praise with God's marvellous deeds include 26:7; 31:21; 75:1; 89:5a; 96:3–4; and 145:3–5.

This general category of wonders actually includes the next two types of God's works: praise is due both for His creation and His salvation. Although Psalm 19 does not mention praise directly, by stating that "the heavens declare the glory of God" (v. 1), David classifies **creation** as God's "glory" (כָּבוֹד, *kavowd*), and His glory clearly qualifies for our praise (96:2–4). Psalm 33 begins with praise (vv. 1–2) then treats the theme of creation (vv. 6, 9). Possibly the psalmist was thinking about creation when he said, "I will shout for joy because of the works of Your hands" (92:4b, HCSB).[30] In 148:5 praise for the work of creation is directly in view: "Let them praise the name of the LORD: for he commanded, and they were created." As David contemplated the creation of his own body,[31] he said, "I will praise thee; for I am fearfully and wonderfully made" (139:14a).

---

[29] Usually the Hebrew term is נִפְלָאוֹת, *niphla'owth*, a feminine plural niphal participle, though there are a few synonyms used in Psalms (for example, in 88:10).

[30] "It is at least possible that "the works of Thy hands" could refer to the works of creation." Leupold, 659.

[31] Modern science has discovered and informed us regarding many more marvelous facts about the human body. See, for example, Alan L. Gillen, Frank J. Sherwin III, and Alan C. Knowles, *The Human Body: An Intelligent Design,* 2nd ed. (n.p.: Creation Research Society, 2001). Even secular, evolutionary books about the body present this information. See *The Incredible Machine* (n.p.: National Geographic Society, 1986).

Theological Themes of Psalms

The psalmists, however, concentrate much more on praising God for His work of deliverance or **salvation**. The psalmist tells himself, "hope thou in God: for I shall yet praise him for the help [יְשׁוּעָה, *yeshuw‘ah*; "salvation"] of his countenance" (42:5b, 11b; 43:5b).[32] In Psalm 50 God makes a promise: "I will deliver thee, and thou shalt glorify me" (v. 15b). David says, "May the Lord be praised [בָּרוּךְ, *baruwk*; "blessed"]! Day after day He bears our burdens; God is our salvation" (68:19, HCSB). Other passages that link praise with salvation include 70:4; 71:14–15; 96:2; 106:47; and 118:21. In a psalm that refers to praise seven times in its description of various works of deliverance that the Lord provided, the writer finishes with a question and a challenge: "Who is wise? Let him give heed to these things" (107:43a, NASB).

(6) *There is an obligation to communicate praise to others.* By its very nature praise must be shared, either conveyed to its object (by acknowledging or in thanking) or publicized to some third-party audience.[33] Psalms has much to say about the latter activity. Words indicating this act of communication frequently occur within the contexts of divine praise: there are seven Hebrew verbs of particular importance.[34] Table 25:3 lists these with their close English equivalents and notes the important references. The two main verbs are סָפַר (*saphar*, "declare") and נָגַד (*nagad*; "tell"), used synonymously in 19:1. Although used frequently and each with various meanings, the remaining five verbs occur about three times each to indicate

---

[32] See the NET Bible note on this verse. It understands this refrain as referring to "the saving acts associated with God's presence/intervention." ESV renders this clause, "for I shall again praise him, my salvation and my God."

[33] Mays has stated that "Praise in the psalms has an evangelical function." That is, "Praise is proclamation; it witnesses to the present and coming reign of the Lord." He argues that "It is right to deem this proclamation 'evangelical,' because its content has unmistakable connections with the message of prophecy and the preaching of Jesus ...." He makes application to the church: "What this means is that the church as it praises God with the psalms is prophet and evangelist to the world" (pp. 68f.). See 96:2 for the gospel emphasis: "Proclaim good tidings of His salvation from day to day" (NASB). The verb used here is בָּשַׂר (*basar*, "bring news"), usually translated in the LXX by εὐαγγελίζομαι (*euangelizomai*; "announce good news").

[34] Because of the close synonymy of these terms, the English versions often interchange their translations for them, making it difficult for the reader to recognize which Hebrew word appears in a particular verse. For example, in 145:11 KJV has "They shall **speak** of the glory of thy kingdom, and **talk** of thy power," but the first verb is אָמַר (*'amar*, "say"), and the second is דָּבַר (*davar*, "speak").

the publicity of God's praise. Psalm 40:5 uses three of the seven verbs to indicate the broadcasting of praise (v. 3) for God's works: "Many, O LORD my God, are thy wonderful works ...: if I would **declare** and **speak** of them, they are more than can be numbered [**told**, ESV]." Furthermore, in connecting praise with publishing, the psalmists often mention the instruments of speech, with or without one of the verbs: the mouth (34:1; 40:3; 71:8; 89:1; 109:30), the lips (51:15; 63:5; 71:23; 119:171), and the tongue (51:14; 126:2).

Table 25.3 Hebrew Verbs in Psalms for Communicating Praise

Hebrew	English	References Connected to Praising
ספר (*saphar*)	tell	9:1, 14; 22:22; 26:7; 40:3–5; 66:16–17; 71:14–15; 78:3–6; 79:13; 96:3–4; 102:21; 107:21–22
נגד (*nagad*)	declare	9:11; 30:9; 40:3–5; 51:15; 64:9–10; 71:17–18 (see v. 22); 75:9; 92:1–2; 145:4
שמע (*shama'*)	proclaim	26:7; 66:8; 106:2
ידע (*yada'*)	make known	89:1; 105:1; 145:12
זכר (*zakar*)	mention	20:7; 45:17; 71:16
אמר (*'amar*)	say	35:27; 40:17; 145:11a
דבר (*davar*)	speak	40:3–5; 145:11b, 21

(7) *Praise naturally connects to music.* A number of times in this book, the psalmists link divine praise with music, either vocal or instrumental. The verb זמר (*zamar*), charted in the previous chapter about rejoicing, is often translated as "sing praise/s":[35] the KJV does this 25 times in Psalms. For example, "Praise ye the LORD: for it is good to **sing praises** unto our God; for it is pleasant; and praise is comely" (147:1). Furthermore, that verb of singing occurs in the same verse with ידה (*yadah*; "praise" or "thank") ten times: for example, "I will praise thee, ... I will sing unto thee ..." (57:9). The noun תְּהִלָּה (*tehillah*; "praise") occurs with the verb שׁיר (*shiyr*; "sing") or noun שִׁיר (*shiyr*; "song") three times (40:3; 106:12; 149:1). Additionally, David says, "with my song will I praise him" (28:7b), and "I will praise the name of God with a song" (69:30). The ESV translates the second half of 95:2 as "let us make a joyful noise to him with songs of praise!" The lyre and harp serve as additional means of praising: "Give thanks to the LORD with the lyre; Sing praises to Him with a harp of ten strings" (33:2, NASB). The psalmist says, "yea, upon the harp [or "lyre"] will I praise thee" (43:4b). The

---

[35] The BDB entry begins with the gloss "make music in praise of God."

Theological Themes of Psalms

"psaltery" used to praise God in 71:22 is a harp. The instrumental climax for this proposition occurs in the last psalm, which lists eight instruments (150:3–5).

New Testament Echoes

In the New Testament praise is a common theme, expressed by about half a dozen verbs and four nouns.[36] Additionally, the New Testament uses a post-classical verb (εὐχαριστέω, *eukharisteō*), a noun (εὐχαριστία, *eukharistia*), and an adjective (εὐχάριστος, *eukharistos*)[37] that clearly mean "to be thankful," "thankfulness," and "thankful." The noun appears together with one of the words for "praise," verifying the association of gratitude and praise mentioned above (second proposition): "**Blessing** ["Praise" in the NIV], and glory, and wisdom, and **thanksgiving**, and honour, and power, and might, be unto our God for ever and ever" (Rev. 7:12). Paul tells us about the natural men: "Because that, when they knew God, they **glorified** him not as God, neither were **thankful** ..." (Rom. 1:21a). This statement affirms both the obligation for all creatures to praise God and the fact that this duty nonetheless runs contrary to human nature (first and third propositions).

The New Testament affirms also propositions four and five, praising the Lord for His attributes and His works. In the first chapter of Ephesians Paul uses a phrase three times, almost like a refrain, to magnify two of God's attributes: "the praise of the glory of his grace" (v. 6); "the praise of his glory" (vv. 12, 14).[38] Peter, writing about the work of Christ in salvation, tells us that its purpose is "that ye should shew forth the praises of him who hath called you out of darkness into his marvellous light" (1 Pet. 2:9b). Connected to this kind of praise is the thanksgiving for God's works of conquering enemies and ruling: "We give thee thanks, O Lord God Almighty, which art,

---

[36] For a list of these with selected references, see Brice L. Martin, "Praise," *ISBEr*, 3:929f.

[37] These Greek terms are not used in the LXX translation of Psalms, but a later Greek translation by Aquila uses the noun to translate several occurrences of תּוֹדָה (*towdah*; "thanksgiving") in Psalms. See Hans Conzelmann, "εὐχαριστέω, εὐχαριστία, εὐχάριστος," *TDNT*, 9:409.

[38] "The glory of God is the manifested excellence of God, and the glory of any one of his attributes is the manifestation of that attribute as an object of praise." Charles Hodge, *A Commentary on Ephesians* (1856; reprint, Carlisle, Penn.: The Banner of Truth Trust, 1991), 15.

260

and wast, and art to come; because thou hast taken to thee thy great power, and hast reigned" (Rev. 11:17). The sixth proposition (about communicating) appears in the imperatives for praise and thanksgiving: for example, "And a voice came out of the throne, saying, Praise our God, all ye his servants, and ye that fear him, both small and great" (Rev. 19:5); "In every thing give thanks: for this is the will of God in Christ Jesus concerning you" (1 Thess. 5:18). James refers to the tongue as an instrument of praise for God (3:9). After an exhortation to be thankful, Paul echoes the proposition concerning music: "teaching and admonishing one another in psalms and hymns and spiritual songs, singing with grace ["thankfulness," NASB] in your hearts to the Lord" (Col. 3:16).

David has written a fitting conclusion to the discussion of this theme: "My mouth shall speak the praise of the LORD: and let all flesh bless his holy name for ever and ever" (145:21).

26

Worship

In one sense the whole book of Psalms is about worship, the recognition of God's character and works and the resultant honoring of Him for these.[1] This is true because the components of worship include prayer and preaching or theological instruction,[2] essentially covering the whole book. In an earlier work I identified the overall theme of the book as "spiritual worship of the true God."[3] In this chapter, however, the focus is on the passages in Psalms that speak explicitly about the theme of worship: bowing and serving, the sacrificial ritual, and the places of worship.

It is natural for those who have experienced God's work of deliverance to want to worship Him and His Messiah. Praise and other expressions of joy form a part of mankind's divine worship. In fact, praise is at the center of godly worship. God has, however, prescribed certain ritual forms as an additional part of His requirement for mankind to worship Him properly. Of course, we are familiar with baptism and communion mandated for the New Testament church. In primeval times God instituted animal sacrifices as a ritual for Adam's family (Gen. 4:4–5). At Sinai God instituted an elaborate ritual of sacrifices and other ceremonies (for example, Lev. 1–7; Num. 7, 15; Deut. 16).

There are 96 verses (almost 4% of the verses in the book) occurring in 58 different psalms that mention this theme. These verses are distributed most heavily in Books I and II, and least in Book III. Critics usually refer to

---

[1] "Worship is seen as reverent devotion and service to God motivated by God's saving acts in history." Ralph P. Martin, "Worship," *ISBEr*, 4:1118.

[2] See Geoffrey W. Bromiley, "Worship," *ZPEB*, 5:969.

[3] Robert D. Bell, *The Theological Messages of the Old Testament Books* (Greenville, S. C.: Bob Jones University Press, 2010), 222, 495.

the ritualistic practices of Israel's religion as "the cult";[4] one finds many occurrences of the words "cult" and "cultic" in their works.[5] In light of the fact that these critics usually consider the original setting of individual psalms to be part of the ritual of the second temple in post-exilic Judah, it is most significant that there are not many more references to sacrifice and other temple ritual in the book.[6] If, as the Scriptures teach, David is the author of the majority of these poems, we would not expect him to mention more frequently these aspects since Solomon's temple had not yet been built and David himself did not always have access to the tabernacle, which was located at Gibeon during his days (1 Chron. 16:39–40).

Vocabulary of Worship

Table 26.1 charts the six main words for the theme of worship, three verbs and three nouns, occurring a total of 74 times. The totals at the bottom of the table indicate the distribution of each term according to the five Books of Psalms. Table 26.2 lists a dozen other words associated with ritual worship with a total of 59 occurrences for this particular theme. Three additional terms mentioned below are not in the list because they occur just once each. The grand total in Psalms is 137 usages, only 0.7% of the words in the book. Many of these words occur additional times in Psalms but with other meanings not associated with worship.

The one word that in general means "worship" is חוה (*khawah*; used 165x in the OT), a word that literally means "to bow down." In many cases it refers simply to one person bowing before another creature: for example,

---

[4] Sigmund Mowinckel has defined the cult "as the socially established and regulated holy acts and words in which the encounter and communion of the Deity with the congregation is established, developed, and brought to its ultimate goal." *The Psalms in Israel's Worship*, trans. D. R. Ap-Thomas (Oxford: Basil Blackwell, 1962), 1:15.

[5] The words "cult" and "cultic" occur 319x in Hans-Joachim Kraus, *Theology of the Psalms*, trans. Keith Crim (Minneapolis: Augsburg, 1986). They appear 894x in his two-volume commentary. By contrast these two terms appear only 39x in Kidner's commentary, and just 8x in Futato's work.

[6] This has been acknowledged by the critics themselves. "The presentation of the sacrifice has constituted a special theme in the cultic life of Jerusalem. It is, however, astonishing how little is in fact said in the Psalms on this theme." Kraus then speaks of the "difficulty [of] understanding how it is that there are so few references to the sacrifices, and that ... these are so general" (*Theology*, 93).

Table 26.1 Key Terms for Worship

Hebrew words:	חוה *khawah* **bow**	עבד *'avad* **serve**	זבח *zavakh* **sacrifice**	זֶבַח *zevakh* **sacrifice**	הֵיכָל *heykal* **temple**	בֵּית *beyth* **house**
Psalm						
2:		11				
4:			5	5		
5:	7				7	7
18:		43				
22:	27, 29	30				
23:						6
26:						8
27:			6	6	4	4
29:	2				9	
36:						8
40:				6		
42:						4
45:	11					
48:					9	
50:			14, 23	5, 8		
51:				16, 17, 19		
52:						8
54:			6			
55:						14
65:					4	4
66:	4					13
68:					29	
69:						9
72:	11	11				
79:					1	
81:	9					
84:						4, 10
86:	9					
92:						13
93:						5
95:	6					
96:	9					
97:	7	7				
99:	5, 9					
100:		2				
102:		22				
106:	19	36	37, 38	28		
107:			22	22		
116:			17	17		19
118:						26
122:						1, 9
132:	7					
134:						1
135:						2
138:	2				2	
totals:	**17** (4/3/2/6/2)	**8** (3/1/0/4/0)	**9** (2/3/0/2/2)	**11** (3/5/0/1/2)	**8** (3/3/1/0/1)	**21** (5/6/2/2/6)

Theological Themes of Psalms

Table 26.2 Additional Terms Connected to Worship

Hebrew	English	#	References	Totals: Ps./all
אֹהֶל	tabernacle	6	15:1; 27:5, 6; 61:4; 76:2; 78:60	18/349
חָצֵר	court	8	65:4; 84:2, 10; 92:13; 96:8; 100:4; 116:19; 135:2	9/191
כָּרַע	kneel	2	72:9; 95:6	3/36
מִזְבֵּחַ	altar	5	26:6; 43:4; 51:19; 84:3; 118:27	5/403
מִנְחָה	offering	5	20:3; 40:6; 72:10; 96:8; 141:2	6/211
מִקְדָּשׁ	sanctuary	5	68:35; 73:17; 74:7; 78:69; 96:6	5/75
מִשְׁכָּן	dwelling	8	26:8; 43:3; 46:4; 74:7; 78:60; 84:1; 132:5, 7	11/139
נְדָבָה	offering	2	54:6; 119:108	4/26
סֹךְ	shelter	2	27:5; 76:2	3/4
עֹלָה	holocaust	7	20:3; 40:6; 50:8; 51:16, 19; 66:13, 15	7/288
קֹדֶשׁ	sanctuary	7	20:2; 63:2; 68:17, 24; 74:3; 134:2; 150:1	45/470
קְטֹרֶת	incense	2	66:15; 141:2	2/60

when Joseph's brothers first came to Egypt, they bowed down to him in politeness since they regarded him as a high Egyptian official (Gen. 42:6). In other cases it refers to worshipping without the accompanying bowing: for example, in 1 Samuel 15 Saul desired to worship Yahweh by sacrificing to Him, not to prostrate himself literally (vv. 25, 30, 31). In Psalms the word occurs seventeen times, translated by the KJV as "worship" sixteen times and as "fall down" once (72:11). In two cases the worship is offered to false gods (81:9; 106:19). Parallelism in two passages makes it clear that the verb עָבַד ('avad, "serve")[7] occurs as an equivalent for the act of worshipping: 72:11; 97:7. The synonym for "bow" is "kneel" (כָּרַע, kara'), two of its three occurrences in Psalms indicating worship: 72:9 and 95:6, where an additional synonym (בָּרַךְ, barak) occurs.

Eight terms occur in Psalms referring to the sacrificial ritual of worship prescribed in the Old Testament. Most of these are quite common,

---

[7] This verb is frequent in the OT (over 2000x) with additional meanings such as "work" and "perform"; however, in Psalms it occurs just 8x, always in the sense of "worship." Furthermore it could legitimately be argued that the noun עֶבֶד ('eved), "servant," could be a way of designating a worshipper of Yahweh. This would be especially true in the case of Psalm 119, containing 14 of its 37 sg forms in the book (not counting 105:17 that mentions Joseph as a slave). These, however, have not been figured into the statistics of this chapter.

half of them with over a hundred occurrences each, but in Psalms they are relatively rare. The verb for "sacrifice" (זבח, *zavad*) occurs nine times in Psalms (out of 134x for the OT), and it accompanying noun (זֶבַח, *zevakh*) appears eleven times. The others are "gift" or "meal [grain] offering" (מִנְחָה, *minkhah*),[8] "burnt offering" or "holocaust"[9] (עֹלָה, *'owlah*; just seven out of 288x in the OT), "sin offering" (חֲטָאָה, *kheta'ah*; 40:6), "whole burnt offering" (כָּלִיל, *kaliyl*; 51:19), "freewill offering" (נְדָבָה, *nedavah*), and "incense" (קְטֹרֶת, *qetowreth*).[10]

Nine of the terms refer in some way to the place of worship. The מִזְבֵּחַ (*mizbeyakh*, "altar") is the place of sacrifice, referenced five times in the book (for example, "bullocks upon thine altar" in 43:4). In David's time we regard the term "tabernacle" as the designation for the place of worship; then beginning with Solomon we call that place the "temple." The Hebrew word for this is הֵיכָל (*heykal*; 13x in Psalms, 80x in OT), which can also mean "palace": for example, notice "ivory palaces" and "the king's palace" in 45:8, 10; also 144:12. Twice in Psalms the term refers to God's kingly palace in heaven: "The LORD is in his holy temple, the LORD's throne is in heaven …" (11:4a); "I called upon the LORD …: he heard my voice out of his temple …" (18:6a). The other eight occurrences in the book concern the place of worship on earth.

The most common Hebrew word for the tabernacle is אֹהֶל (*'owhel*), "tent," a word used 349 times. Just six of its eighteen uses in Psalms refer to the place of worship. Usually, the psalmists use the term "house" (בַּיִת, *beyth*) when speaking about the tabernacle or temple. This is a very common word (in the OT over 2000x, in Psalms 53x). The context of 21 passages[11] indicates that the psalmists are speaking about God's temple; that is, "the house of God" (note 42:4; 52:8; 55:14).

---

[8] This word appears in 45:12 to indicate a gift of tribute for Solomon's queen. Its other five uses, however, are in contexts of divine worship.

[9] The KJV usually translates this word as "burnt offering." This animal sacrifice was completely consumed by fire on the altar, thus the term "holocaust."

[10] This word literally means "smoke" and thus the smoke of a burning sacrifice in 66:15; in 141:2 it refers to the sweet smelling incense used in worship.
Not counted in the statistics, one additional verse mentions a pagan worship ritual: "drink offerings of blood" (16:4).

[11] Not counting its use as part of the title in 30:1. The word statistics in this chapter exclude the Psalm titles.

Theological Themes of Psalms

By means of parallelism and other aspects of context, we can identify five additional terms the psalmists employ to refer to the tabernacle or temple. The Hebrew word חָצֵר (*khatseyr*) means "village" (without a wall; in 10:8) or "courtyard"; the plural is used eight times in Psalms for the temple "courts"; for example, "bring an offering, and come into his courts" (96:8b). Two terms identify the place of worship as a "holy place" or "sanctuary": מִקְדָּשׁ (*miqdash*) and קֹדֶשׁ (*qowdesh*), a total of twelve times (for example, 74:7 and 134:2).[12] Another name for the tabernacle in the Pentateuch was מִשְׁכָּן (*mishkan*; for example, Exod. 25:9), a term associated with what theologians refer to as the Shekinah glory but one that could simply refer to any "dwelling place" (for example, "their dwelling places" in 49:11). Eight of its eleven occurrences in Psalms refer to the temple,[13] five of them using the plural: for example, "they have defiled by casting down the dwelling place of thy name to the ground" (74:7b), and "How amiable are thy tabernacles, O LORD of hosts" (84:1). In two passages the tabernacle is called a סֹךְ (*sowk*), "shelter" or "pavilion" (27:5; 76:2).[14] Because of the parallelism in verses like 20:2 and 116:19, it is possible to regard some of the references to Zion and Jerusalem in Psalms[15] as additional ways of mentioning the temple.

---

[12] The first noun is plural in 68:35 and 73:17, perhaps an intensive use to indicate grandeur. For the first reference, see Steveson, 260. Possibly there is an allusion to God's heavenly temple, as suggested by Norman C. Habel, *Yahweh Versus Baal: A Conflict of Religious Cultures* (New York: Bookman Associates, 1964), 91, n. 52; and Goldingay, 2:333. But 73:17 is clearly speaking about the temple in Jerusalem. Most likely, the plural simply indicates the various holy areas connected to the temple: "the Temple with its sacred precincts, ... something otherwise found only in 73:17 or in the analogous plural 'the holy dwellings' in 43:3; 46:[4]; 84:[1]; 132:5, 7." Hossfeld & Zenger, 15B:167. The second noun (קֹדֶשׁ)occurs 470x in the OT, meaning "holiness," semantically referring to a state of apartness or consecration. In seven of its 45 uses in Psalms it denotes a place of holiness.

[13] In 26:8b the Hebrew reads literally "the place of the dwelling of Your glory," a clear reference to the Shekinah (Steveson, 108). English translations, however, usually render the noun "dwelling" as a verb: "LORD, I have loved ... the place where thine honour dwelleth."

[14] In 76:2 סֹךְ (*sowk*) is parallel to מְעֹנָה (*me'ownah*), "den," another possible case of a word referring to the place of worship.

[15] The totals are 38 for Zion and 17 for Jerusalem in the book. These have not been included in the statistics of this chapter.

By determining which sections contain three or more instances of the vocabulary for worship, we can establish the key passages for this theme. Two of these contain seven terms each: 27:4–6 and 51:16–19. Six contain four each, representing all five Books of Psalms: 40:6 in Book I, 66:13–15 and 72:9–11 in Book II, 84:1–4 in Book III, 96:6–9 in Book IV, and 116:17–19 in Book V. The six passages that contain three terms each are 5:7; 20:2–3; 22:27–30; 65:4; 106:36–38; 132:5–7. Psalm 50 contains five cases of the vocabulary, but the verses are scattered throughout the poem (vv. 5, 8, 14, 23); 68 is similar with four words (vv. 17, 24, 29, 35).

Propositions

These key passages teach us seven truths. (1) *True worship takes place in the presence of the living God Himself.* In human societies there are fan clubs and personality cults that can exist independent and sometimes far removed from the hero who is the object of adoration. As people idolize and glorify this person, his or her presence is only represented by a picture or maybe even a statue. Yahweh, however, as the living God characterizes Himself as the ever present I AM (Exod. 3:14).[16] The fact that the Psalms are filled with prayers indicates that the psalmists were well aware of the Lord's presence. In Psalm 5 David declares to the Lord that "The foolish shall not stand in thy sight" (v. 5a); then he says, "But as for me, I will come into thy house in the multitude of thy mercy: and in thy fear will I worship toward thy holy temple" (v. 7). That David is welcome in God's house makes sense only if God who has accepted him is truly present.[17] Why would David long to "dwell in the house of the LORD all the days of [his] life" (27:4a), if it were

---

[16] "The best translation for Exodus 3:14 seems ... to be this: 'I am present is what I am.'" J. Barton Payne, *The Theology of the Older Testament* (Grand Rapids: Zondervan, 1962), 148. God's answer to Moses in this verse concerning His identification is literally "I am [that] I AM." The Hebrew word אֲשֶׁר (*'esher*), "that," in this verse should not be translated; it is a function word necessary to link the predicate to the preceding subject with its linking verb ("I am," one word in Hebrew), required in Hebrew because "I am I am" would sound like a redundancy. An apt illustration of how this name I AM works is in John 6:20. When the disciples on the Sea of Galilee during the night were frightened by seeing a figure walking on the water toward their boat, Jesus simply said "I am; be not afraid" (literal translation). Hearing that familiar voice, they immediately knew that Jesus was *present* with them.

[17] "So he mixes his confidence over free access into God's presence with awe and humility" (Ross, 1:251).

not for the Lord's presence there? In 26:8 David says explicitly that God's glory, His Shekinah, is there in the sanctuary.[18] Another explicit reference occurs in Psalm 95: "Let us come before his presence with thanksgiving" (v. 2a); then a few sentences later the psalmist writes about worship, bowing, and kneeling (v. 6). That divine presence is salvation itself (42:5). Psalm 22 is also especially instructive: all of mankind will worship before Yahweh (vv. 27, 29), kneeling before Him (v. 29) and serving (another word for worship) Him (v. 30). The psalmist says, "my soul longeth, yea, even fainteth for the courts of the LORD: my heart and my flesh crieth out for the living God" (84:2). Note his awareness of the living God, the One present, at the temple.[19]

(2) *The God who is present has Himself prescribed the nature of the worship He accepts.* It is not left up to mankind to choose how to worship the Creator. The method of veneration for God does originate from creative initiative on our part. The Pentateuch lays down numerous regulations about priests, sacrifices, and other elements involved in the ritual of worship. God warned Moses to be careful concerning the stipulated details: "And look that thou make them after their pattern, which was shewed thee in the mount" (Exod. 25:40). The psalmists acknowledge this both by using the same terms for the sacrifices that the Pentateuch prescribed (such as the holocaust, the voluntary offering,[20] and the meat [grain] offering) and by referring to "sacrifices of righteousness" (4:5; 51:19), meaning the ones God approved.[21]

---

[18] Calvin says, "we know how frequently expressions of this kind are employed in Scripture to bear testimony to the presence of God" (1:446). "People would go to the sanctuary ... to witness his wonderful works that confirmed his presence in their midst .... The evidence of the divine presence dwelling there made it a glorious place, but they also knew that in the Holy of Holies the glory of the LORD dwelt" (Ross, 1:616).

[19] "The ancient worshipers ... felt the presence of God in the temple and even in Jerusalem, as nowhere else." Boice, 2:691.

[20] The term נְדָבָה (*nedavah*) was translated by the KJV as "freely" in 54:6; this was followed by NASB with "willingly." Many other translations, however, have rendered the prepositional phrase בִּנְדָבָה (*binedavah*) as "with a freewill offering" (ASV, RSV, NRSV, ESV, NET).

[21] The term occurs only in Deuteronomy 33:19 and twice in Psalms. Commentators generally regard "sacrifices of righteousness" as meaning those that reflect the proper motive, not hypocritically. See for example, Delitzsch, 1:115. Some understand this to refer to "a broken spirit; a broken and a contrite heart" (51:17), not animal sacrifices. See for example, Rawlinson, 1:23. I understand this, however,

Another way we know the truth of this proposition would be occurrences of the so-called "liturgies at the gate,"[22] where someone asks, "Who may sojourn in Your tent?" (15:1, literal translation) or "Who shall ascend into the hill of the LORD? or who shall stand in his holy place?" (24:3); then the answer provides stipulations of ethical behavior (15:2–5; 24:4). Yahweh's control of worship is evident in His choice of Zion as the place (132:13–14). In Psalm 20 the prayer of the people is that Yahweh would approve the sacrificial offering of the king (v. 3),[23] indicating the need of the king to meet a preset requirement in his ritual worship.

(3) *True worship includes sacrifices.* It has been the habit of humanists to speculate about the evolutionary origin of sacrifice (usually either as a gift to the gods or as food for them), and basically their theories claim that the imagination of ancient humans about gods was the determining factor.[24] Scripture, however, makes clear that God initiated sacrifices, not man: the first human family offered sacrifices, and God evaluated positively or negatively the offerings of Abel and Cain (Gen. 4:4–5), seemingly possible only if God had mandated both the practice and what was acceptable. The detailed system of Mosaic sacrifices that God prescribed on Mount Sinai confirms that this was His program. Using the psalmists as His mouthpiece, the Holy Spirit commands (2MP impv) sacrifices[25] in Psalm 4:5 and the

---

to mean sacrifices that conform to God's standard, in regard to both heart attitude and the instructions the Lord has specifically given: "not only the sacrifices performed correctly according to the ritual; not only the sacrifices due on account of sins that have been committed …; but true sacrifices performed with a disposition in accordance with the will of God, and the meaning of the law." Moll, 70.

[22] See, for example, Horst Dietrich Preuss, *Old Testament Theology*, trans. Leo G. Perdue (Louisville: Westminster John Knox, 1996), 2:64.

[23] The Hebrew verb in 20:3b is the piel of דשׁן (*dashan*), literally "regard as fat," translated as "accept" (KJV, ASV, NET, NIV) or "regard with favor" (RSV, NRSV, ESV).

[24] For a review of theories, see Gary A. Anderson, "Sacrifice and Sacrificial Offerings (OT)," *ABD*, 5:871–72.

[25] It is recognized that "many psalms … express an intense devotion to the temple" and that there are "psalms which more specifically refer to sacrifice in the temple as an essential part of worship" (such as 4, 20, 27, 54, 66, and 118). Norman Whybray, *Reading the Psalms As a Book*, JSOTSup 222 (Sheffield: Sheffield Academic, 1996), 101.

binding of a sacrifice[26] to the altar in 118:27. Critics have claimed, however, that in ancient Israel a faction arose that opposed what they have called "the cult." They have identified several passages in the Psalms that supposedly expressed a sentiment against sacrifices: 40:6–8; 50:7–14; 51:16–17; 69:30–31; 141:2. But the key to a proper understanding of these passages is in the text of Psalm 51: David recognizes that he cannot simply cover his blatant sin with the ritual of an animal sacrifice (v. 16); he must repent in godly inward sorrow (v. 17); then being forgiven by a merciful God, he can offer the Lord the sacrifices the Law has stipulated (v. 19).[27]

(4) *True worship includes gifts to the One honored.* Since worship begins with an acknowledgment of worthy character and great deeds, usually done for the benefit of the worshiper, it is natural for this person to give something as a token of gratitude. Deuteronomy 16:17 states this principle: "Every man shall give as he is able, according to the blessing of the LORD thy God which he hath given thee." In Psalm 68 David declares that at the place of worship Yahweh will receive gifts even from kings (vv. 18, 29). The psalmist says, "let all that be round about [Yahweh] bring presents unto him that ought to be feared" (76:11b). If we understand Solomon as a type of Christ in Psalm 72, then "the kings of Tarshish and of the isles shall bring presents: the kings of Sheba and Seba shall offer gifts" (v. 10). The "offering" in 96:8 could be understood as "gift" (NEB).[28] The thank offering (תּוֹדָה, *towdah*), discussed in the chapter about praise, is relevant as corroboration for this proposition.

(5) *The worship of Yahweh excludes any worship of others.* Yahweh is a jealous God. He does not tolerate those who would worship Him along with other gods; He wants complete devotion from those who have entered into a covenant relationship with Him just as a husband requires fidelity from his wife. Some of the verses in Psalms on the topic of worship are negative; that

---

[26] The Hebrew word in this verse is (חַג, *khag*), "festival," understood by translators to mean "a festival sacrifice," a metonymy (as happens also with this word in Exod. 23:18). See the NET note on this verse.

[27] "As Psalm 50 teaches that God wants sacrifices from a grateful heart, Psalm 51 teaches that God wants sacrifices from a broken and repentant heart." Futato, 186. See also Whybray, 105–06; and Barnes, 2:90–91.

[28] See the entry in *HALOT* for מִנְחָה (*minkhah*): "A. (37 times) **gift, present.**" They list 72:10 and 96:8 as examples for this meaning. Ross translates this noun as "gift" in 96:8 (3:130, 140).

is, they deal with the wrong kind of worship. Yahweh speaks directly to Israel in Psalm 81:6–16 and forbids them to "worship any strange [foreign] god" (v. 9b). David affirms his loyalty to Yahweh by repudiating a ritual for pagan gods: "their drink offerings of blood will I not offer" (16:4b). The psalmist remembers and deliberates about disobedient Israel who sacrificed to false gods (106:28) that were dead in contrast to the living God, and even offered the blood of their children to the idols that represented demons (vv. 37–38). Thus Israel "worshiped" (חוה, *khawah*) an image (v. 19) and "served" (עבד, *'avad*) idols (v. 36). Of course, all of this angered Yahweh (v. 40). The condemnation is not just for Israel, His covenant nation, but for all mankind, whom He will eventually shame and disgrace[29] because of their idolatry (97:7).

(6) *It is a pleasure for the righteous to worship Yahweh.* Although we could certainly contend that it is the duty of the redeemed to worship their God and Savior, the psalmists testify that gathering with the people of God to worship together in God's house is a wonderful delight. The psalmist says, "I was glad when they said unto me, Let us go into the house of the LORD" (122:1). David called this experience with other worshipers "sweet fellowship" (55:14, NASB), and another psalmist refers to the joy even in the trip with the multitude to God's house (42:4). Indeed, he could testify that "a day in thy courts is better than a thousand" (84:10). Under inspiration the psalmists use the אַשְׁרֵי (*'asherey*, "blessed") formula to declare as fortunate the person who spends time at the sanctuary (65:4; 84:4). David regards those who are in God's presence as experiencing something like Eden in the past or like the future millennial kingdom (36:8–9).[30] David himself loves God's house (26:8) and desires to live there permanently (23:6b; 61:4).[31] Though the first verb in 61:4 is גוּר (*guwr*), "to sojourn" or live temporarily, in 23:6 the idea expressed is that of an enduring residence.[32]

---

[29] The word translated "confounded" by the KJV "means not merely ashamed, but disappointed, defeated, and confounded." Alexander, 408.

[30] "In the presence of God they are satisfied physically and spiritually." In fact, "the sanctuary was a reminder of the garden in Eden"; and it "also had a typological meaning for the future messianic age ...." Ross, 1:792–93.

[31] "I will be a permanent guest in your home" (NET).

[32] The Hebrew word usually translated "dwell" in this verse is problematic. The Masoretic spelling וְשַׁבְתִּי (*weshavtiy*) should mean "and I will return," its root being the verb שׁוּב (*shuwv*). Delitzsch has solved this case by pointing out that this

Theological Themes of Psalms

(7) *The coming Messiah will be worshiped as God.* The messianic typology of Psalm 72 leads us to the remarkable fact that the coming Messiah will receive worship as divine. The two verbs for worship occur together: "And let all kings bow down to him, all nations serve him" (v. 11; HCSB). This language does not really fit Solomon, who is merely a type of the coming Christ.[33] The New Testament makes clear what the Holy Spirit was indicating when He spoke about Yahweh's future reigning from Zion (for example, 99:1–2): Ephesians 4:8 applies what was said about Yahweh in 68:18 to Christ; Hebrews 1:6 informs us that angels will worship Christ, whereas 97:7 speaks of "gods" worshiping Yahweh ("LORD" in vv. 1 and 5). The Messiah is Yahweh Himself and will receive the worship due to God.

New Testament Echoes

The New Testament mentions worship frequently. The Greek verb (προσκυνέω, *proskuneō*) for this concept occurs sixty times. A second term is (λατρεύω, *latreuō*), usually translated in the KJV as "serve," occurs 21 times. A study of these passages and their parallels confirms each of the seven propositions. (1) Revelation makes clear that in heaven the worship of God takes place in His presence, "before the One seated on the throne" (HCSB) (4:10; 7:11). (2) Jesus told the Samaritan woman that the Father is seeking for worshipers according to His standard: those that worship "in spirit and in truth" (John 4:23–24). Paul speaks negatively about "self-made religion," a person's own ritual of worship, invented by himself (Col. 2:23). (3) In Hebrews 10:1-10 we have a description of worshipers presenting sacrifices (vv. 1–2) and then the truth that Christ's body is now the "once for all" sacrifice (v. 10) we need for our worship. Paul says that Christ "hath given

---

is a example of the *constructio praegnans*, where a verb has been joined to a preposition that does not fit in order to indicate an ellipsis of a second verb that does connect with the preposition. This verb "return" should be coupled to the preposition אֶל ('*el*, "to"), not the preposition בְּ (*be*, "in"), which fits with (*y-sh-b*, "to dwell"); therefore, David was saying, "I will return [and consequently dwell] in God's house," the words in brackets being the ellipsis (1:332).

[33] Calvin interprets this verse correctly: "the whole world will be brought in subjection to the authority of Christ. The kingdom of Judah was unquestionably never more flourishing than under the reign of Solomon; but even then there were only a small number of kings who paid tribute to him, and what they paid was inconsiderable in amount" (3:111). See also NASB's marginal note on 72:2 about the pronouns there.

274

himself for us an offering and a sacrifice to God for a sweetsmelling savour" (Eph. 5:2).

(4) The gift that Paul received from the Philippians he regarded as "a fragrant offering, a sacrifice acceptable and pleasing to God" (4:18; ESV), really an act of worship by giving to God.[34] (5) Of course, the New Testament regards worship of anyone or anything else as totally unacceptable to the Lord (Rom. 1:22–25; Rev. 9:20). (6) Jude 24 describes the saints, who in the future will stand before God (obviously in worship), as then having "exceeding joy." (7) When Jesus met the disciples after His resurrection, they "held him by the feet, and worshipped him" (Matt. 28:9). Luke tells us that "they worshipped him, and returned to Jerusalem with great joy" (24:52).

May our exhortation to one another ever be, "O come, let us worship and bow down; let us kneel before the LORD our maker" (95:6).

---

[34] Paul defines "their gift as a sacrificial offering to God." David E. Garland, "Philippians," in *EBC*, 12:259.

27

Life

The saints, who delight in worshiping their Savior, know that their joy in that activity will not end with death. In their praise and worship, God's redeemed people look forward to the fulfillment of the promise of eternal life (Titus 1:2). True life is eternal life. The life Jesus proclaimed in John 14:6 was really eternal life. Life after death is not a late theological concept in the Old Testament. What God did for Enoch (near the beginning of time) in taking him bodily to heaven (Gen. 5:24; Heb. 11:5) was a indicator for the righteous that their future would involve an existence in God's presence. In the Old Testament where we have records of those close to God in this life (men like Abraham and David), we do not see instances when they lamented an end to that fellowship with their loving Redeemer as they approached the transition of death in their old age.[1] Indeed, the evidence is that they had the same hope that Paul had when he said, "absent from the body, ... present with the Lord" (2 Cor. 5:8).

Over two thousand years ago the Sadducees of the time of Jesus denied the afterlife and bodily resurrection (Matt. 22:23), presumably because Moses did not mention these in his writings. In recent centuries liberal scholarship has claimed on the basis of the earlier Old Testament writings that the Israelites did not believe in the afterlife until they were influenced during a late period by Persian religious concepts.[2] Among

---

[1] "An unbroken relationship with God tended to carry with it the assurance that death could not sever the relationship." E. F. Harrison, "Life," ISBEr, 3:130.

[2] For example, Millar Burrows says, "The modern mind thinks of the future life ... in terms of the immortality of the soul. The Hebrew conception of personality makes no such sharp division between the body and soul ..."; and "As we have seen, the emergence of any hope for the individual after death was a relatively late phenomenon in Old Testament religion." An Outline of Biblical Theology (Philadelphia: Westminster, 1946), 193, 203.

Theological Themes of Psalms

conservative expositors of Scripture there has even been an appeal to the concept of progressive revelation to explain why the Old Testament does not say more about life after death.[3]

It is important, however, to evaluate the Pentateuch in light of the time Moses was writing God's revelation to the Israelites. They had just come out of Egypt, a place where a great deal of emphasis was put on what happened in the afterlife to Pharaoh and his servants. The Israelites were traveling to Canaan, where the civilization clearly believed in the afterlife as evidenced from their literature discovered archaeologically at Ugarit.[4] We should rather say that the Pentateuch just assumes that the Israelites believed in life after death. If they had not believed in the immorality of the soul, why would God find it necessary to forbid them to communicate with the dead (Lev. 20:27; Deut. 18:11–12)? Job, who was contemporary with the Patriarchs, certainly possessed a hope in the resurrection of the body (Job 19:25–27), and David knew that he would again be with his child who had died (2 Sam. 12:23b).

Much of the Biblical evidence for the immorality of the soul is actually in Psalms. What does this book say about eternal life? It actually begins with the very first word of the book: "Blessed." Before we get to that word, however, it is necessary to grasp the meaning of certain key verses in the book.

---

[3] For example, Joseph Hammond claims that for the OT saint, "little was revealed to him concerning the life beyond the grave.... Thus death remained a terror and a calamity, even to the most religious Jew, until, about the time of Daniel, the doctrine of the resurrection began to be preached (Dan. 12:1–3), and the life beyond the grave to take a more cheerful aspect." *II. Kings*, in *The Pulpit Commentary*, ed. H. D. M. Spence and Joseph S. Exell (New York: Funk and Wagnalls, n.d.), 411. Concerning the incident in 2 Kings 20 about Hezekiah's sickness, Robert Jamieson says, "his great grief might arise partly from the love of life, partly from the obscurity of the Mosaic dispensation, where life and immortality had not been fully brought to light ...." *A Commentary on the Old and New Testaments*, by Robert Jamieson, A. R. Fausset , and David Brown (Grand Rapids: Eerdmans, 1948), 2:579–80.

[4] "According to the Bible, man originally had a true concept of deity which he proceeded to distort.... But some of this truth was, and is, always mingled in all religions.... [A] distorted concept of immortality antedates the Bible in written records of the Egyptians and Babylonians, and some notion of resurrection from the dead was a part of Sumerian mythology." Elmer B. Smick, "Ugaritic and the Theology of the Psalms," in *New Perspectives on the Old Testament*, ed. J. Barton Payne (Waco, Texas: Word Books, 1970), 115.

Key Passages about the Afterlife

Various interpreters have argued that the psalmists speak only about God's blessings in this life, His deliverance of the righteous from an early death, and His cutting short the life of the wicked in the here and now. In other words, Psalms does not address life after death. The book, however, contains four important passages which when properly interpreted in context clearly provide teaching about the afterlife that the Holy Spirit revealed to the psalmists.[5] This information at the same time informs us about what an Old Testament saint like David believed personally.

Psalm 17:15

David concludes his prayer for vindication and deliverance by declaring, "As for me, I will behold thy face in righteousness: I shall be satisfied, when I awake, with thy likeness" (17:15). He has been contrasting himself (vv. 3, 4b–6a) with the wicked (vv. 9–12), whom he recognizes as prospering in the present (v. 14).[6] They are "men of the world, which have their portion in this life." The position of the pronoun at the beginning of verse 15 ("As for me") climaxes the contrast between them. The waking David mentions must refer either to bodily resurrection[7] or, preferably, a new consciousness of God's very presence after a brief unconsciousness experienced in death. It is true that "thy face" (פָּנֶיךָ, *paneyka*) may refer to God's presence in an abstract manner (for example, 4:6), but the following term "thy likeness" (תְּמוּנָתֶךָ, *temuwnatheka*) would indicate that David is speaking about seeing God directly as Moses did (Exod. 34:5–6a; Num.

---

[5] A. B. Davidson singled out these four as "typical passages" that sought to resolve the problem of the wicked who prosper and the righteous who suffer. *The Theology of the Old Testament*, ed. S. D. F. Salmond (New York: Charles Scribner's Sons, 1914), 458–66. J. Barton Payne developed that discussion, stressing an order of progressive revelation. *The Theology of the Older Testament* (Grand Rapids: Zondervan, 1962), 204. I did not find the argument for progressive revelation convincing.

[6] This last verse is difficult to interpret. See Ross, 1:428–29. What is clear, however, is that what they own is only temporal, in this present, earthly existence. David's enemies "find their 'portion,' a material goal, in this life." Steveson, 70.

[7] VanGemeren recognizes that "that the psalmist by inspiration is looking for a greater experience with God that can only be a part of the postresurrection world" (p. 200).

12:8),[8] something that the saints expect in heaven (1 Cor. 13:12; 1 John 3:2; Rev. 22:4).[9]

Psalm 37

David wrote a wisdom psalm (one addressing man rather than one praying to God) in which he counsels godly persons not to be frustrated about the prosperity of the wicked (37:1). As the psalm progresses, the Holy Spirit promises five times that evildoers will be "cut off" (vv. 9, 22, 28, 34, 38; different forms of the same verb כרת, *karath*); in contrast the righteous will "inherit the earth" (vv. 9, 11, 22, 29, 34; the verb ירש, *yarash*, plus אֶרֶץ, *'erets*). This contradicts our present experience where we see the wicked prospering and the righteous often being disinherited; therefore, David must be speaking about a future period[10] in which the righteous will inherit the earth and the wicked will be absent from it,[11] a situation described by a later revelation: "And many of them that sleep in the dust of the earth shall awake, some to everlasting life, and some to shame and everlasting contempt" (Dan. 12:2). Consistent with this is God's instruction to Jeremiah, who never had any offspring and who died in exile, to hide in a jar the deeds to a piece of land in Israel that he would later inherit (Jer. 32:9–15). Furthermore, David identifies the righteous heirs as "the meek" (v. 11); Christ's promise no doubt alludes to this psalm (Matt. 5:5). This understanding of the psalm finds special significance in the fact that on the fourth mention of the land or earth

---

[8] "In a psalm with Mosaic echoes, seeing God's likeness reminds us of Exod 33:18-23; Num 12:8; and Deut 34:10." Grogan, 64.

[9] Moll acknowledges an "undeniable reference" to what God did for Moses and that "In the present context a glance is given into *eternity*." The doctrinal conclusion he draws from the psalm is that "He who has God has *life*. This truth enters only into the *experience* of the soul which has communion with God." The source of comfort for that person is the knowledge of "beholding *in the future that form* of God, in which those who are completely blessed, will see Him as He is" (pp. 133–34). Even a critic like W. O. E. Oesterley can sum up what he thinks is the psalmist's "unexpressed thought": "How can communion with the ever-living God be broken by death?" *The Psalms* (New York: Macmillan, 1939), 1:161.

[10] Even the critic Kraus admits that the reference to the inheritance of the land is "in the eschatological sense" according to Isaiah 57:13 (1:406).

[11] "While David undoubtedly thought of occupying the Promised Land, there is also an eschatological fulfillment. In the millennial kingdom, believers will indeed 'inherit the earth' ...." Steveson, 149.

David says that the righteous will "dwell therein for ever" (v. 29b). He was proclaiming something that was truly eternal.

Psalm 49:15

In another wisdom psalm after the author has spoken about the foolish in relation to Sheol and death (49:14), he exclaims, "But God will redeem my soul from the power of the grave: for he shall receive me" (v. 15). This verse is one of the clearest in the Old Testament regarding the saint's hope for the afterlife. There is an allusion here: the Hebrew verb translated "receive" is לקח (*laqakh*), the same verb used in Genesis 5:24 ("God took him.") for the translation of Enoch. A later writer would use this verb again four times in the account of Elijah's departure from this life (2 Kings 2:3, 5, 9, and 10). Even a critical scholar like Mitchell Dahood, who on the basis of his Ugaritic studies has acknowledged that Psalms has much to say about the afterlife, notes that this writer "is stating his belief in 'assumption.'"[12] Now the psalmist was not really expecting a bodily assumption to heaven as Elijah experienced; rather he had the same hope Paul had (2 Cor. 5:8), that at death God would take his soul, his essential self, to heaven. Modern Christians use this same kind of language ("The Lord *took* him home.") to indicate not that the departed loved-one was bodily transported to heaven but that the soul has gone to heaven.

Once we understand verse 15, we realize that verse 9 is not just talking about a long life in this world but about eternal life. The grammar of verses 7–9 has given Bible translators problems. The difficult connection in thought between verses 7 and 8 has led commentators and translators to insert the word "that" at the beginning of verse 9 while subordinating verse 8 (by using dashes or parentheses) as a parenthetic idea. They have thus missed noticing a remarkable declaration of hope. Normal grammatical usage (a jussive followed by a model imperfect) would require verse 9 to say, "But let him still live for ever! He should not see the pit" (literal translation). Because we already know from verse 8 that redemption's price is too great for man himself to pay, by implication God Himself must have furnished a ransom so that a person could possess the eternal life that God ordered in verse 9.

---

[12] *Psalms I*, vol. 16 of The Anchor Bible, ed. William Foxwell Albright and David Noel Freedman (New York: Doubleday, 1966), 301.

Theological Themes of Psalms
Psalm 73:24–26

In still another wisdom psalm a different author confesses that because of envy he had almost abandoned his trust in God (73:2–3).[13] Then he testifies that what secured for him the correct perspective was God's revelatory word, apparently heard proclaimed at the temple (v. 17). Facts about the future for the wicked (vv. 18–20) stabilized this saint as he also understood the truth of his relationship with God: "Thou shalt guide me with thy counsel, and afterward receive me to glory" (v. 24). Starting with this verse, we learn several key facts based on the interpretation of four elements in verses 24–26.[14] (1) The first element is the word אַחַר (*'akhar*), "afterward," which can be either a preposition ("behind" or "after") or an adverb. In this context the preposition makes no sense.[15] The adverb, however, would point to a contrast between the two verbs ("guide" and "take"), both Hebrew imperfects. The first imperfect thus indicates what happens in the ongoing present;[16] the second is used for the future. The psalmist knows the truth that God is guiding him in the **present** and in the **future** heaven awaits him. By mentioning "heaven" and "earth," verse 25 confirms that there is a sharp and clear distinction between this present life on earth and some kind of future existence.

(2) The next element is כָּבוֹד (*kavowd*), "glory," a noun referring to the place where the psalmist expects to be taken. We are in the habit of referring to heaven as "glory" (for example, "gone to glory"),[17] but this is not

---

[13] "He had well-nigh slipped from the rock of faith into the abyss of scepticism" (Rawlinson, 2:70).

[14] Tate refers to "this enigmatic verse," with each of the last three words posing a problem (pp. 230, 236). These three words are the first three elements above.

[15] What would "behind glory" mean? The LXX followed by the Vulgate did, however, treat it as a preposition in the sense of "with glory." But changing the meaning of the preposition still does not get rid of the difficulty.

[16] The rabbinic Aramaic Targum interprets verse 24a by adding, "… in this world." David M. Stec, *The Targum of Psalms: Translated, with a Critical Introduction, Apparatus, and Notes,* vol. 16 of The Aramaic Bible (Collegeville, Minn: Liturgical Press, 2004), 103.

[17] Kidner is insistent that this psalmist was thinking here of eternity: "We may well conclude that if eternal life was visible to a discerning eye even in the saying

the case for the language of the Old Testament. If we recognize, however, that this word can be a reference to the Shekinah, a clearly established Old Testament usage (Exod. 40:35; 1 Kings 8:11), then the author is speaking about God's very presence, and He is clearly visible in heaven.[18]

(3) At the end of verse 24 there is an allusion again to Enoch in the verb "receive" or "take" (לקח, *laqakh*), indicating the transfer of the soul into God's presence, here called "glory." The object of this verb, "me," cannot have reference to the psalmist's body in the sense of a bodily rapture like Enoch's experience. In this context he says that "My flesh and my heart faileth" (v. 26a), knowing that his body and mind are deteriorating toward death.[19] That would mean that the "me" refers to his soul, the essence of his personality, that would be taken to God's presence in heaven.[20]

(4) The last element is the phrase "my portion for ever" (v. 26c). The expression לְעוֹלָם, *le'owlam*, "forever," appears 92x in Psalms. Although the noun can have the meaning "ancient" (for example, "ancient doors," 24:7,

---

'I am the God of Abraham, … Isaac, and … Jacob', as our Lord pointed out, here it lies open for all to see" (16:292).

[18] "And after a life of divine guidance there will come an acceptance into His immediate presence 'in glory.' True, this glory is not defined more fully for the present, but it is, nevertheless, a marvelous and wonderful prospect" (Leupold, 530). Some other commentators who recognize this interpretation of the word "glory" include Barnes (2:261), Rawlinson (2:72), VanGemeren (p. 566), Mays (p. 243), Boice (2:615), Eaton (p. 267), and Steveson (p. 284). Moll points out that "it is best to consider [the word] as the accusative of the end striven after …, namely, the glory of God …, into which the Psalmist hopes to be taken up, Gen. v. 24; Ps. xlix. 16…. It is, to be sure, only since Grotius, that we find in some expositors the limitation of these words to the *earthly* life" (p. 416).

[19] "… he seems to have placed himself by imagination in the situation where his strength would be all gone—in sickness, in weakness, in sorrow, on the bed of death. He asks himself now what would be his strength then, … and he answers without hesitation, and with entire confidence, that he could rely on God …. Even then, when heart and flesh should fail, when all the powers of mind and body should be exhausted, the love of God would survive, and he would find strength and joy in Him." Barnes, 2:262.

[20] "So guided, the Lord's Chosen One will at last … be 'taken' or 'received' into glory; although this could be understood of eventual victory on earth, a heavenly destiny is more probably in mind …. In v. 26 again, some understand the failing of flesh and heart as a temporary suffering within earthly life; but, as in v. 24b, the prospect could be of an eternal bliss beyond the body's death …." Eaton, 267.

NASB), when connected to the preposition, however, it means "for all time." Because of an indication of approaching death in the first part of this verse, the psalmist must have in mind an eternal inheritance, something involving the afterlife. His present life was not showing much promise (v. 14);[21] therefore, hope lay in what was in store for him in eternity.[22]

Vocabulary Involved with the Afterlife

A further benefit of studying these four portions is that they add to our confidence in identifying the vocabulary relevant for the theme of eternal life. Their clear teaching about the afterlife encourages a search of the whole book for further information. David's reference in 17:15 to an existence after death (whether in resurrection or immediate presence in heaven) leads us to investigate the occurrences of the noun for "life" (חַיִּים, *khayyim*)[23] and the verb "to live" (חָיָה, *khayah*) to determine which ones refer to the afterlife. Table 27.1 charts 21 cases out of the 30 occurrences of the noun in Psalms where it probably refers to eternal life. For example, in 21:4 parallel to the "life" David requested from God is the phrase "length of days for ever and ever," indicating that God gave the king everlasting life.[24] The verb occurs 31 times in the book, and in 23 of these contexts it can in refer to life beyond present earthly existence. For example, in 22:26 the mention of לָעַד (*la'ad*, "forever") in the clause "May your hearts live forever" (ESV)[25] would indicate

---

[21] "Of each and all, however vigorous they may now be, it will be true that 'flesh and heart' will 'fail;' of each and all it is true that when this shall occur, none but God can be the portion and the strength of the soul." Barnes, 2:262.

[22] Appendix C catalogues thirteen expressions that refer to perpetuity and in many cases to eternity itself, especially in connection with God's attributes.

[23] "Though Daniel 12:2 is often given in the lexicons as the only place where *hayyîm* means eternal life, Dahood sees it in many places and more than once refers to the Ugaritic antecedent in 2 Aqht VI 27–29." Smick, 108.

[24] "But life here is a pregnant word, as appears by its parallel, 'length of days for ever and ever.' It reaches into the life eternal, and therefore includes the life that comes by the new birth from above." Murphy, 167. Having studied similar wording in the Ugaritic texts, Dahood says, "it follows with considerable probability that *hayyîm* here, as well as in Prov. xii 28, means 'eternal life'" (1:132).

[25] "The phrase … has a jussive sense …. It is a benediction, praying God's *everlasting* blessing on those who join the Lord in praising the Father, v. 26" (my emphasis). Steveson, 94–95.

Table 27.1 Key Terms Pointing to the Concept Eternal Life

Psalm	חַיִּים khayyim — life	חָיָה khayah — to live	נֶפֶשׁ nephesh — soul	אַשְׁרֵי 'ashrey — fortunate	בְּרַךְ barak — to bless
1:				1	
2:				12	
5:					12
6:			4		
16:	11		10		
21:	4				
22:		26			
23:	6				
25:			20		
26:	9		9		
27:	1, 4				
28:					9
29:					11
30:	5				
32:				1, 2	
33:			20	12	
34:	12		22	8	
36:	9				
37:					22
40:				4	
41:		2	4	1	
42:	8				
45:					2
49:		9	8, 15		
54:			4		
56:	13		13		
62:			1, 5		
63:	4				
64:	1				
65:				4	
66:	9		16		
67:					1, 6, 7
69:	28	32	18		
71:		20	23		
72:		15			
80:		18			
84:				4, 5, 12	
85:		6			
86:			2, 13		
89:		48	48	15	
94:				12	
103:	4				
104:	33				
106:				3	
109:			31		28
112:				1	2
115:					12 [3], 13, 15
116:	9		4, 8		
119:		[13x]†		1, 2	

Hebrew words:	חַיִּים khayyim	חָיָה khayah	נֶפֶשׁ nephesh	אַשְׁרֵי 'ashrey	בָרַךְ barak
Psalm	life	to live	soul	fortunate	to bless
128:	5			1, 2	4, 5
133:	3				
134:					3
138:		7			
144:				15b	
146:	2			5	
147:					13
totals:	21 (9/6/0/2/4)	23 (2/4/3/0/14)	22 (7/9/3/0/3)	22 (8/1/4/2/7)	19 (4/4/0/0/11)

† 119:37, 40, 50, 77, 88, 93, 116, 144, 149, 154, 156, 159, 175

an afterlife. Psalm 49:9 with its reference to living "forever" serves to confirm this understanding of the verb.

In Psalm 37 David's clear contrast of the wicked being "cut off" while the righteous inherit the earth indicates to us a blessing (v. 22) for the latter group that involves something after death. This directs us, therefore, to investigate the 74 uses of בָרַךְ (barak, "bless") and the 26 uses of אַשְׁרֵי ('ashrey, "blessed")26 to determine which ones may refer to the afterlife. Table 27.1 logs the results of the study: 19 instances for the former and 22 for the latter. For example, 2:12 proclaims as fortunate "all they that put their trust in" the Son, a blessing that is realized only truly after this present life, for now in this life many of the saints suffer pain and poverty. Psalm 5:12a declares that "For thou, Lord, wilt bless the righteous ...." Surely this has reference to heaven and eternity. Additionally, three of the nine uses of the noun בְּרָכָה (berakah, "blessing") refer to something beyond earthly bliss: "For thou hast made him most blessed for ever: thou hast made him exceeding glad with thy countenance" (21:6); "He shall receive the blessing from the Lord, and righteousness from the God of his salvation" (24:5); and "... for there the Lord commanded the blessing, even life for evermore"

---

26 This latter term is not used as a description of God, only of mankind. It is translated into English as "blessed" or "happy," but probably the best rendering would be "fortunate" of "privileged." In life sometimes those who appear fortunate or privileged turn out in the long run to be cursed by the very assets they treasured. A rich man may eventually be cursed because of his wealth; a beautiful woman may find that her attractiveness, which others envy, leads to her being kidnapped and sexually abused. When the Lord, however, declares someone as "fortunate," as happens in Psalms and in the Beatitudes, then that person has real, lasting assets, what the human heart truly wishes for. For a discussion that concludes that "truly happy" is the best translation, see Michael L. Brown, "אַשְׁרֵי," NIDOTTE, 1:570–71.

(133:3b). Note that 21:6 follows the verse that just mentioned "length of days for ever and ever"!

Because we realize in Psalm 49 that the psalmist expected to be taken to heaven apart from his body, the redemption of the soul, that is mentioned twice (vv. 8, 15), must have reference to the immaterial part of man. This alerts us that the word נֶפֶשׁ (*nephesh*), "soul,"[27] can refer to the immaterial part of man that being separated from the body is able to have an existence in the afterlife after death. It would therefore be profitable to look among the term's 144 occurrences in Psalms for additional cases where the Holy Spirit refers to the soul apart from the body. Because of the connection of "redemption" and "soul" in Psalm 49, passages relating to the salvation of the soul would be key candidates for consideration. Including the two cases in Psalm 49, Table 27.1 charts a total of 22 instances. For example, when David prays for God to rescue or to deliver his soul (6:4; 25:20; 69:18; 86:2),[28] was he not concerned about a salvation beyond a temporal preservation from bodily death? David makes a special request in 26:9 that God would "not sweep [his] soul away with sinners, nor [his] life with bloodthirsty men" (ESV). He wants to be spared "from a common fate with them," but he must know that all die; therefore, what he is really asking for is deliverance from

---

[27] This Hebrew word has three primary meanings in the Old Testament: (1) "life" (for example, "the life of the flesh" in Lev. 17:11), (2) "person" ("that person shall be cut off" in Gen. 17:14, NASB), and (3) "self" ("my soul [=I] shall not abhor you" in Lev. 26:11b). See D. C. Fredericks, "נֶפֶשׁ," *NIDOTTE*, 3:133. I disagree with Bruce K. Waltke's conclusion that "the OT presents man as physical only" ("*nepesh*," *TWOT*, 2:591). Since we recognize that the essence of a human person (meaning 2) is fundamentally identified with one's inner, immaterial part (the real "I"), by synecdoche (whole for a part) the word in many cases refers to a person's soul.

[28] An additional case would be 116:4b, where the anonymous psalmist prays, "O LORD, I beseech thee, deliver my soul." The commentators interpret this as a rescue from physical death (Barnes, 3:160; Kidner, 16:443; Futato, 362). Because of the reference to Sheol in verse 3 and the verb "deliver" (a synonym of "redeem"), it is possible that the psalmist had something in mind beyond physical death. What confirms this is his later comment that "Precious in the sight of the LORD is the death of his saints" (v. 15). We need to realize that for the natural man his fear of death is connected to an innate sense (which he often tries to suppress) that after death he must face a judge who will call him to account. The terrors of physical death pale in comparison to the horror of a final helplessness in eternal death as a judgment from one's Creator.

eternal condemnation when he faces the Judge in the afterlife.[29] David affirms in 34:22 this exemption from judgment and couples it with salvation of the soul: "The LORD redeems the soul of His servants, And none of those who take refuge in Him will be condemned" (NASB).[30] Is this not spiritual salvation, what the Bible refers to as justification by faith (Rom. 3:28)? Furthermore, David ends Psalm 109 with the same truth about the soul: "For he [Yahweh] shall stand at the right hand of the poor, to save him from those that condemn his soul" (v. 31).[31] David's reference to "those that condemn" becomes understandable for us in light of Zechariah 3, which presents Satan is the accuser of the saints.[32] The plural ("those") in 109:31 indicates that demons and evil men join Satan as accusers, those that would condemn God's forgiven and regenerated children.

Although it does not employ any of the key terms, Psalm 73 verifies, nevertheless, (1) that there is **life** after death in God's presence (v. 24), (2) that God transports the saint's **soul**, his immaterial part, to heaven (v. 24), and (3) that the ultimate **blessing** is to enjoy God's very presence in the inheritance of paradise. Asaph establishes this last point by referring to the Shekinah ("glory" in v. 24), by asking, "Whom have I in heaven *but thee?*" (v. 25), and then by exclaiming, "God *is* the strength of my heart, and my portion for ever" (v. 26b).[33]

---

[29] "When the LORD begins to judge the wicked, whether in his lifetime or at the end of the age, he does not want to be judged with them." Ross, 1:617. "He did not wish to be associated with them when he died or was dead. He had preferred the society of the righteous; and he prayed that he might die as he had lived, united in feeling and in destiny with those who feared and loved God." Barnes, 1:235.

[30] "In the last stanza the psalm moves beyond mere deliverance or blessing in this life to speak of death and, by implication, also of life beyond the grave. In this context it speaks of redemption and deliverance from God's final condemnation or judgment (vv. 21–22)." Boice, 1:298.

[31] Rawlinson points out that "The salvation is not always from the death of the body, or there could have been no martyrs; but in all cases it is a deliverance of the soul" (3:22).

[32] See Boice, 3:890.

[33] "In the midst of the natural life of perishableness and of sin, a new, individual life which is resigned to God has begun within [the poet], and in this he has the pledge that he cannot perish, so truly as God, with whom it is closely united, cannot perish." Delitzsch, 2:322. This is the greatest blessing!

Propositions

If the above exegesis and theological argumentation are correct, then there are at least 104 verses[34] in Psalms that declare truths about the afterlife for the saints. (1) The first theological proposition is that *there is indeed an existence for mankind beyond this life*. The book presents two aspects of this hope: (a) the resurrection of the body (16:10; 22:29; 56:13; 71:20;[35] 89:48) and (b) the soul taken to heaven (17:15; 49:15; 73:24).[36] The majority of the verses that indicate this proposition, however, do not distinguish which aspect the psalmist has in mind. For example, when David says, "weeping may endure for a night, but joy cometh in the morning" (30:5b), the "life" of 30:5a must be eternal life.[37] When he asks the rhetorical question in 34:12, the "life" to which he refers must relate to the hope of resurrection or presence in heaven in the intermediate state since the persons he addresses are already alive in an earthly sense. In Psalm 119 when the poet says "quicken me" or "revive me" (NASB, NET), seven times (vv. 37, 40, 88, 149, 154, 156, and 159) there is something in the context to show that he is asking God for life following his earthly departure. For example, his associating this life with God's immutable attributes (righteousness, v. 40; lovingkindness, vv. 88,

---

[34] Counting the separate verses from the table (i.e., counting only once a verse with multiple occurrences of a key term) plus two cases of בְּרָכָה (*barakah*, "blessing"; 133:3 contained a key word as well so was already counted) and 17:15 (which did not contain any of the key terms).

[35] "It is tempting to read verse 20 as a statement about resurrection, but in the Hebrew text the first two lines speak of 'us' rather than 'me'. Israel, like the psalmist, has seen its disasters, but its revivals too; he can have the same confidence. Pressed to its conclusion, this hope makes little sense if it stops short of resurrection; but the psalmist shows no sign of looking further than a new lease of life." Kidner, 15:272. Broyles admits, "Within the horizon of the NT, claims like **from the depths of the earth** (i.e., the underworld of Sheol) **you will bring me up** could denote resurrection" (p. 293).

[36] "It is clear …, in a small but significant number of psalms, that the ultimate destiny of the believing psalmist was in continued fellowship with God. He is convinced that the fellowship with God that he experienced during his lifetime would not be terminated at death but would go on and, indeed, in some way would be consummated." Grogan, 423.

[37] "The morning will come; a morning without clouds; a morning when the sources of sorrow will disappear. This often occurs in the present life; it will always occur to the righteous in the life to come." Barnes, 256.

149, 159; justice, v. 149; and compassion, v. 156) could point to a request for eternal life.[38] Because we understand that spiritual regeneration results from the power of God's word, the mention of that word in connection to the poet's being made alive (vv. 37,[39] 50, 77, 93, 116, 144, 149, 154, 156, 159, and 175) implies that the Holy Spirit is referring to eternal life.[40]

(2) *The afterlife for the saints is in God's very presence.* When David made the bold statement in 11:7 that "The upright will behold His face" (NASB), he knew under inspiration that he would see God in heaven.[41] Additionally, three verses from our list refer to this fact: (a) after referring to "the path of [eternal] life," David says, "in thy presence is fullness of joy" (16:11); (b) after referring to everlasting life ("all the days of my life"), David says, "I will dwell in the house of the LORD for ever" (23:6);[42] and (c) his one desire is "that I may dwell in the house of the LORD all the days of my [eternal] life, to behold the beauty of the LORD, and to enquire in his temple" (27:4).

---

[38] "That the faithful remain living even after the death of the body is assured, argues Calvin, through God's divine nature, especially his immutability." Herman J. Selderhuis, *Calvin's Theology of the Psalms* (Grand Rapids: Baker Academic, 2007), 174. "It is true, that when through our own fault we become estranged from God, we are also as it were cut off from the fountain of life; but no sooner are we reconciled to Him than he begins again to pour down his blessings upon us. Whence it follows that true believers, as they are regenerated by the incorruptible seed, shall continue to live after death, because God continues unchangeably the same." Calvin, 4:123.

[39] NIV and NET have "word" (rather than "way") based on the Aramaic Targum.

[40] In two additional cases the references to "dust" (v. 25) and "affliction" (v. 107) would signal that these are requests for God to preserve his earthly life, a deliverance from a premature death.

[41] "The psalmists knew the experience of seeing God with the inward eye in worship (e.g. 27:4; 63:2); but there is little doubt that they were led to look beyond this to an unmediated vision when they would be ransomed and awakened from death 'to behold (his) face in righteousness' (cf. 16:8–11; 17:15; 23:6; 49:15; 73:23ff.; 139:18)." Kidner, 15:91.

[42] "By this concluding sentence he manifestly shows that he does not confine his thoughts to earthly pleasures or comforts; but that the mark at which he aims is fixed in heaven, and to reach this was his great object in all things." Calvin, 1:399.

(3) The saints will stand before God uncondemned and redeemed. The psalmist testifies about God's work of salvation: "Come and hear, all ye that fear God, and I will declare what he hath done for my soul" (66:16). In this third proposition the possibility for the saints' being uncondemned is the other side of their being redeemed; for those who have sinned, it is impossible to have one without the other. The concepts occur together in 32:1–2 and 34:22. Escape from condemnation appears in 16:10; 26:9; and 109:31, each of which mention the soul. The terms for redemption and soul occur together in 34:22; 49:8, 15; 69:18; and 71:23.[43] In 103:4 David blesses Yahweh for redeeming his "life from destruction,"[44] a reference to spiritual salvation. The psalmists refer to the redemption of the soul additionally by using various synonyms: deliver (6:4; 56:13; 86:13; 116:8), guard or preserve (25:20; 86:2), heal (41:4), save (116:4, NASB & HCSB), and uphold (54:4). Possessing this redemption is truly the blessed state, fortunate for the saints. Table 27.1 lists 41 cases where the two words "fortunate" and "to bless" refer to this kind of bliss. For example, 65:4a exclaims, "Blessed is the man whom thou choosest, and causest to approach unto thee, that he may dwell in thy courts." Is this not a reference to God's elect and the saint in heaven? Furthermore, that privileged condition is connected to faith in 2:12b ("Blessed are all they that put their trust in him").

New Testament Echoes

The specific mention of "eternal life" occurs 43 times in the New Testament, especially in the Gospel of John (17x). This statistic is based on seven different combinations of the Greek noun ζωή (*zōay*, "life") and adjective αἰώνιος (*aiōnios*, "eternal"). The KJV reflects some of the variations and thus has the exact expression "eternal life" only 26 times, but some other English translations render each of the 43 as "eternal life" (RSV, NRSV, ESV, HCSB). Of course, there are various other ways the New Testament expresses the concept: "live forever" (for example, John 6:51) or just simply "life" (for example, "narrow *is* the way, which leadeth unto life," Matt. 7:14; "Christ … hath brought life and immortality to light," 2 Tim. 1:10). Thus the first proposition stands: believers possess "the hope of eternal life" (Tit. 3:7c).

---

[43] In 72:14 the redemption refers to the King's deliverance of the poor from injustices their enemies inflict on them. See VanGemeren, 553.

[44] "While not an explicit statement, the phrase implies the resurrection of the believing dead." Steveson, 393.

Theological Themes of Psalms

The second is echoed in Christ's words to His disciples: "I go to prepare a place for you.... I will come again, and receive you unto myself; that where I am, there ye may be also" (John 14:2b–3). Jude 24 is another echo: God is able "to present you faultless before the presence of his glory." Affirmation of the third proposition, uncondemned (forgiven) and redeemed, appears most clearly in Ephesians: "In whom we have redemption through his blood, the forgiveness of sins" (1:7a). Galatians 3:13a is also significant: "Christ hath redeemed us from the curse of the law," the law that would have condemned us!

We conclude where Psalms begins: "Blessed is the man ..." (1:1). The Bible, taken as a whole, makes clear that the greatest blessing for any person lies in the afterlife, where the righteous experience paradise, free from the condemnation laid out for the wicked. The Korahite psalmist has expressed the hope of mankind when he wrote, "so that he may live forever and not see the Pit" (49:9, HCSB).

28

Sovereignty

The bliss of eternal life that the saints will experience is necessarily bound up with the promised kingdom and reign of God's Messiah. Because the Old Testament as well as the New indicates that the Messiah is Himself Yahweh,[1] in Psalms many of the references to Yahweh's sovereignty and His kingship[2] are actually messianic. The theme of sovereignty itself begins in Psalm 2, where Yahweh (God the Father) says, "Yet have I set my king upon my holy hill of Zion" (v. 6), and it continues through other royal psalms (20, 21, 45, 72, 89, 101, 110, 132, 144)[3] as well as in various verses all the way to Psalm 149, which tells of the messianic "King" (v. 2) and His coming in judgment of the "nations" and "peoples" (vv. 7–9, NASB).[4] Providentially,

---

[1] The OT concept of the divine Messiah appears most clearly in Isaiah 9:6 ("The mighty God") and Micah 5:2 ("whose goings forth have been from of old, from everlasting"). Of course, there are various additional pointers to this truth, as Christ Himself indicated in Mark 12:35–37.

[2] John Luther Mays asks the question, "Is there in the psalms some one central, organic characterization of God out of which all the rest unfolds and to which all the variety can be treated?" His answer is "that an organizing center for the theology of the psalms can be found in the sentence *Yhwh malak*" ("The LORD reigneth"). *The Lord Reigns: A Theological Handbook to the Psalms* (Louisville: Westminster John Knox, 1994), 12–13. Allan Harman concurs: "It is hardly surprising that the central fact of Israel's faith, that the Lord was their king, should be so prominent in the songs of the people" (1:72).

[3] Many would classify Psalm 18 as one of these. Appendix B, however, regards this psalm as primarily an individual Thanksgiving song because of verses 1-6 and 16-19. The psalm is composite, and certainly some verses clearly fit what would be expected in a royal psalm.

[4] It is normal to understand these verses as referring to "the saints" (v. 5), Messiah's people, but since each of these verses begins with an infinitive, "It is not

293

the crowd on Palm Sunday quoted 118:26, "Blessed be he that cometh in the name of the LORD" (Matt. 21:9), and the Lord Jesus used this reference again when He prophesied how Jerusalem would greet Him at the divine visitation of His Second Coming (Matt. 23:39). Thus this theme of messianic sovereignty is the primary eschatological theology in Psalms. Normally, we do not think of Psalms as a book about the "last things."[5] By meditating, however, on the concept of sovereignty (identified by some special terms) and by connecting this to the Messiah, we discover that Psalms has much to say about the destiny of our planet, namely the coming messianic King and His future work.

There is, however, a complicating factor for this theological theme: many psalms speak of Yahweh's sovereignty in heaven (for example, 2:4; 11:4) and furthermore would indicate that He is presently and eternally "the King" (for example, 5:2; 29:10b; 47:2; 84:3b). We could call this "original sovereignty" to distinguish it. Original sovereignty is certainly linked to creation (for example, 24:1–2; 89:11–12), and as the Creator, Yahweh owns everything (50:10–12) and superintends all nature (65:6–13; 104:7–17) and mankind (33:13–19; 75:7b; 147:6).[6] In the introductory second Psalm, however, Yahweh, the original Sovereign, anoints His representative on earth, establishing a messianic kingship. The Davidic nature of Psalms points to a focus on God's viceroy, the Anointed, the "Christ" (Greek for "anointed"). The reason for this is the Davidic Covenant, in which Yahweh made an eternal promise about the throne of the Seed of David (89:3–4, 28–29, 34–37). God fulfilled an important part of that promise with His act of incarnation, God with us in the flesh in the person of Christ Jesus, the son of David and thus that Seed. But just as mankind has been in rebellion to the sovereignty of the Creator, there has been rebellious resistance to the Anointed (2:2–3).

---

clear who is the subject of the actions, whether the Lord or his people. The reference to the sword might favor the latter. However, the psalms ascribing kingship to the Lord make it clear that the victory is the Lord's (cf. 96:13; 98:1–3, 8). He will avenge, punish, and bind ...." VanGemeren, 1007. On the other hand, Scripture clearly pictures the avenging King coming with heavenly armies (Rev. 19:11–16), which could be "the saints."

[5] "At first sight the book of Psalms appears to have a somewhat thin eschatology." But "there is more here of eschatological significance than might appear on a cursory reading." Grogan, 418.

[6] "... the creator God is a sovereign who exercises his rule over the world and over his human creatures in particular." Harman, 70.

The essential connection between the two rebellions finds its counterpart in the blending of original and messianic sovereignty. Thus we may treat the two as one theme and thereby concentrate on its fundamental eschatological focus. Psalm 2 itself does not really conform to some historical context in David's life,[7] but properly interpreted it speaks to all mankind ("nations," "peoples," "kings," "rulers") and refers to future events (vv. 8–9). The New Testament indicates to us that this Psalm realizes its fulfillment in Christ (Acts 4:25–26; 13:33; Heb. 1:5a; 5:5) and in His future coming in judgment (Rev. 19:15). These future events of sovereignty over all nations and universal judgment and rule will appear as themes in many other psalms which speak of Yahweh's reigning (for example, 93:1; 99:1).

Vocabulary of Sovereignty

When we think of sovereignty, the words "king" and "lord" naturally come to mind. By searching for these terms in Psalms, we discover a significant number of psalms that refer to this theme. Not every occurrence of the word מֶלֶךְ (*melek*, "king") is relevant: 24 out of the 40 uses of the singular refer to God's or the Messiah's kingship. The same is true for the word אָדוֹן (*'adown*, "lord")[8] with 10 of its 13 uses in Psalms. On the other hand all 54 uses of אֲדֹנָי (*'Adownay*, "Lord")[9] have significance for the subject of sovereignty.[10] Of course, the term "kingdom" naturally refers to sovereignty, but the two Hebrew words for this are relatively rare in Psalms: מַלְכוּת (*malkuwth*) and מְלוּכָה (*meluwkah*).[11] Actually, the second word probably means "kingship" or "dominion,"[11] a reference to ruling power rather than the realm of a king; it occurs only in 22:28 but 23 other times in the Old Testament. Another Hebrew word for "dominion" is מֶמְשָׁלָה (*memshalah*;

---

[7] "A greater, however, than David or Solomon was needed to justify the full fury of these threats and the glory of these promises." Kidner, 15:66.

[8] "The most common synonyms to *'ādôn* equate it with rulership or kingship." Gordon H. Johnson, "אָדוֹן," *NIDOTTE*, 1:257.

[9] This word is a special form of אָדוֹן (*'adown*), literally "my Lords," with the plural indicating a special honor or majesty for God. After the time of Moses the "my" part of the term seems to lose its force, the term becoming simply "Lord"; therefore, we find God referring to Himself as "Lord" (for example, Amos 9:8).

[10] "The use of this title indicates that he is the sovereign master, and everyone else is a servant." Ross, 1:205.

[11] VanGemeren, 249.

103:22; 114:2; 145:13). The verb related to מֶלֶךְ (*melek*) is מלך (*malak*, "to reign"), a very common Hebrew word but occurring just six times in the book. Its synonym is מָשַׁל (*mashal*, "to rule"), used with God as its subject five of its ten times in Psalms. In 103:19 this verb appears with the noun מַלְכוּת (*malkuwth*) and the word כִּסֵּא (*kissey'*, "throne"), indicating that this is another term signifying sovereignty. In Psalms "throne" occurs 18 times, 14 of which refer to God's authority.

Additionally, some other key passages signal important words for this theme. Psalm 47:7–9 associates the terms "King," "to reign," and "throne" with גּוֹיִם (*gowyim*, "nations") and עַמִּים (*'ammiym*, "peoples"). The plural of these words occurs in Psalms often in contexts that indicate universal divine sovereignty rather than David's limited authority over the nation and people of Israel (for example, 33:10; 96:10). The noun אֻמִּים (*'ummiym*, "peoples"), a synonym for עַמִּים (*'ammiym*), occurs just once in 117:1. Earlier in Psalm 47 the King (v. 2) and the nations (v. 3) are mentioned alongside of לְאֻמִּים (*le'ummiym*), another word for "peoples"; in this context of sovereignty an additional name of God appears: עֶלְיוֹן (*'Elyown*, "Most High"),[12] associated with sovereignty also in 83:18.[13]

David asks a question in 24:10, "Who is this King of glory?" His answer provides us with another divine title that indicates sovereignty: יהוה צְבָאוֹת (*Yahweh tseva'owth*, "The LORD of Hosts"). This title or variations of it occur 15 times in Psalms. The mention of "kings" bringing tribute to the Messiah (68:29) or fearing God's glory (102:15) alerts us that the use of מְלָכִים (*melakiym*, "kings") can be another indication of a sovereignty passage.[14] Table 28:2 classifies 11 out of the 24 occurrences of "kings" in Psalms

---

[12] This name "gave witness to an absolute right to lordship and majesty over the entire world, in contrast to the claims of all gods and supernatural powers." Hans-Joachim Kraus, *Theology of the Psalms*, trans. Keith Crim (Minneapolis: Augsburg, 1986), 25. Harman agrees: "It emphasises the majesty of God, and it mainly appears in contexts in which universal claims are made in connection with Israel's God" (1:130).

[13] Table 28.3 below list 21 cases of this title in Psalms. NIV and NET include two more occurrences (7:8, 10) by understanding עָלַי and עַל (*'alay* & *'al*; the main word usually translated as a preposition) as shortened forms of עֶלְיוֹן (*'Elyown*, "Most High"). See Dahood, 1:45–46.

[14] In 68:29 "David now looks into the future to when the Lord sets up His kingdom and rules the earth from Jerusalem." Steveson, 259. 102:13–16 have reference to the future when God will appear in His glory to exert His sovereignty

Table 28.1 Key Terms for Sovereignty

Hebrew words:	מֶלֶךְ *melek* King	אֲדֹנָי *'Adownay* Lord	כִּסֵּא *kissey'* throne	גּוֹים *gowyiym* nations	עַמִּים *'ammiym* peoples
Psalm					
2:	6	4		1, 8	
5:	2				
7:					8
9:			4, 7	5, 15, 17, 19, 20	11
10:	16			16	
11:			4		
16:		2			
18:				43, 49	47
20:	9				
22:		30		27, 28	
24:	7, 8, 9, 10 [2]				
29:	10				
30:		8			
33:				10	10
35:		17, 22, 23			
37:		13			
38:		9, 15, 22			
39:		7			
40:		17			
44:	4	23			
45:	1, 5		6		5, 17
46:				6, 10	
47:	2, 6, 7		8	8	1, 3, 9
48:	2				
49:					1
51:		15			
54:		4			
55:		9			
57:		9			9
59:		11		5, 8	
62:		12			
66:		18		7	8
67:				2	3 [2], 4, 5 [2]
68:	24	11, 17, 19, 20, 22, 32			30
69:		6			
71:		5, 16			
72:				11, 17	
73:		20, 28			
74:	12				
77:		2, 7			14
78:		65			
79:		12		6	
82:				8	
84:	3				

over kings and nations. See Kidner, 16: 394. Rawlinson refers to the plain reality of v. 15 "if extended to the establishment on earth of the new and heavenly Jerusalem" and cross-references Rev. 21 (p. 371).

Hebrew words: Psalm	מֶלֶךְ *melek* King	אֲדֹנָי *'Adownay* Lord	כִּסֵּא *kissey'* throne	גּוֹיִם *gowyiym* nations	עַמִּים *'ammiym* peoples
86:		3, 4, 5, 8, 9, 12, 15		9	
89:		49, 50	4, 14, 29, 36		
90:		1, 17			
93:			2		
94:				10	
95:	3				
96:				3, 10	3, 7, 10, 13
97:			2		6
98:	6			2	9
99:	4				1, 2
102:				15	22
103:			19		
105:					1
108:					3
109:		21			
110:		5		6	
113:				4	
117:				1	
130:		2, 3, 6			
132:			11, 12		
140:		7			
141:		8			
144:					2
145:	1				
149:	2			7	
totals:	24 (9/8/2/3/2)	54 (13/17/15/2/7)	14 (3/2/4/3/2)	34 (13/9/3/5/4)	31 (4/14/1/10/2)

Table 28.2 Additional Terms Connected to Sovereignty

Hebrew	English	#	References	Totals: Ps./all
מלך	to reign	6	47:8; 93:1; 96:10; 97:1; 99:1; 146:10	6/351
מַלְכוּת	kingdom	6	45:6; 105:13; 145:11, 12, 13 [2]	6/91
משׁל	to rule	5	22:28; 59:13; 66:7; 89:9; 103:19	10/81
מֶמְשָׁלָה	dominion	3	103:22; 114:2; 145:13	5/17
לְאֻמִּים	peoples	11	2:1; 7:7; 9:8; 47:3; 57:9; 65:7; 67:4 [2]; 108:4; 148:11; 149:7	14/30
מְלָכִים	kings	11	2:10; 48:4; 68:29; 72:11; 76:12; 102:15; 110:5; 138:4; 144:10; 148:11; 149:8	24/282
ישׁב	to reign	15	2:4; 9:4, 7, 11; 22:3; 29:10 [2]; 33:14; 55:19; 61:7; 80:1; 99:1; 102:12; 113:5; 123:1; 132:14	54/1041

as relevant to this theme. Finally, 9:7, which mentions God's "throne," speaks of Yahweh sitting or dwelling (ישׁב, *yashav*); a number of translations render this as "sits enthroned" (ESV, RSV, NEB, NRSV, HCSB), thus recognizing a specialized use of this very common Hebrew verb—"to reign."[15] In fact, 9:4b says, "thou satest in the throne judging right." In Psalms 15 out of 54 usages of ישׁב have this particular meaning.[16] The three tables below (30.1, 30.2, and 30.3) chart the main words and the less frequent ones.

Table 28.3 Additional Names and Titles Related to Sovereignty in Psalms

Hebrew	English	#	References
אָדוֹן Lord		10	8:1, 9; 12:4; 45:11; 97:5; 110:1; 114:7; 135:5; 136:3; 147:5
עֶלְיוֹן Most High		21	7:17; 9:2; 18:13; 21:7; 46:4; 47:2; 50:14; 57:2; 73:11; 77:10; 78:17, 35, 56; 82:6; 83:18; 87:5; 91:1, 9; 92:1; 97:9; 107:11
יהוה צְבָאוֹת LORD of hosts		15	24:10; 46:7, 11; 48:8; 59:5; 69:6; 80:4, 7, 14, 19; 84:1, 3, 8, 12; 89:8

Propositions

The verses listed in the three tables come from 88 different psalms.[17] A study of these verses and their contexts leads to the following scenario. The sovereign God, the Creator of the universe (33:6–9), established His viceroy on earth (2:6) in a Davidic line of kings (89:3–4). But mankind has rebelled against this sovereignty (2:2–3); however, Psalms prophesies what God will do to reestablish His sovereignty on earth by using the Messiah. This prophecy consists of seven propositions.

(1) *The Lord will descend to earth in a glorious personal appearance.* David, acknowledging mankind's evil (144:8, 10b, 11b) and insignificance (v. 4), prays for Yahweh to "come down" (v. 5a). A similar request for the King to appear in majesty occurs in 45:3–4. In Psalm 72, connected to Solomon but actually fulfilled in the Messiah, the author announces that "He shall come down like rain upon the mown grass: as showers *that* water the

---

[15] Note the following translations of this one word: "reigns" (NIV, NLT), "rules" (NET, NAB, CEV), and "is enthroned" (NJB, JPS).

[16] "In places where the Lord is said to dwell in heaven or in Zion, the thought is that he is enthroned." Walter C. Kaiser, *"yashab,"* TWOT, 1:411–12.

[17] J. H. Eaton lists eleven standard royal psalms (2, 18, 20, 21, 45, 72, 89, 101, 110, 132, 144), 38 "psalms with clearly royal content," and 23 "less clear cases," for a total of 72. There are a number of differences from my list (for example, 3, 4, 101). *Kingship and the Psalms,* Studies in Biblical Theology (Second Series) 32 (Naperville, Ill.: Alec R. Allenson, n.d.), vii.

earth" (v. 6).[18] The glory of that appearance is affirmed in 102:16b.[19] Another way of referring to that glory is to speak about a theophanic appearance by using the term יָפַע (yapha', "shine forth"). Such a request occurs in 80:1, a psalm that repeatedly uses the sovereign name LORD of Hosts, and in 94:1, a context of sovereign judgment of the whole earth; 50:2 states the future reality[20] of this appearance in a universal setting ("the earth from the rising of the sun unto the going down thereof"). Using some synonyms for glory, Moses made a similar request in 90:16–17a. Psalm 96:13 explicitly states that Yahweh "is coming" (HCSB, NASB, NRSV, NJB).[21] When David brought the ark to Jerusalem, the psalm celebrating the incident contained the same expression (1 Chron. 16:33), but since the ark represented God's presence, that occasion was a type of something future, an anticipation of what would eventually happen.[22] There may be one more very significant verse stating this proposition if the Septuagint translators were correct in their understanding of the unpointed text: "The God of the gods shall appear in Zion" (84:7).[23]

---

[18] "Psalm 72 is called a direct messianic psalm because it uses the future tense throughout the psalm and also because it uses frequent hyperbole. King Solomon, who wrote this psalm according to the ancient heading, could not have fulfilled its terms, even in all his glory. Instead, Solomon's reign can supply only the imagery, language, and line of descent for the one and only proper occupant of the throne in his peaceful and prosperous rule and reign to come." Walter C. Kaiser, Jr., *Preaching and Teaching the Last Things: Old Testament Eschatology for the Life of the Church* (Grand Rapids: Baker Academic, 2011), 64.

[19] "The psalmist declares his confidence that God will … come in majestic power to restore Jerusalem…. What actually happened when Jerusalem was restored in the late sixth century BC was only a foreshadowing of the ultimate city of God." Harman, 2:731.

[20] Broyles classifies Psalm 50 as prophetic with allusions to what God did in the past at Sinai (p. 223). The verb in this verse is a prophetic perfect.

[21] These translations understand the Hebrew participle as a *futurum instans*, referring to something about to happen. See *IBHS*, 627 (§37.6f).

[22] Concerning 96:13 Mays asks, "to what does it refer? To a historical or a liturgical or an eschatological event?" His answer is "that these alternatives are not mutually exclusive for Old Testament faith…. The past 'comings' of the LORD have a future. The liturgy remembers and anticipates" (p. 309).

[23] Literal translation of the Greek. RSV, NRSV, NAB, NJB, and NEB follow this reading, which is supported by Aquila and the Syriac Peshitta. Kidner (16:337) and Steveson (p. 330) agree with the LXX.

(2) *The Lord will defeat all His enemies.* Messiah's glorious advent as a warrior means doom for God's enemies. Psalm 24, a worship liturgy, celebrates the entrance of the glorious King into His temple,[24] but it pictures Him as a victorious warrior: "The LORD strong and mighty, the LORD mighty in battle" (v. 8). Consistent with the military picture of the Sovereign is the title "Lord of hosts" (v. 10), "hosts" being the Hebrew term for "armies" (צְבָאוֹת, *tseva'owth*). Psalm 68, which frequently uses the sovereign title "Lord" (6x), begins with David's request: "Let God arise, let his enemies be scattered" (v. 1a). God was a warrior in past events to deliver Israel (vv. 7–8, also 78:65), giving hope for a future victory (v. 21). God's victory march enters His capital with captives and gifts. Other requests for the divine warrior to appear occur in 45:3–4 and 59:5 ("Awake to punish all the nations," NASB). The theme of defeating God's enemies occurs also in 149:6–9.

(3) *The Lord will rescue and regather national Israel to their promised land.* The victory over His enemies results in the liberation of God's people and their return to their ancient inheritance. The prophets Isaiah and Ezekiel spoke frequently about this ingathering,[25] but the psalmists mention this as well. A general request occurs in 106:47, which could refer to an exile now past or one happening in modern times. In 107:2–3, however, the reference to "lands" and all points of the compass would indicate an eschatological event.[26] Although English translations render the verbs of 147:2 ("build" and "gather") as present tense, Hebrew grammar would allow the future tense here: "building Jerusalem, Yahweh will gather the outcasts of Israel" (my translation). The expression "outcasts of Israel" occurs only two other times

---

[24] It is common for commentators to associate this psalm with the procession of the ark into Jerusalem (2 Sam. 6), but there is no reference to the ark in the psalm. For an argument that the psalm prophesies an event yet future, see James D. Smart, "The Eschatological Interpretation of Psalm 24," *JBL* 52 (1933): 175–180. He points out that "If the gates and doors which are to be lifted up for the entrance of Yahweh were no existing ones but rather those of the New Jerusalem of the last days, a real meaning would be given to terming them 'the everlasting doors'. It must be admitted that there is nothing in vv. 7–10 which does not harmonize with an eschatological interpretation" (p. 178).

[25] See David C. Mitchell, *The Message of the Psalter: An Eschatological Programme in the Book of Psalms*, JSOTSup 252 (Sheffield: Sheffield Academic, 1997), 352–54.

[26] Mitchell acknowledges this: "Book V opens with thanksgiving for the accomplished fact of Israel's final ingathering from all the nations …" (p. 295).

301

Theological Themes of Psalms

in the Old Testament: Isaiah 11:12 and 56:8, prophetic verses that have their fulfillment in the millennium.[27] In both verses we find synonymous verbs (אסף, 'asaph; קבץ, qavats) for "gather" (כנס, kanas) in 147:2, and the first verse mentions the idea of Israel returning "from the four corners of the earth." David prophesied that the salvation for Israel brought about by the Sovereign in Zion would include a return from "captivity" (14:7; 53:7).

(4) *The Lord Himself will judge the whole world.* Another important event following the defeat of enemies is the Messiah's judgment of the nations that have been in rebellion against both Him and God's sovereignty. The purpose of the "coming" announced in 96:13 is His worldwide judgment. The request for the Lord to perform this act appears in Psalm 82:8a ("Arise, O God, judge the earth"). The prophecy is stated in 82:1, where God takes His place in court as the Judge of "rulers" (NASB),[28] those who had been given the responsibility of implementing justice in the world. That request shows up again in 94:2 in slightly different words ("Lift up thyself, thou judge of the earth"). By using the words עַמִּים ('ammiym, "peoples") and תֵּבֵל (teyveyl, "world"),[29] the psalmists announce the universality of Yahweh's judgment (7:7–8; 9:8; 96:10, 13). Thus a day is coming when mankind will exclaim, "Verily there is a reward for the righteous: verily he is a God that judgeth in the earth" (58:11). The psalmist uses the prophetic perfect to indicate the certainty of this future event: "Thou didst cause judgment to be heard from heaven; the earth feared, and was still, When God arose to judgment, to save all the meek of the earth" (76:8–9).[30]

---

[27] J. Barton Payne classifies the fulfillment of Isa. 11:11–12 as millennial. *Encyclopedia of Biblical Prophecy: The Complete Guide to Scriptural Predictions and Their Fulfillment* (New York: Harper & Row, 1973), 300. Steveson regards Isa. 56:3–8 as ultimately fulfilled in the millennium (pp. 477–79).

[28] Many other translations understand this as a reference to "gods" because the Hebrew word is (אֱלֹהִים, 'Elowhiym); then this would be a reference to "the tutelary deities of the nations" (Mitchell, 85). The context here and in vv. 7–8, however, require that Asaph is speaking about God's representatives who govern the nations. "But here it would appear, from the scope of the passage, that this name of the Divine Being is applied to those who occupy the exalted station of princes." Calvin, 3:330.

[29] Poetic OT texts use this noun to convey the global concept of earth. See Christopher J. H. Wright, "תֵּבֵל," *NIDOTTE*, 4:272–73.

[30] "This is the end-time …." Kidner, 16:304.

302

(5) *The Lord will establish His universal reign.* After dispensing a just vengeance on a rebellious word, God will reaffirm His universal sovereignty over the earth. The messianic sovereignty will be universal. The proclamation that He reigns first occurs in Psalm 47:8, where "God" (אֱלֹהִים, *'Elowhiym*) is the subject of the verb, which is in the perfect tense. The exclamation "Yahweh reigns" (יהוה מָלָךְ, *YHWH malak*) occurs four times with the verb in the perfect tense (93:1; 96:10; 97:1; 99:1) and once with an imperfect verb ("The LORD shall reign for ever," 146:10a). The last reference is clearly future; however, the perfect tenses are statements that some event has just begun.[31] The Holy Spirit has already written the script for the inauguration of Christ's millennial reign! The contexts of these five psalms with perfect tenses make it clear that they are describing something that has not happened in history and is not true now: Psalm 2:1–3 portrays what has been happening in human history—rebellion against the Lord's sovereignty. Note the following expressions: "He subdues peoples under us" (47:3a, HCSB); "The princes of the peoples gather as the people of the God of Abraham" (47:9a, ESV);[32] "the world also shall be established that it shall not be moved" (96:10b; also 93:1a);[33] "all the peoples see his glory" (97:6b, NIV); "let the peoples tremble" (99:1b, NASB). When has the whole world seen God's glory? When has there been the fear of God all over the world? We await His kingdom!

(6) *This reign is characterized by absolute justice.* The King of the earth is also the good shepherd, who in complete righteousness will rule over the flock of His people. Psalm 89:14 proclaims the features of the King's government: "Justice and judgment are the habitation of thy throne: mercy and truth shall go before thy face." David asserts that God's governing verdicts in the kingdom will always be just: "And he shall judge the world in righteousness, he shall minister judgment to the people in uprightness" (9:8). The Messiah's scepter, the emblem of His ruling, is characterized by "justice"

---

[31] This short sentence "does not simply affirm Jehovah's sovereignty as a general truth, but announces the fact that he has just become king or begun to reign, *i. e.* manifested himself anew in his regal character." Alexander, 397.

[32] Steveson interprets both these statements from Psalm 47 as looking "forward to the millennial kingdom" to events that "take place in the kingdom reign of Christ when Israel becomes the dominant nation in the earth" (pp. 188–89).

[33] "When God takes his throne, and manifestly reigns, the earth is at once 'established,' settled, placed on a firm footing." That is, "it can suffer no violent agitation or disturbance." Rawlinson, 294, 320.

(45:6, HCSB); the Hebrew term for this, מִישׁוֹר (*miyshowr*), appears also in 67:4 ("for thou shalt judge the people righteously"). The prayer in 72:1 indicates that God is the source of this attribute: "O God, grant the king the ability to make just decisions!" (NET). Just as God gave wisdom to Solomon, He will also endow the Messiah.[34] This characteristic shows up in the kingship psalms as well: "He will judge the peoples with equity" (96:10c, ASV); "He will judge the world with righteousness" (98:9b, ASV).

(7) *In this reign there will be universal worship of the King.* In appropriate recognition of the goodness of their Sovereign, all the peoples and nations of the earth will show their devotion to the Messiah with proper veneration. Psalm 2 tells the kings of the earth to "worship the LORD with reverence" (v. 11, NASB). The psalmists expressed their desire for this to happen: "let all the people praise thee" (67:3b); "May all the earth worship You" (66:4a, literal translation).[35] In fact, they repeatedly command universal veneration: "Bless our God, O peoples" (66:8a, NASB); "... sing unto the LORD, all the earth. Sing unto the LORD, bless his name ..." (96:1b–2a); "O worship the LORD ..., fear before him, all the earth" (96:9); "Bless the LORD, all his works in all places of his dominion" (103:22a); "O praise the LORD, all ye nations: praise him, all ye people" (117:1). David prophesies that this will happen for the Messiah: "all the kindreds of the nations shall worship before thee" (22:27b); "All nations whom thou hast made shall come and worship before thee, O Lord [note the use of the sovereign title]; and shall glorify thy name" (86:9). In several places the psalmists mention the gathering of the nations to Zion for this worship (47:9; 65:1–2; 102:21–22).

New Testament Echoes

Focused on eschatology, the Olivet Discourse and the book of Revelation restate each of these seven propositions. (1) "And then shall appear the sign of the Son of man in heaven: and then shall all the tribes of the earth mourn, and they shall see the Son of man coming in the clouds of heaven with power and great glory" (Matt. 24:30). "Behold, he cometh with clouds;

---

[34] Kidner notices the appropriate link: "the ability to deal justly is seen as God-given (as both Solomon's prayer for wisdom in 1 Kgs 3, and the prophecy of the Spirit-filled Messiah in Isa. 11 emphasize) ..." (15:274).

[35] Based on the fact that the LXX used an imperative verb, indicating that they understood the Hebrew form to be a jussive. See Hossfeld & Zenger's translation (15B:143).

and every eye shall see him, and they also which pierced him: and all kindreds of the earth shall wail because of him. Even so, Amen" (Rev. 1:7). (2) "And I saw heaven opened, and behold a white horse; and he that sat upon him ... doth ... make war.... And he was clothed with a vesture dipped in blood .... And the armies which were in heaven followed him upon white horses .... And out of his mouth goeth a sharp sword, that with it he should smite the nations ..." (Rev. 19:11–15a).

(3) "And he shall send his angels with a great sound of a trumpet, and they shall gather together his elect from the four winds, from one end of heaven to the other" (Matt. 24:31). Jerusalem "had a wall great and high, and had twelve gates, and at the gates twelve angels, and names written thereon, which are the names of the twelve tribes of the children of Israel" (Rev. 21:12). (4) "When the Son of man shall come in his glory, ... then shall he sit upon the throne of his glory: And before him shall be gathered all nations: and he shall separate them one from another ..." (Matt. 25:31–32). He "was called Faithful and True, and in righteousness he doth judge ..." (Rev. 19:11).

(5) "And the seventh angel sounded; and there were great voices in heaven, saying, The kingdoms of this world are become the kingdoms of our Lord, and of his Christ; and he shall reign for ever and ever" (Rev. 11:15). (6) "Great and marvellous are Your works, O Lord God, the Almighty; Righteous and true are Your ways, King of the nations" (Rev. 15:3b, NASB). (7) "Who shall not fear thee, O Lord, and glorify thy name? ... for all nations shall come and worship before thee ..." (Rev. 15:4).

A fitting conclusion is the passage that solicits our worship for Yahweh while uniting the original sovereignty of God with our Lord's future messianic sovereignty: "Sing praises to God, sing praises; Sing praises to our King, sing praises. For God is the King of all the earth; Sing praises with a skillful psalm. God reigns over the nations, God sits on His holy throne" (47:6–8, NASB).

Appendix A

Names of God in Psalms

Table A1.1 Occurrences of יהוה (Yahweh) in Psalms

Psalm Verses	Number of Times in the Psalm
1: 2 6	2
2: 2 7 11	3
3: 1 3 4 5 7 8	6
4: 3[2] 5 6 8	5
5: 1 3 6 8 12	5
6: 1 2 3[2] 4 8 9[2]	8
7: 1 3 6 8[2] 17[2]	7
8: 1 9	2
9: 1 7 9 10 11 13 16 19 20	9
10: 1 3 12 16 17	5
11: 1 4[2] 5 7	5
12: 1 3 5 6 7	5
13: 1 3 5	3
14: 2 4 6 7	4
15: 1 4	2
16: 2 5 7 8	4
17: 1 13 14	3
18: 1 2 3 6 13 15 18 20 21 24 28 30 31 41 46 49	16
19: 7[2] 8[2] 9[2] 14	7
20: 1 5 6 7 9	5
21: 1 7 9 13	4
22: 8 19 23 26 27 28	6
23: 1 6	2
24: 1 3 5 8[2] 10	6
25: 1 4 6 7 8 10 11 12 14 15	10
26: 1[2] 2 6 8 12	6
27: 1[2] 4[3] 6 7 8 10 11 13 14[2]	13
28: 1 5 6 7 8	5
29: 1[2] 2[2] 3[2] 4[2] 5[2] 7 8[2] 9 10[2] 11[2]	18
30: 1 2 3 4 7 8 10[2] 12	9
31: 1 5 6 9 14 17 21 23[2] 24	10
32: 2 5 10 11	4
33: 1 2 4 5 6 8 10 11 12 13-18 20 22	13
34: 1 2 3 4 6 7 8 9 10 11 15 16 17 18 19 22	16
35: 1 5 6 9 10 22 24 27	8
36: 5 6	2
37: 3 4 5 7 9 17 18 20 23 24 28 33 34 39 40	15
38: 1 15 21	3
39: 4 12	2
40: 1 3 4 5 9 11 13[2] 16	9

307

Appendix A

Psalm Verses	Number of Times in the Psalm
41:1 2 3 4 10 13	6
42:8	1
43:	0
44:	0
45:	0
46:7 8 11	3
47:2 5	2
48:1 8	2
49:	0
50:1	1
51:	0
52:	0
53:	0
54:6	1
55:16 22	2
56:10	1
57:	0
58:6	1
59:3 5 8	3
60:	0
61:	0
62:	0
63:	0
64:10	1
65:	0
66:	0
67:	0
68:16 20 26	3
69:6 13 16 31 33	5
70:1 5	2
71:1 5 16	3
72:18	1
73:28	1
74:18	1
75:8	1
76:11	1
77:	0
78:4 21	2
79:5	1
80:8 19	2
81:10 15	2
82:	0
83:16 18	2
84:1 2 3 8 11[2] 12	7
85:1 7 8 12	4
86:1 6 11 17	4
87:2 6	2
88:1 9 13 14	4
89:1 5 6 8[2] 5 18 46 51 52	10
90:13	1
91:2 9	2
92:1 4 5 8 9 13 15	7
93:1[2] 3 4 5	5
94:1 3 5 11 14 17 18 22 23	9
95:1 3 6	3
96:1 2[2] 4 5 7[2] 8 9 10 13	11
97:1 5 8 9 10 12	6
98:1 2 4 5 6 9	6

308

Psalm Verses	Number of Times in the Psalm
99:1 2 5 6 8 9[2]	7
100:1 2 3 5	4
101:1 8	2
102:1 12 15 16 19 21 22	7
103:1 2 6 8 13 17 19 20 21 22[2]	11
104:1[2] 16 24 31[2] 33 34 35	9
105:1 3 4 7 19	5
106:1[2] 2 4 16 25 34 40 47 48	10
107:1 2 6 8 13 15 19 21 24 28 31 43	12
108:3	1
109:14 15 20 21 26 27 30	7
110:1 2 4	3
111:1 2 4 10	4
112:1 7	2
113:1[2] 2 3 4 5	6
114:	0
115:1 9 10 11[2] 12 13 14 15 16	10
116:1 4[2] 5 6 7 9 12 13 14 15 16 17 18 19	15
117:1 2	2
118:1 4 6 7 8 9 10 11 12 13 15 16[2] 20 23 24 25[2] 26[2] 27 29	22
119:1 12 31 33 41 52 55 57 64 65 75 89 107 108 126 137 145 149 151 159 166 169 174	23
120:1 2	2
121:2 5[2] 7 8	5
122:1 4 9	3
123:2 3	2
124:1 2 6 8	4
125:1 2 4 5	4
126:1 2 3 4	4
127:1[2] 3	3
128:1 4 5	3
129:4 8[2]	3
130:1 5 7[2]	4
131:1 3	2
132:1 2 5 8 11 13	6
133:3	1
134:1[3] 2 3	5
135:1[2] 2 3 5 6 13[2] 14 19[2] 20[3] 21	15
136:1	1
137:4 7	2
138:4 5[2] 6 8[2]	6
139:1 4 21	3
140:1 4 6[2] 7 8 12	7
141:1 3 8	3
142:1[2] 5	3
143:1 7 9 11	4
144:1 3 5 15	4
145:3 8 9 10 14 17 18 20 21	9
146:1 2 5 7 8[3] 9 10	9
147:2 6 7 11 12	5
148:1 5 7 13	4
149:1 4	2
150:	0
Totals: **689** (273/32/44/105/235)	

Appendix A

Table A1.2 Titles for Yahweh in Psalms

Heb. words: Psalm	אֱלֹהִים 'Elowhiym God	אֵל 'Eyl God	אֲדֹנָי 'Adownay Lord	יָהּ Yah Yah	עֶלְיוֹן 'Elyown Most High
2:			4		
3:	2 7				
4:	1				
5:	2 10	4			
7:	1 3 9 10 11	11			17
8:			1 9		
9:	17				2
10:	4 13	11 12			
13:	3				
14:	1 2 5				
16:		1	2		
17:		6			
18:	6 21 28 29 31 46	2 30 32 47			13
19:		1			
20:	1 5 7				
21:					7
22:	2	1[2] 10	30		
24:	5				
25:	2 5 22				
27:	9				
29:		3			
30:	2 12		8		
31:	14	5			
33:	12				
35:	23 24		17 22 23		
36:	1 7				
37:	31		13		
38:	15 21		9 15 22		
39:			7		
40:	3 5 8 17		17		
41:	13				
42:	1 2[2] 3 4 5 6 10 11[2]	2 8 9			
43:	1 2 4[3] 5[2]	4			
44:	1 4 8 20 21		23		
45:	2 6 7[2]		11		
46:	1 4 5[2] 7 10 11				4
47:	1 5 6 7 8[2] 9[2]				2
48:	1 3 8[2] 9 10 14[2]				
49:	7 15				
50:	1 2 3 6 7[2] 14 16 23				14
51:	1 10 14[2] 17[2]		15		
52:	7 8[2]	1 5			
53:	1 2[2] 4 5[2] 6				
54:	1 2 3 4		4		
55:	1 14 16 19 23	19	9		
56:	1 4[2] 7 9 10 11 12 13				
57:	1 2 3 5 7 11	2	9		2
58:	6 11				
59:	1 5[2] 9 10[2] 13 17[2]		11		
60:	1 6 10[2] 12				

310

Heb. words: Psalm	אֱלֹהִים 'Elowhiym God	אֵל 'Eyl God	אֲדֹנָי 'Adownay Lord	יָהּ Yah Yah	עֶלְיוֹן 'Elyown Most High
61:	1 5 7				
62:	1 5 7[2] 8 11		12		
63:	1 11	1			
64:	1 7 9				
65:	1 5 9				
66:	1 3 5 8 10 16 19 20		18		
67:	1 3 5 6[2] 7				
68:	[26x]†	19 20[2] 24 35	11 17 19 20 22 23	4 18	
69:	1 3 5 6 13 29 30 32 35		6		
70:	1 4 5				
71:	4 11[2] 12 17 18 19[2] 22		5 16		
72:	1 18[2]				
73:	1 26 28	11 17	20 28		11
74:	1 10 12 22	8			
75:	1 7 9				
76:	1 6 9 11				
77:	1 3 13[2] 16	9 13 14	2 7	11	10
78:	7 10 19 22 31 35 56 59	7 8 18 19 34 35 41	65		17 35 56
79:	1 9 10		12		
80:	3 4 7 14 19	10			
81:	1[2] 4 10				
82:	1 8				6
83:	1 12 13	1			18
84:	3 7 8[2] 9 10 11	2			18
85:	4	8			
86:	2 10 12 14	15	3 4 5 8 9 12 15		
87:	3				5
88:	1				
89:	8	7 26	49 50	8	
90:	17	2	1 17		
91:	2				1 9
92:	13				1
94:	7 22 23	1[2]		7 12	
95:	7				
97:			5		9
98:	3				
99:	5 8 9[2]	8			
101:	3				
102:		24		18	
104:	1 33	21		35	
105:	7			45	
106:	47 48	14 21		1 48	
107:		11			11
108:	1 5 7 11[2] 13				
109:	1 26		21		
110:			1 5		
111:				1	
112:				1	
113:	5			1 9	
114:			7		
115:	2 3			17 18[2]	

Appendix A

Heb. words:	אֱלֹהִים 'Elowhiym God	אֵל 'Eyl God	אֲדֹנָי 'Adownay Lord	יָהּ Yah Yah	עֶלְיוֹן 'Elyown Most High
Psalm					
116:	5			19	
117:				2	
118:	28	27 28		5[2] 14 17 18 19	
119:	115				
122:	9			4	
123:	2				
130:			2 3 6	3	
135:	2		5	1 3 4 21	
136:	2	26	3		
139:		17 23			
140:		6	7		
141:			8		
143:	10				
144:	9 15				
145:	1				
146:	2 5 10	5		1 10	
147:	1 7 12		5	1 20	
148:				1 14	
149:		6		1 9	
150:		1		1 6[2]	

totals: **351** (48/198/59/18/28) **68** (16/13/20/8/10) **63** (15/18/14/3/12) **43** (0/2/2/7/32) **21** (4/4/8/4/1)

†1 2 3 4 5 6 7 8[3] 9 10 15 16 17 18 21 24 26 28[2] 31 32 34 35[2]

Table A1.3 Additional Titles for God in Psalms

Hebrew	English	References	Totals: Ps./all
אֱלוֹהַּ God	God	18:31; 50:22; 114:7; 139:19	4/58
שַׁדַּי Almighty	Almighty	68:14; 91:1	2/48
יְהוָה צְבָאוֹת Yahweh [of] Armies	Yahweh [of] Armies	24:10; 46:7, 11; 48:8;, 69:7; 84:1, 3, 1	8/247
אֱלֹהִים צְבָאוֹת God [of] Armies	God [of] Armies	80:7, 14	2/2
אֱלֹהִים יְהוָה צְבָאוֹת Yahweh GOD [of] Armies	Yahweh GOD [of] Armies	59:5; 80:4, 19; 84:8	4/4

Appendix B

Types of Psalms

Critical scholarship has focused on genre classification of the Psalms since the time of Hermann Gunkel (1862-1932). Of course, his approach was based on his theory of form criticism (specifically, *Sitz im Leben* or "setting in life"), and it has been characterized by an overemphasis on the belief that the Psalms originated as compositions for post-exilic temple worship. The books of Samuel and Chronicles as well as the psalm titles would indicate, however, that the majority of psalms were individual compositions even before Solomon's temple was built. Gunkel's student Sigmund Mowinckel (1884-1965) went even further in his speculation, claiming that many psalms celebrated a yearly king-enthronement festival in Israel. The theories of these two critics have not really contributed to our true understanding of Psalms.[1]

It is obvious, nevertheless, from the text of the psalms themselves and from their titles that there are different types or categories of these poems. For example, since at least the 6th century AD Christians have recognized one group of seven as penitential (6, 32, 38, 51, 102, 130, and 143).[2] Distinguishing these categories can be important because it contributes to holistic interpretation, but difficulties arise because the types do not follow some

---

[1] This is contrary to Walter Brueggemann's evaluation of their work along with the writings of Claus Westermann as gains: "great insight" and a "major advance in Psalms study." He does admit, however, that their theories are somewhat problematic. *The Message of the Psalms: A Theological Commentary* (Minneapolis: Augsburg, 1984), 17-18.

[2] "... seven psalms of penitents are taught in the book." *Cassiodorus: Explanation of the Psalms*, trans. P. G. Walsh, no. 51 of Ancient Christian Writers: The Works of the Fathers in Translation, ed. Walter J. Burghardt and Thomas Comerford Lawler (New York: Paulist, 1990), 511. Six of these are laments in the table below; Psalm 32 has been classified as thanksgiving.

313

strict form without any room for individuality[3] and because many psalms are mixed in character.[4] In general, however, the contents of the psalms, their mood, and their literary structures allow for identification of about eight genres that 20th century critics and conservatives have proposed for classification.[5] (1) Laments are prayers that express some sort of grief, though almost all of them speak also about confidence, joy, and praise. (2) Hymns are poems expressing primarily joy and praise to God. (3) Thanksgiving songs praise God for answers to prayer. (4) Royal psalms are those that focus on the promised messianic King or on His type. (5) Zion songs eulogize God's choice of Jerusalem as His throne. (6) Wisdom psalms are poems that have many of the characteristics that we find in the book of Proverbs. Two lesser categories are (7) poems simply expressing an affirmation of trust or confidence and (8) hymns with clear indications of a worship liturgy. Recognizing widespread disagreement, I have provided in the following Table A2 a single label for each psalm based on some consensus from many sources, critical and conservative.

---

[3] Tremper Longman III observes that "the lack of consensus identifying the specific genres of the psalms can be explained partly by the fluid nature of genre …." "Psalms," in *A Complete Literary Guide to the Bible*, ed. Leland Ryken and Tremper Longman III (Grand Rapids: Zondervan, 1993), 246. Robert Alter speaks of the "refashioning of genre": "writers tend to be restive [difficult to restrict] within the limits of genre, repeatedly find ways to juggle and transform generic conventions, formulaic or otherwise, and on occasion push genre beyond its own formal or thematic limits." "Psalms," in *The Literary Guide to the Bible*, ed. Robert Alter and Frank Kermode (Cambridge: Harvard University Press, 1987), 247.

[4] For example, "Psalm 32 is most akin to the thanksgiving psalms of the individual …, but it forms a combination of features unlike any other psalm. Most notably, it incorporates a confession of sin … [making it one of the penitential psalms] and a divine oracle, along with an overall didactic … emphasis [like a wisdom psalm]. Its liturgical setting is implied …." Broyles, 161. Another example would be Psalm 68, which "includes prayers (vv. 1–3, 28–31), hymnic praise (vv. 4–6, 19–20, 32–35), thanksgiving (vv. 7–10, 15–18), and oracles (vv. 11–14, 21–23)." VanGemeren, 513–14.

[5] "Any attempt … to effect a systematic generic classification based on a commonality of theme, mood, occasion and style is bound to be more an exercise in convenience than precision. The choice of categories will be influenced by subjective or exegetical factors …." Nahum M. Sarna, "Psalms, Book of," *Encyclopaedia Judaica* (New York: Macmillan, 1971), 13:1314. Sarna himself employs for his classification five of the types that appear below in Table A2.

Table A2 Types of Psalms (I=individual; C=communal)[6]

Psalm	Lament	Hymn	Thanks	Royal	Zion	Wisdom	Other[7]
1						•	
2				•			
3	I						
4	I						
5	I						
6	I						
7	I						
8		•					
9	I						
10	I						
11							trust
12	C						
13	I						
14	I						
15							liturgy
16							trust
17	I						
18				I			
19						•	
20				•			
21				•			
22	I						
23							trust
24							liturgy
25	I						
26	I						
27	I						
28	I						
29		•					
30			I				
31	I						

[6] Concerning laments and thanksgiving songs, many books on Psalms make a distinction between individual (I) and community (C) categories. Although the table reflects this trait, it is really better not to generate additional genres.

[7] Though there are more trust psalms (8 examples) and liturgical psalms (8) than Zion psalms (6), I have put the former two groups together in a column labeled "Others" because they are not as commonly identified as the Zion ones.

315

Appendix B

Psalm	Lament	Hymn	Thanks	Royal	Zion	Wisdom	Other[7]
32			I				
33		•					
34			I				
35	I						
36	I						
37							•
38	I						
39	I						
40	I						
41			I				
42	I						
43	I						
44	C						
45				•			
46					•		
47		•					
48					•		
49						•	
50							liturgy
51	I						
52	I						
53	I						
54	I						
55	I						
56	I						
57	I						
58	C						
59	I						
60	C						
61	I						
62							trust
63	I						
64	I						
65			C				
66			I				
67			C				
68							liturgy
69	I						
70	I						
71	I						

Psalm	Lament	Hymn	Thanks	Royal	Zion	Wisdom	Other[7]
72				•			
73						•	
74	C						
75			C				
76					•		
77	I						
78						•	
79	C						
80	C						
81							liturgy
82							liturgy
83	C						
84					•		
85	C						
86	I						
87					•		
88	I						
89				•			
90	C						
91							trust
92			I				
93		•					
94	C						
95		•					
96		•					
97		•					
98		•					
99		•					
100		•					
101				•			
102	I						
103		•					
104		•					
105		•					
106		•					
107			C				
108	I						
109	I						
110				•			
111						•	

Appendix B

Psalm	Lament	Hymn	Thanks	Royal	Zion	Wisdom	Other[7]
112						•	
113		•					
114		•					
115							liturgy
116			I				
117		•					
118			C				
119						•	
120	I						
121							trust
122					•		
123	C						
124			C				
125							trust
126	C						
127						•	
128						•	
129	C						
130	I						
131							trust
132				•			
133						•	
134							liturgy
135		•					
136		•					
137	C						
138			I				
139		•					
140	I						
141	I						
142	I						
143	I						
144				•			
145		•					
146		•					
147		•					
148		•					
149		•					
150		•					
Totals:	64 [49/15]	27	15 [9/6]	10	6	12	16

Appendix C

"Forever" Hebrew Vocabulary

Psalms uses some form of the word עוֹלָם ('owlam, "always") 143 times, 32.6% of its 439 occurrences in the Old Testament. The close synonym עַד ('ad, "always") occurs 29 times, 60.4% of its occurrences. Another synonym is נֶצַח (netsakh, "perpetual"), occurring 18 times in Psalms. Table A3.1 plots the 150 verse references for five common combinations of these terms.

Table A3.1 Key Forever Expressions

Hebrew:	לְעוֹלָם	עוֹלָם only	עוֹלָם וָעֶד	לְעַד	לָנֶצַח
Psalm	le'owlam forever	'owlam always	'owlam wa'ed ever & ever	la'ad forever	lanetsakh forever
5:	11				
9:	7		5	18	6, 18
10:			16		11
12:	7				
15:	5				
19:				9	
21:			4	6	
22:				26	
24:		7, 9			
29:	10				
30:	6, 12				
31:	1				
33:	11				
37:	18, 27, 28			29	
41:	12				
44:	8				23
45:	2		6, 17		
48:			14		
49:	8, 11				9
52:	9		8		5
55:	22				
61:		7		8	
66:		7			
68:					16
71:	1				
72:	17, 19				

Appendix C

Hebrew:	לְעוֹלָם	עוֹלָם only	עוֹלָם וָעֶד‡	לָעַד	לָנֶצַח
Psalm	le'owlam forever	'owlam always	'owlam wa'ed ever & ever	la'ad forever	lanetsakh forever
73:	26	12			
74:					1, 10, 19
75:	9				
77:					8
78:	69	66			
79:	13				5
81:	15				
85:	5				
86:	12				
89:	28, 36, 52	1, 2, 37		29	46
92:	8				
100:	5				
102:	12				
103:	9				9
104:	31		5		
105:	8	10			
106:	1				
107:	1				
110:	4				
111:	5, 8, 9			3, 8, 10	
112:	6	6		3, 9	
113:		2			
115:		18			
117:	2				
118:	1, 2, 3, 4, 29				
119:	[9x]†		44		
121:		1			
125:	1	2			
131:		3			
135:	13				
136:	1–26 [26x]				
138:	8				
139:		24			
143:		3			
145:			1, 2, 21		
146:	6, 10				
148:	6			6	
totals:	92	19	12	13	14
	(13/9/10/7/53)	(2/2/5/2/8)	(3/4/0/1/4)	(5/1/1/0/6)	(3/4/6/1/0)

* Includes three cases where the spelling is לְעֹלָם (le'owlam): 75:9; 92:8; 136:3.

‡ In five cases לְ precedes עוֹלָם (le'owlam, "forever"): 9:5; 119:44; 145:1, 2, 21. In an additional case it is spelled לְעֹלָם (45:17).

† 119:89, 93, 98, 111, 112, 142, 144, 152, 160

Additional expressions using the three words for "always" include עַד־עוֹלָם ('ad-'owlam, "until always"), עַד הָעוֹלָם ('ad ha'owlam, "until the always"), מֵעוֹלָם (mey'owlam, "from long ago"), עוֹלָמִים ('owlamiym, "ages"), עֲדֵי־עַד ('edey-'ad, "until always"), and נֶצַח by itself (netsakh, "perpetual"). Two further synonymous expressions are לְדֹר וָדֹר (ledowr

320

wadowr, literally "for age and age" or "for all generations") and דֹּר וָדֹר (*dowr wadowr*, "age and age"). Table A3.2 lists the references for these.

Table A3.2 Additional "Forever" Expressions in Psalms

Hebrew	English	#	References
עַד־עוֹלָם	until always	6	18:50; 48:8; 89:4; 90:2; 103:17; 106:31
עַד הָעוֹלָם	until the always	4	28:9; 41:13; 106:48; 133:3
מֵעוֹלָם	from long ago	7	25:6; 41:13; 90:2; 93:2; 103:17; 106:48; 119:52
עוֹלָמִים	ages	3	61:4; 77:5; 145:13 (spelled עֹלָמִים)
עֲדֵי־עַד	until always	4	83:17; 92:7; 132:12, 14
לְדֹר וָדֹר	for age and age	12	10:6; 33:11; 49:11; 77:8; 79:13; 85:5; 89:1; 102:12; 106:31; 119:90; 135:13; 146:10
דֹּר וָדֹר	age and age	3	45:17; 61:6; 100:5
נֶצַח only	perpetual	3	13:1; 16:11; 74:3

A total of 73 different psalms contain one or more references to the ideas of long ago, perpetuity, permanence, or eternity. In 21 cases a verse uses two of these expressions. All totaled 171 verses refer to these concepts.

Index of Authors

Theological Themes of Psalms

Index of Comments on Psalm Passages

Theological Themes of Psalms